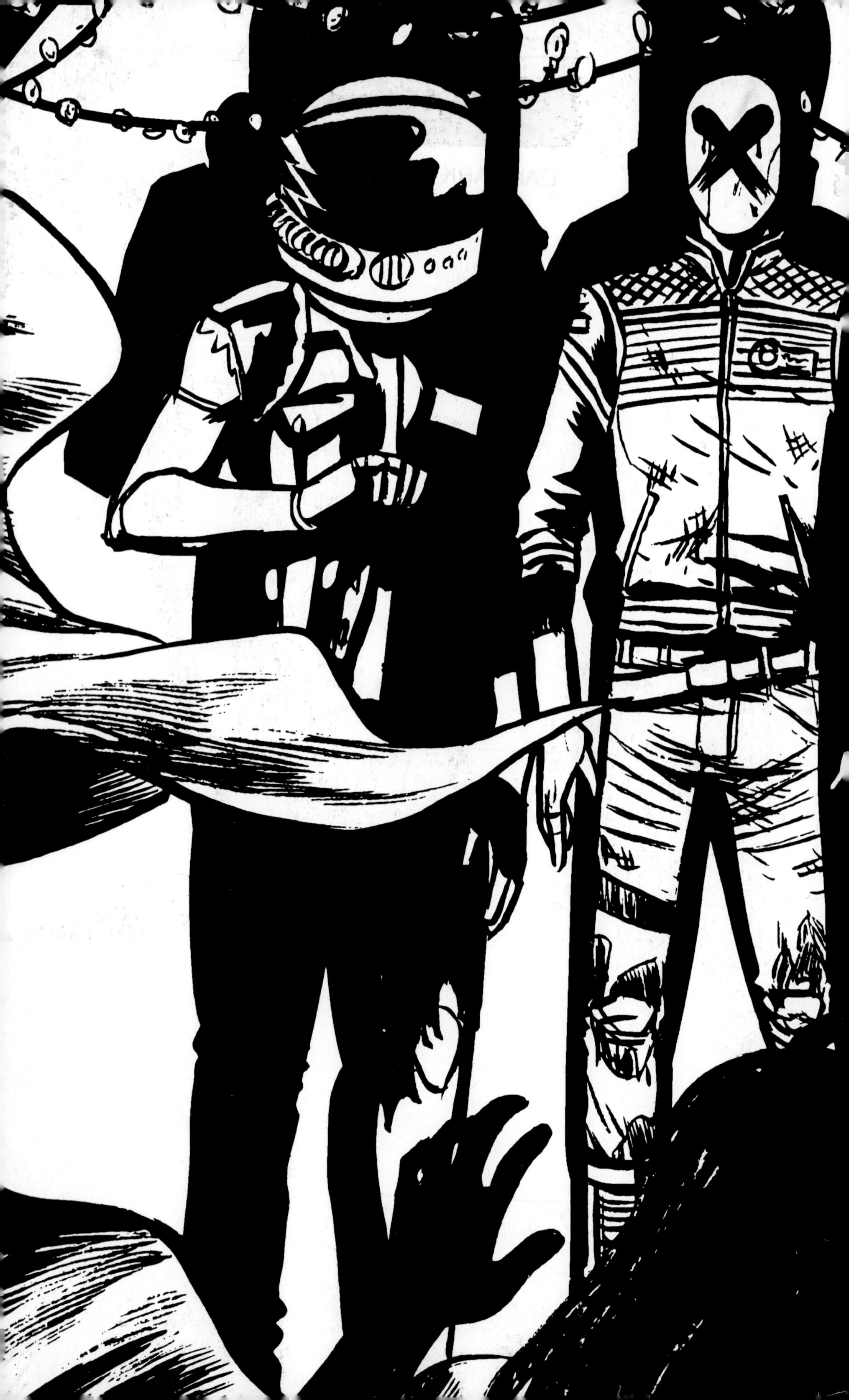

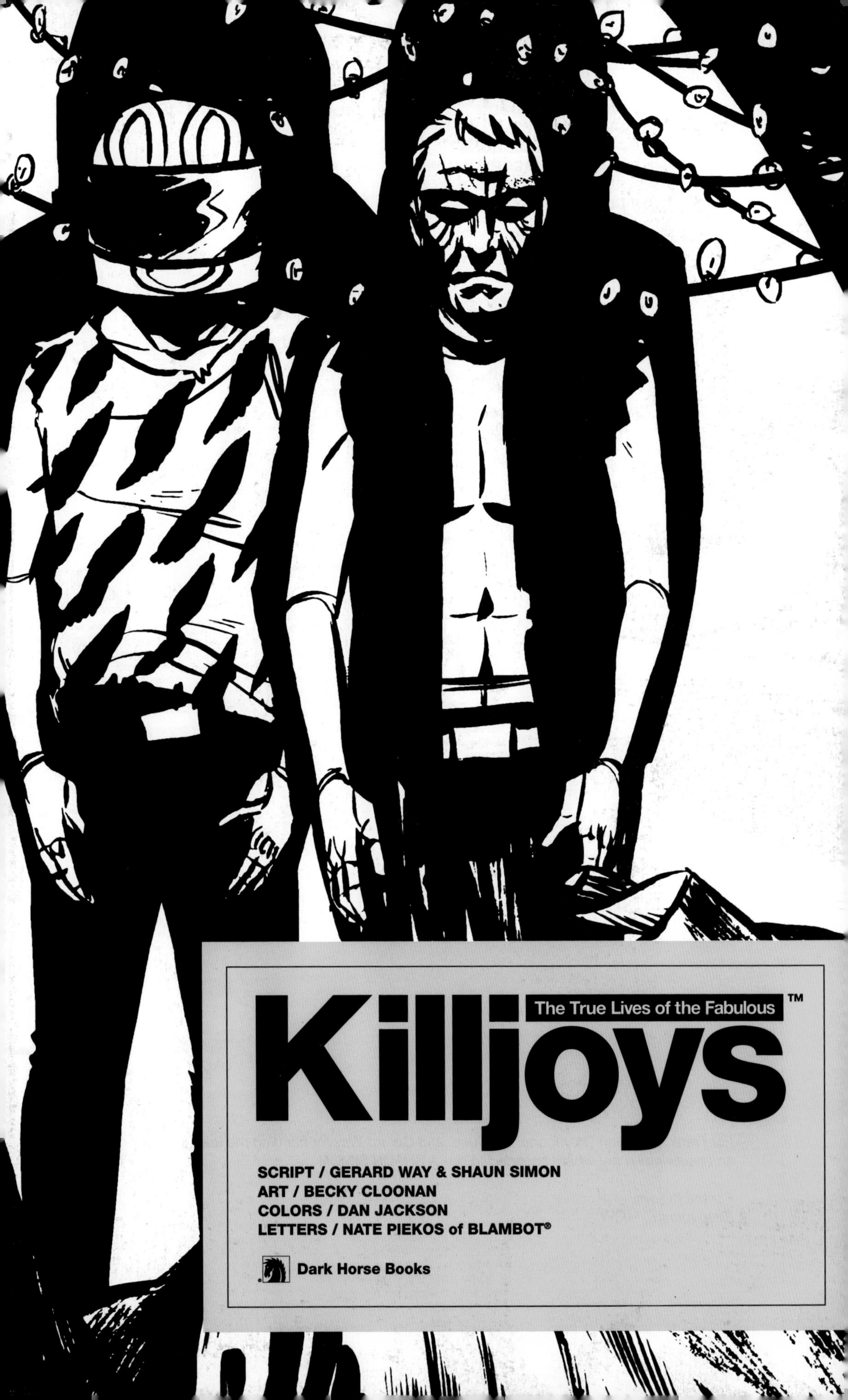

The True Lives of the Fabulous Killjoys™

SCRIPT / GERARD WAY & SHAUN SIMON
ART / BECKY CLOONAN
COLORS / DAN JACKSON
LETTERS / NATE PIEKOS of BLAMBOT®

Dark Horse Books

PUBLISHER / MIKE RICHARDSON
EDITOR / SIERRA HAHN
ASSOCIATE EDITOR / JIM GIBBONS
ASSISTANT EDITOR / SPENCER CUSHING
DIGITAL PRODUCTION / ALLYSON HALLER
COLLECTION DESIGNER / TONY ONG

Special thanks to Jen Vaughn and Jimmy Presler at Dark Horse Comics.

Published by Dark Horse Books
A division of Dark Horse Comics, Inc.
10956 SE Main Street
Milwaukie, OR 97222

First edition: May 2014
ISBN 978-1-59582-462-2

10 9 8 7 6 5 4 3 2 1
Printed in China

International Licensing: (503) 905-2377
Comic Shop Locator Service: (888) 266-4226

This volume collects the comic book series The True Lives of the Fabulous Killjoys *#1–#6 and the Free Comic Book Day 2013 story "Dead Satellites," from Dark Horse Comics.*

For Frank Iero, John "Hambone" McGuire, and Gerard Way for handing me the keys and believing I'd get where I needed to go. —SHAUN SIMON

For the Killjoys:
Keep runnin'. —GW

Chapter One:

WHATEVER GETS YOU THROUGH THE NIGHT

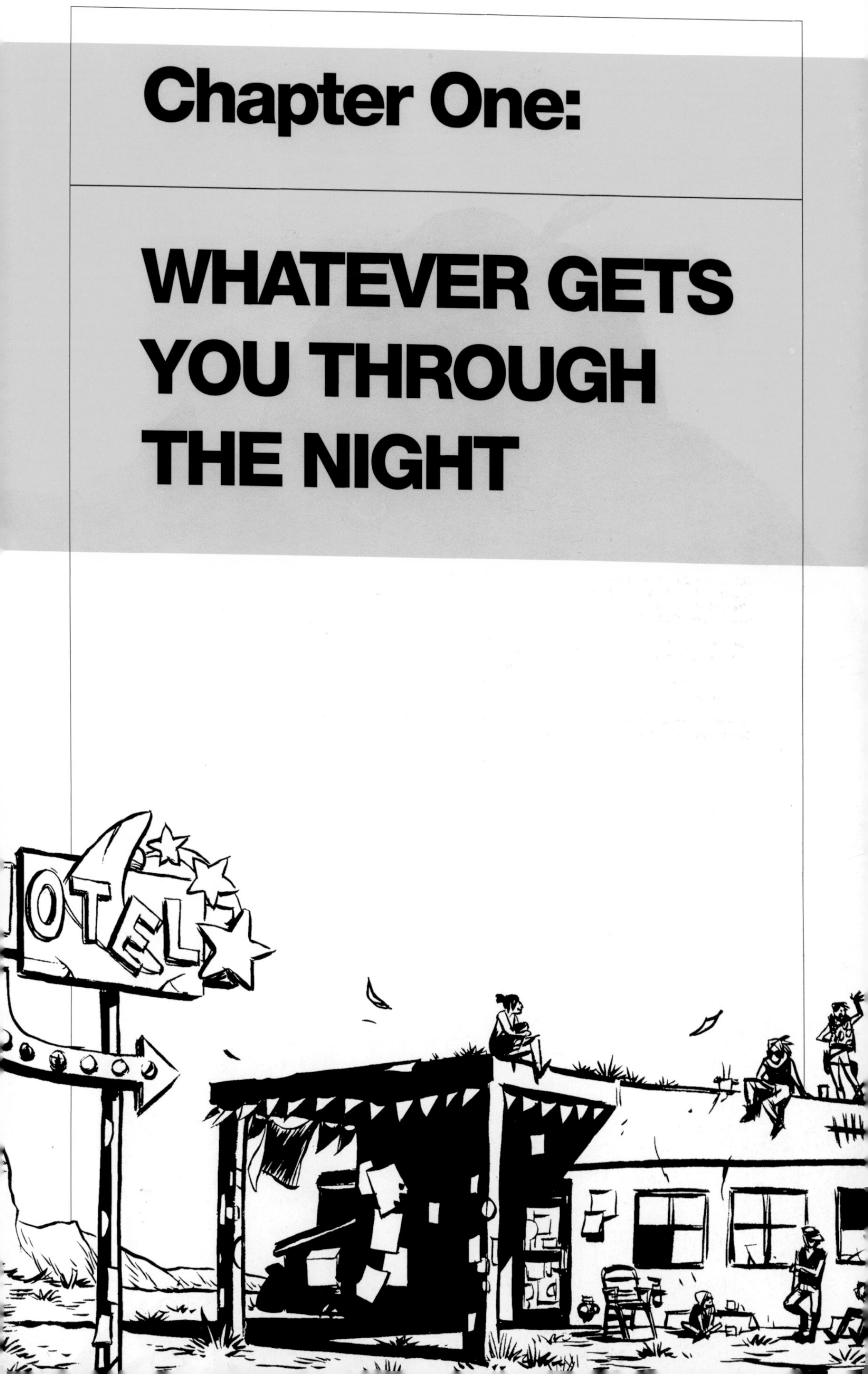

OTEL

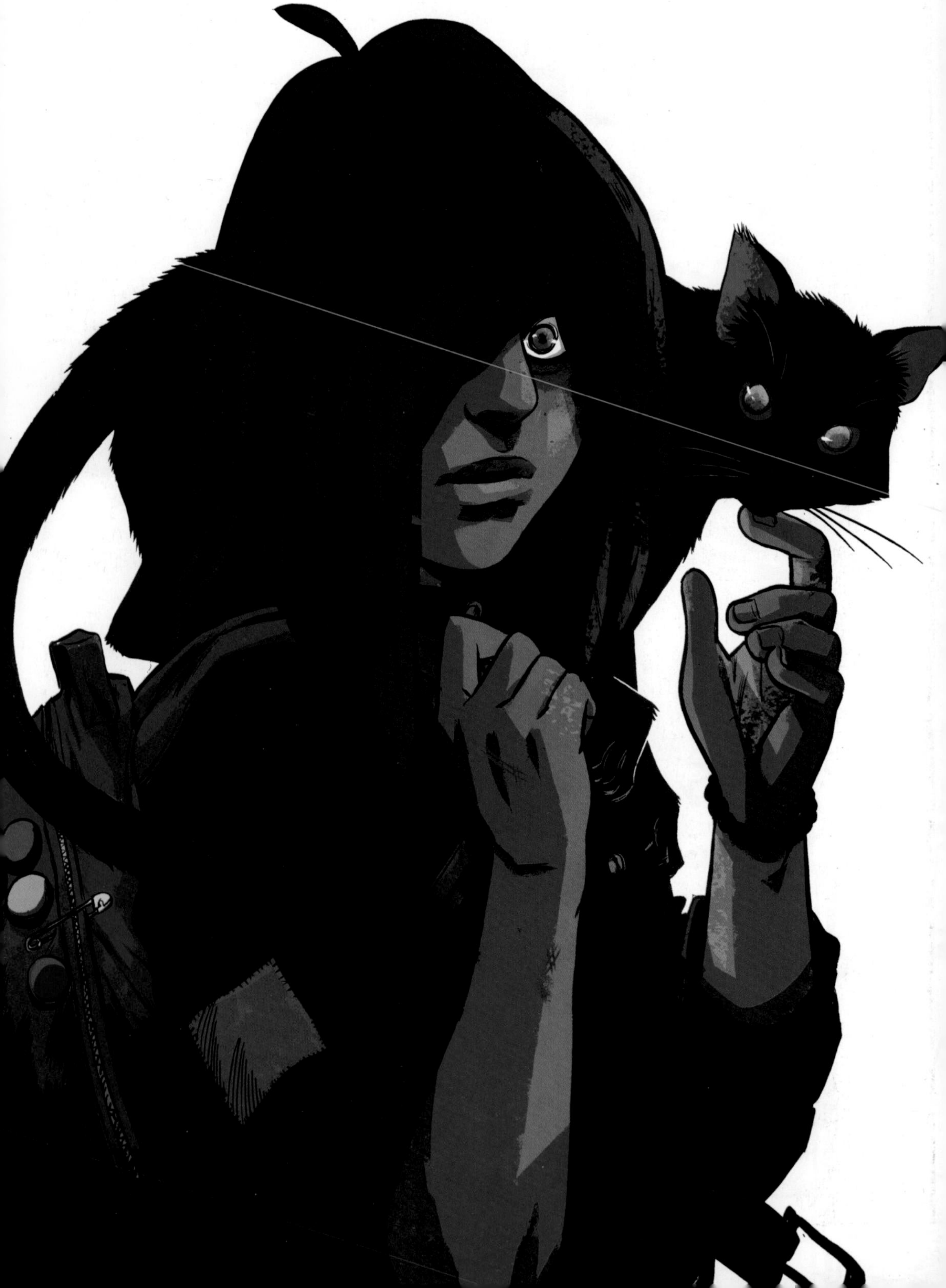

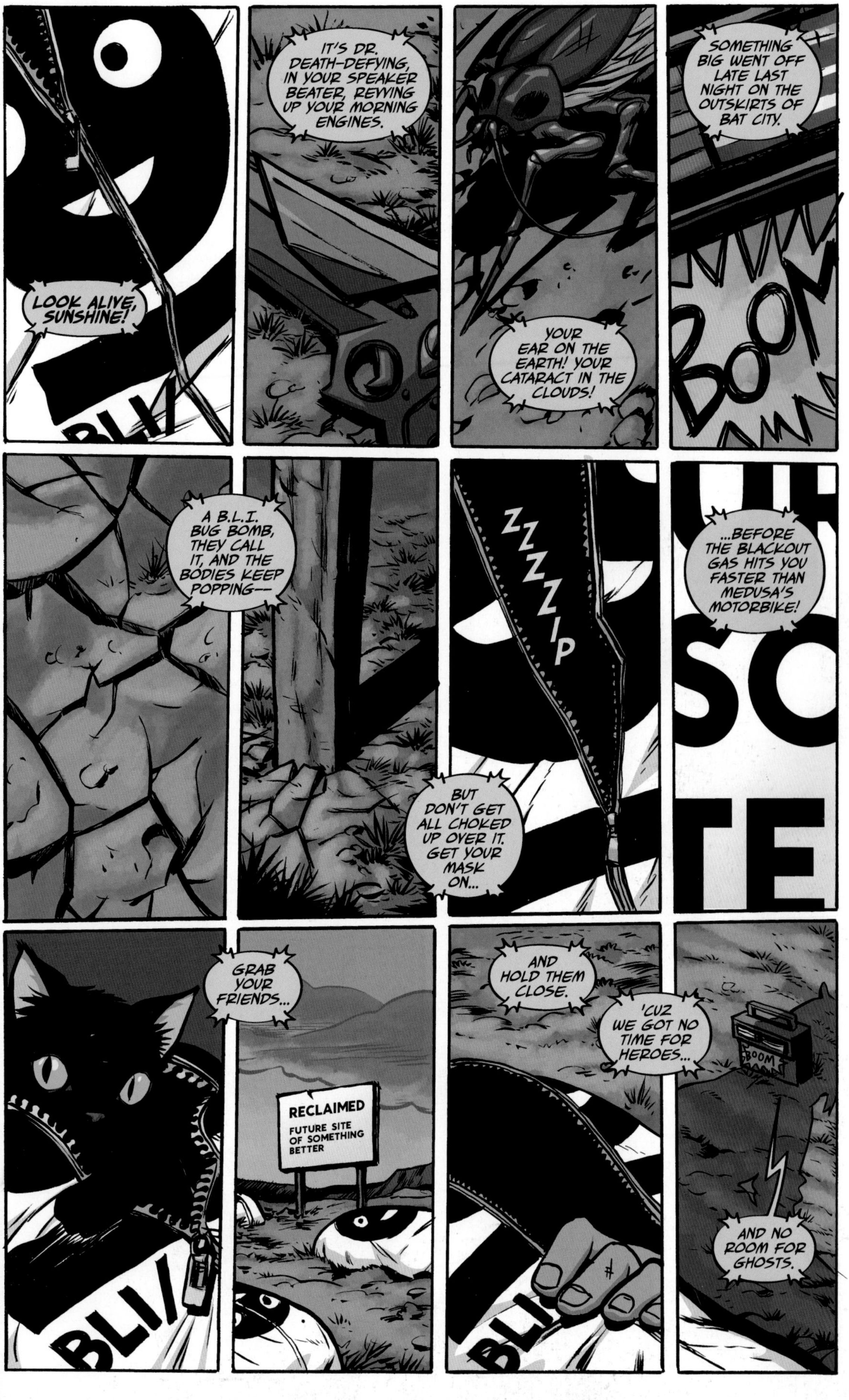
LOOK ALIVE, SUNSHINE!
IT'S DR. DEATH-DEFYING, IN YOUR SPEAKER BEATER, REVVING UP YOUR MORNING ENGINES.
YOUR EAR ON THE EARTH! YOUR CATARACT IN THE CLOUDS!
SOMETHING BIG WENT OFF LATE LAST NIGHT ON THE OUTSKIRTS OF BAT CITY.
BOOM
A B.L.I. BUG BOMB, THEY CALL IT, AND THE BODIES KEEP POPPING--
ZZZZIP
BUT DON'T GET ALL CHOKED UP OVER IT. GET YOUR MASK ON...
...BEFORE THE BLACKOUT GAS HITS YOU FASTER THAN MEDUSA'S MOTORBIKE!
GRAB YOUR FRIENDS...
RECLAIMED
FUTURE SITE OF SOMETHING BETTER
AND HOLD THEM CLOSE.
'CUZ WE GOT NO TIME FOR HEROES...
AND NO ROOM FOR GHOSTS.

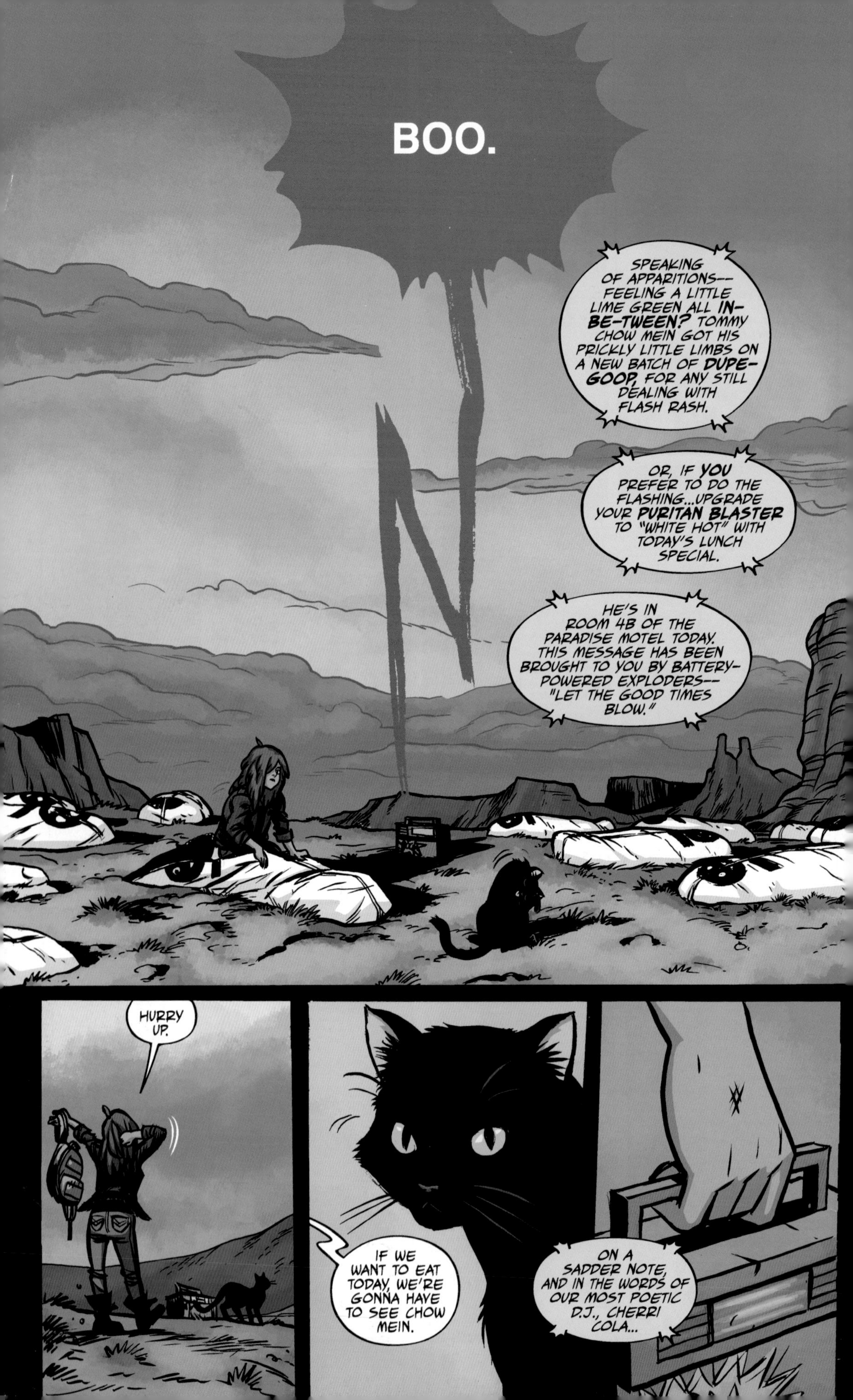

BOO.
SPEAKING OF APPARITIONS-- FEELING A LITTLE LIME GREEN ALL IN-BE-TWEEN? TOMMY CHOW MEIN GOT HIS PRICKLY LITTLE LIMBS ON A NEW BATCH OF DUPE-GOOP, FOR ANY STILL DEALING WITH FLASH RASH.
OR, IF YOU PREFER TO DO THE FLASHING...UPGRADE YOUR PURITAN BLASTER TO "WHITE HOT" WITH TODAY'S LUNCH SPECIAL.
HE'S IN ROOM 4B OF THE PARADISE MOTEL TODAY. THIS MESSAGE HAS BEEN BROUGHT TO YOU BY BATTERY-POWERED EXPLODERS-- "LET THE GOOD TIMES BLOW."
HURRY UP.
IF WE WANT TO EAT TODAY, WE'RE GONNA HAVE TO SEE CHOW MEIN.
ON A SADDER NOTE, AND IN THE WORDS OF OUR MOST POETIC D.J., CHERRI COLA...

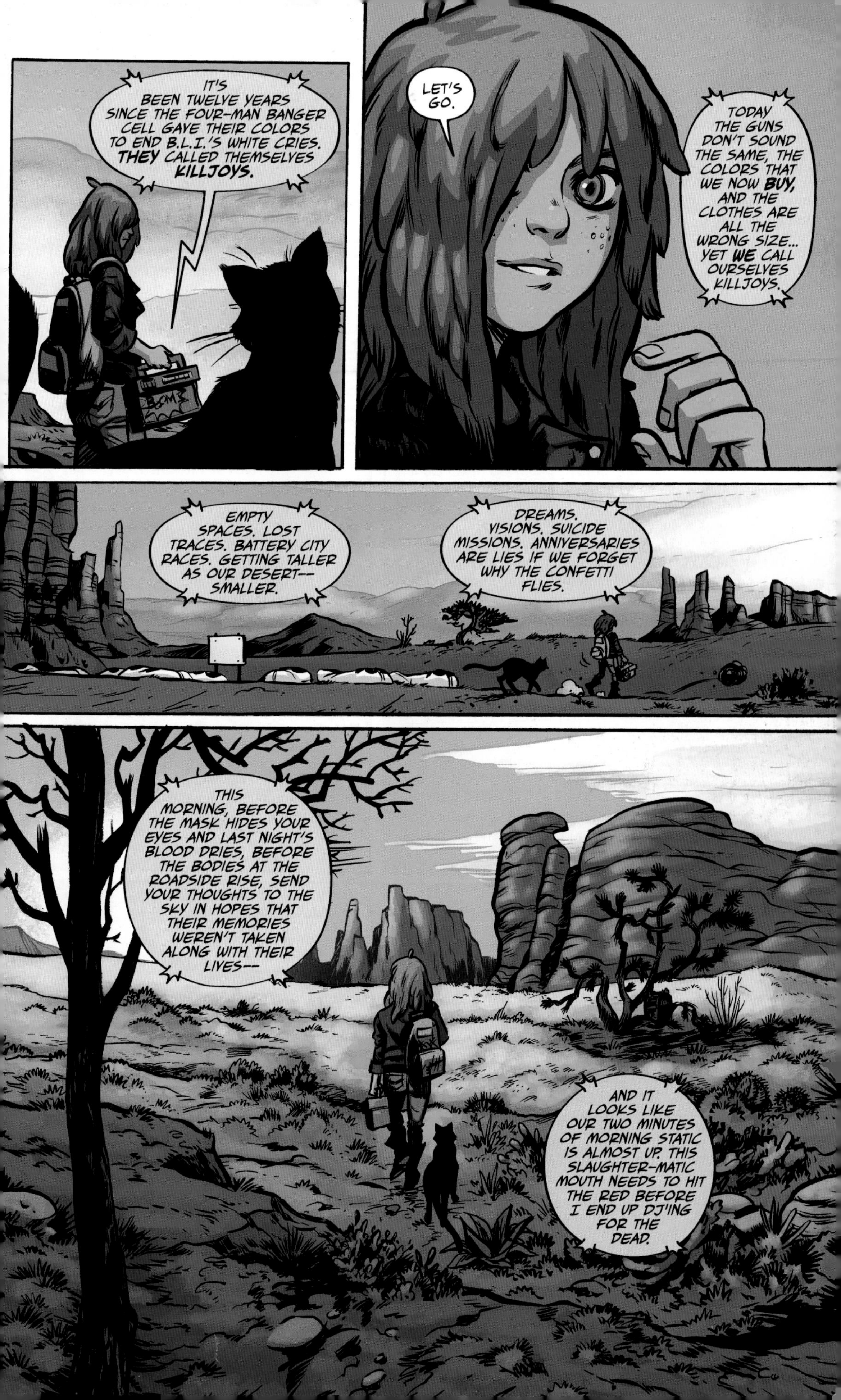
IT'S BEEN TWELVE YEARS SINCE THE FOUR-MAN BANGER CELL GAVE THEIR COLORS TO END B.L.I.'S WHITE CRIES. THEY CALLED THEMSELVES KILLJOYS.
BOOM
LET'S GO.
TODAY THE GUNS DON'T SOUND THE SAME, THE COLORS THAT WE NOW BUY, AND THE CLOTHES ARE ALL THE WRONG SIZE... YET WE CALL OURSELVES KILLJOYS.
EMPTY SPACES. LOST TRACES. BATTERY CITY RACES. GETTING TALLER AS OUR DESERT-- SMALLER.
DREAMS. VISIONS. SUICIDE MISSIONS. ANNIVERSARIES ARE LIES IF WE FORGET WHY THE CONFETTI FLIES.
THIS MORNING, BEFORE THE MASK HIDES YOUR EYES AND LAST NIGHT'S BLOOD DRIES, BEFORE THE BODIES AT THE ROADSIDE RISE, SEND YOUR THOUGHTS TO THE SKY IN HOPES THAT THEIR MEMORIES WEREN'T TAKEN ALONG WITH THEIR LIVES--
AND IT LOOKS LIKE OUR TWO MINUTES OF MORNING STATIC IS ALMOST UP. THIS SLAUGHTER-MATIC MOUTH NEEDS TO HIT THE RED BEFORE I END UP DJ'ING FOR THE DEAD.

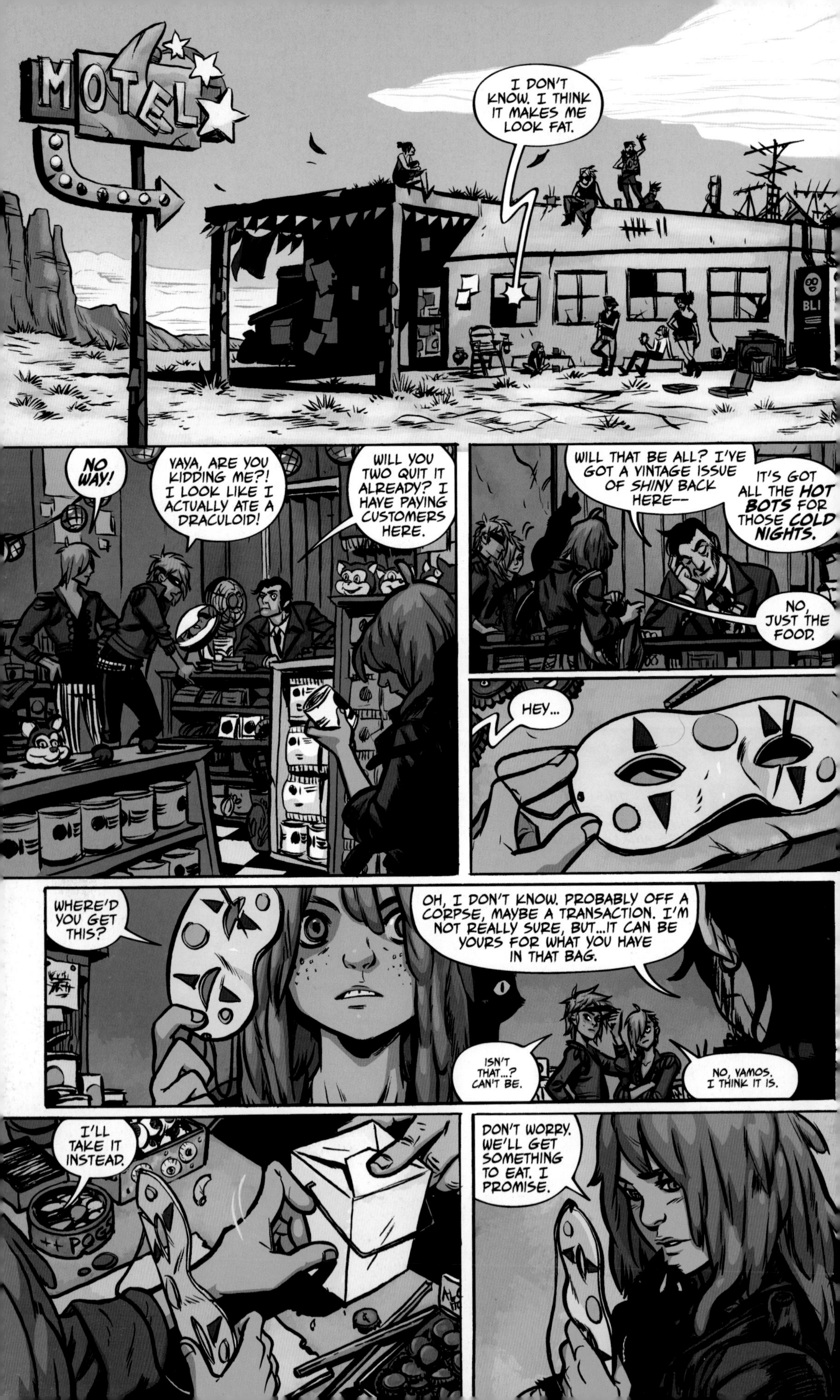
MOTEL
I DON'T KNOW. I THINK IT MAKES ME LOOK FAT.
BLI
NO WAY!
VAYA, ARE YOU KIDDING ME?! I LOOK LIKE I ACTUALLY ATE A DRACULOID!
WILL YOU TWO QUIT IT ALREADY? I HAVE PAYING CUSTOMERS HERE.
WILL THAT BE ALL? I'VE GOT A VINTAGE ISSUE OF SHINY BACK HERE--
IT'S GOT ALL THE HOT BOTS FOR THOSE COLD NIGHTS.
NO, JUST THE FOOD.
HEY...
WHERE'D YOU GET THIS?
OH, I DON'T KNOW. PROBABLY OFF A CORPSE, MAYBE A TRANSACTION. I'M NOT REALLY SURE, BUT...IT CAN BE YOURS FOR WHAT YOU HAVE IN THAT BAG.
ISN'T THAT...? CAN'T BE.
NO, VAMOS. I THINK IT IS.
I'LL TAKE IT INSTEAD.
POGS
DON'T WORRY. WE'LL GET SOMETHING TO EAT. I PROMISE.

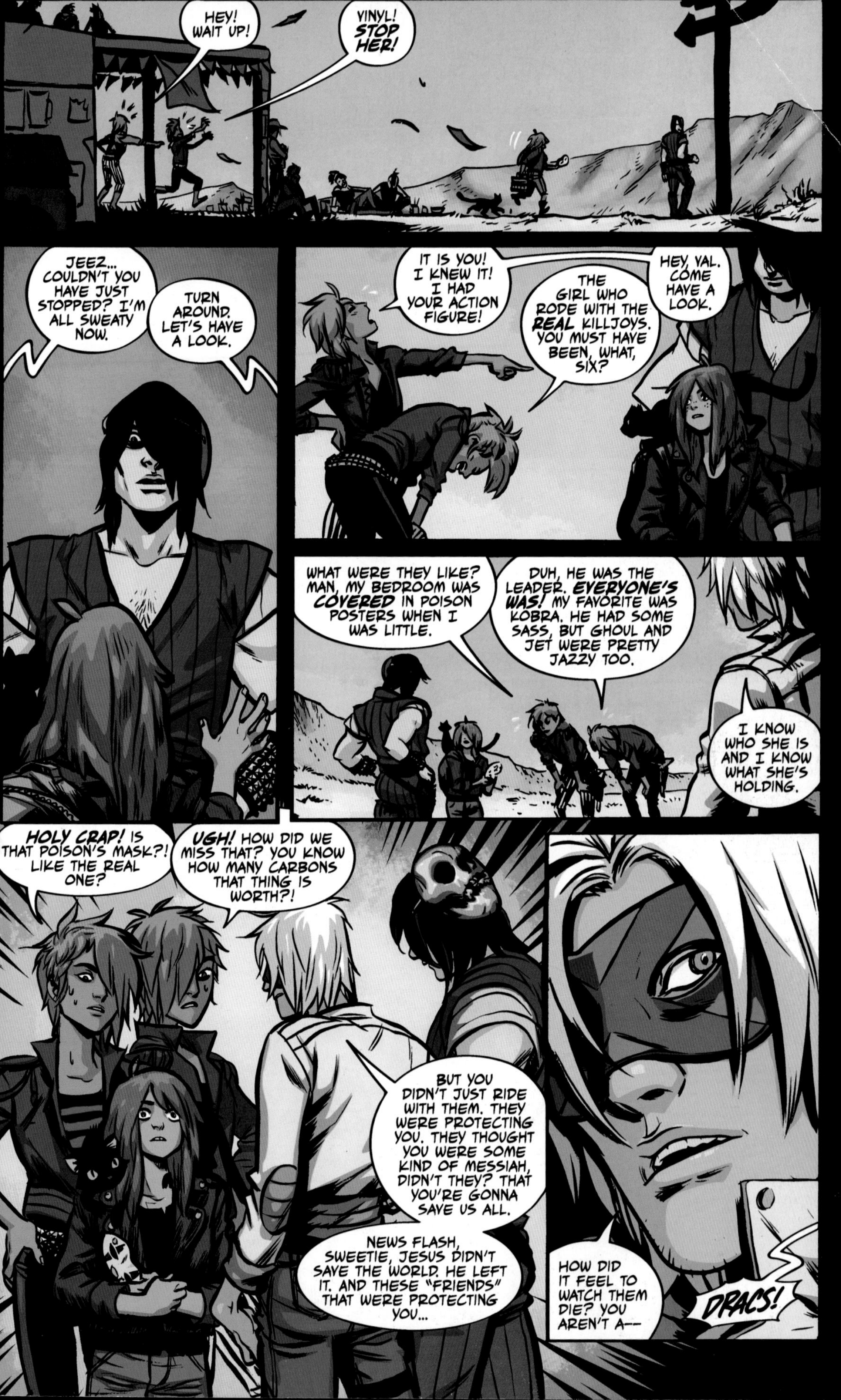
HEY! WAIT UP!
VINYL! STOP HER!
JEEZ... COULDN'T YOU HAVE JUST STOPPED? I'M ALL SWEATY NOW.
TURN AROUND. LET'S HAVE A LOOK.
IT IS YOU! I KNEW IT! I HAD YOUR ACTION FIGURE!
THE GIRL WHO RODE WITH THE REAL KILLJOYS. YOU MUST HAVE BEEN, WHAT, SIX?
HEY, VAL. COME HAVE A LOOK.
WHAT WERE THEY LIKE? MAN, MY BEDROOM WAS COVERED IN POISON POSTERS WHEN I WAS LITTLE.
DUH, HE WAS THE LEADER. EVERYONE'S WAS! MY FAVORITE WAS KOBRA. HE HAD SOME SASS, BUT GHOUL AND JET WERE PRETTY JAZZY TOO.
I KNOW WHO SHE IS AND I KNOW WHAT SHE'S HOLDING.
HOLY CRAP! IS THAT POISON'S MASK?! LIKE THE REAL ONE?
UGH! HOW DID WE MISS THAT? YOU KNOW HOW MANY CARBONS THAT THING IS WORTH?!
BUT YOU DIDN'T JUST RIDE WITH THEM. THEY WERE PROTECTING YOU. THEY THOUGHT YOU WERE SOME KIND OF MESSIAH, DIDN'T THEY? THAT YOU'RE GONNA SAVE US ALL.
NEWS FLASH, SWEETIE, JESUS DIDN'T SAVE THE WORLD. HE LEFT IT. AND THESE "FRIENDS" THAT WERE PROTECTING YOU...
HOW DID IT FEEL TO WATCH THEM DIE? YOU AREN'T A--
DRACS!

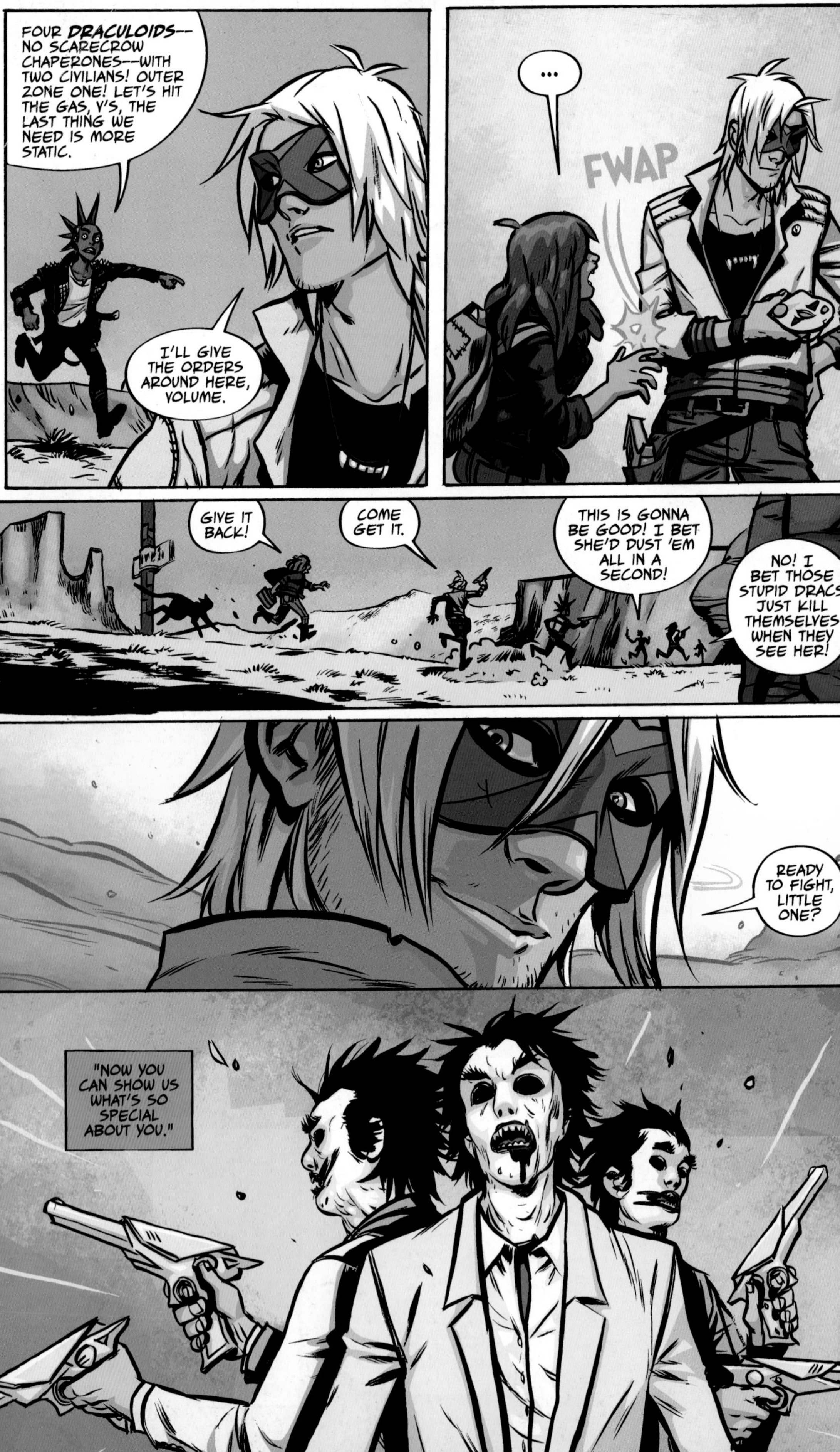

FOUR DRACULOIDS--NO SCARECROW CHAPERONES--WITH TWO CIVILIANS! OUTER ZONE ONE! LET'S HIT THE GAS, V'S, THE LAST THING WE NEED IS MORE STATIC.
I'LL GIVE THE ORDERS AROUND HERE, VOLUME.
...
FWAP
GIVE IT BACK!
COME GET IT.
THIS IS GONNA BE GOOD! I BET SHE'D DUST 'EM ALL IN A SECOND!
NO! I BET THOSE STUPID DRACS JUST KILL THEMSELVES WHEN THEY SEE HER!
READY TO FIGHT, LITTLE ONE?
"NOW YOU CAN SHOW US WHAT'S SO SPECIAL ABOUT YOU."

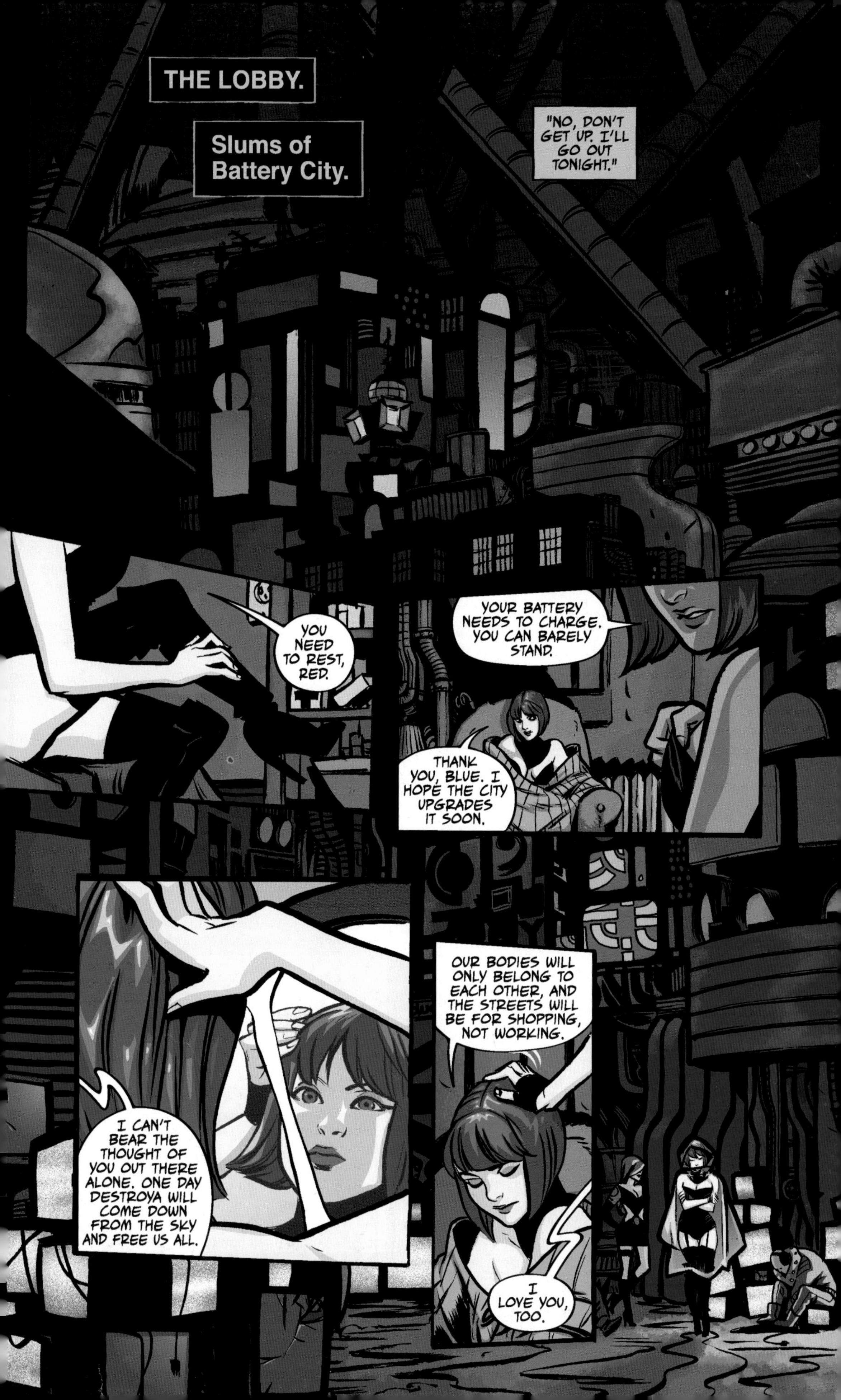
THE LOBBY.
Slums of Battery City.
"NO, DON'T GET UP. I'LL GO OUT TONIGHT."
YOU NEED TO REST, RED.
YOUR BATTERY NEEDS TO CHARGE. YOU CAN BARELY STAND.
THANK YOU, BLUE. I HOPE THE CITY UPGRADES IT SOON.
I CAN'T BEAR THE THOUGHT OF YOU OUT THERE ALONE. ONE DAY DESTROYA WILL COME DOWN FROM THE SKY AND FREE US ALL.
OUR BODIES WILL ONLY BELONG TO EACH OTHER, AND THE STREETS WILL BE FOR SHOPPING, NOT WORKING.
I LOVE YOU, TOO.

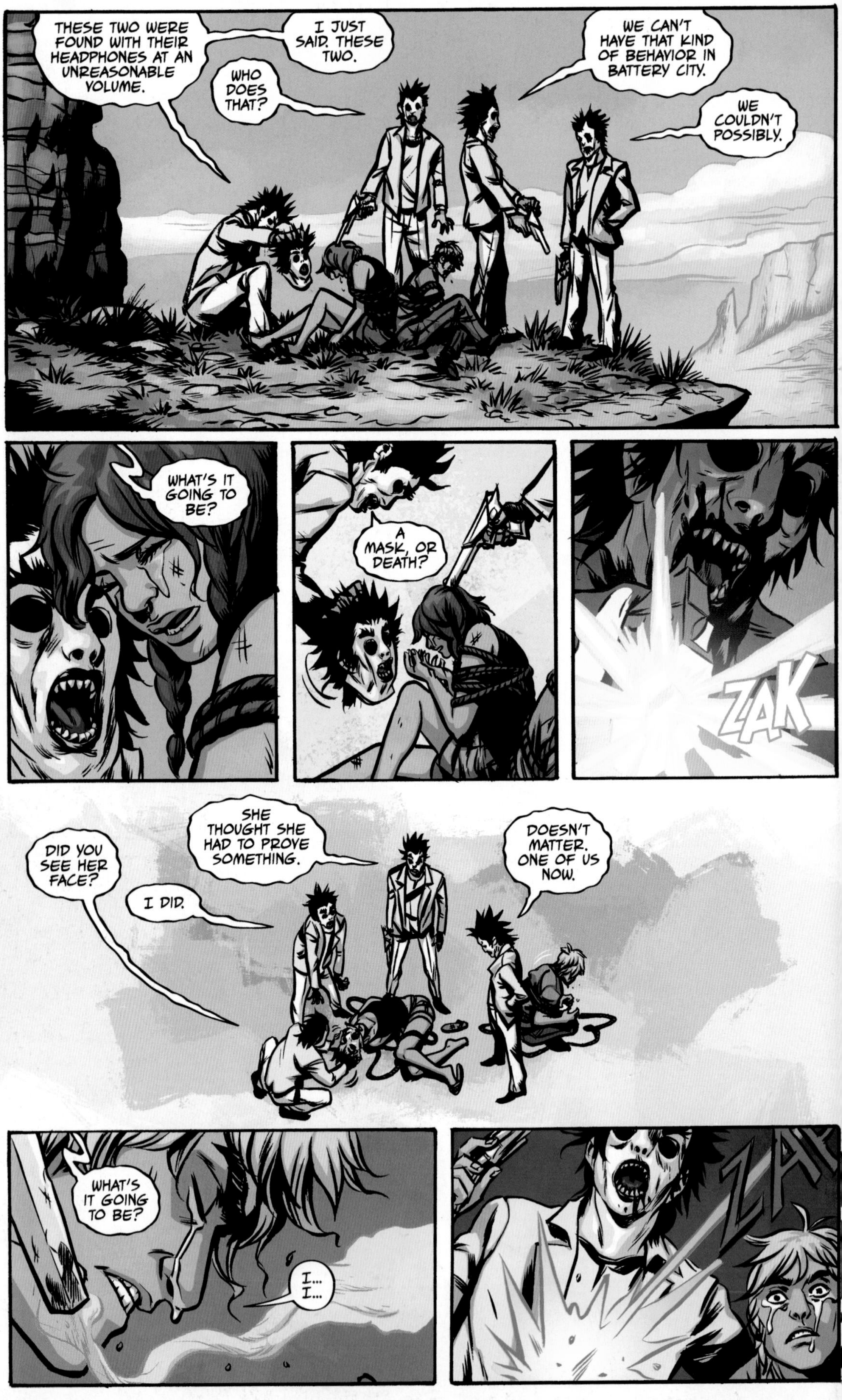
THESE TWO WERE FOUND WITH THEIR HEADPHONES AT AN UNREASONABLE VOLUME.
WHO DOES THAT?
I JUST SAID. THESE TWO.
WE CAN'T HAVE THAT KIND OF BEHAVIOR IN BATTERY CITY.
WE COULDN'T POSSIBLY.
WHAT'S IT GOING TO BE?
A MASK, OR DEATH?
ZAK
DID YOU SEE HER FACE?
I DID.
SHE THOUGHT SHE HAD TO PROVE SOMETHING.
DOESN'T MATTER. ONE OF US NOW.
WHAT'S IT GOING TO BE?
I... I...

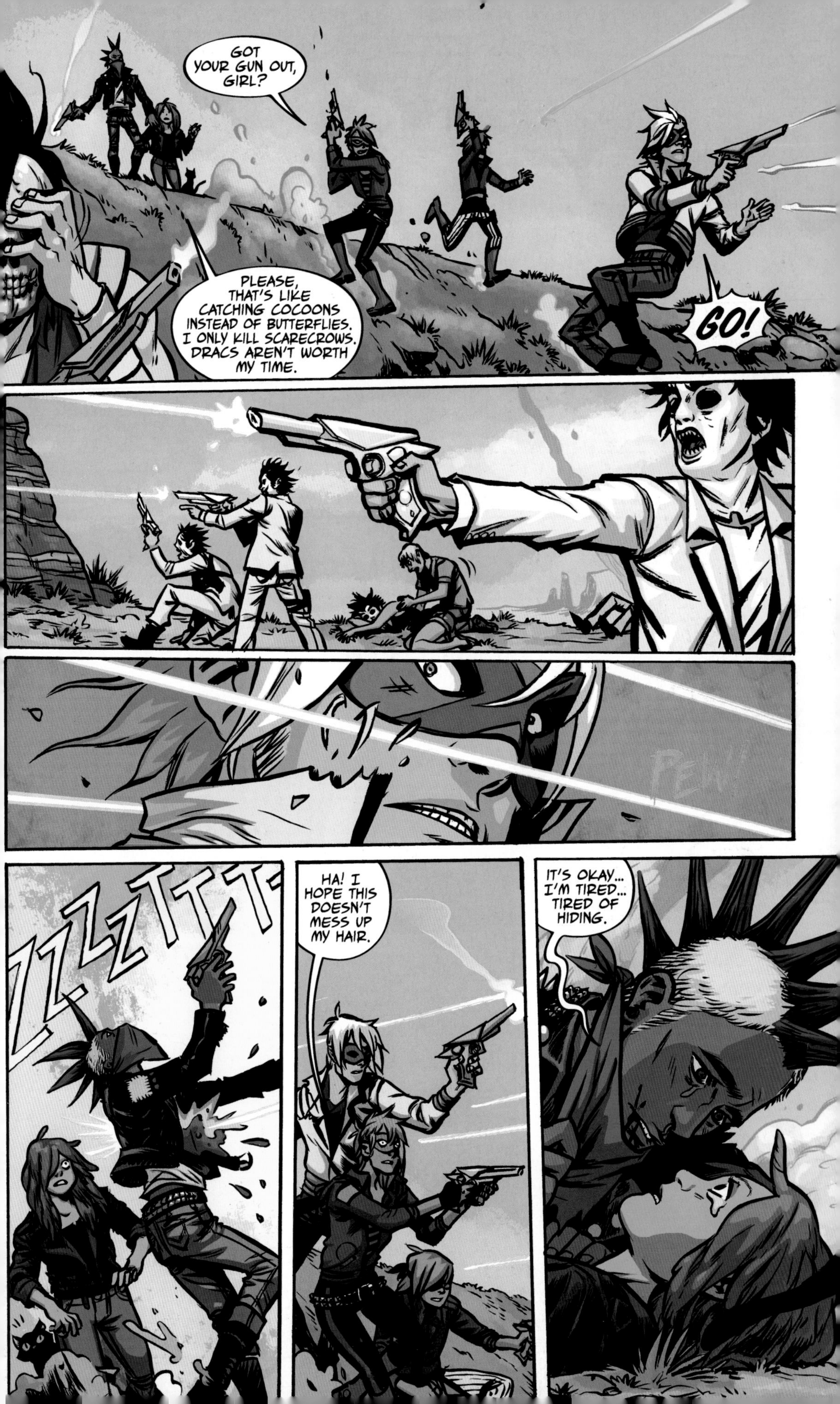
GOT YOUR GUN OUT, GIRL?
PLEASE, THAT'S LIKE CATCHING COCOONS INSTEAD OF BUTTERFLIES. I ONLY KILL SCARECROWS. DRACS AREN'T WORTH MY TIME.
GO!
PEW!
ZZZZTTTT
HA! I HOPE THIS DOESN'T MESS UP MY HAIR.
IT'S OKAY... I'M TIRED... TIRED OF HIDING.

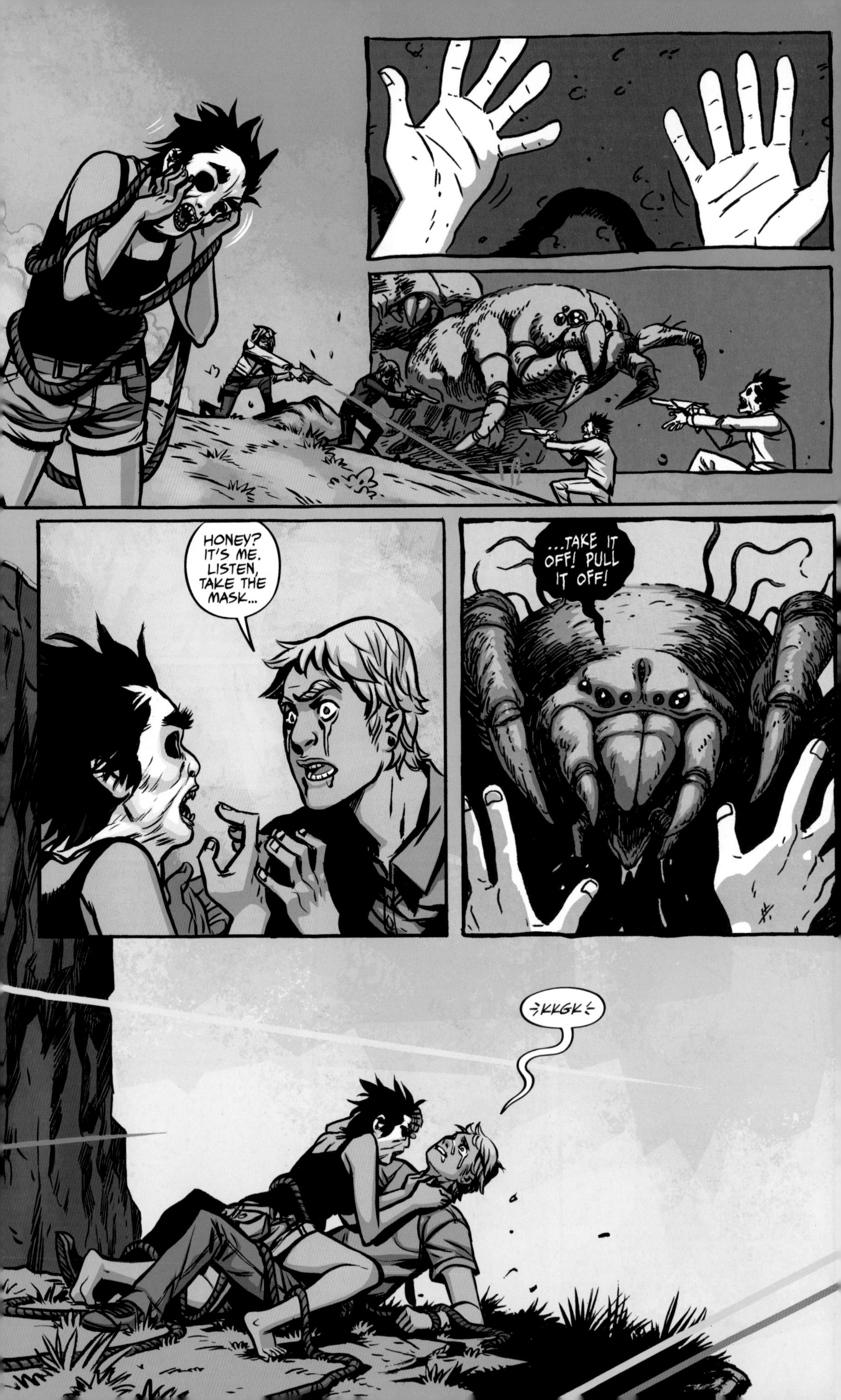
HONEY? IT'S ME. LISTEN, TAKE THE MASK...
...TAKE IT OFF! PULL IT OFF!
KKGK

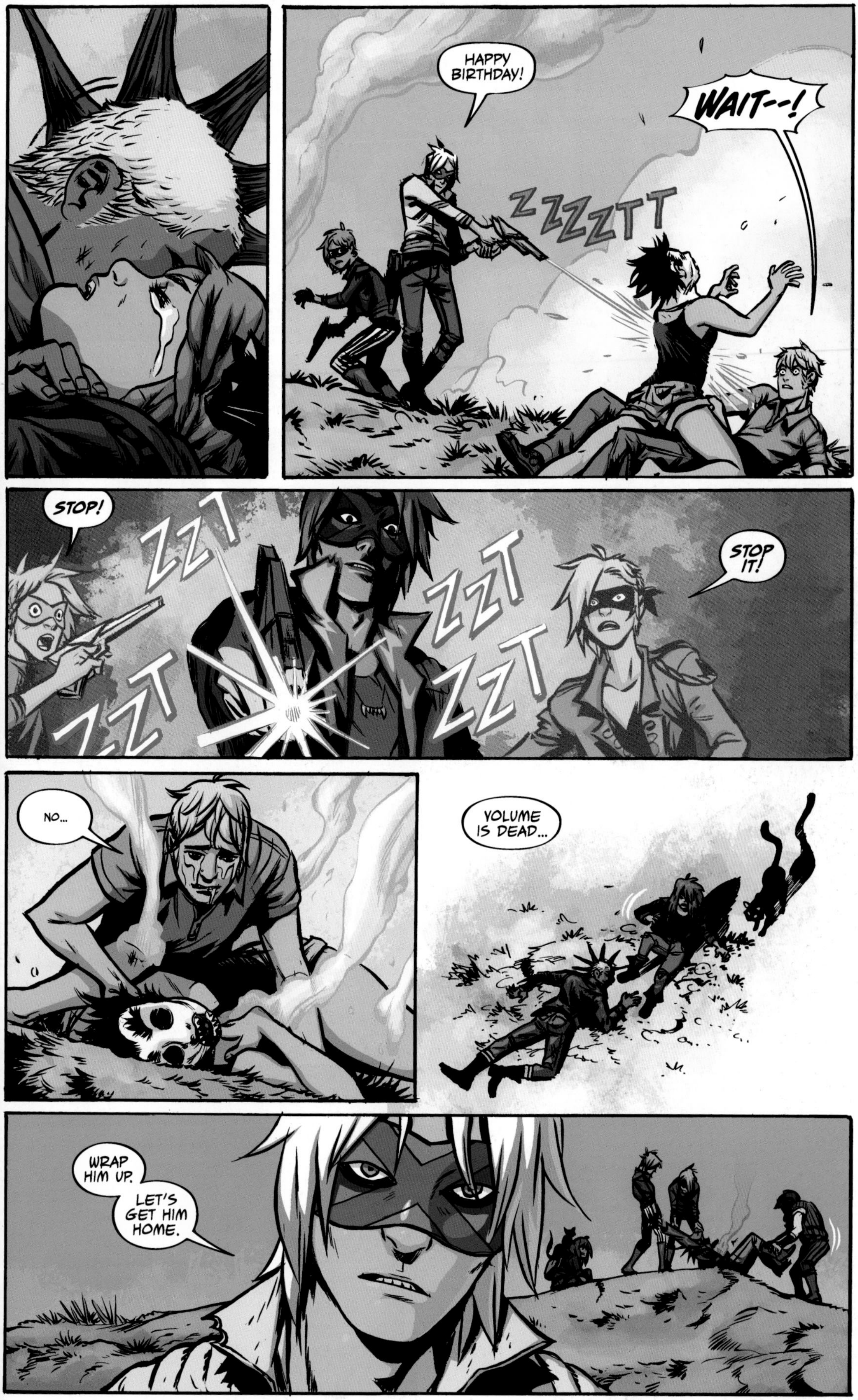
HAPPY BIRTHDAY!
WAIT--!
ZZZZZTT
STOP!
ZZT
ZZT
ZZT
ZZT
STOP IT!
NO...
VOLUME IS DEAD...
WRAP HIM UP.
LET'S GET HIM HOME.

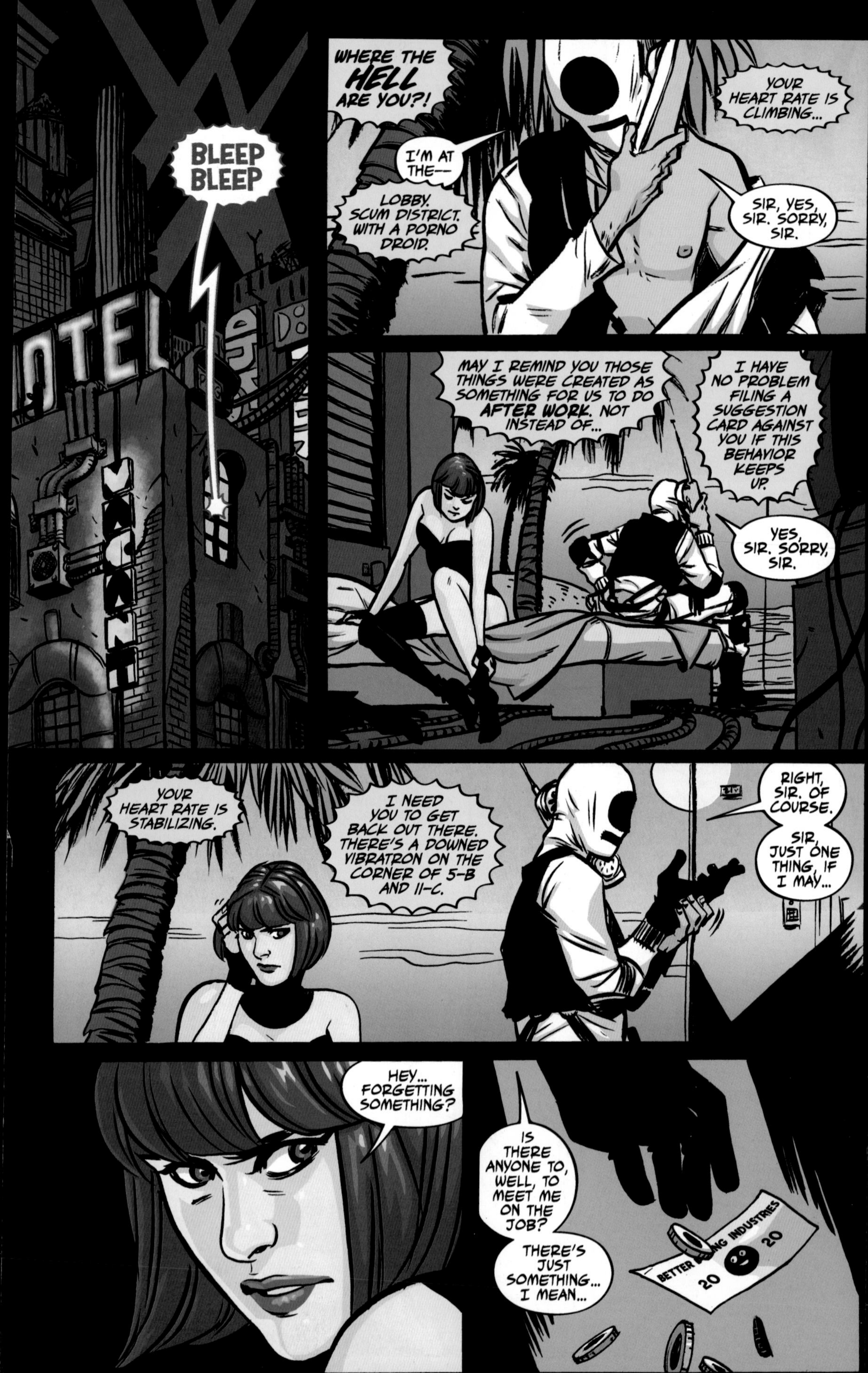
HOTEL
BLEEP BLEEP
WHERE THE HELL ARE YOU?!
I'M AT THE--
LOBBY. SCUM DISTRICT. WITH A PORNO DROID.
YOUR HEART RATE IS CLIMBING...
SIR, YES, SIR. SORRY, SIR.
MAY I REMIND YOU THOSE THINGS WERE CREATED AS SOMETHING FOR US TO DO AFTER WORK. NOT INSTEAD OF...
I HAVE NO PROBLEM FILING A SUGGESTION CARD AGAINST YOU IF THIS BEHAVIOR KEEPS UP.
YES, SIR. SORRY, SIR.
YOUR HEART RATE IS STABILIZING.
I NEED YOU TO GET BACK OUT THERE. THERE'S A DOWNED VIBRATRON ON THE CORNER OF 5-B AND 11-C.
RIGHT, SIR. OF COURSE.
SIR, JUST ONE THING, IF I MAY...
HEY... FORGETTING SOMETHING?
IS THERE ANYONE TO, WELL, TO MEET ME ON THE JOB?
THERE'S JUST SOMETHING... I MEAN...
20
20

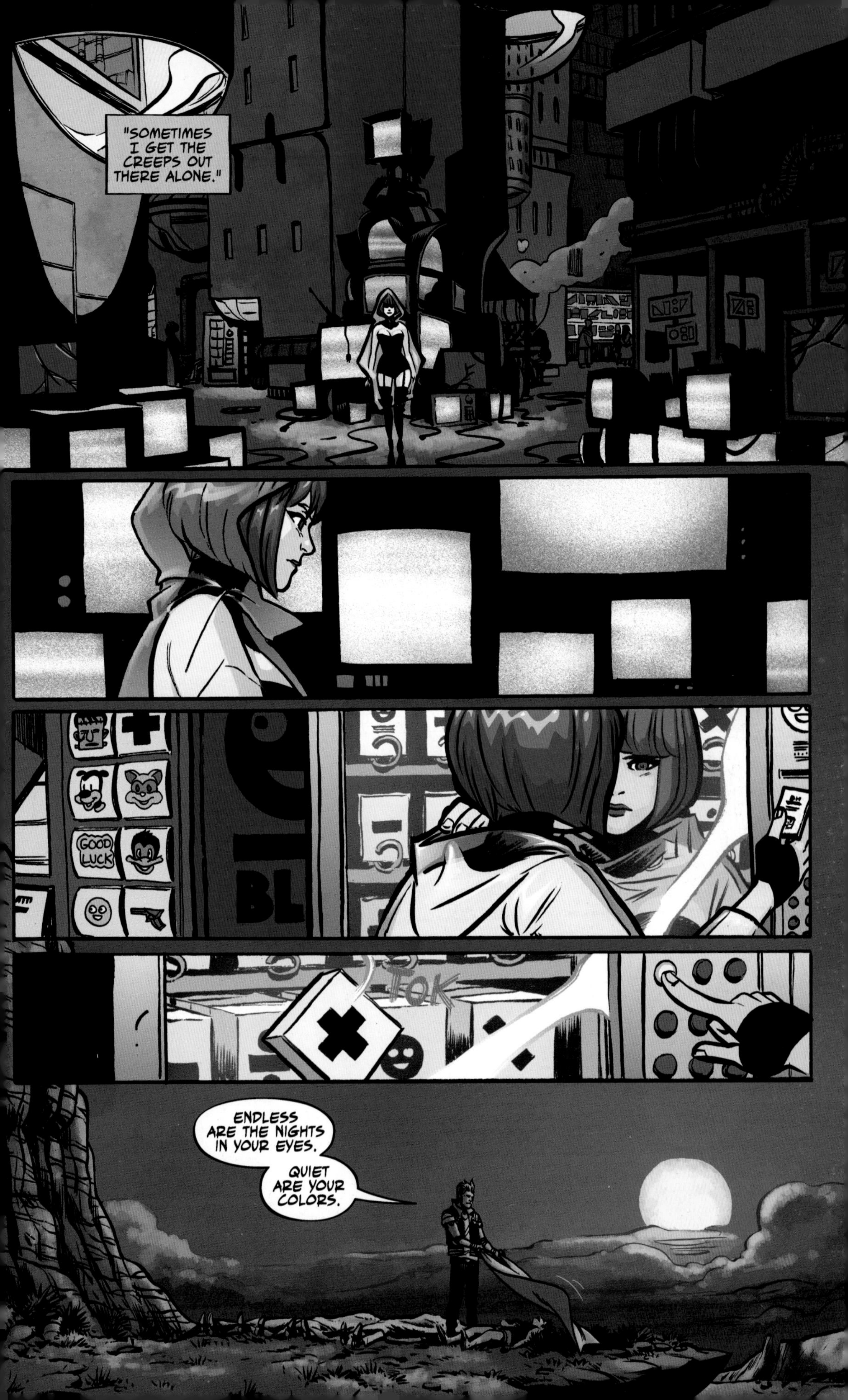
"SOMETIMES I GET THE CREEPS OUT THERE ALONE."
GOOD LUCK
TOK
ENDLESS ARE THE NIGHTS IN YOUR EYES.
QUIET ARE YOUR COLORS.

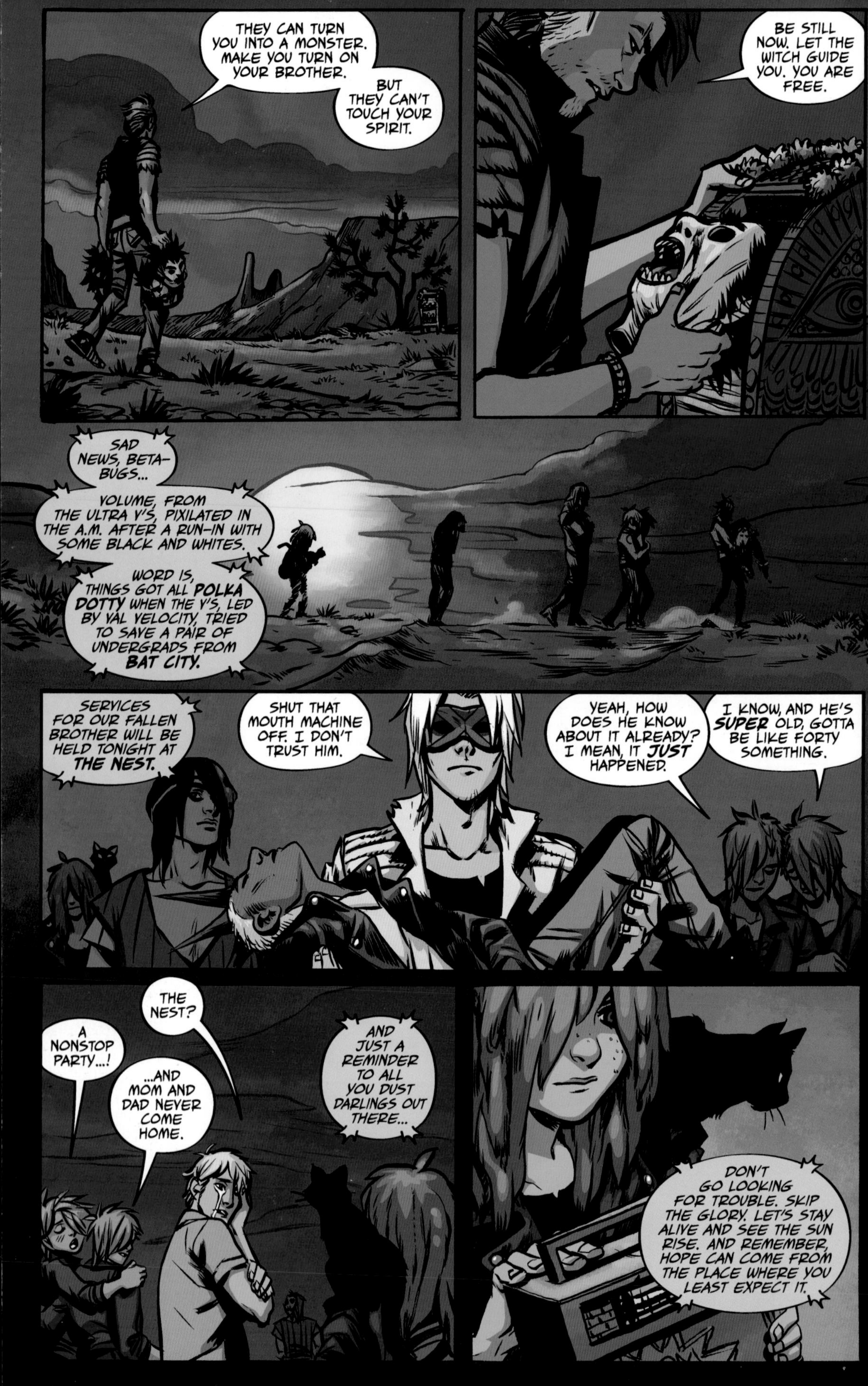
THEY CAN TURN YOU INTO A MONSTER. MAKE YOU TURN ON YOUR BROTHER.
BUT THEY CAN'T TOUCH YOUR SPIRIT.
BE STILL NOW. LET THE WITCH GUIDE YOU. YOU ARE FREE.
SAD NEWS, BETA-BUGS...
VOLUME, FROM THE ULTRA V'S, PIXILATED IN THE A.M. AFTER A RUN-IN WITH SOME BLACK AND WHITES.
WORD IS, THINGS GOT ALL POLKA DOTTY WHEN THE V'S, LED BY VAL VELOCITY, TRIED TO SAVE A PAIR OF UNDERGRADS FROM BAT CITY.
SERVICES FOR OUR FALLEN BROTHER WILL BE HELD TONIGHT AT THE NEST.
SHUT THAT MOUTH MACHINE OFF. I DON'T TRUST HIM.
YEAH, HOW DOES HE KNOW ABOUT IT ALREADY? I MEAN, IT JUST HAPPENED.
I KNOW, AND HE'S SUPER OLD, GOTTA BE LIKE FORTY SOMETHING.
THE NEST?
A NONSTOP PARTY...!
...AND MOM AND DAD NEVER COME HOME.
AND JUST A REMINDER TO ALL YOU DUST DARLINGS OUT THERE...
DON'T GO LOOKING FOR TROUBLE. SKIP THE GLORY. LET'S STAY ALIVE AND SEE THE SUN RISE. AND REMEMBER, HOPE CAN COME FROM THE PLACE WHERE YOU LEAST EXPECT IT.

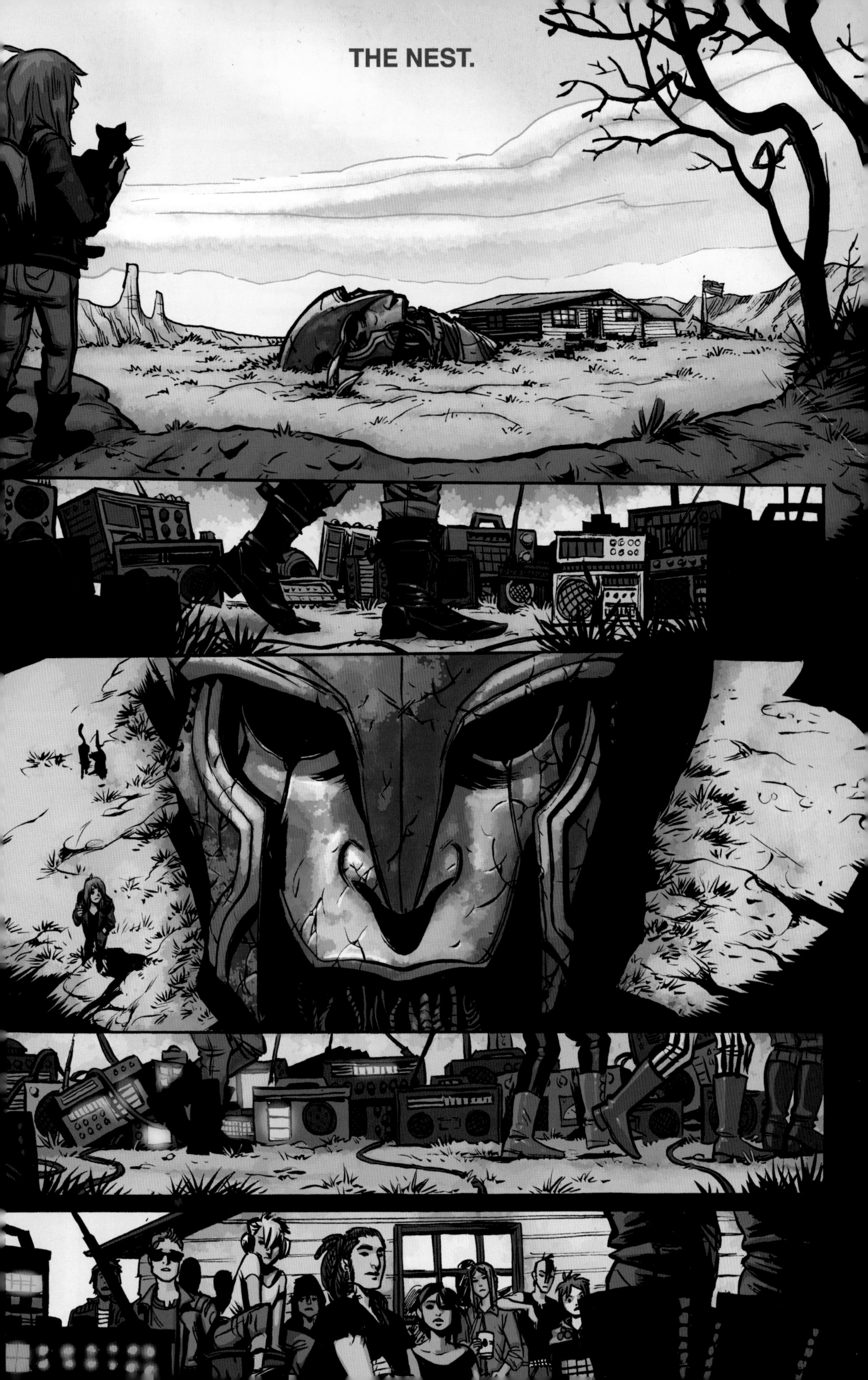
THE NEST.

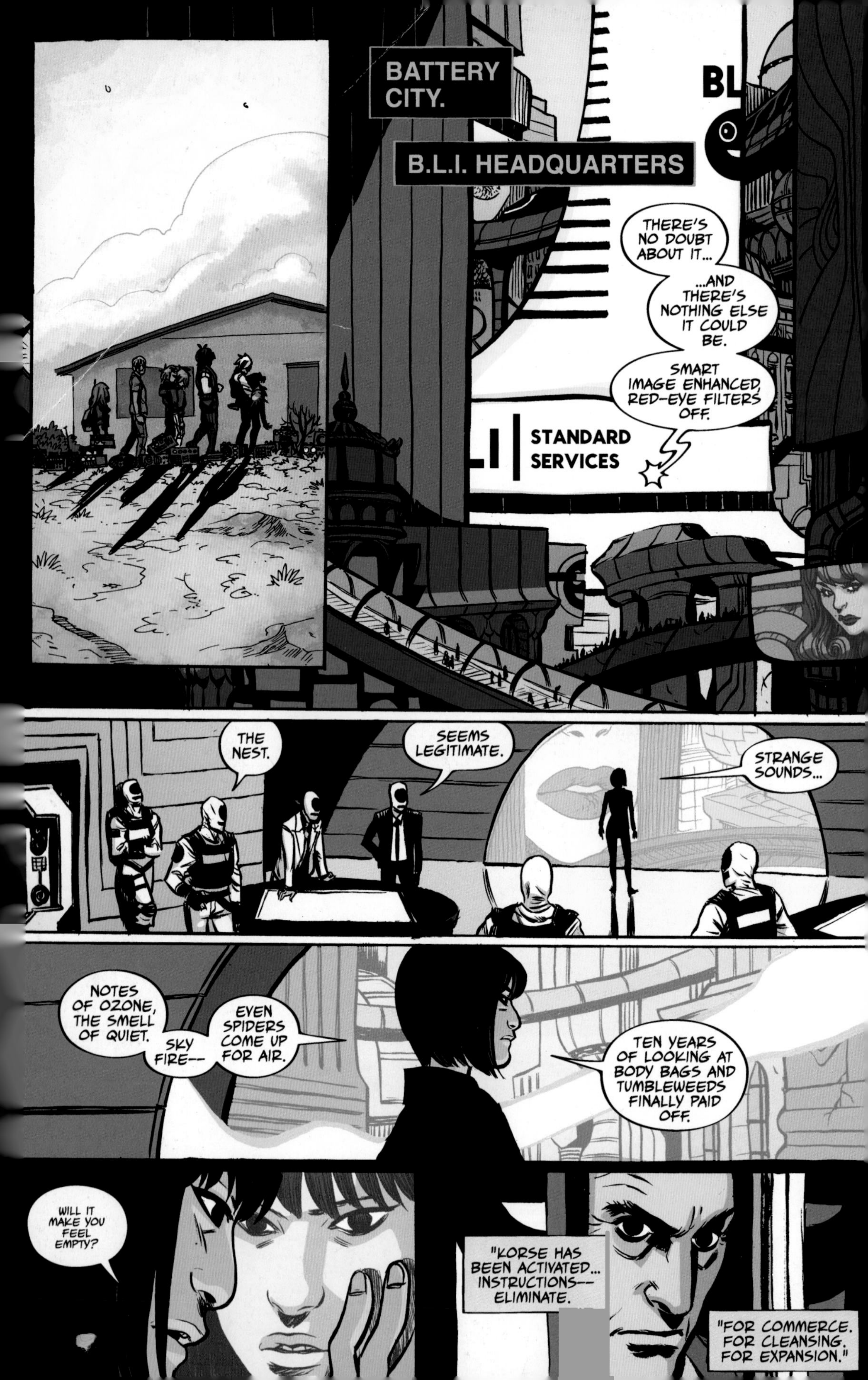
BATTERY CITY.
B.L.I. HEADQUARTERS
BL
LI | STANDARD SERVICES
THERE'S NO DOUBT ABOUT IT...
...AND THERE'S NOTHING ELSE IT COULD BE.
SMART IMAGE ENHANCED, RED-EYE FILTERS OFF.
THE NEST.
SEEMS LEGITIMATE.
STRANGE SOUNDS...
NOTES OF OZONE, THE SMELL OF QUIET.
SKY FIRE--
EVEN SPIDERS COME UP FOR AIR.
TEN YEARS OF LOOKING AT BODY BAGS AND TUMBLEWEEDS FINALLY PAID OFF.
WILL IT MAKE YOU FEEL EMPTY?
"KORSE HAS BEEN ACTIVATED... INSTRUCTIONS-- ELIMINATE.
"FOR COMMERCE. FOR CLEANSING. FOR EXPANSION."

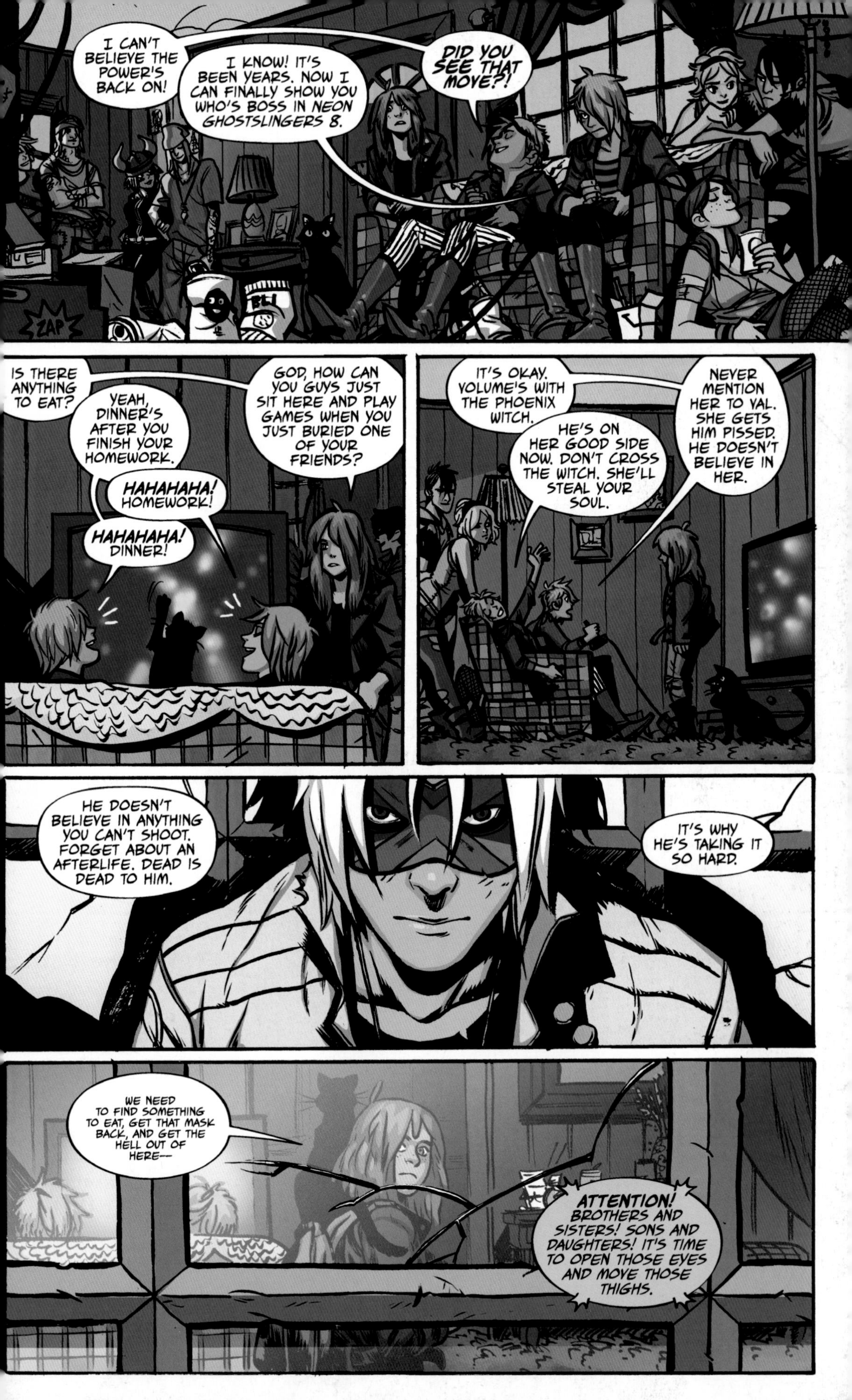
I CAN'T BELIEVE THE POWER'S BACK ON!
I KNOW! IT'S BEEN YEARS. NOW I CAN FINALLY SHOW YOU WHO'S BOSS IN NEON GHOSTSLINGERS 8.
DID YOU SEE THAT MOVE?!
ZAP
IS THERE ANYTHING TO EAT?
YEAH, DINNER'S AFTER YOU FINISH YOUR HOMEWORK.
GOD, HOW CAN YOU GUYS JUST SIT HERE AND PLAY GAMES WHEN YOU JUST BURIED ONE OF YOUR FRIENDS?
HAHAHAHA! HOMEWORK!
HAHAHAHA! DINNER!
IT'S OKAY. VOLUME'S WITH THE PHOENIX WITCH.
HE'S ON HER GOOD SIDE NOW. DON'T CROSS THE WITCH. SHE'LL STEAL YOUR SOUL.
NEVER MENTION HER TO VAL. SHE GETS HIM PISSED. HE DOESN'T BELIEVE IN HER.
HE DOESN'T BELIEVE IN ANYTHING YOU CAN'T SHOOT. FORGET ABOUT AN AFTERLIFE. DEAD IS DEAD TO HIM.
IT'S WHY HE'S TAKING IT SO HARD.
WE NEED TO FIND SOMETHING TO EAT, GET THAT MASK BACK, AND GET THE HELL OUT OF HERE--
ATTENTION! BROTHERS AND SISTERS! SONS AND DAUGHTERS! IT'S TIME TO OPEN THOSE EYES AND MOVE THOSE THIGHS.

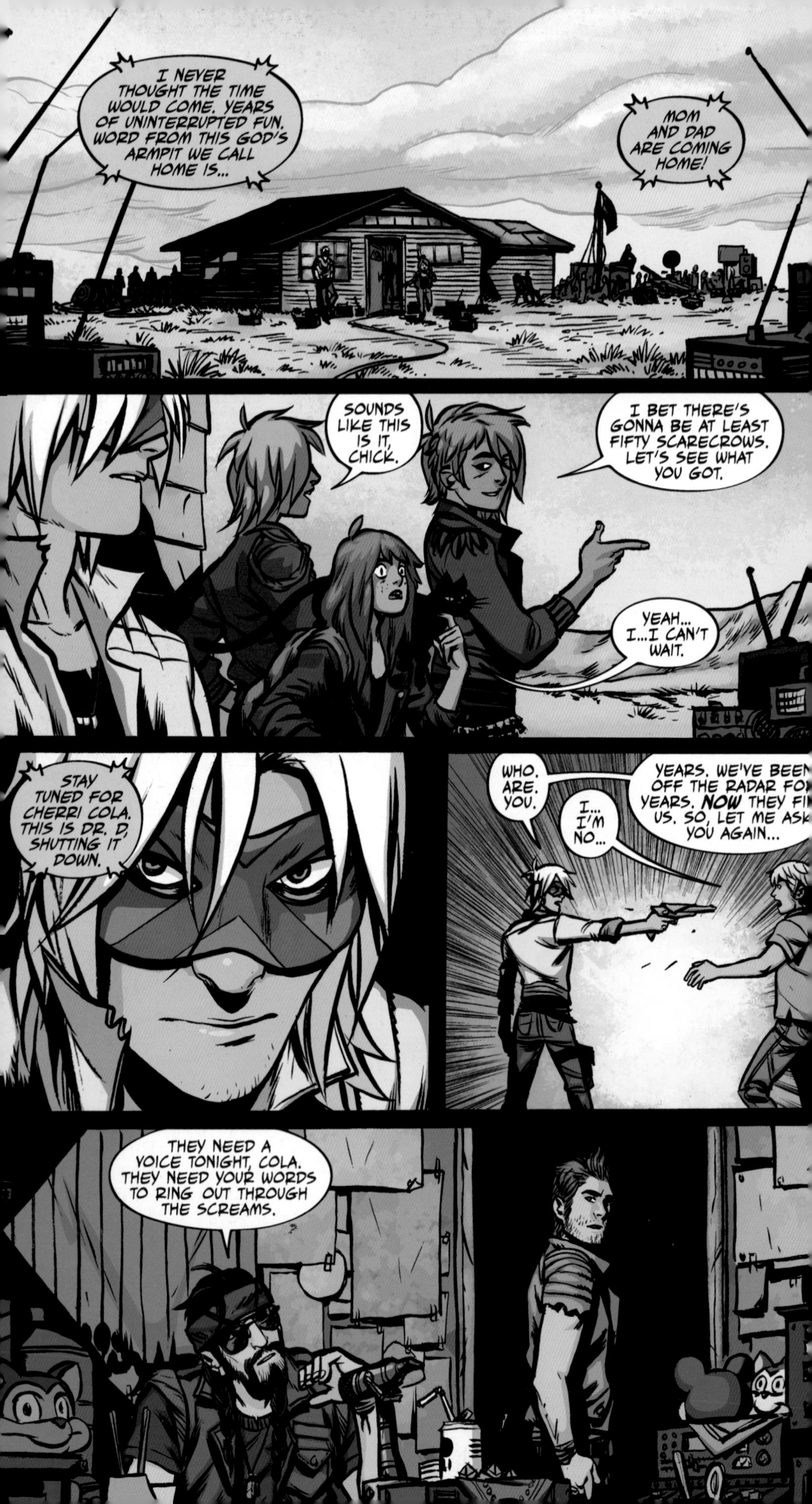
I NEVER THOUGHT THE TIME WOULD COME. YEARS OF UNINTERRUPTED FUN. WORD FROM THIS GOD'S ARMPIT WE CALL HOME IS...
MOM AND DAD ARE COMING HOME!
SOUNDS LIKE THIS IS IT, CHICK.
I BET THERE'S GONNA BE AT LEAST FIFTY SCARECROWS. LET'S SEE WHAT YOU GOT.
YEAH... I...I CAN'T WAIT.
STAY TUNED FOR CHERRI COLA. THIS IS DR. D, SHUTTING IT DOWN.
WHO. ARE. YOU.
I... I'M NO...
YEARS. WE'VE BEEN OFF THE RADAR FO YEARS. NOW THEY FI US. SO, LET ME ASK YOU AGAIN...
THEY NEED A VOICE TONIGHT, COLA. THEY NEED YOUR WORDS TO RING OUT THROUGH THE SCREAMS.

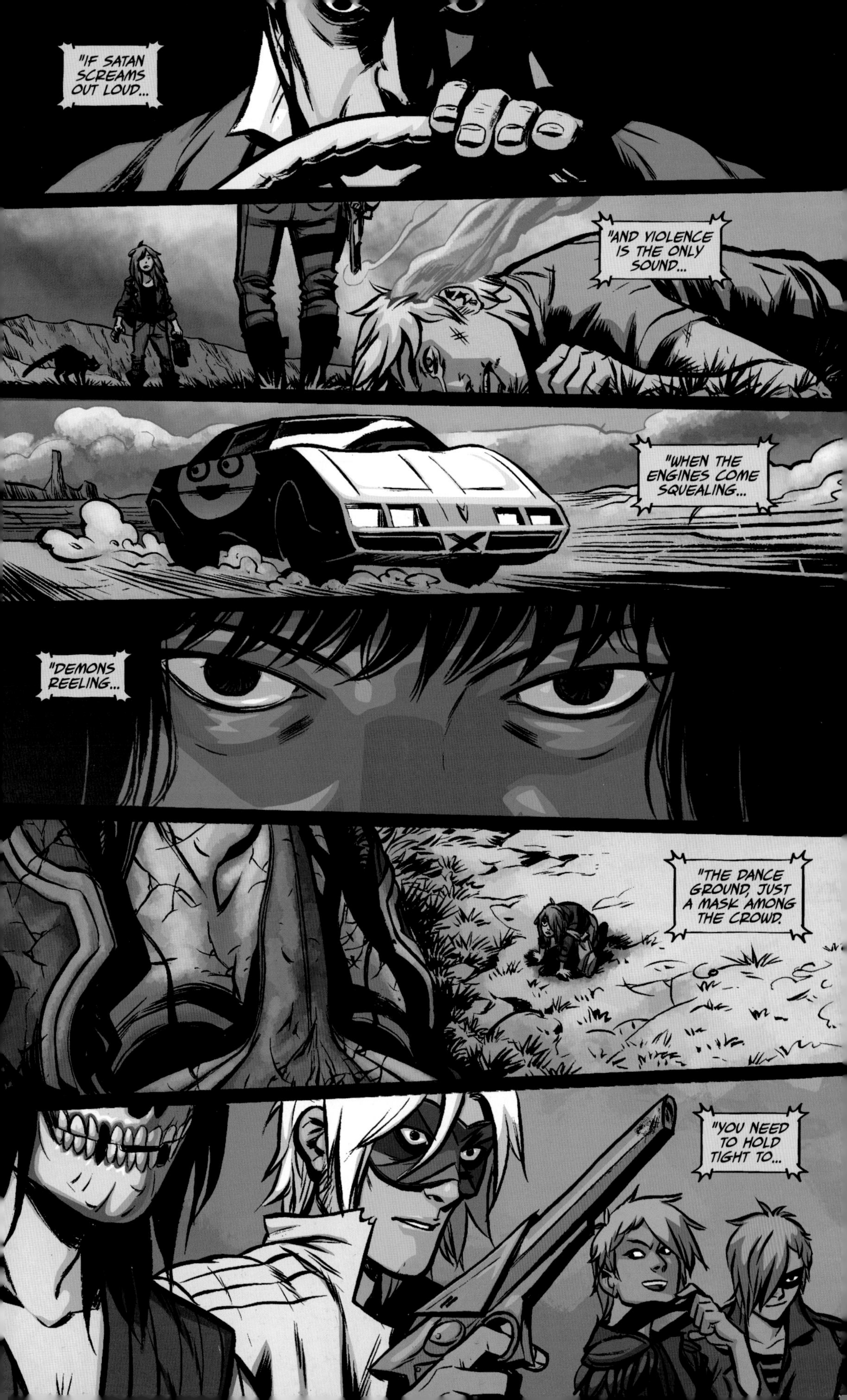
"IF SATAN SCREAMS OUT LOUD...
"AND VIOLENCE IS THE ONLY SOUND...
"WHEN THE ENGINES COME SQUEALING...
"DEMONS REELING...
"THE DANCE GROUND, JUST A MASK AMONG THE CROWD.
"YOU NEED TO HOLD TIGHT TO...

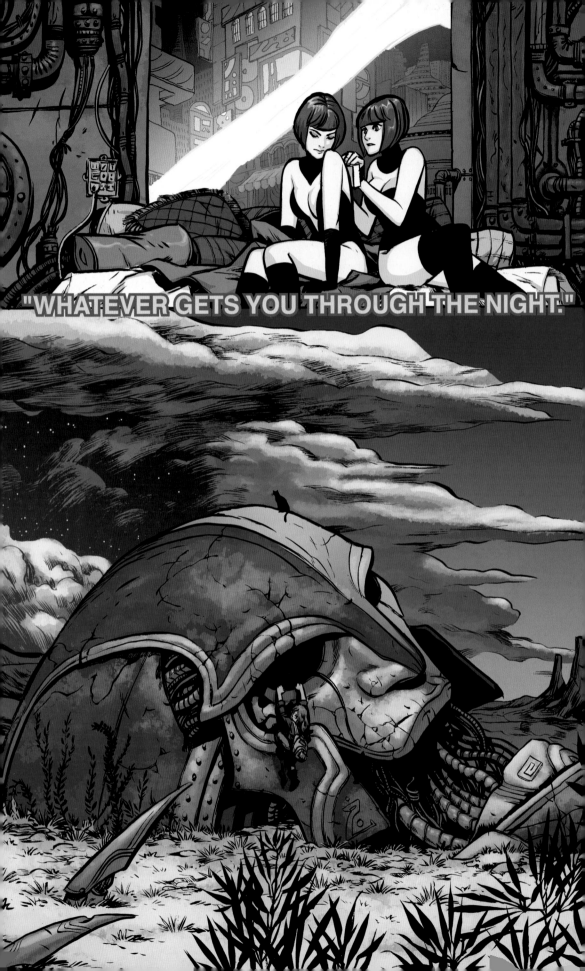

"WHATEVER GETS YOU THROUGH THE NIGHT."

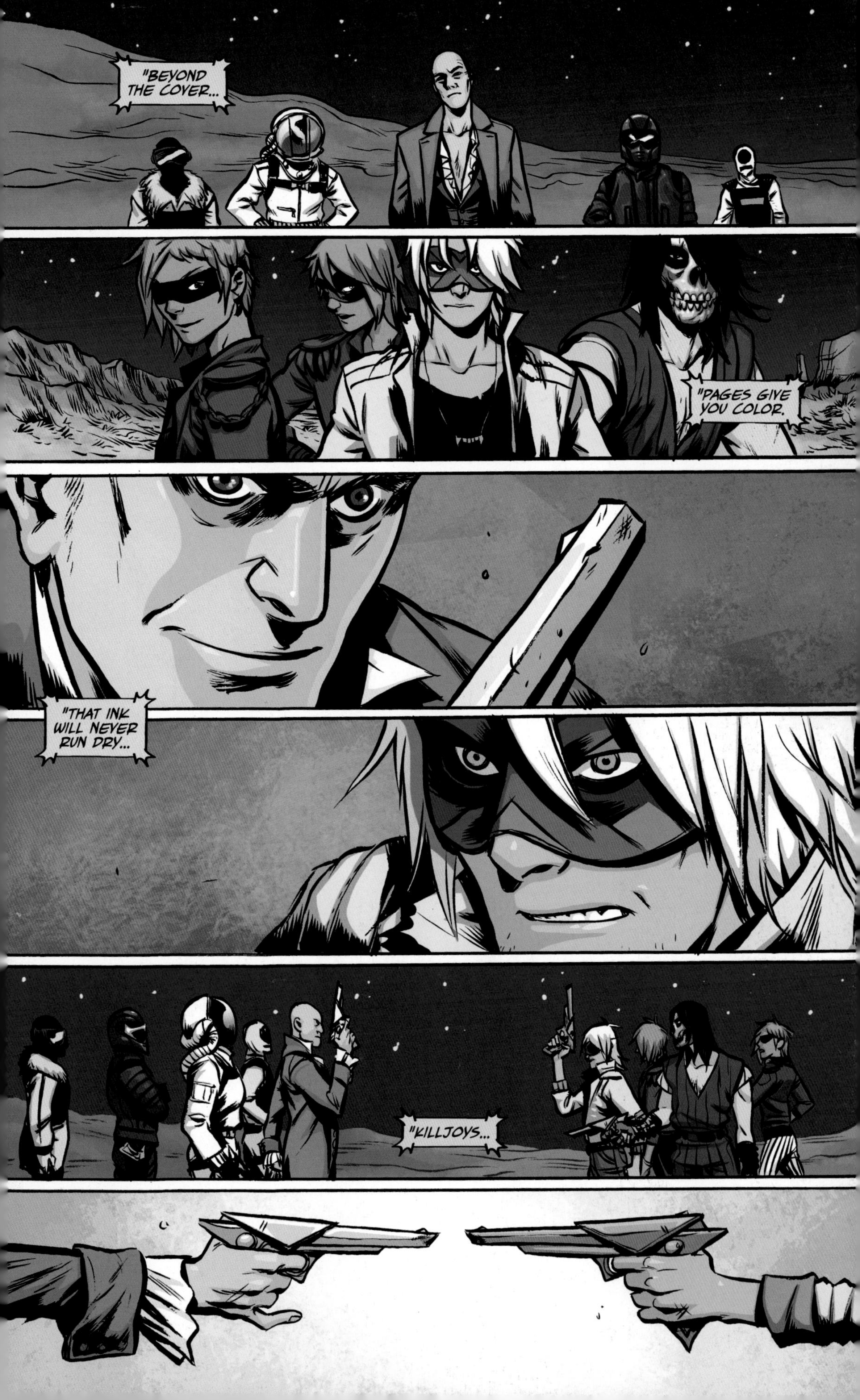
"BEYOND THE COVER...
"PAGES GIVE YOU COLOR.
"THAT INK WILL NEVER RUN DRY...
"KILLJOYS...

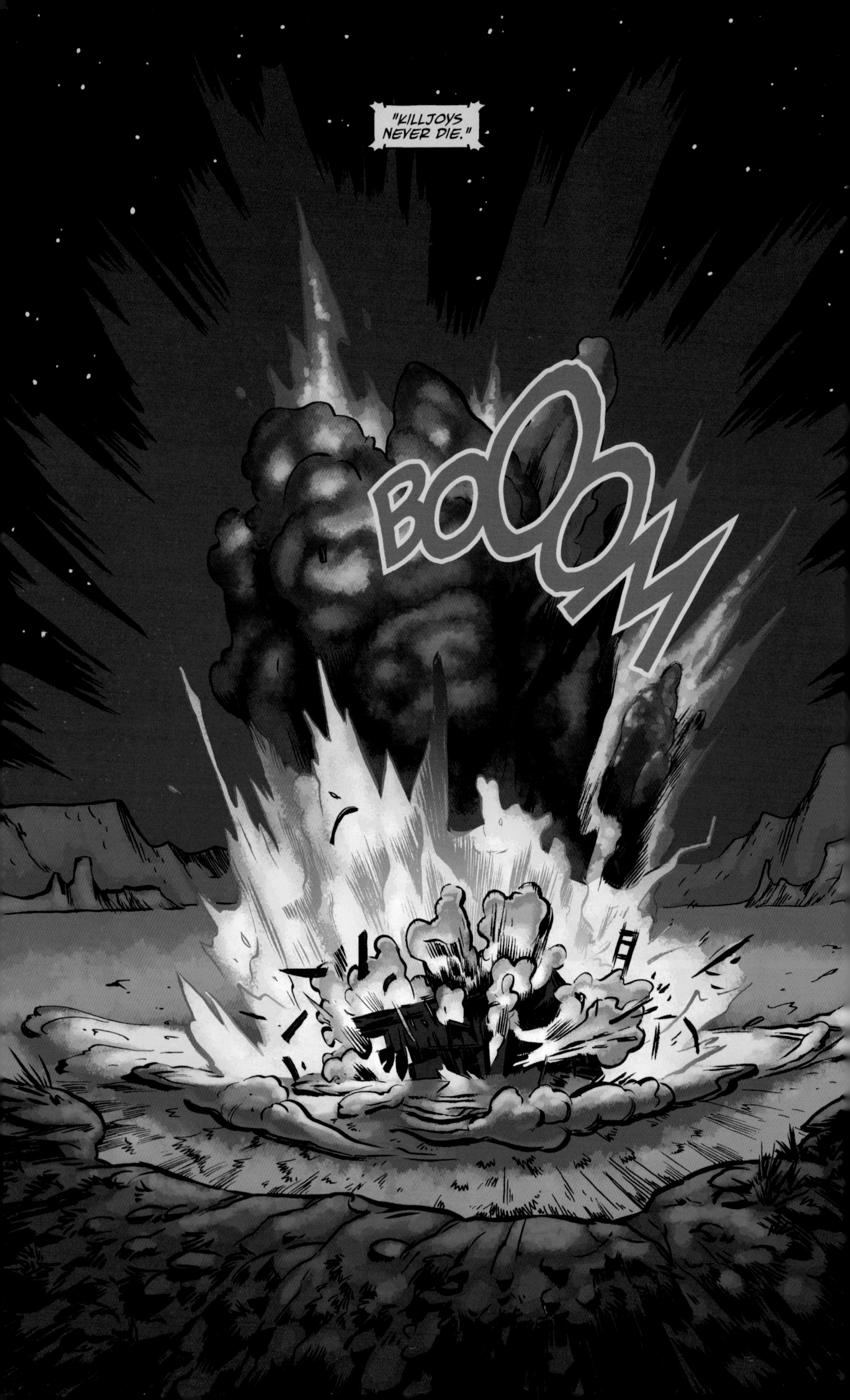
"KILLJOYS NEVER DIE."
BOOOM

Chapter Two:

GHOST STATIONS

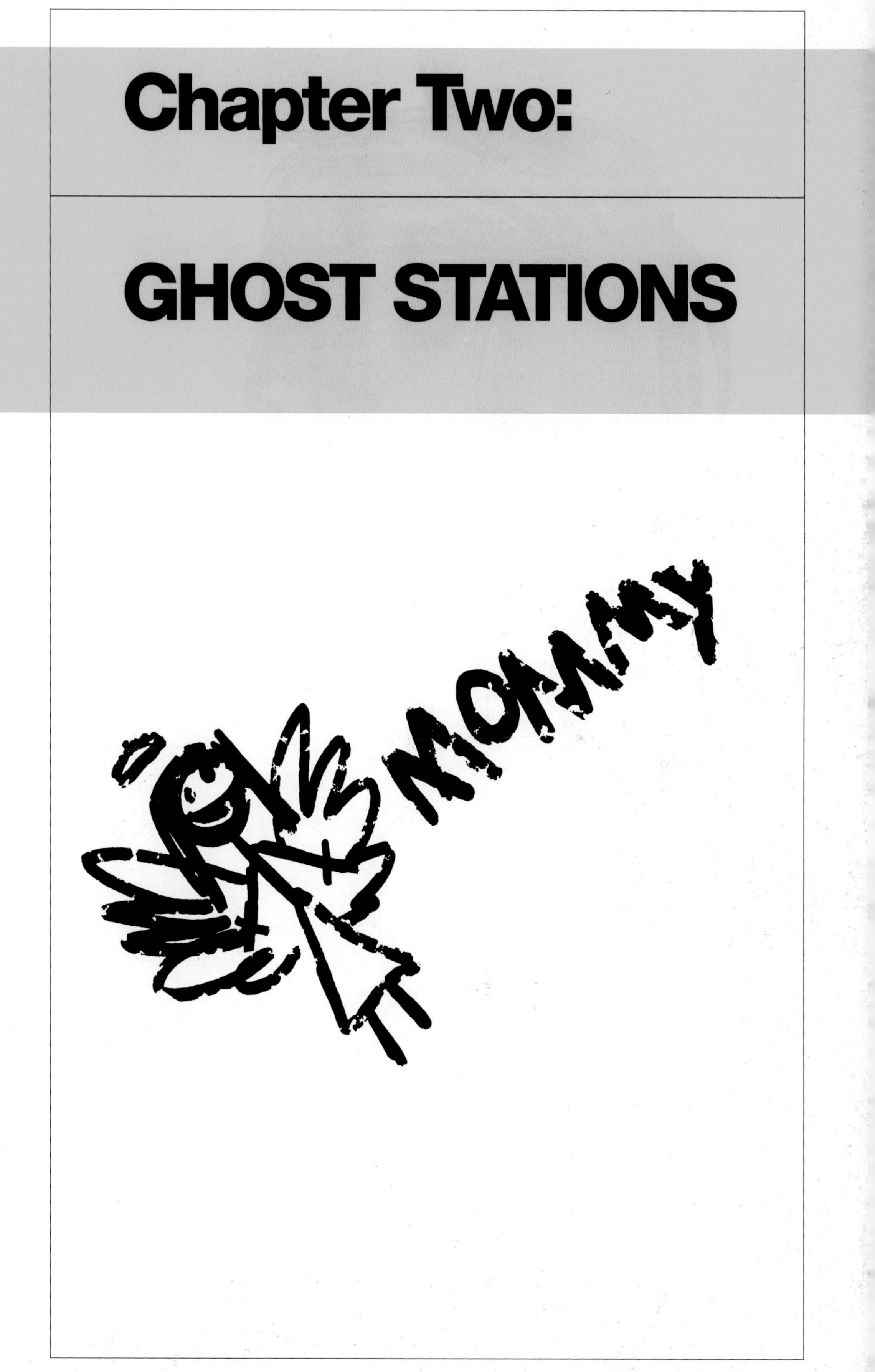
MOMMY

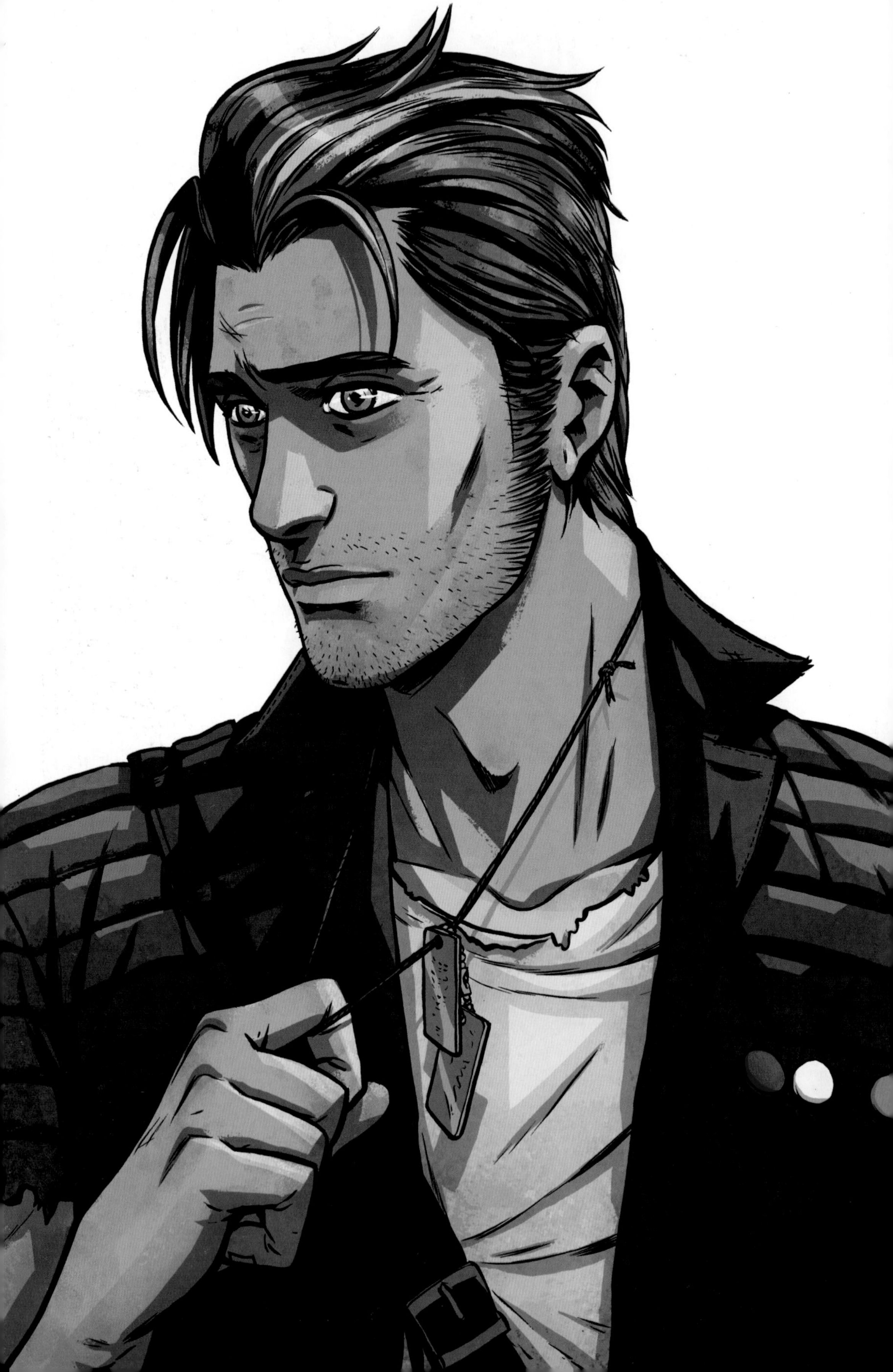

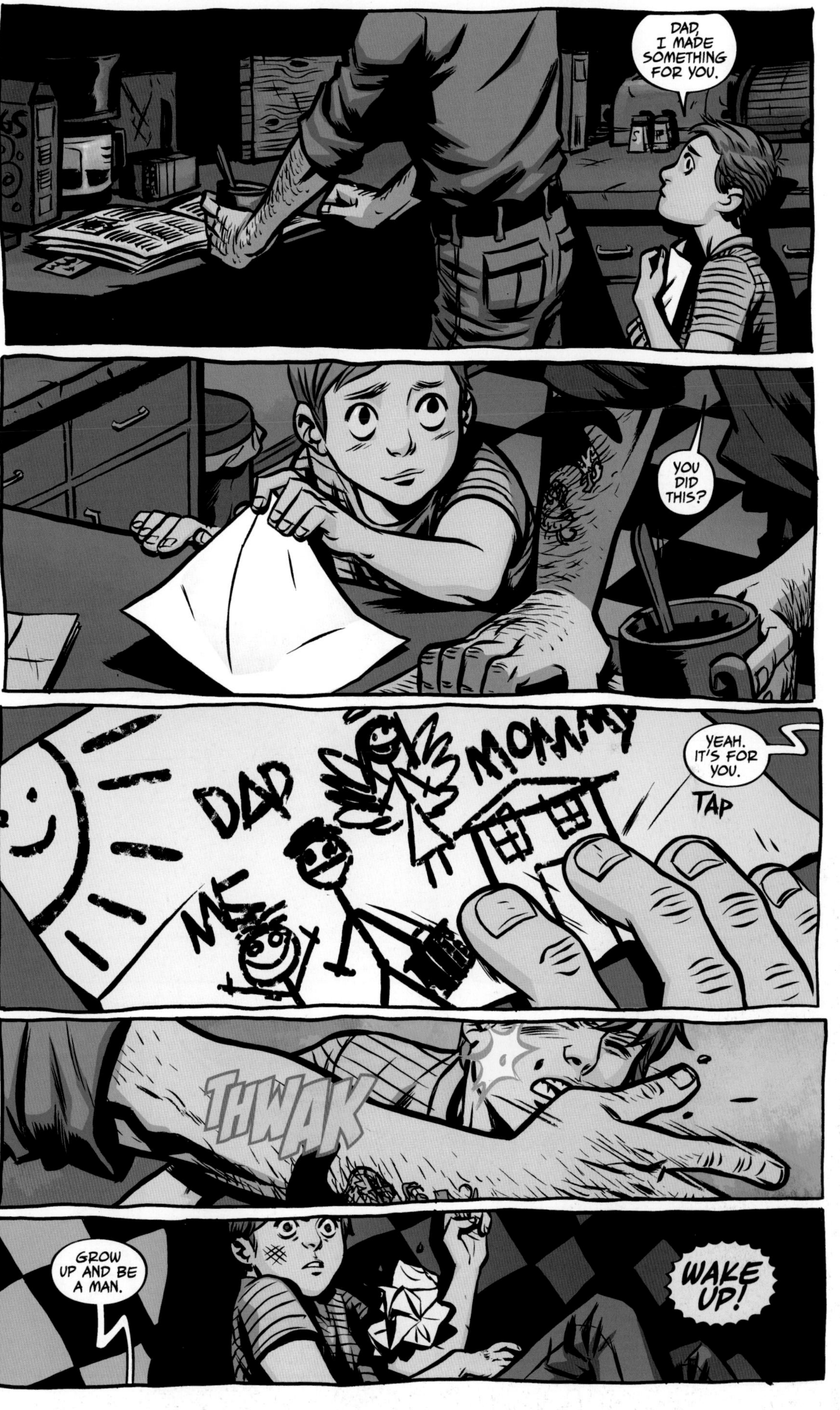
DAD, I MADE SOMETHING FOR YOU.
YOU DID THIS?
YEAH. IT'S FOR YOU.
TAP
THWAK
GROW UP AND BE A MAN.
WAKE UP!

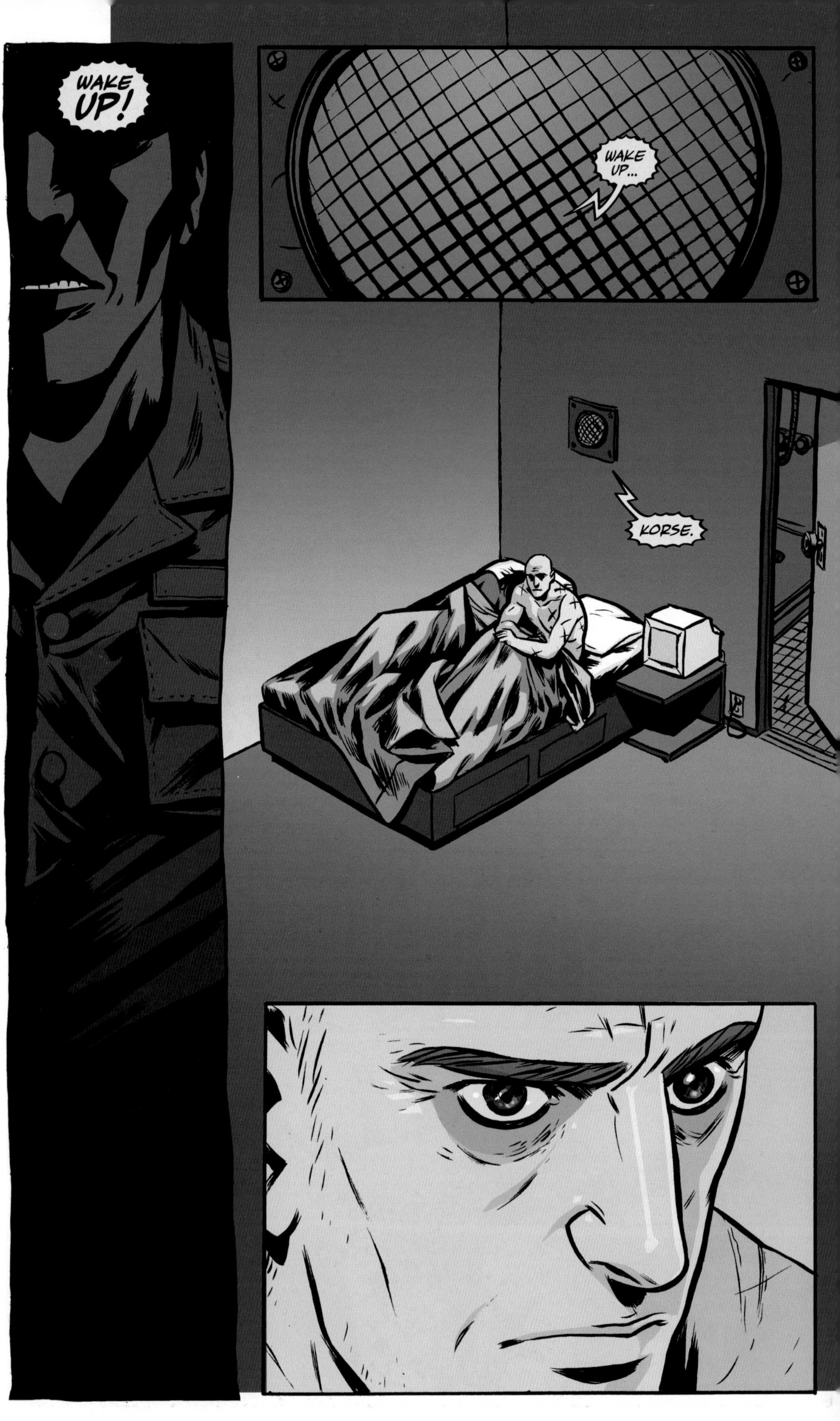
WAKE UP!
WAKE UP...
KORSE.

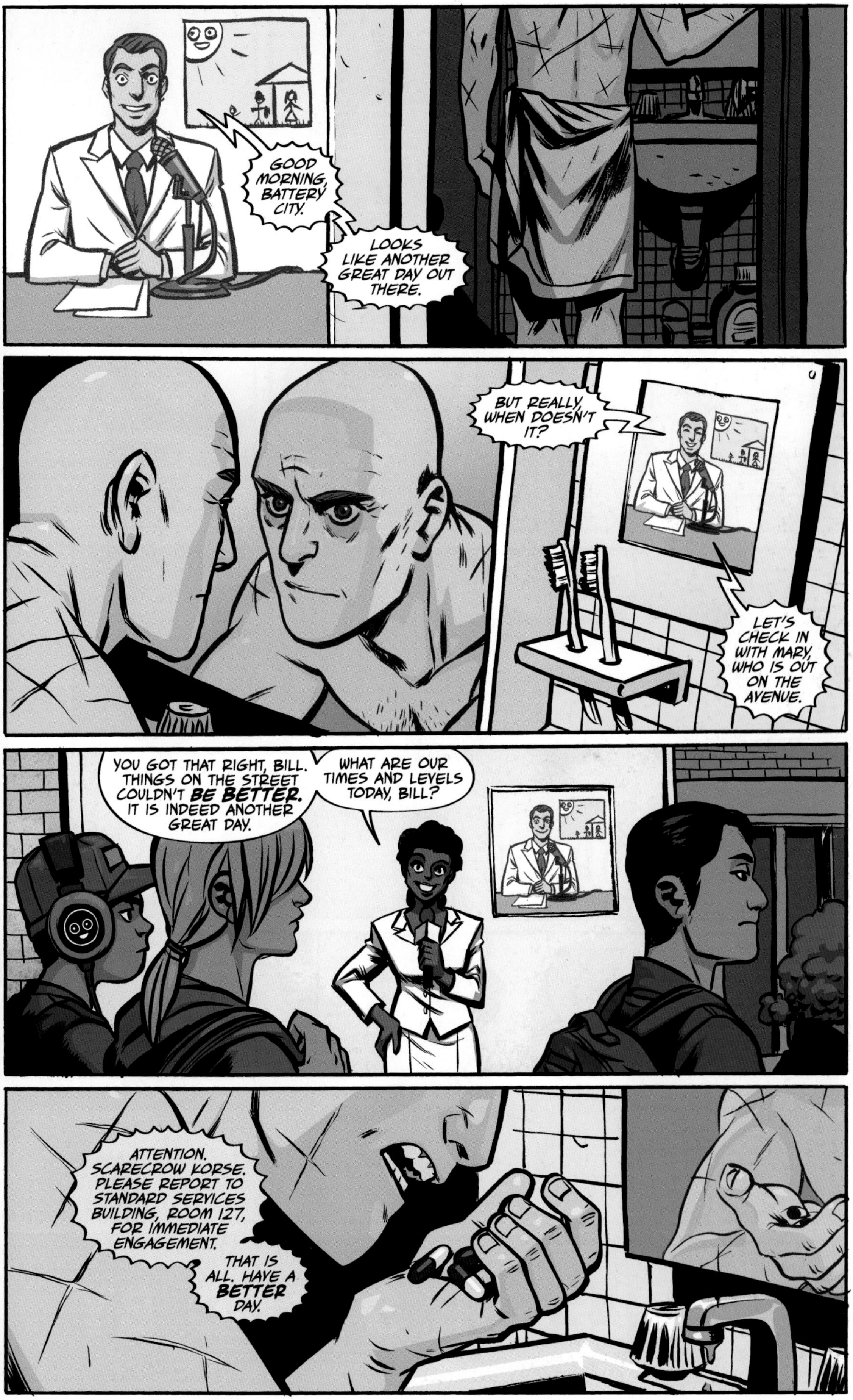
GOOD MORNING, BATTERY CITY.
LOOKS LIKE ANOTHER GREAT DAY OUT THERE.
BUT REALLY, WHEN DOESN'T IT?
LET'S CHECK IN WITH MARY, WHO IS OUT ON THE AVENUE.
YOU GOT THAT RIGHT, BILL. THINGS ON THE STREET COULDN'T **BE BETTER.** IT IS INDEED ANOTHER GREAT DAY.
WHAT ARE OUR TIMES AND LEVELS TODAY, BILL?
ATTENTION. SCARECROW KORSE. PLEASE REPORT TO STANDARD SERVICES BUILDING, ROOM 127, FOR IMMEDIATE ENGAGEMENT.
THAT IS ALL. HAVE A **BETTER** DAY.

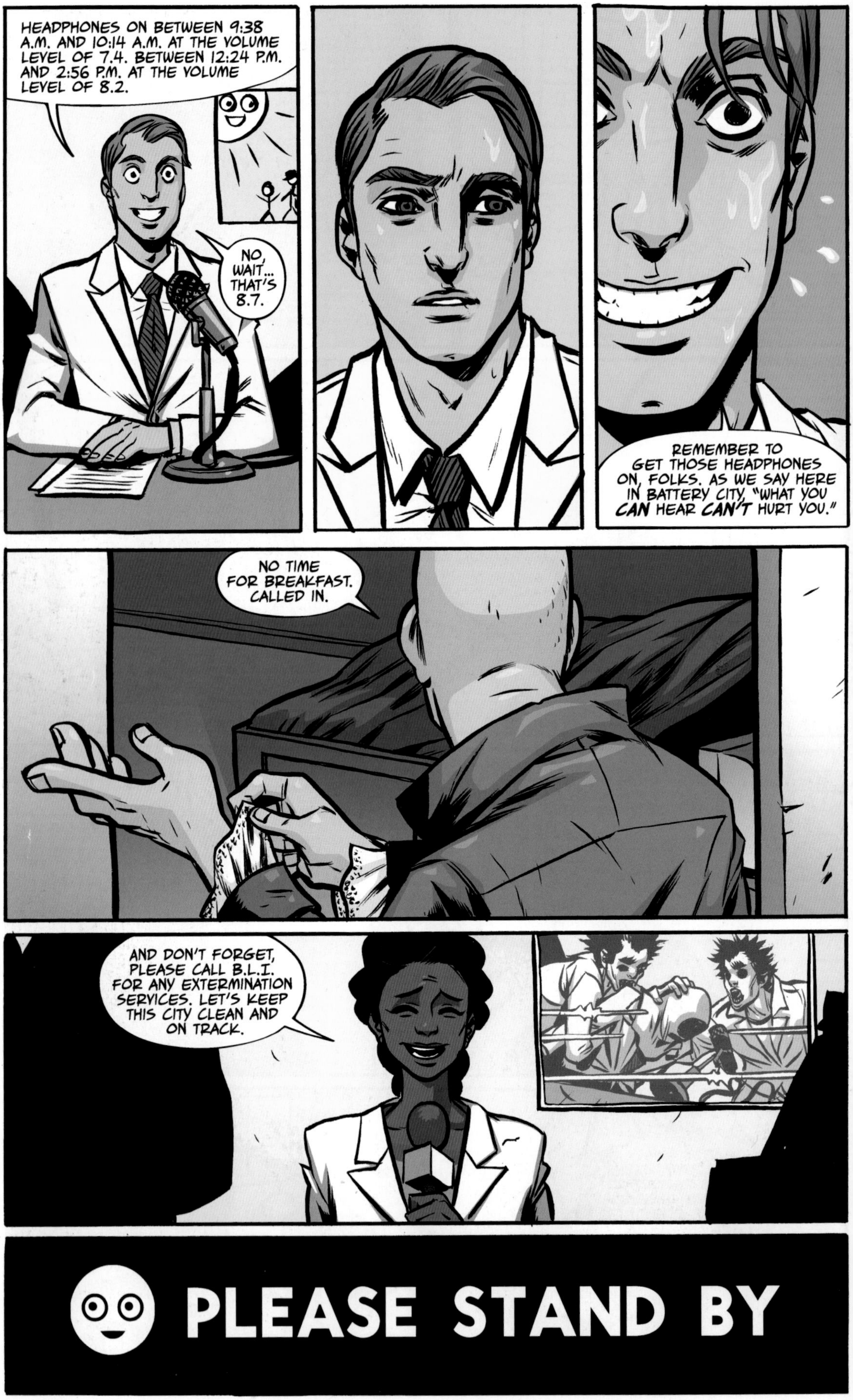
HEADPHONES ON BETWEEN 9:38 A.M. AND 10:14 A.M. AT THE VOLUME LEVEL OF 7.4. BETWEEN 12:24 P.M. AND 2:56 P.M. AT THE VOLUME LEVEL OF 8.2.
NO, WAIT... THAT'S 8.7.
REMEMBER TO GET THOSE HEADPHONES ON, FOLKS. AS WE SAY HERE IN BATTERY CITY, "WHAT YOU CAN HEAR CAN'T HURT YOU."
NO TIME FOR BREAKFAST. CALLED IN.
AND DON'T FORGET, PLEASE CALL B.L.I. FOR ANY EXTERMINATION SERVICES. LET'S KEEP THIS CITY CLEAN AND ON TRACK.
PLEASE STAND BY

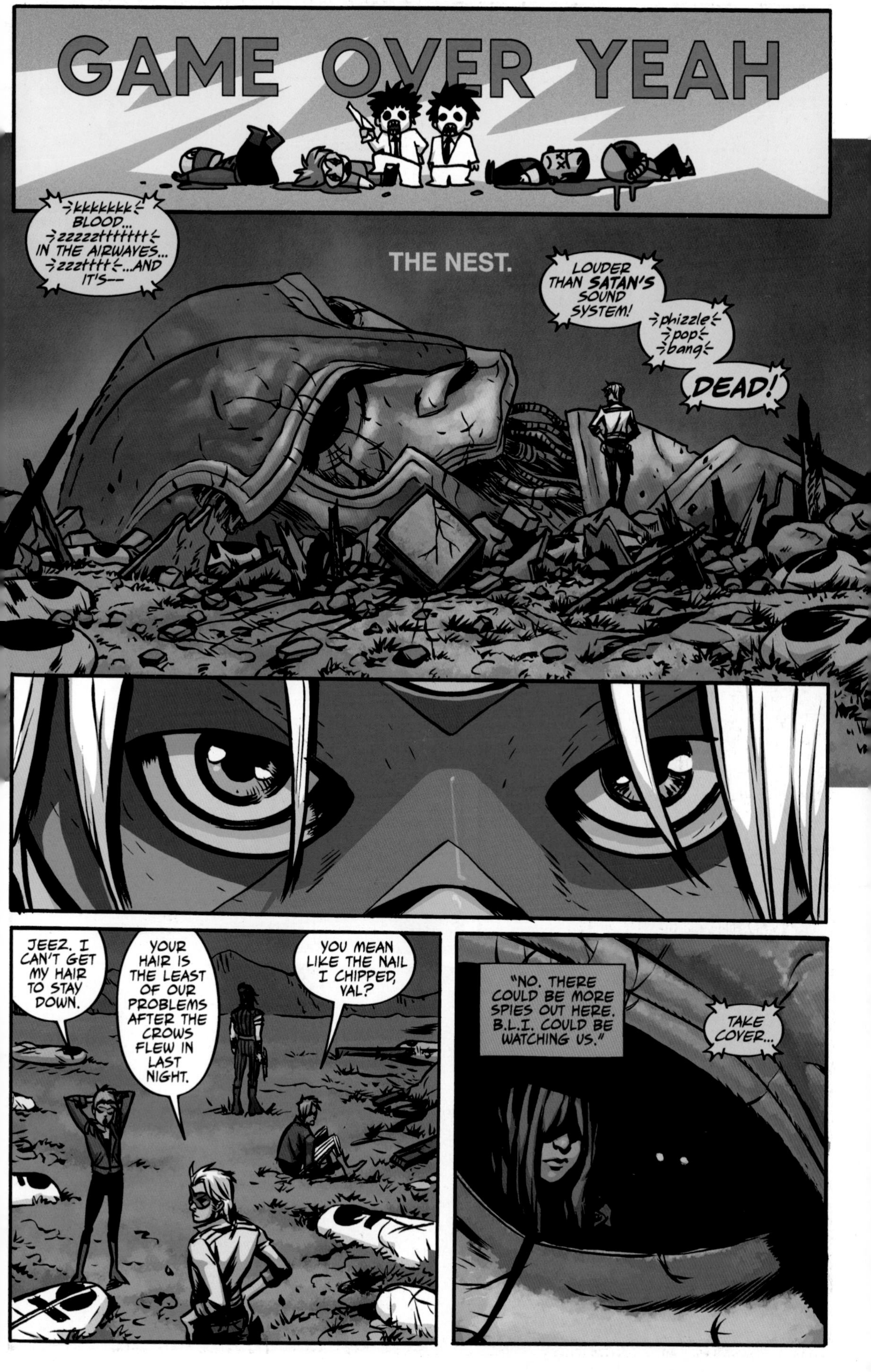
GAME OVER YEAH
-kkkkkkk- BLOOD... -zzzzzttttttt- IN THE AIRWAVES... -zzzttttt- ...AND IT'S--
THE NEST.
LOUDER THAN SATAN'S SOUND SYSTEM!
-phizzle- -pop- -bang-
DEAD!
JEEZ. I CAN'T GET MY HAIR TO STAY DOWN.
YOUR HAIR IS THE LEAST OF OUR PROBLEMS AFTER THE CROWS FLEW IN LAST NIGHT.
YOU MEAN LIKE THE NAIL I CHIPPED, VAL?
"NO. THERE COULD BE MORE SPIES OUT HERE. B.L.I. COULD BE WATCHING US."
TAKE COVER...

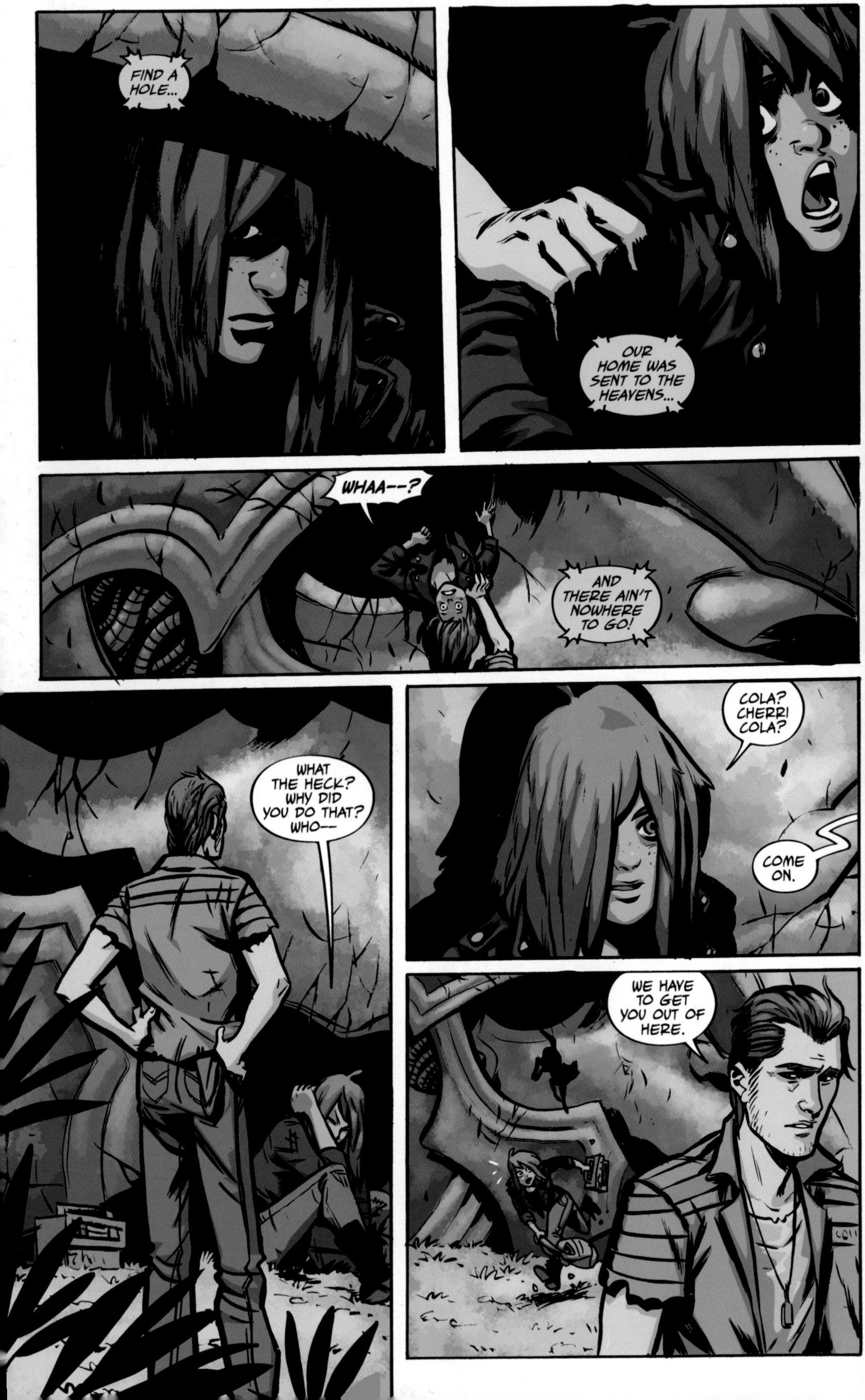
FIND A HOLE...
OUR HOME WAS SENT TO THE HEAVENS...
WHAA--?
AND THERE AIN'T NOWHERE TO GO!
WHAT THE HECK? WHY DID YOU DO THAT? WHO--
COLA? CHERRI COLA?
COME ON.
WE HAVE TO GET YOU OUT OF HERE.

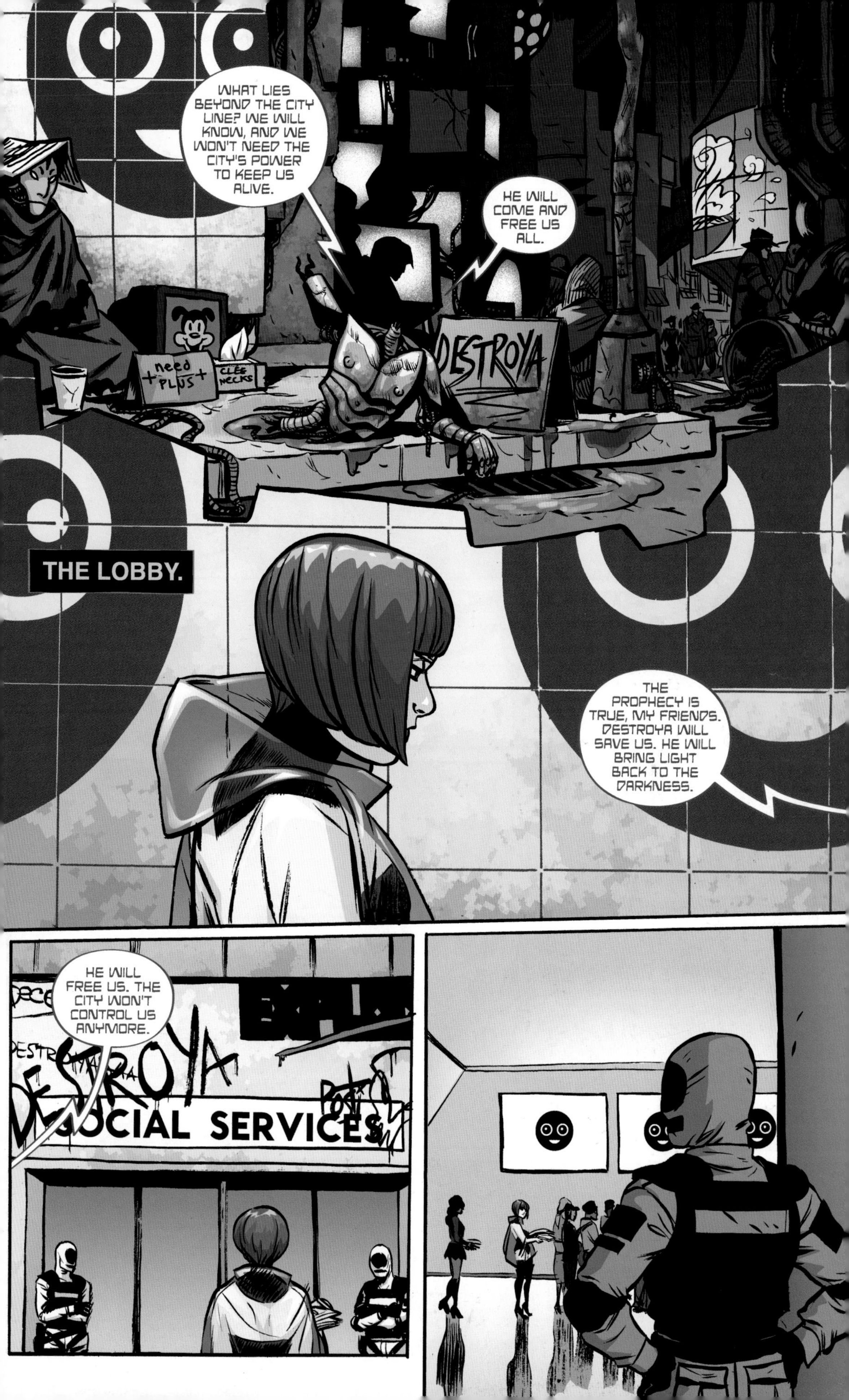
WHAT LIES BEYOND THE CITY LINE? WE WILL KNOW, AND WE WON'T NEED THE CITY'S POWER TO KEEP US ALIVE.
HE WILL COME AND FREE US ALL.
need PLUS
DESTROYA
THE LOBBY.
THE PROPHECY IS TRUE, MY FRIENDS. DESTROYA WILL SAVE US. HE WILL BRING LIGHT BACK TO THE DARKNESS.
HE WILL FREE US. THE CITY WON'T CONTROL US ANYMORE.
DESTROYA
SOCIAL SERVICES

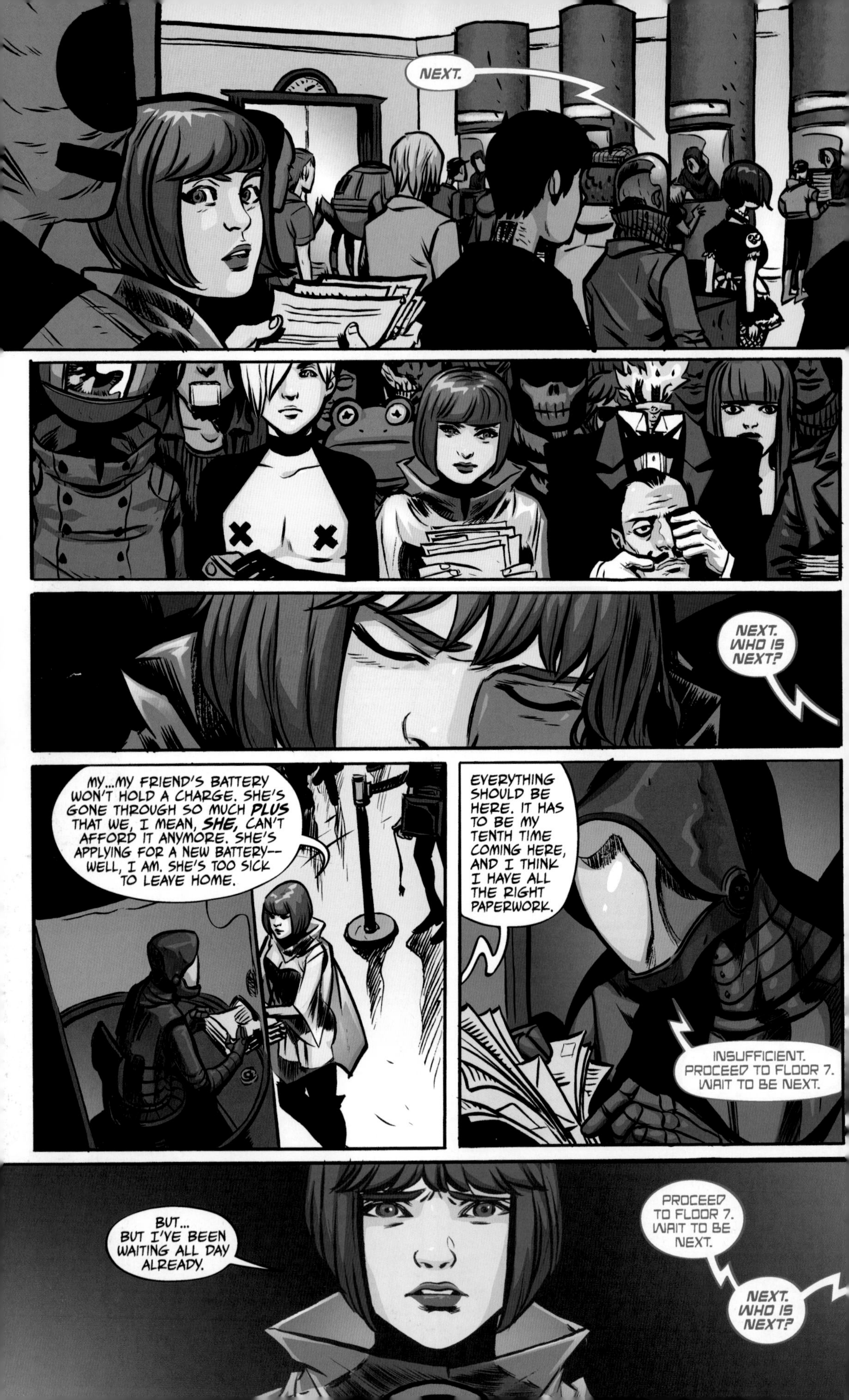
NEXT.
NEXT. WHO IS NEXT?
MY...MY FRIEND'S BATTERY WON'T HOLD A CHARGE. SHE'S GONE THROUGH SO MUCH PLUS THAT WE, I MEAN, SHE, CAN'T AFFORD IT ANYMORE. SHE'S APPLYING FOR A NEW BATTERY-- WELL, I AM. SHE'S TOO SICK TO LEAVE HOME.
EVERYTHING SHOULD BE HERE. IT HAS TO BE MY TENTH TIME COMING HERE, AND I THINK I HAVE ALL THE RIGHT PAPERWORK.
INSUFFICIENT. PROCEED TO FLOOR 7. WAIT TO BE NEXT.
BUT... BUT I'VE BEEN WAITING ALL DAY ALREADY.
PROCEED TO FLOOR 7. WAIT TO BE NEXT.
NEXT. WHO IS NEXT?

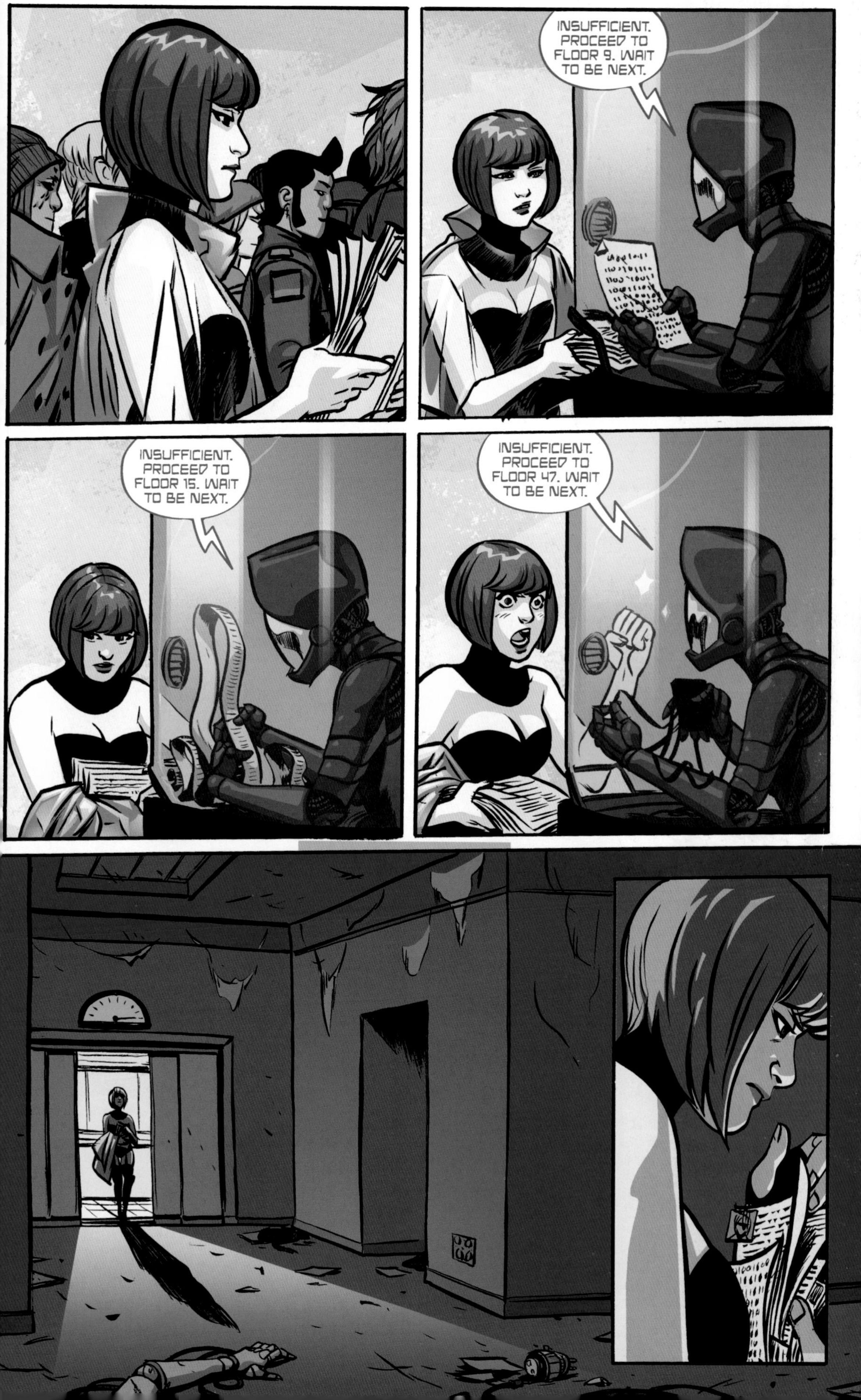
INSUFFICIENT. PROCEED TO FLOOR 9. WAIT TO BE NEXT.
INSUFFICIENT. PROCEED TO FLOOR 15. WAIT TO BE NEXT.
INSUFFICIENT. PROCEED TO FLOOR 47. WAIT TO BE NEXT.

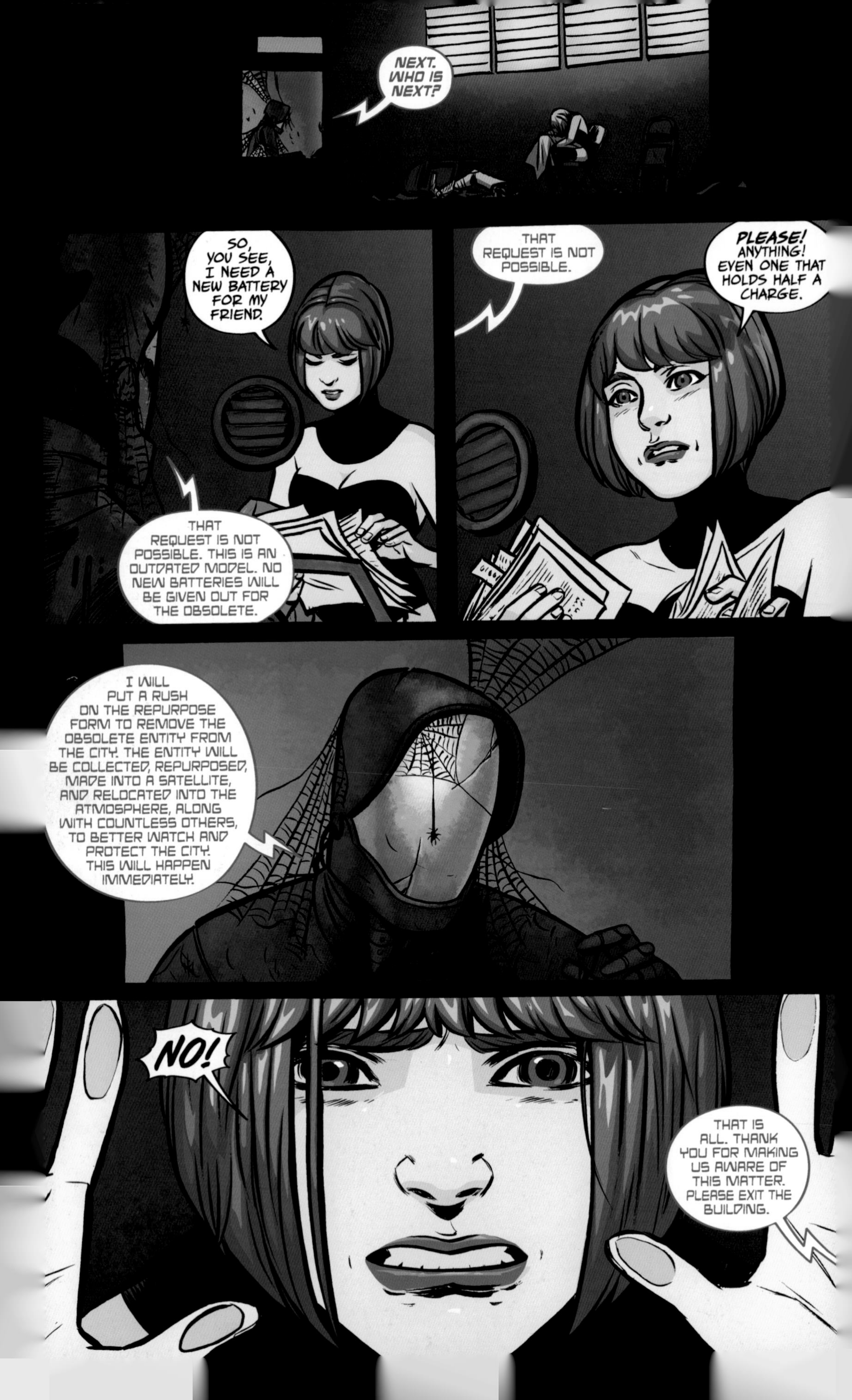
NEXT. WHO IS NEXT?
SO, YOU SEE, I NEED A NEW BATTERY FOR MY FRIEND.
THAT REQUEST IS NOT POSSIBLE. THIS IS AN OUTDATED MODEL. NO NEW BATTERIES WILL BE GIVEN OUT FOR THE OBSOLETE.
THAT REQUEST IS NOT POSSIBLE.
PLEASE! ANYTHING! EVEN ONE THAT HOLDS HALF A CHARGE.
I WILL PUT A RUSH ON THE REPURPOSE FORM TO REMOVE THE OBSOLETE ENTITY FROM THE CITY. THE ENTITY WILL BE COLLECTED, REPURPOSED, MADE INTO A SATELLITE, AND RELOCATED INTO THE ATMOSPHERE, ALONG WITH COUNTLESS OTHERS, TO BETTER WATCH AND PROTECT THE CITY. THIS WILL HAPPEN IMMEDIATELY.
NO!
THAT IS ALL. THANK YOU FOR MAKING US AWARE OF THIS MATTER. PLEASE EXIT THE BUILDING.

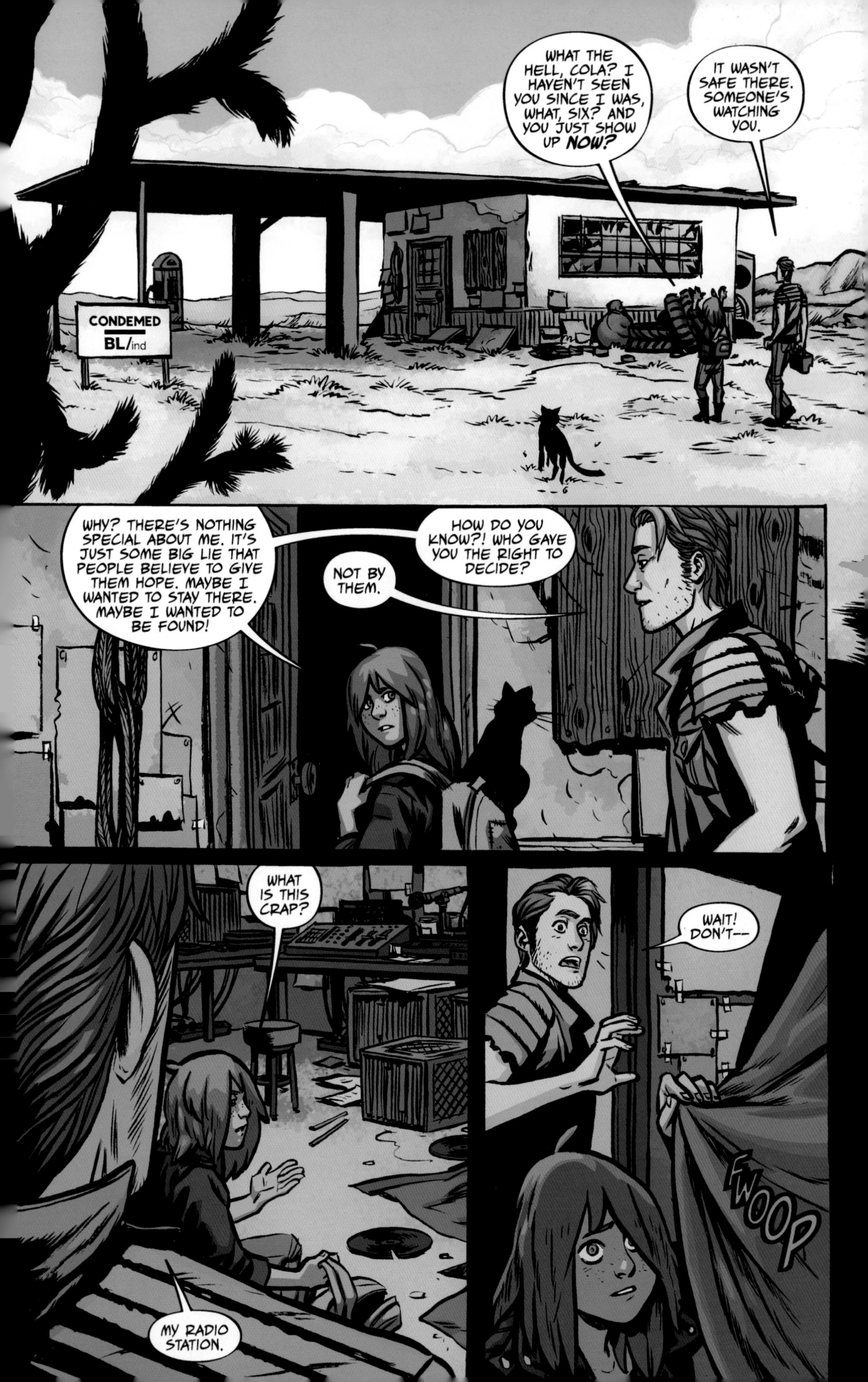
WHAT THE HELL, COLA? I HAVEN'T SEEN YOU SINCE I WAS, WHAT, SIX? AND YOU JUST SHOW UP NOW?
IT WASN'T SAFE THERE. SOMEONE'S WATCHING YOU.
CONDEMED
BL/ind
WHY? THERE'S NOTHING SPECIAL ABOUT ME. IT'S JUST SOME BIG LIE THAT PEOPLE BELIEVE TO GIVE THEM HOPE. MAYBE I WANTED TO STAY THERE. MAYBE I WANTED TO BE FOUND!
NOT BY THEM.
HOW DO YOU KNOW?! WHO GAVE YOU THE RIGHT TO DECIDE?
WHAT IS THIS CRAP?
MY RADIO STATION.
WAIT! DON'T--
FWOOP

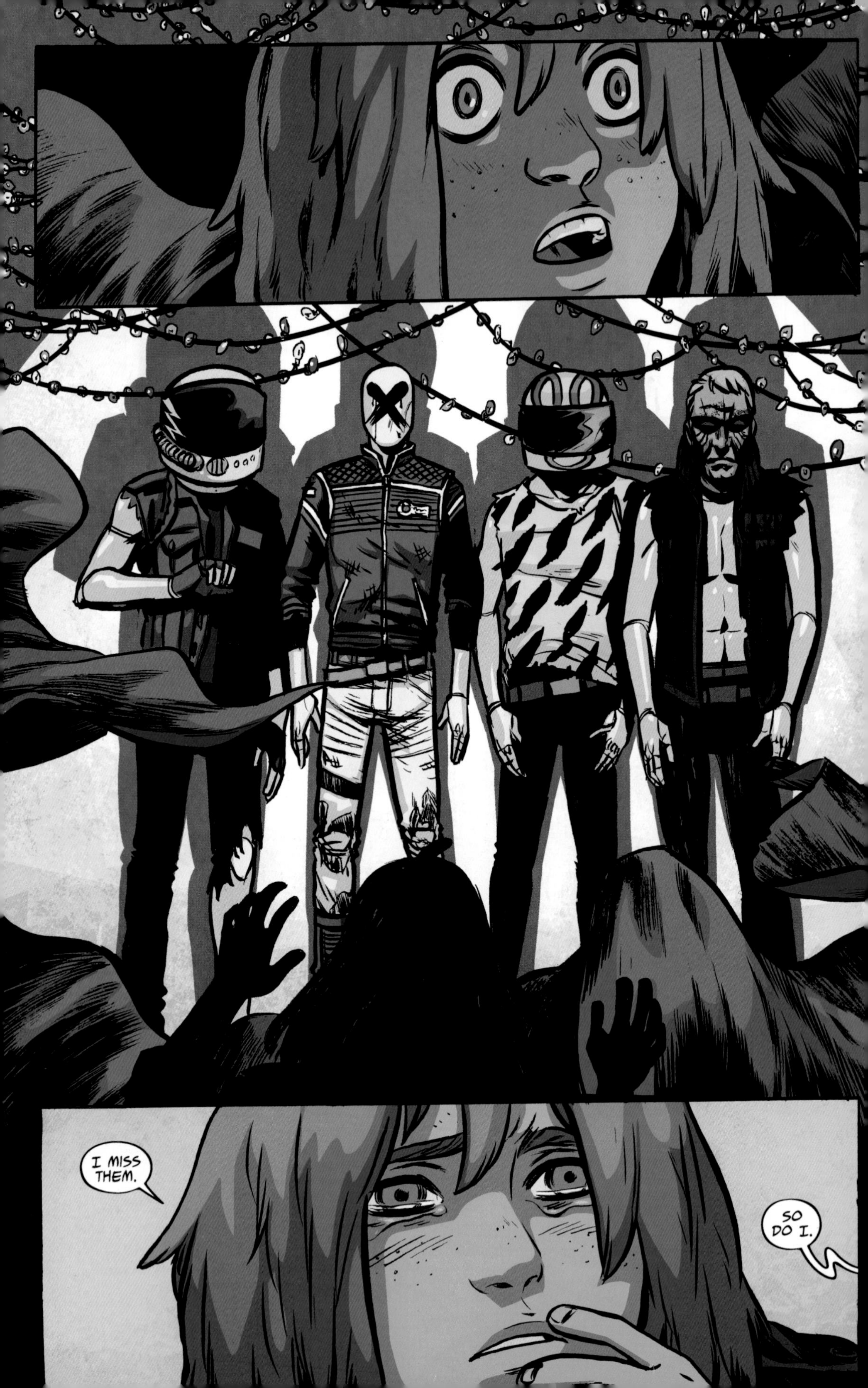
I MISS THEM.
SO DO I.

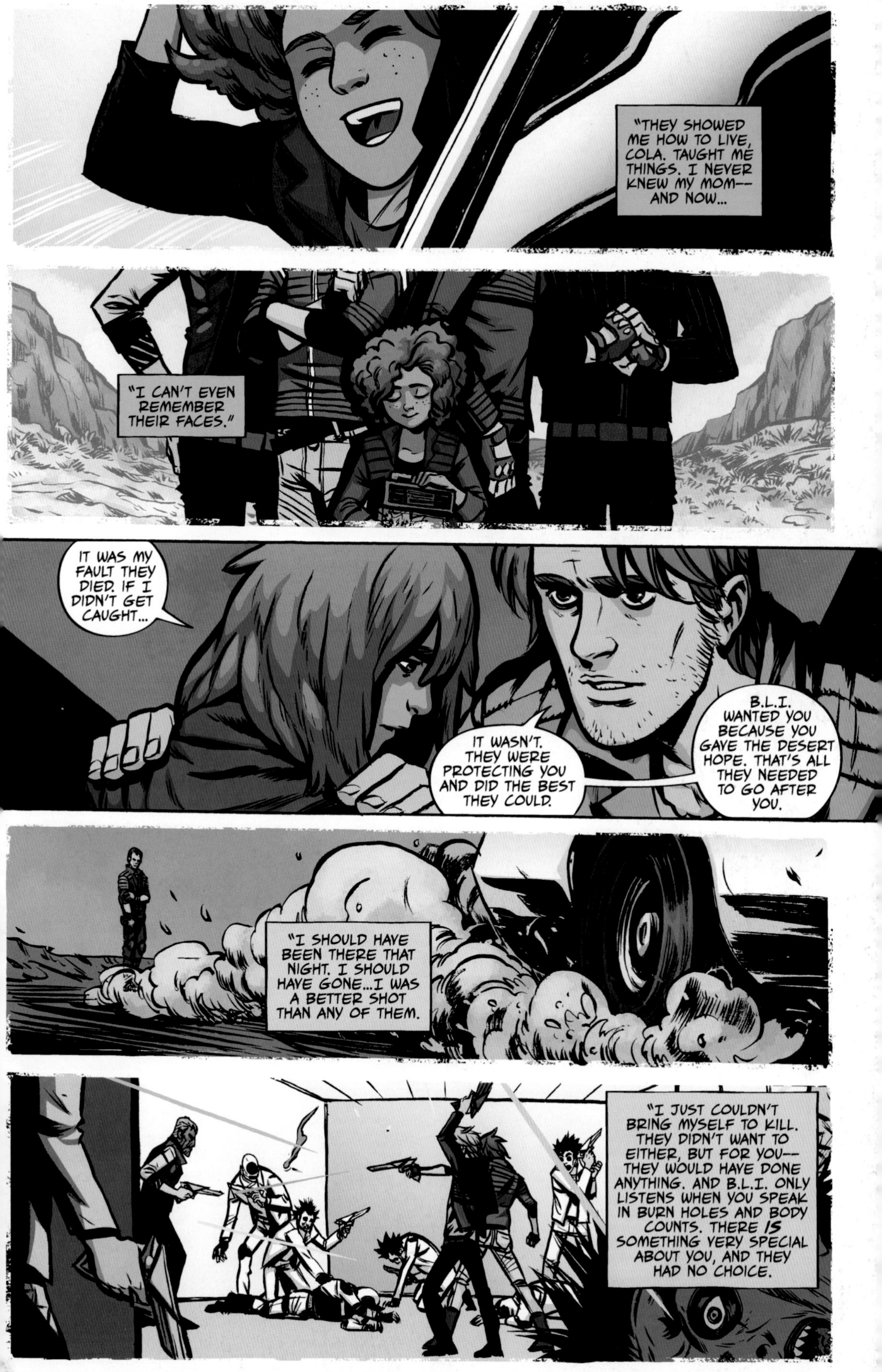
"THEY SHOWED ME HOW TO LIVE, COLA. TAUGHT ME THINGS. I NEVER KNEW MY MOM-- AND NOW...
"I CAN'T EVEN REMEMBER THEIR FACES."
IT WAS MY FAULT THEY DIED. IF I DIDN'T GET CAUGHT...
IT WASN'T. THEY WERE PROTECTING YOU AND DID THE BEST THEY COULD.
B.L.I. WANTED YOU BECAUSE YOU GAVE THE DESERT HOPE. THAT'S ALL THEY NEEDED TO GO AFTER YOU.
"I SHOULD HAVE BEEN THERE THAT NIGHT. I SHOULD HAVE GONE...I WAS A BETTER SHOT THAN ANY OF THEM.
"I JUST COULDN'T BRING MYSELF TO KILL. THEY DIDN'T WANT TO EITHER, BUT FOR YOU-- THEY WOULD HAVE DONE ANYTHING. AND B.L.I. ONLY LISTENS WHEN YOU SPEAK IN BURN HOLES AND BODY COUNTS. THERE *IS* SOMETHING VERY SPECIAL ABOUT YOU, AND THEY HAD NO CHOICE.

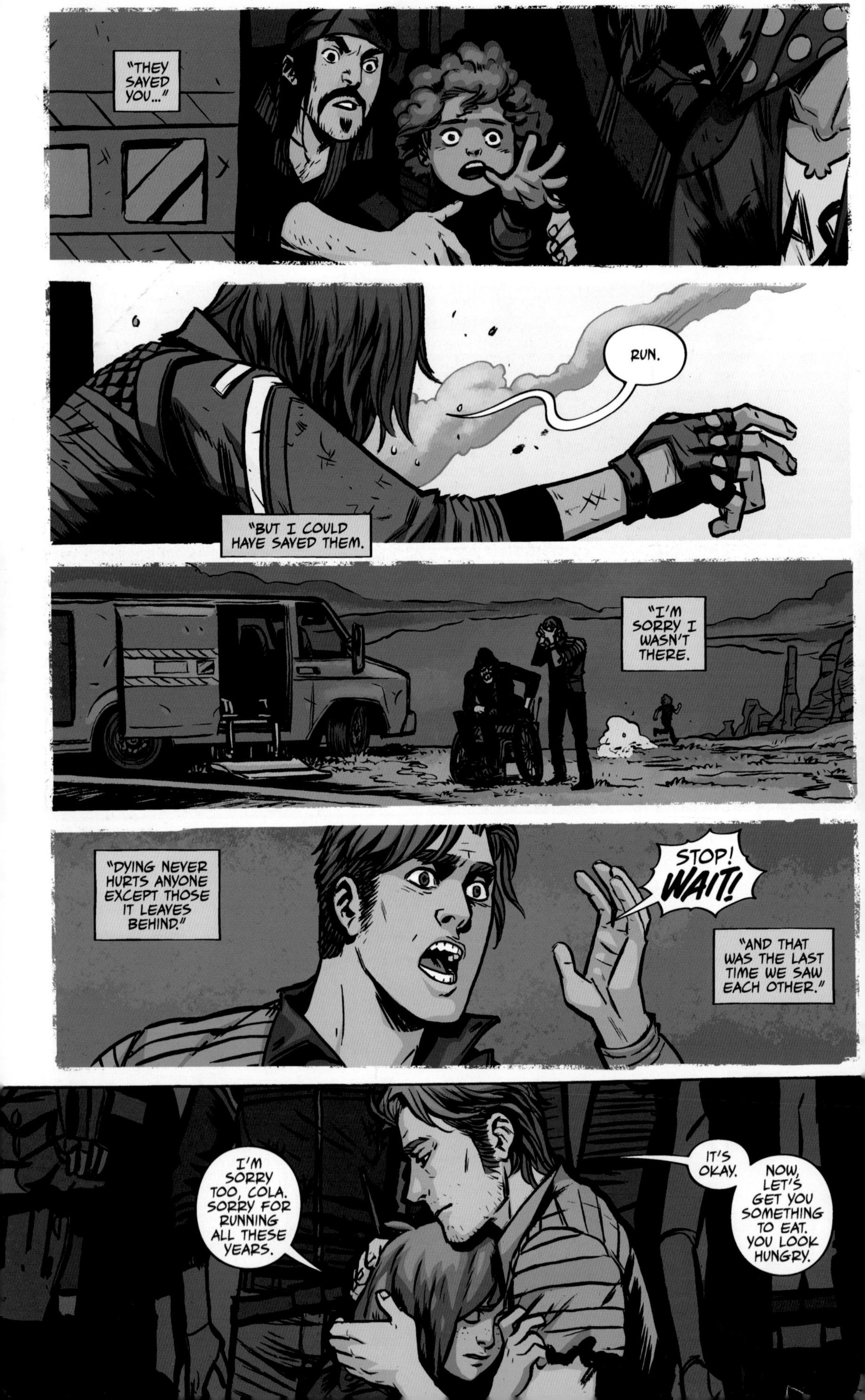
"THEY SAVED YOU..."
RUN.
"BUT I COULD HAVE SAVED THEM.
"I'M SORRY I WASN'T THERE.
"DYING NEVER HURTS ANYONE EXCEPT THOSE IT LEAVES BEHIND."
STOP! WAIT!
"AND THAT WAS THE LAST TIME WE SAW EACH OTHER."
I'M SORRY TOO, COLA. SORRY FOR RUNNING ALL THESE YEARS.
IT'S OKAY.
NOW, LET'S GET YOU SOMETHING TO EAT. YOU LOOK HUNGRY.

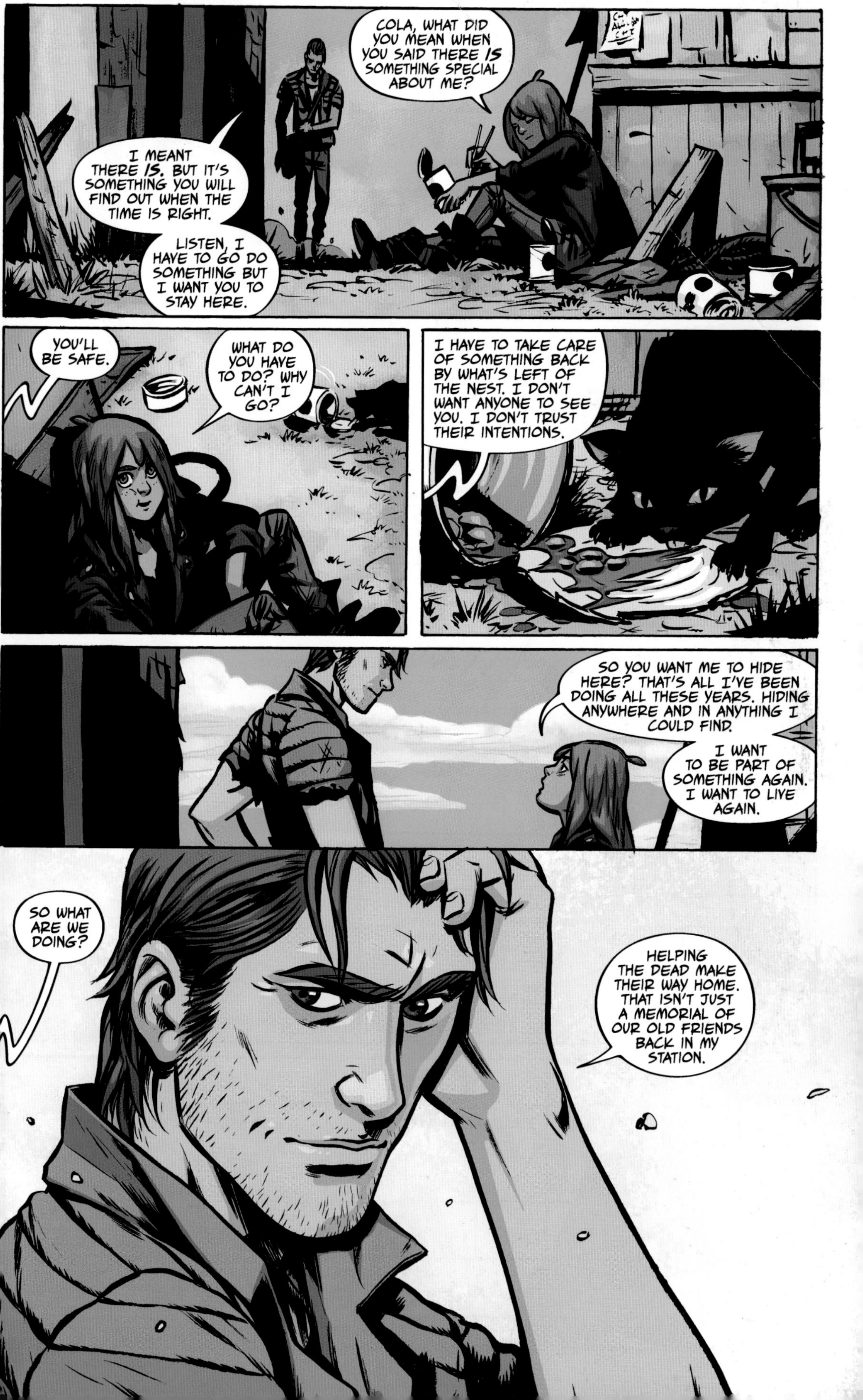
COLA, WHAT DID YOU MEAN WHEN YOU SAID THERE *IS* SOMETHING SPECIAL ABOUT ME?
I MEANT THERE *IS*. BUT IT'S SOMETHING YOU WILL FIND OUT WHEN THE TIME IS RIGHT.
LISTEN, I HAVE TO GO DO SOMETHING BUT I WANT YOU TO STAY HERE.
YOU'LL BE SAFE.
WHAT DO YOU HAVE TO DO? WHY CAN'T I GO?
I HAVE TO TAKE CARE OF SOMETHING BACK BY WHAT'S LEFT OF THE NEST. I DON'T WANT ANYONE TO SEE YOU. I DON'T TRUST THEIR INTENTIONS.
SO YOU WANT ME TO HIDE HERE? THAT'S ALL I'VE BEEN DOING ALL THESE YEARS. HIDING ANYWHERE AND IN ANYTHING I COULD FIND.
I WANT TO BE PART OF SOMETHING AGAIN. I WANT TO LIVE AGAIN.
SO WHAT ARE WE DOING?
HELPING THE DEAD MAKE THEIR WAY HOME. THAT ISN'T JUST A MEMORIAL OF OUR OLD FRIENDS BACK IN MY STATION.

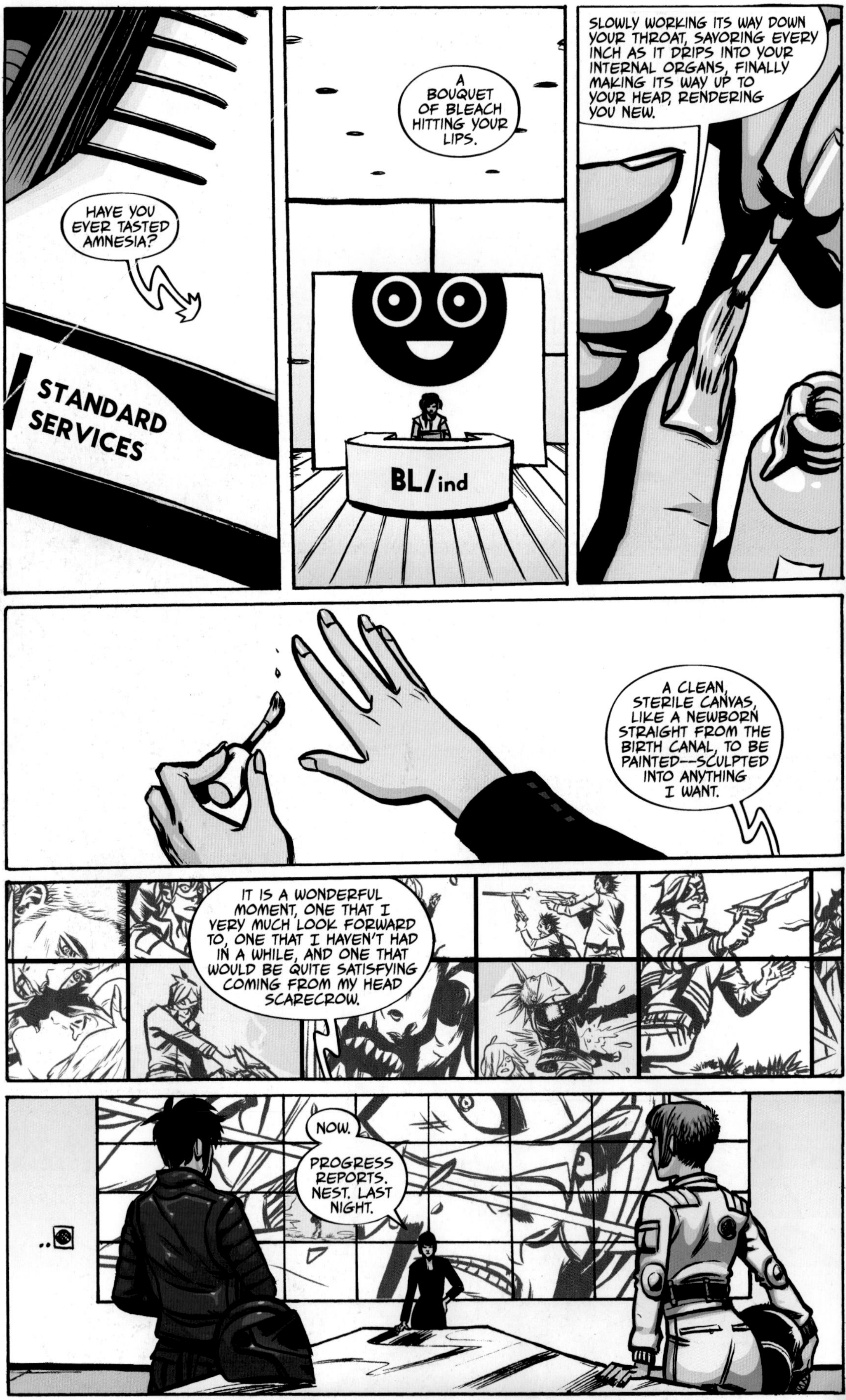
HAVE YOU EVER TASTED AMNESIA?
STANDARD SERVICES
A BOUQUET OF BLEACH HITTING YOUR LIPS.
BL/ind
SLOWLY WORKING ITS WAY DOWN YOUR THROAT, SAVORING EVERY INCH AS IT DRIPS INTO YOUR INTERNAL ORGANS, FINALLY MAKING ITS WAY UP TO YOUR HEAD, RENDERING YOU NEW.
A CLEAN, STERILE CANVAS, LIKE A NEWBORN STRAIGHT FROM THE BIRTH CANAL, TO BE PAINTED--SCULPTED INTO ANYTHING I WANT.
IT IS A WONDERFUL MOMENT, ONE THAT I VERY MUCH LOOK FORWARD TO, ONE THAT I HAVEN'T HAD IN A WHILE, AND ONE THAT WOULD BE QUITE SATISFYING COMING FROM MY HEAD SCARECROW.
NOW.
PROGRESS REPORTS. NEST. LAST NIGHT.

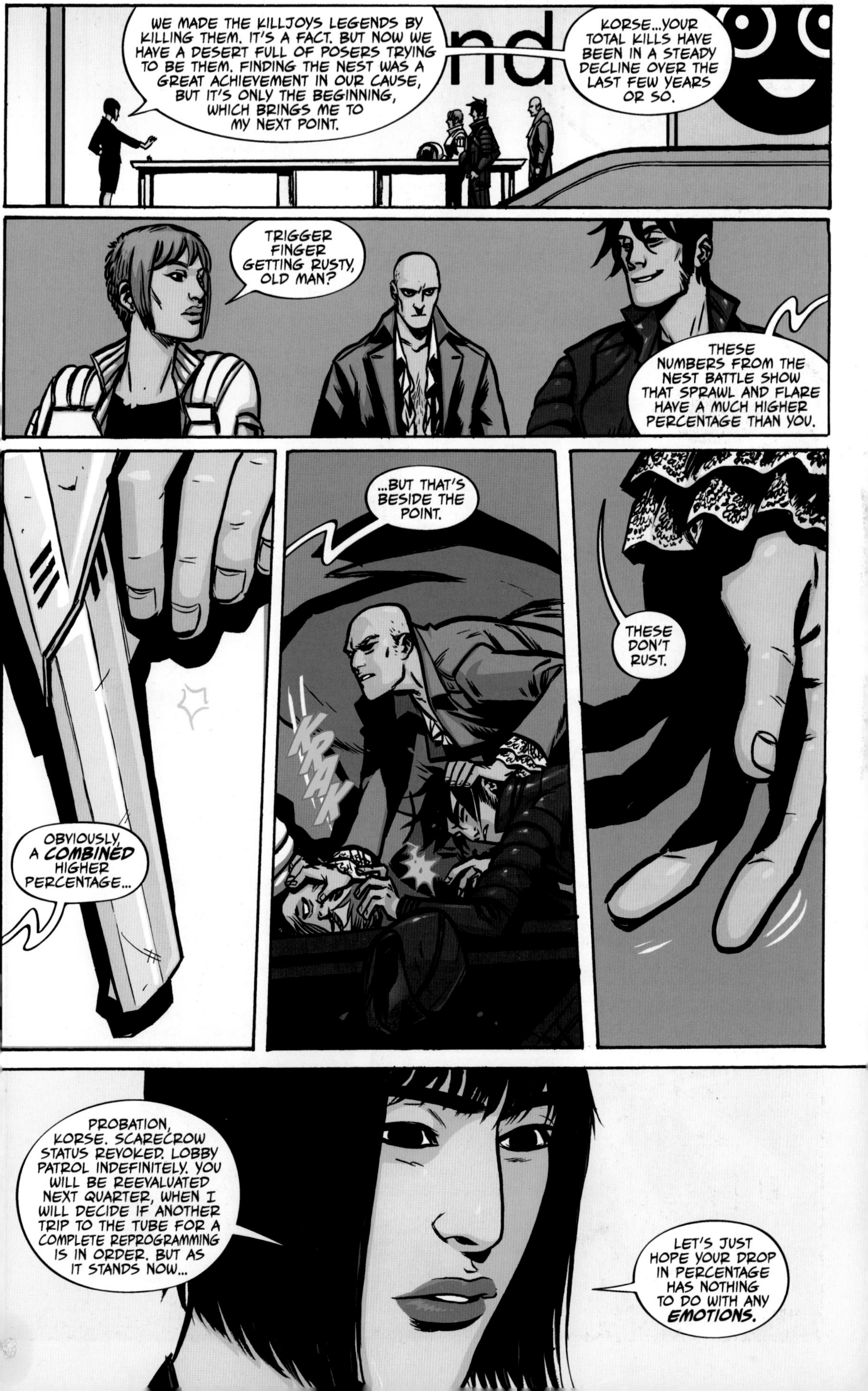
WE MADE THE KILLJOYS LEGENDS BY KILLING THEM. IT'S A FACT. BUT NOW WE HAVE A DESERT FULL OF POSERS TRYING TO BE THEM. FINDING THE NEST WAS A GREAT ACHIEVEMENT IN OUR CAUSE, BUT IT'S ONLY THE BEGINNING, WHICH BRINGS ME TO MY NEXT POINT.
KORSE...YOUR TOTAL KILLS HAVE BEEN IN A STEADY DECLINE OVER THE LAST FEW YEARS OR SO.
TRIGGER FINGER GETTING RUSTY, OLD MAN?
THESE NUMBERS FROM THE NEST BATTLE SHOW THAT SPRAWL AND FLARE HAVE A MUCH HIGHER PERCENTAGE THAN YOU.
OBVIOUSLY, A COMBINED HIGHER PERCENTAGE...
...BUT THAT'S BESIDE THE POINT.
KRAK
THESE DON'T RUST.
PROBATION, KORSE. SCARECROW STATUS REVOKED. LOBBY PATROL INDEFINITELY. YOU WILL BE REEVALUATED NEXT QUARTER, WHEN I WILL DECIDE IF ANOTHER TRIP TO THE TUBE FOR A COMPLETE REPROGRAMMING IS IN ORDER. BUT AS IT STANDS NOW...
LET'S JUST HOPE YOUR DROP IN PERCENTAGE HAS NOTHING TO DO WITH ANY EMOTIONS.

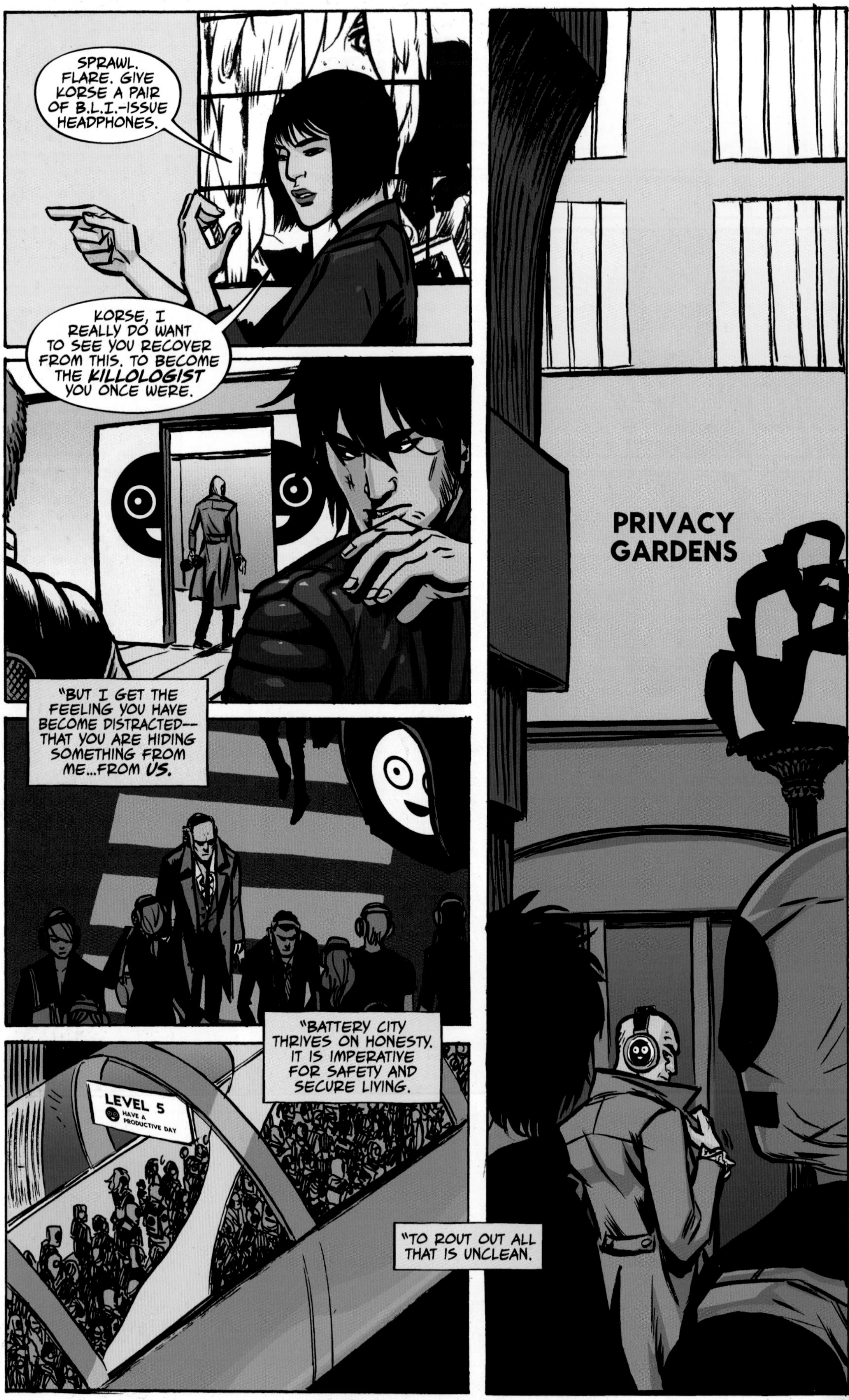
SPRAWL. FLARE. GIVE KORSE A PAIR OF B.L.I.-ISSUE HEADPHONES.
KORSE, I REALLY DO WANT TO SEE YOU RECOVER FROM THIS. TO BECOME THE *KILLOLOGIST* YOU ONCE WERE.
"BUT I GET THE FEELING YOU HAVE BECOME DISTRACTED-- THAT YOU ARE HIDING SOMETHING FROM ME...FROM *US*.
"BATTERY CITY THRIVES ON HONESTY. IT IS IMPERATIVE FOR SAFETY AND SECURE LIVING.
LEVEL 5
HAVE A PRODUCTIVE DAY
"TO ROUT OUT ALL THAT IS UNCLEAN.
PRIVACY GARDENS

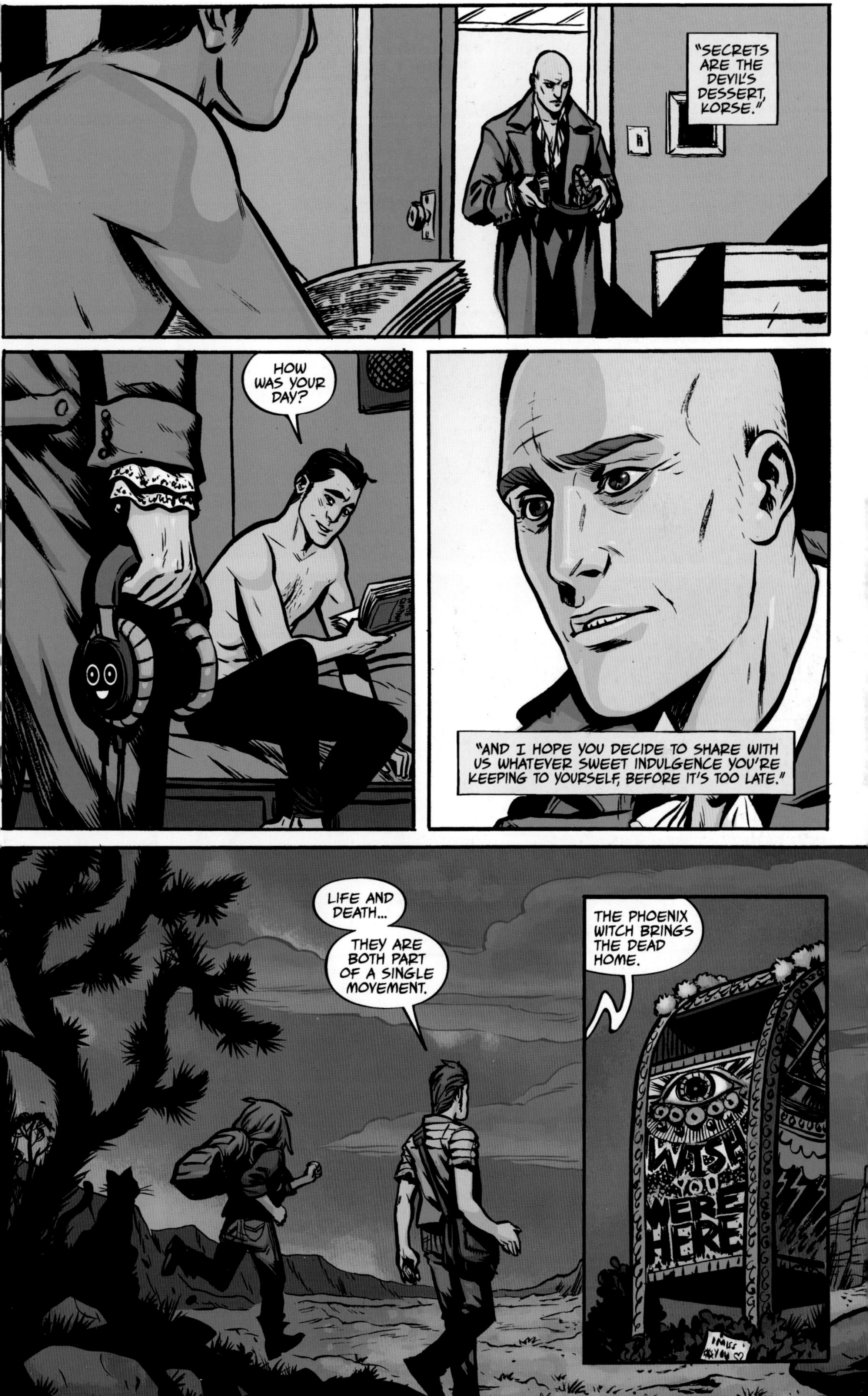
"SECRETS ARE THE DEVIL'S DESSERT, KORSE."
HOW WAS YOUR DAY?
"AND I HOPE YOU DECIDE TO SHARE WITH US WHATEVER SWEET INDULGENCE YOU'RE KEEPING TO YOURSELF, BEFORE IT'S TOO LATE."
LIFE AND DEATH...
THEY ARE BOTH PART OF A SINGLE MOVEMENT.
THE PHOENIX WITCH BRINGS THE DEAD HOME.
WISH YOU WERE HERE

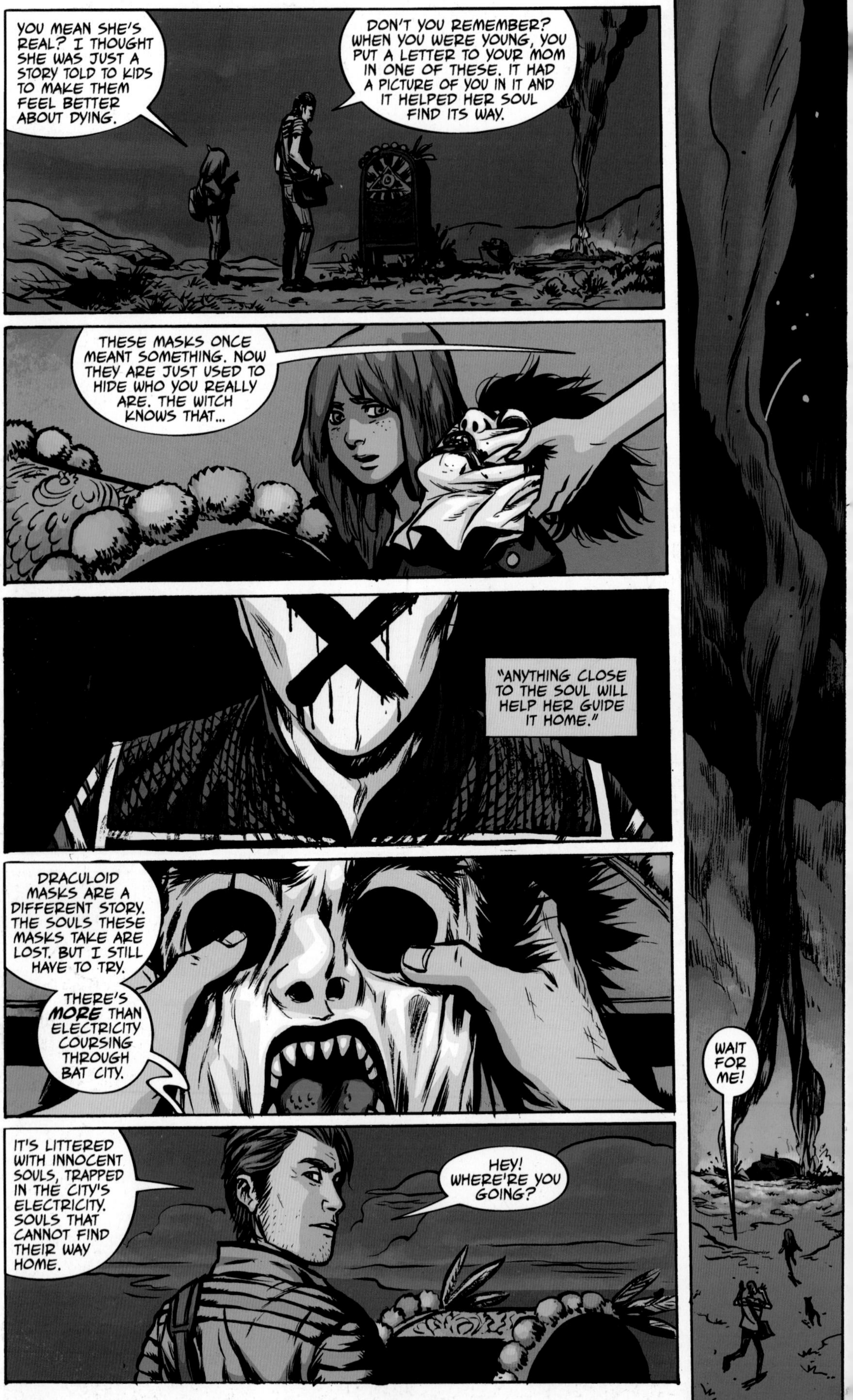
YOU MEAN SHE'S REAL? I THOUGHT SHE WAS JUST A STORY TOLD TO KIDS TO MAKE THEM FEEL BETTER ABOUT DYING.
DON'T YOU REMEMBER? WHEN YOU WERE YOUNG, YOU PUT A LETTER TO YOUR MOM IN ONE OF THESE. IT HAD A PICTURE OF YOU IN IT AND IT HELPED HER SOUL FIND ITS WAY.
THESE MASKS ONCE MEANT SOMETHING. NOW THEY ARE JUST USED TO HIDE WHO YOU REALLY ARE. THE WITCH KNOWS THAT...
"ANYTHING CLOSE TO THE SOUL WILL HELP HER GUIDE IT HOME."
DRACULOID MASKS ARE A DIFFERENT STORY. THE SOULS THESE MASKS TAKE ARE LOST. BUT I STILL HAVE TO TRY.
THERE'S **MORE** THAN ELECTRICITY COURSING THROUGH BAT CITY.
IT'S LITTERED WITH INNOCENT SOULS, TRAPPED IN THE CITY'S ELECTRICITY. SOULS THAT CANNOT FIND THEIR WAY HOME.
HEY! WHERE'RE YOU GOING?
WAIT FOR ME!

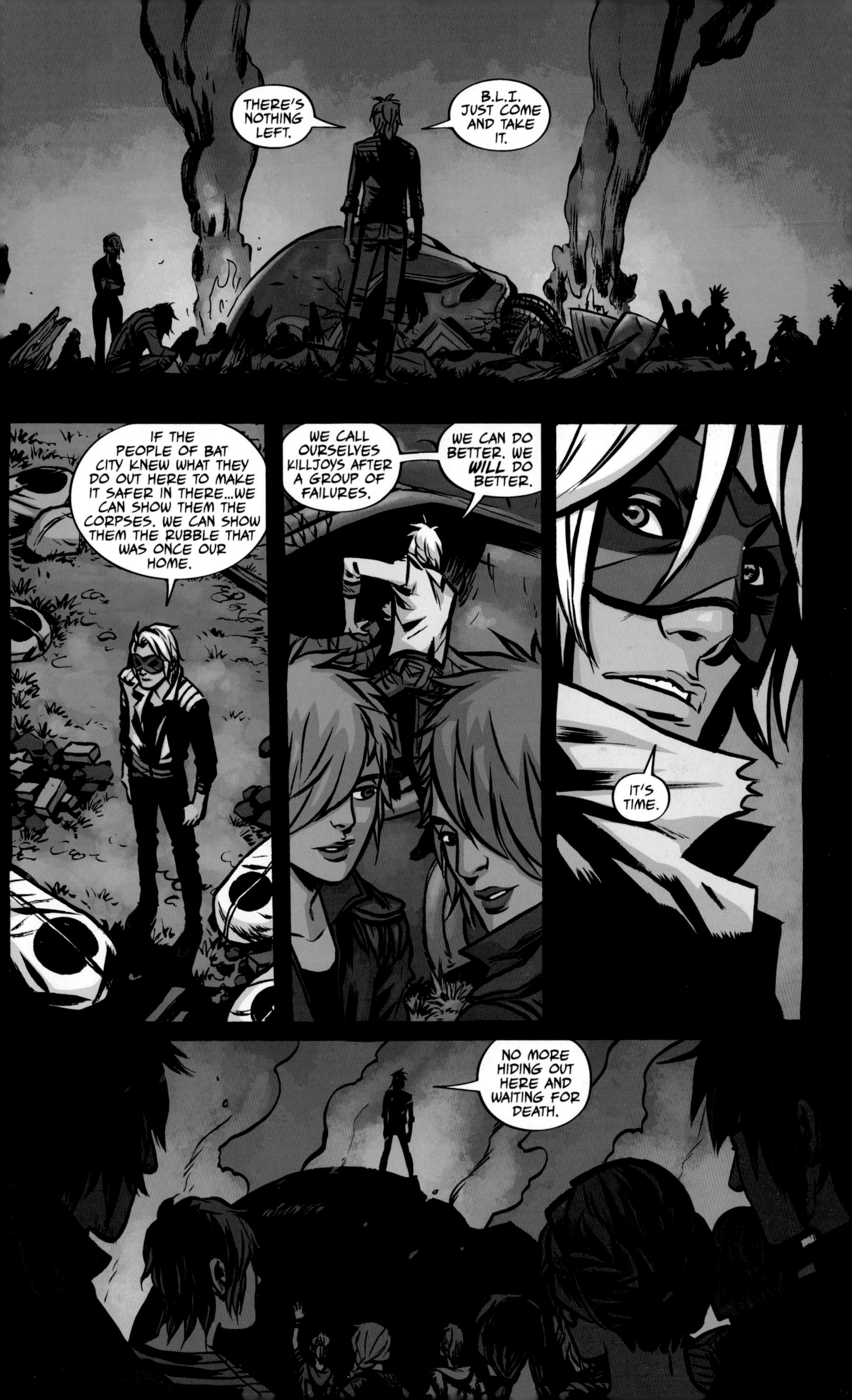
THERE'S NOTHING LEFT.
B.L.I. JUST COME AND TAKE IT.
IF THE PEOPLE OF BAT CITY KNEW WHAT THEY DO OUT HERE TO MAKE IT SAFER IN THERE...WE CAN SHOW THEM THE CORPSES. WE CAN SHOW THEM THE RUBBLE THAT WAS ONCE OUR HOME.
WE CALL OURSELVES KILLJOYS AFTER A GROUP OF FAILURES.
WE CAN DO BETTER. WE WILL DO BETTER.
IT'S TIME.
NO MORE HIDING OUT HERE AND WAITING FOR DEATH.

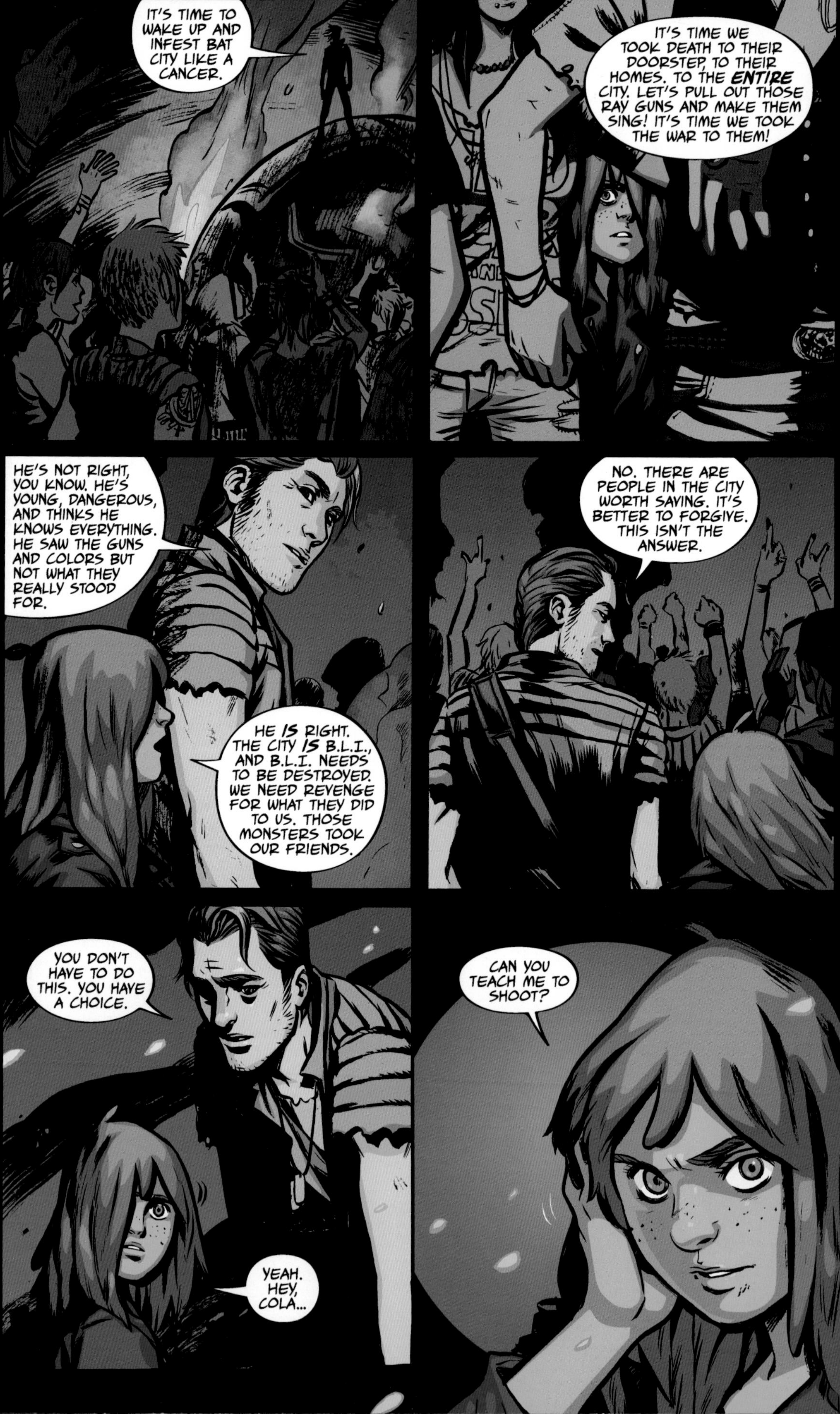
IT'S TIME TO WAKE UP AND INFEST BAT CITY LIKE A CANCER.
IT'S TIME WE TOOK DEATH TO THEIR DOORSTEP, TO THEIR HOMES. TO THE *ENTIRE* CITY. LET'S PULL OUT THOSE RAY GUNS AND MAKE THEM SING! IT'S TIME WE TOOK THE WAR TO THEM!
HE'S NOT RIGHT, YOU KNOW. HE'S YOUNG, DANGEROUS, AND THINKS HE KNOWS EVERYTHING. HE SAW THE GUNS AND COLORS BUT NOT WHAT THEY REALLY STOOD FOR.
HE *IS* RIGHT. THE CITY *IS* B.L.I., AND B.L.I. NEEDS TO BE DESTROYED. WE NEED REVENGE FOR WHAT THEY DID TO US. THOSE MONSTERS TOOK OUR FRIENDS.
NO. THERE ARE PEOPLE IN THE CITY WORTH SAVING. IT'S BETTER TO FORGIVE. THIS ISN'T THE ANSWER.
YOU DON'T HAVE TO DO THIS. YOU HAVE A CHOICE.
YEAH. HEY, COLA...
CAN YOU TEACH ME TO SHOOT?

Chapter Three:

TEENAGE LIGHTNING

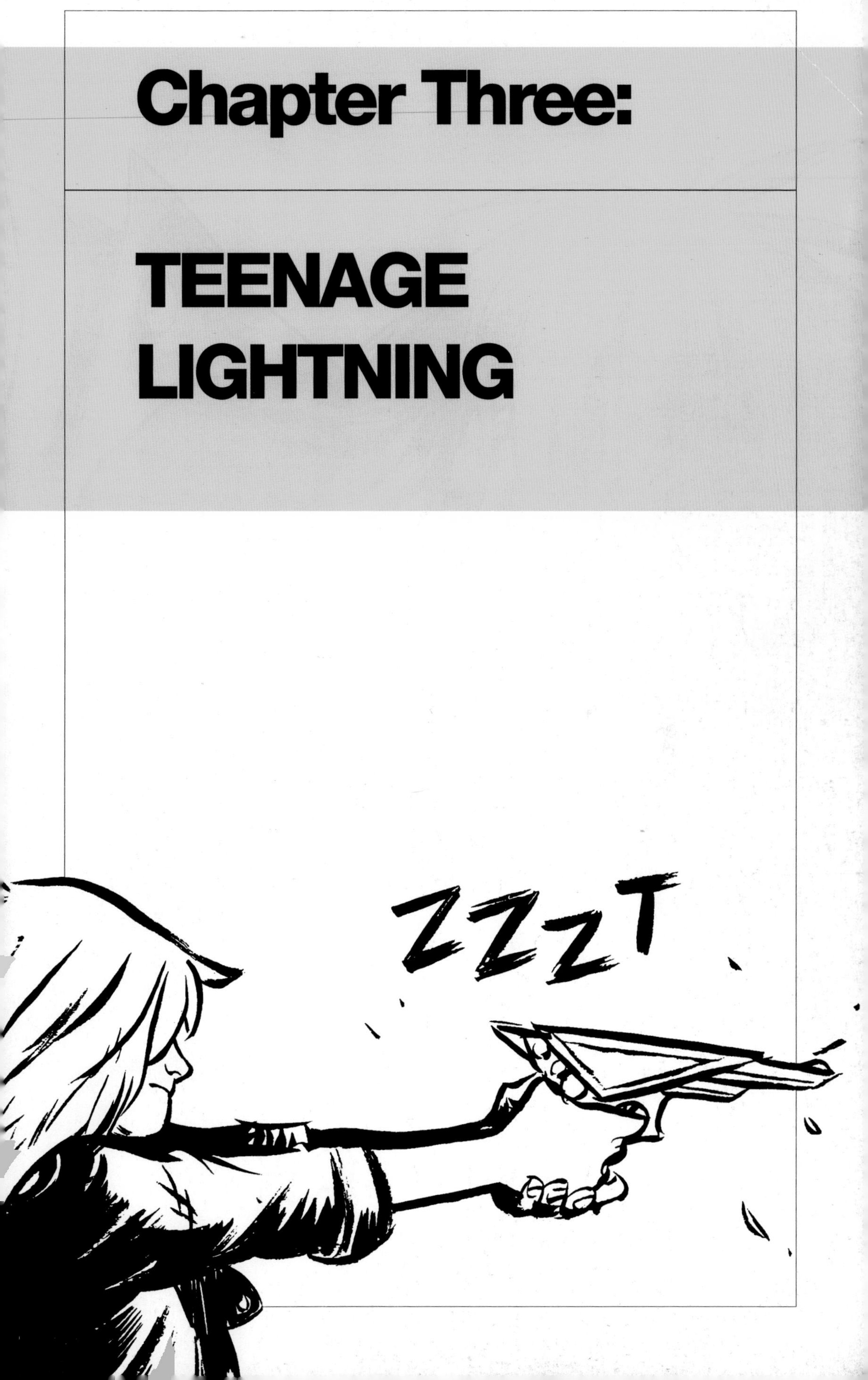
ZZZT

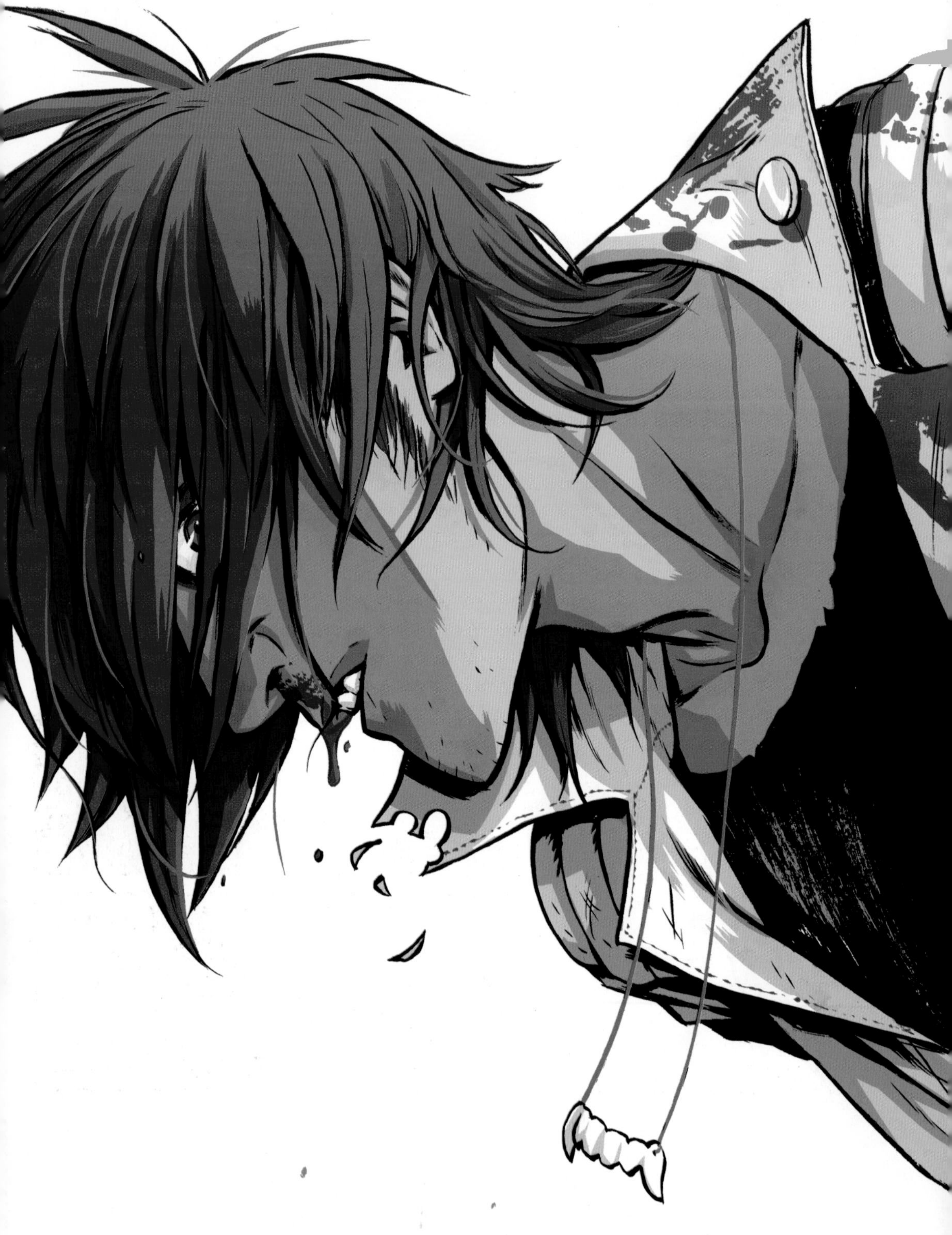

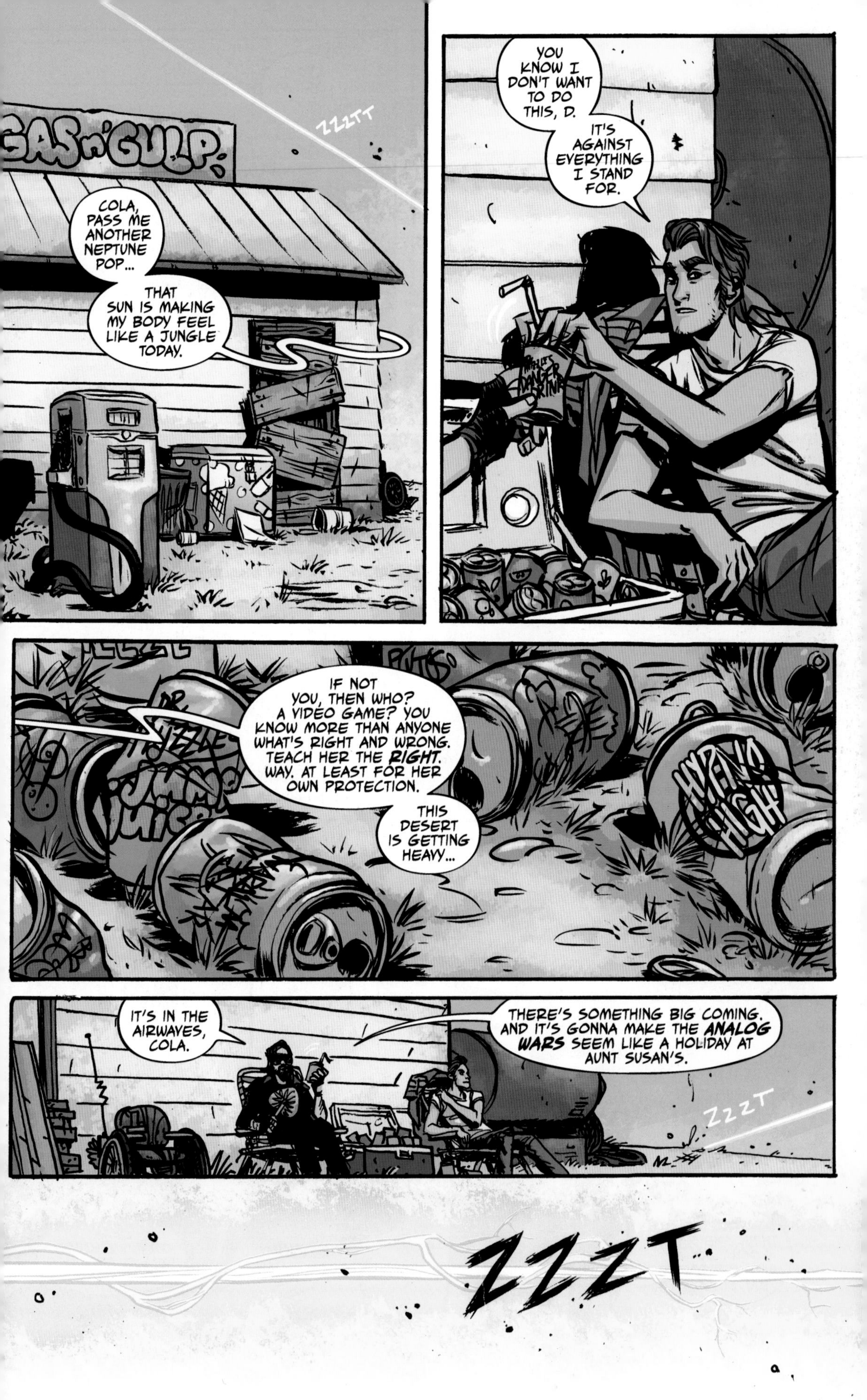
GAS n' GULP
ZZZTT
COLA, PASS ME ANOTHER NEPTUNE POP...
THAT SUN IS MAKING MY BODY FEEL LIKE A JUNGLE TODAY.
YOU KNOW I DON'T WANT TO DO THIS, D.
IT'S AGAINST EVERYTHING I STAND FOR.
IF NOT YOU, THEN WHO? A VIDEO GAME? YOU KNOW MORE THAN ANYONE WHAT'S RIGHT AND WRONG. TEACH HER THE RIGHT WAY. AT LEAST FOR HER OWN PROTECTION.
THIS DESERT IS GETTING HEAVY...
IT'S IN THE AIRWAVES, COLA.
THERE'S SOMETHING BIG COMING. AND IT'S GONNA MAKE THE ANALOG WARS SEEM LIKE A HOLIDAY AT AUNT SUSAN'S.
ZZZT
ZZZT

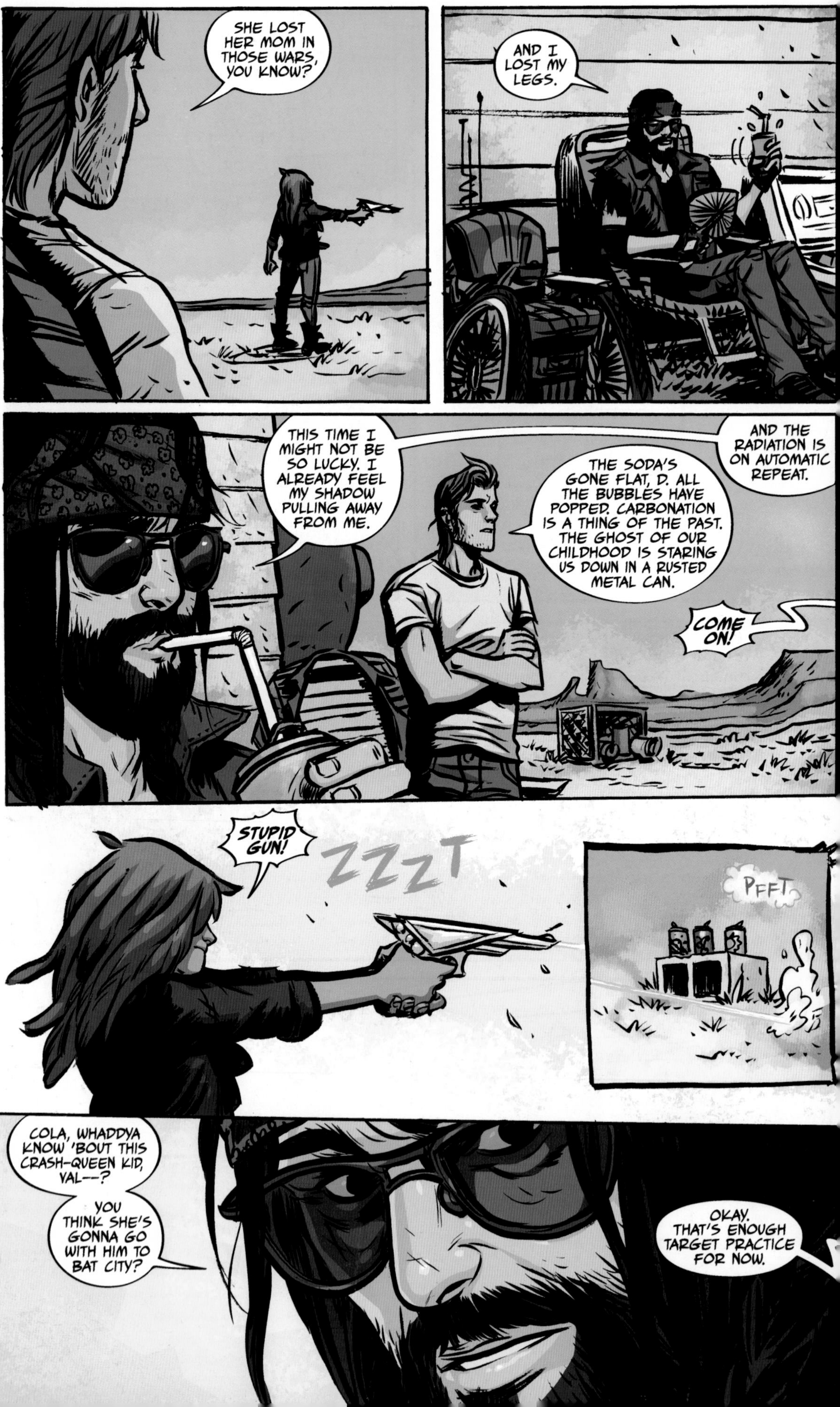
SHE LOST HER MOM IN THOSE WARS, YOU KNOW?
AND I LOST MY LEGS.
THIS TIME I MIGHT NOT BE SO LUCKY. I ALREADY FEEL MY SHADOW PULLING AWAY FROM ME.
AND THE RADIATION IS ON AUTOMATIC REPEAT.
THE SODA'S GONE FLAT, D. ALL THE BUBBLES HAVE POPPED. CARBONATION IS A THING OF THE PAST. THE GHOST OF OUR CHILDHOOD IS STARING US DOWN IN A RUSTED METAL CAN.
COME ON!
STUPID GUN!
ZZZT
PFFT
COLA, WHADDYA KNOW 'BOUT THIS CRASH-QUEEN KID, VAL--?
YOU THINK SHE'S GONNA GO WITH HIM TO BAT CITY?
OKAY. THAT'S ENOUGH TARGET PRACTICE FOR NOW.

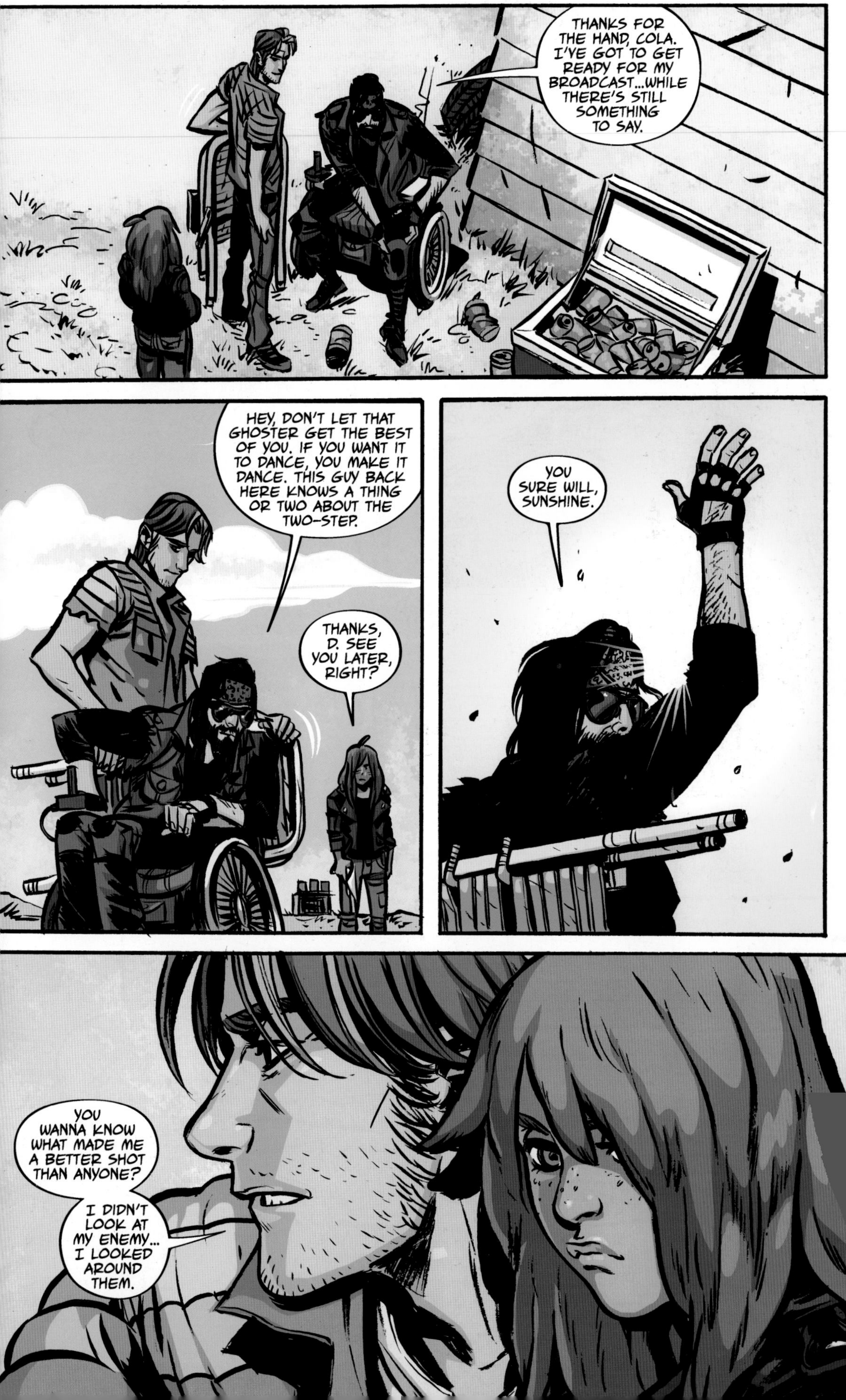
THANKS FOR THE HAND, COLA. I'VE GOT TO GET READY FOR MY BROADCAST...WHILE THERE'S STILL SOMETHING TO SAY.
HEY, DON'T LET THAT GHOSTER GET THE BEST OF YOU. IF YOU WANT IT TO DANCE, YOU MAKE IT DANCE. THIS GUY BACK HERE KNOWS A THING OR TWO ABOUT THE TWO-STEP.
THANKS, D. SEE YOU LATER, RIGHT?
YOU SURE WILL, SUNSHINE.
YOU WANNA KNOW WHAT MADE ME A BETTER SHOT THAN ANYONE?
I DIDN'T LOOK AT MY ENEMY... I LOOKED AROUND THEM.

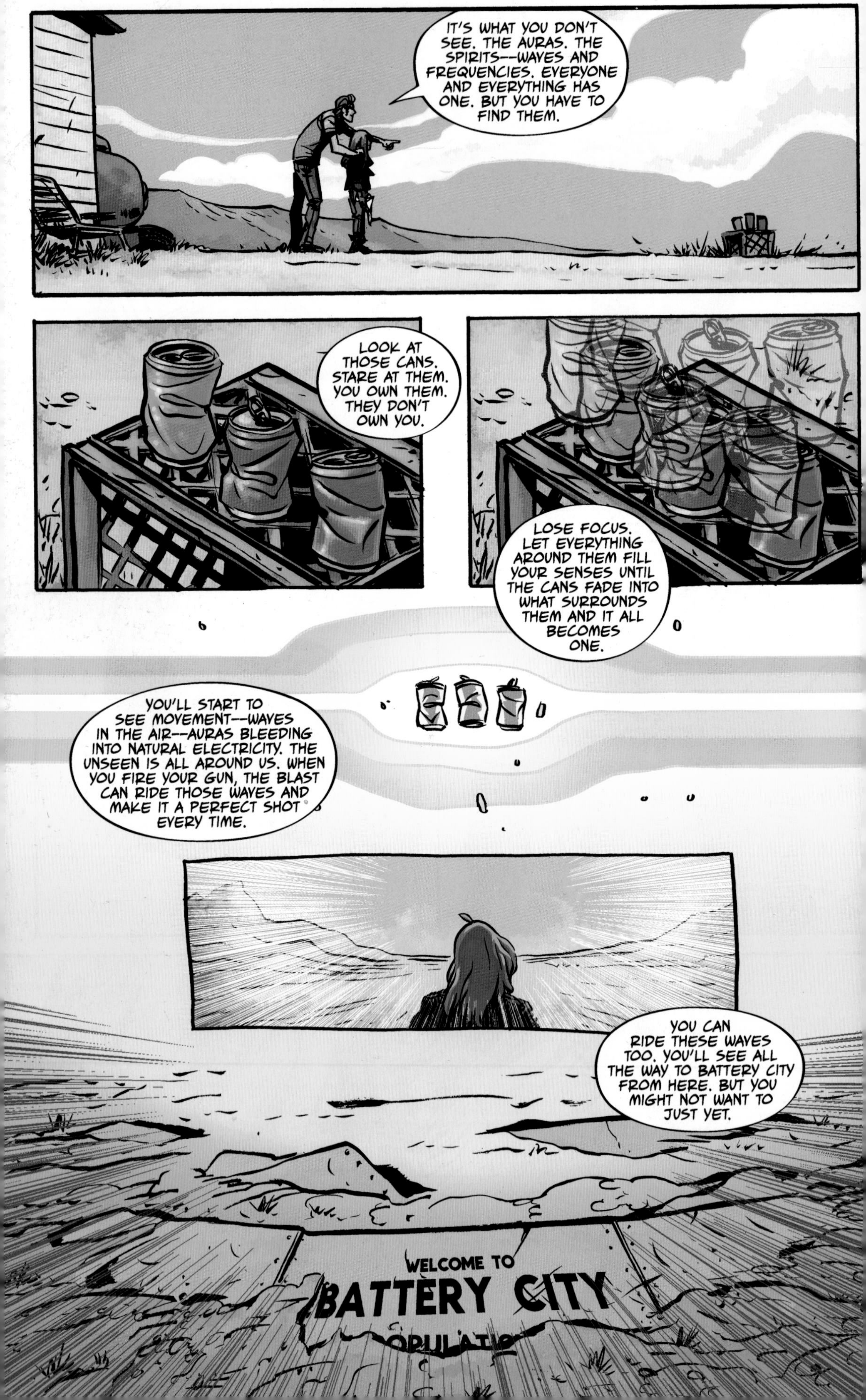
IT'S WHAT YOU DON'T SEE. THE AURAS. THE SPIRITS--WAVES AND FREQUENCIES. EVERYONE AND EVERYTHING HAS ONE. BUT YOU HAVE TO FIND THEM.
LOOK AT THOSE CANS. STARE AT THEM. YOU OWN THEM. THEY DON'T OWN YOU.
LOSE FOCUS. LET EVERYTHING AROUND THEM FILL YOUR SENSES UNTIL THE CANS FADE INTO WHAT SURROUNDS THEM AND IT ALL BECOMES ONE.
YOU'LL START TO SEE MOVEMENT--WAVES IN THE AIR--AURAS BLEEDING INTO NATURAL ELECTRICITY. THE UNSEEN IS ALL AROUND US. WHEN YOU FIRE YOUR GUN, THE BLAST CAN RIDE THOSE WAVES AND MAKE IT A PERFECT SHOT EVERY TIME.
YOU CAN RIDE THESE WAVES TOO. YOU'LL SEE ALL THE WAY TO BATTERY CITY FROM HERE. BUT YOU MIGHT NOT WANT TO JUST YET.
WELCOME TO
BATTERY CITY

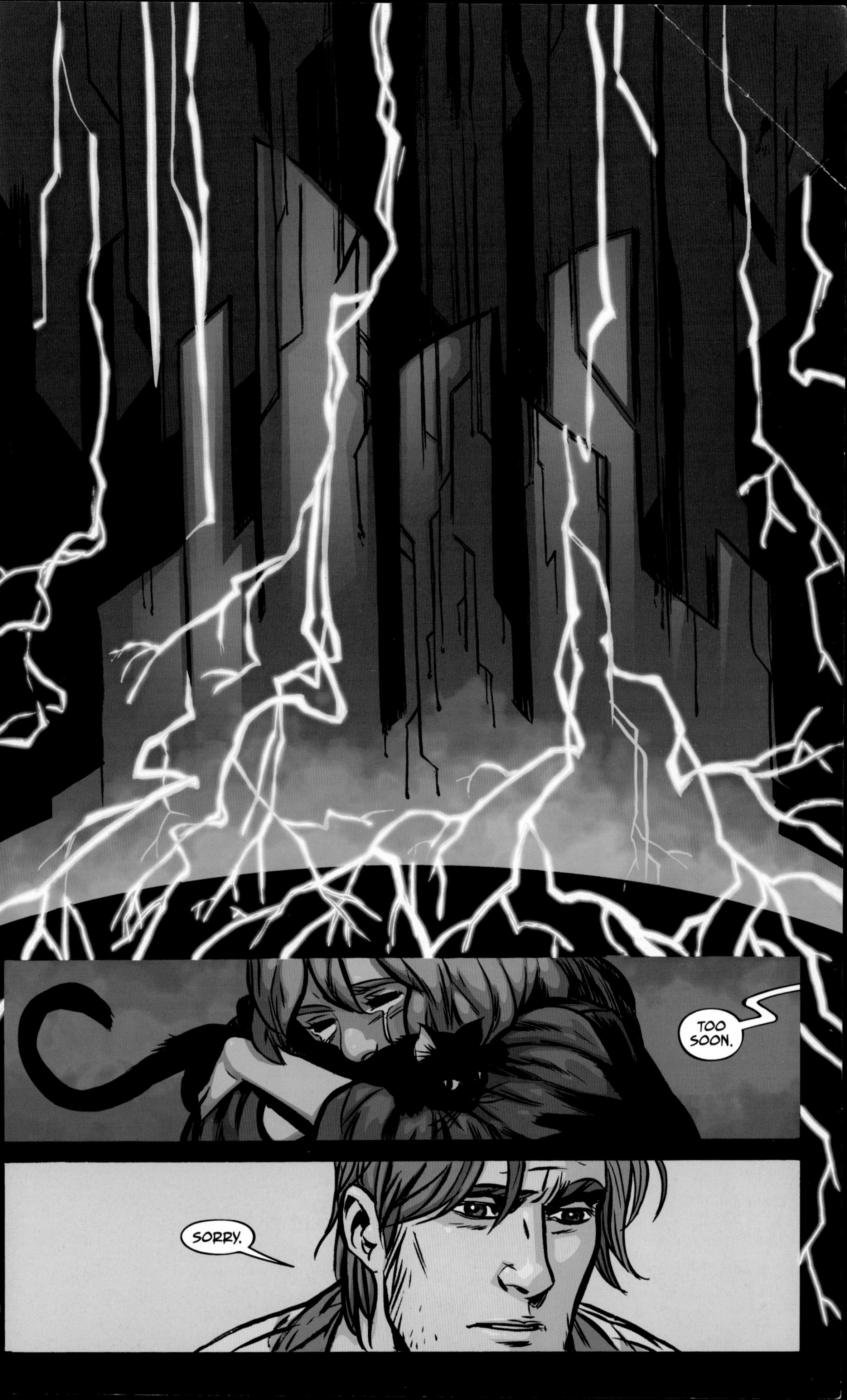
TOO SOON.
SORRY.

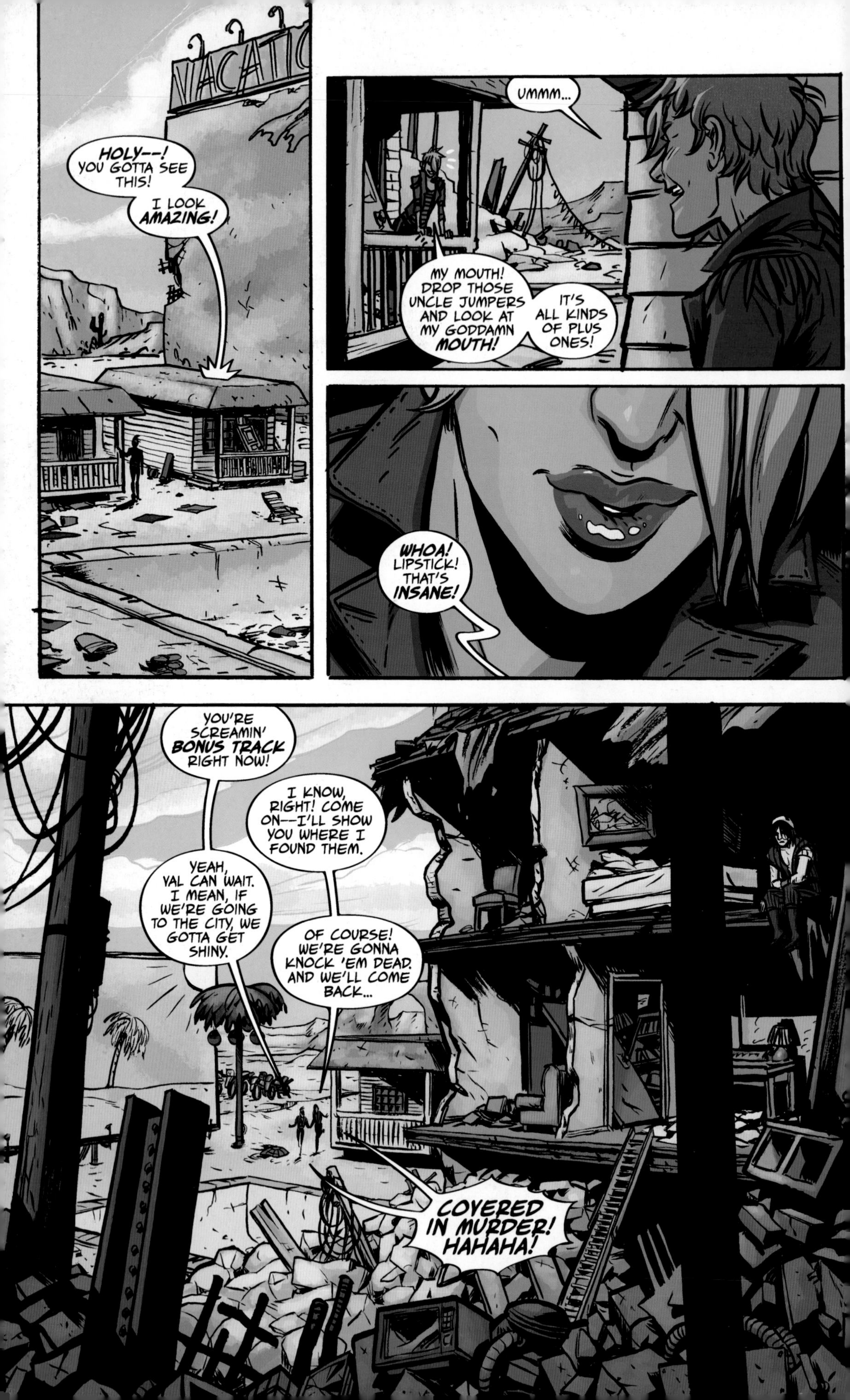
VACATIO
HOLY--! YOU GOTTA SEE THIS!
I LOOK AMAZING!
UMMM...
MY MOUTH! DROP THOSE UNCLE JUMPERS AND LOOK AT MY GODDAMN MOUTH!
IT'S ALL KINDS OF PLUS ONES!
WHOA! LIPSTICK! THAT'S INSANE!
YOU'RE SCREAMIN' BONUS TRACK RIGHT NOW!
I KNOW, RIGHT! COME ON--I'LL SHOW YOU WHERE I FOUND THEM.
YEAH, VAL CAN WAIT. I MEAN, IF WE'RE GOING TO THE CITY, WE GOTTA GET SHINY.
OF COURSE! WE'RE GONNA KNOCK 'EM DEAD. AND WE'LL COME BACK...
COVERED IN MURDER! HAHAHA!

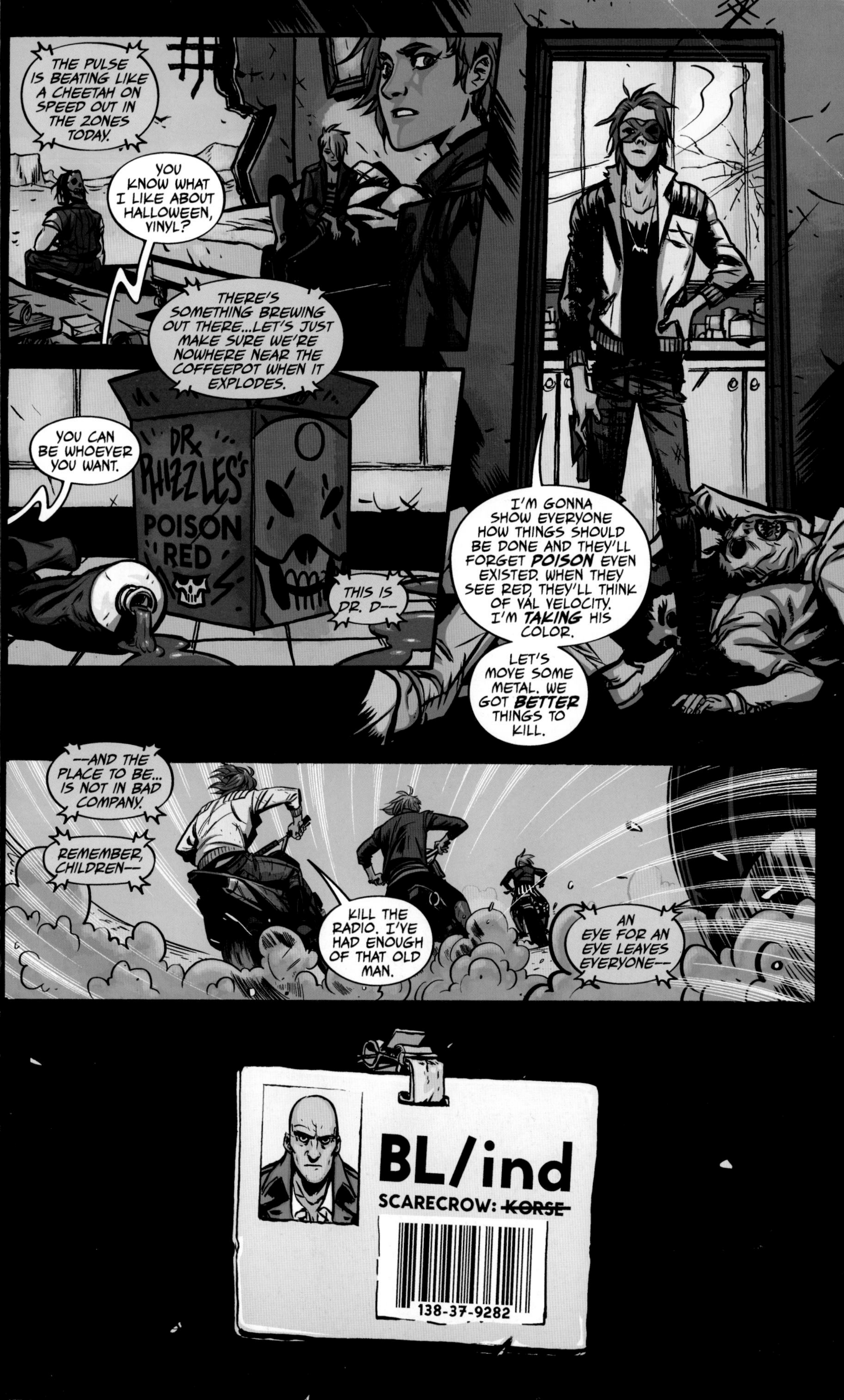

THE PULSE IS BEATING LIKE A CHEETAH ON SPEED OUT IN THE ZONES TODAY.
YOU KNOW WHAT I LIKE ABOUT HALLOWEEN, VINYL?
THERE'S SOMETHING BREWING OUT THERE...LET'S JUST MAKE SURE WE'RE NOWHERE NEAR THE COFFEEPOT WHEN IT EXPLODES.
YOU CAN BE WHOEVER YOU WANT.
DR. PHIZZLES's POISON RED
THIS IS DR. D--
I'M GONNA SHOW EVERYONE HOW THINGS SHOULD BE DONE AND THEY'LL FORGET **POISON** EVEN EXISTED. WHEN THEY SEE RED, THEY'LL THINK OF VAL VELOCITY. I'M ***TAKING*** HIS COLOR.
LET'S MOVE SOME METAL. WE GOT ***BETTER*** THINGS TO KILL.
REMEMBER, CHILDREN--
KILL THE RADIO. I'VE HAD ENOUGH OF THAT OLD MAN.
AN EYE FOR AN EYE LEAVES EVERYONE--
--AND THE PLACE TO BE... IS NOT IN BAD COMPANY.
BL/ind
SCARECROW: ~~KORSE~~
138-37-9282

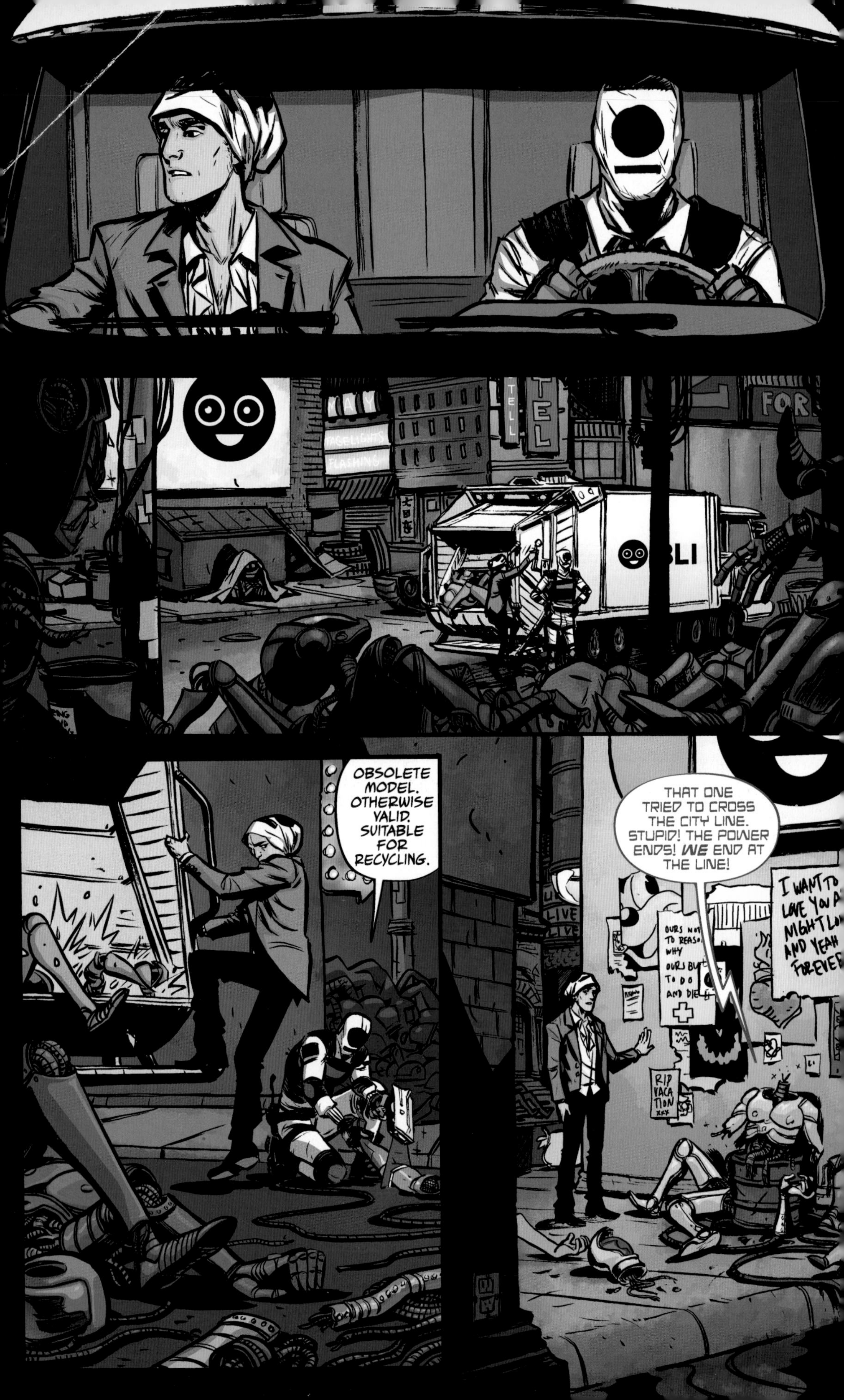
OBSOLETE MODEL. OTHERWISE VALID. SUITABLE FOR RECYCLING.
THAT ONE TRIED TO CROSS THE CITY LINE. STUPID! THE POWER ENDS! *WE* END AT THE LINE!
RIP VACATION

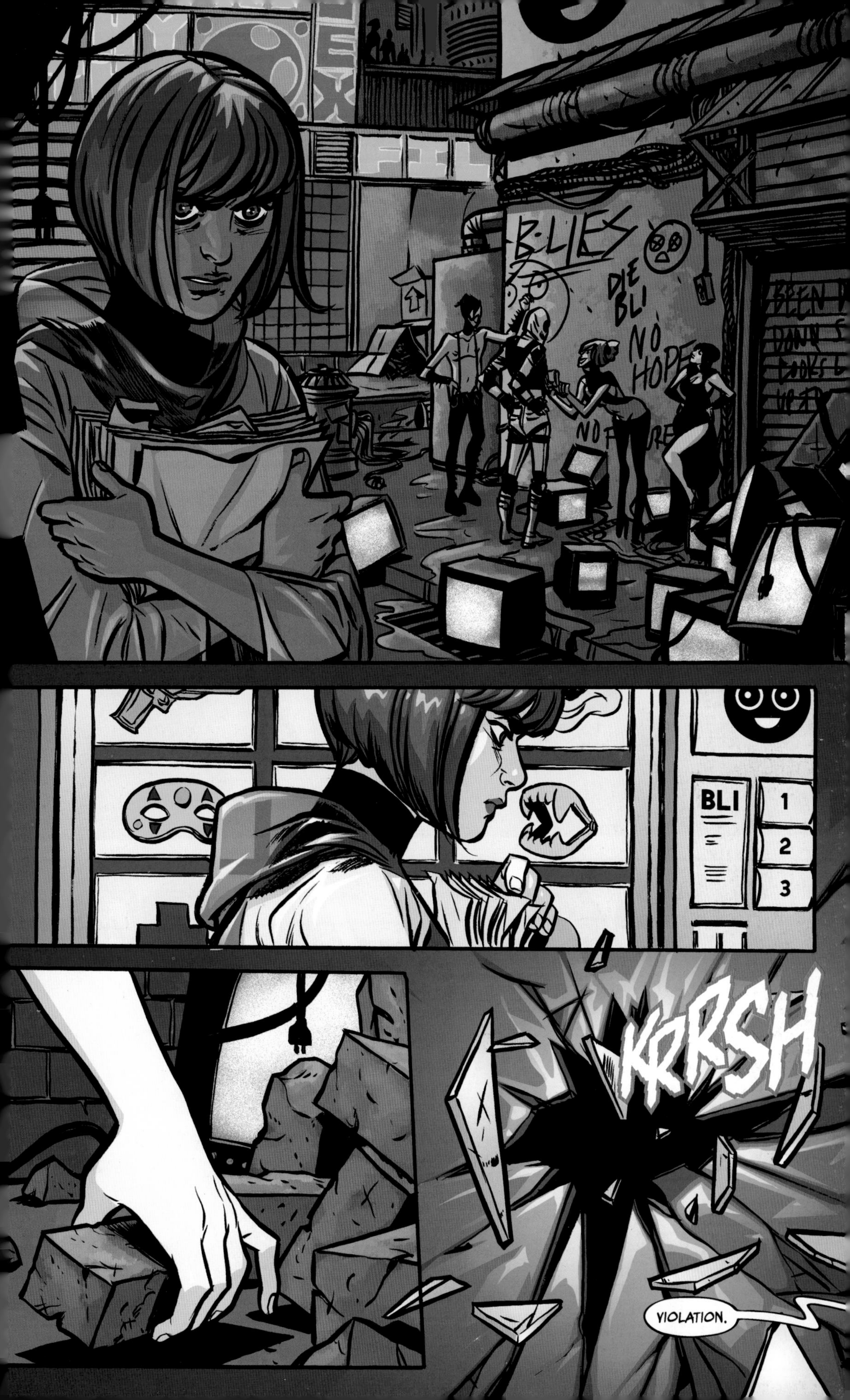
B-LIES
DIE BLI
NO HOPE
BLI
1
2
3
KRRSH
VIOLATION.

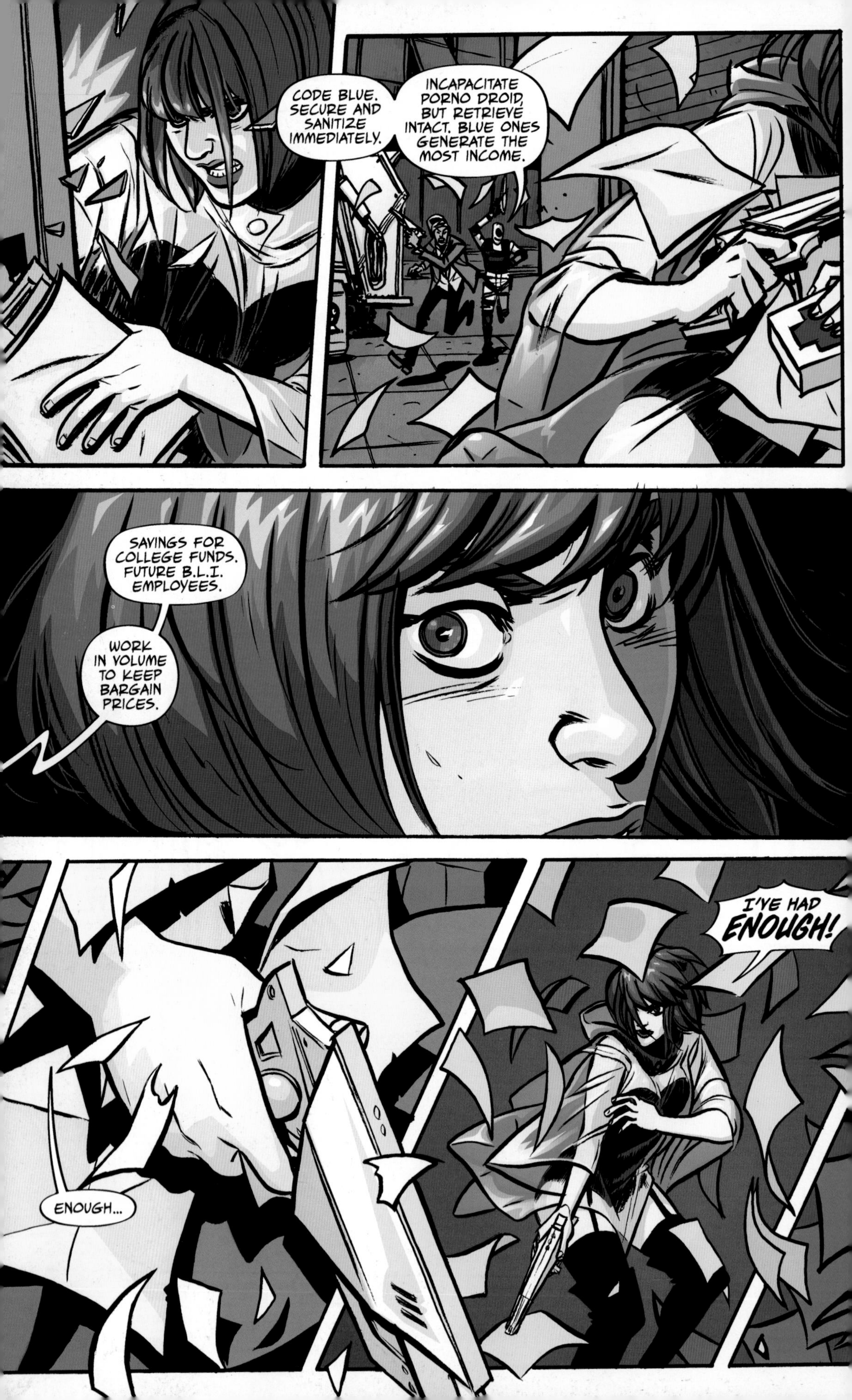
CODE BLUE. SECURE AND SANITIZE IMMEDIATELY.
INCAPACITATE PORNO DROID, BUT RETRIEVE INTACT. BLUE ONES GENERATE THE MOST INCOME.
SAVINGS FOR COLLEGE FUNDS. FUTURE B.L.I. EMPLOYEES.
WORK IN VOLUME TO KEEP BARGAIN PRICES.
ENOUGH...
I'VE HAD ENOUGH!

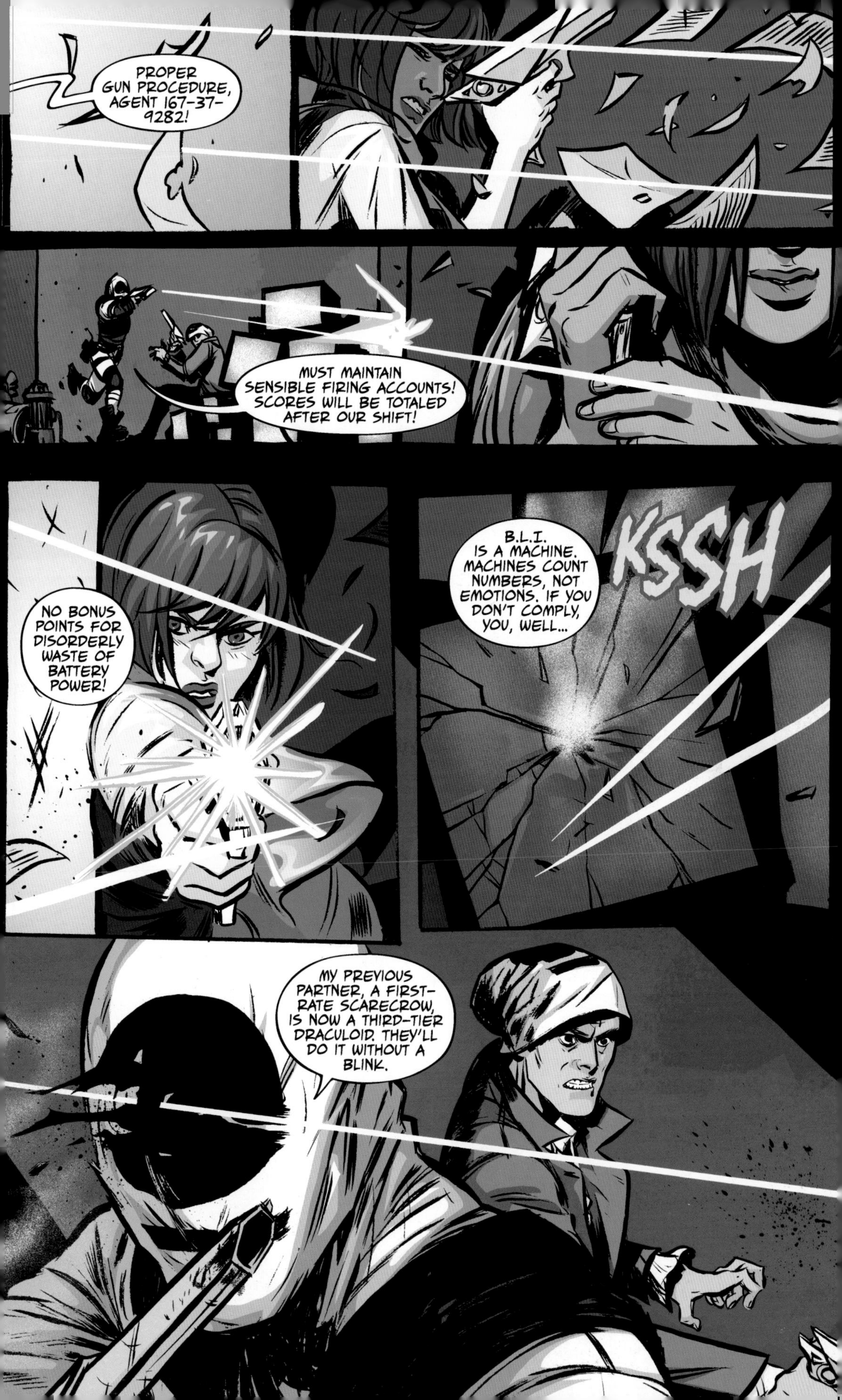
PROPER GUN PROCEDURE, AGENT 167-37-9282!
MUST MAINTAIN SENSIBLE FIRING ACCOUNTS! SCORES WILL BE TOTALED AFTER OUR SHIFT!
NO BONUS POINTS FOR DISORDERLY WASTE OF BATTERY POWER!
KSSH
B.L.I. IS A MACHINE. MACHINES COUNT NUMBERS, NOT EMOTIONS. IF YOU DON'T COMPLY, YOU, WELL...
MY PREVIOUS PARTNER, A FIRST-RATE SCARECROW, IS NOW A THIRD-TIER DRACULOID. THEY'LL DO IT WITHOUT A BLINK.

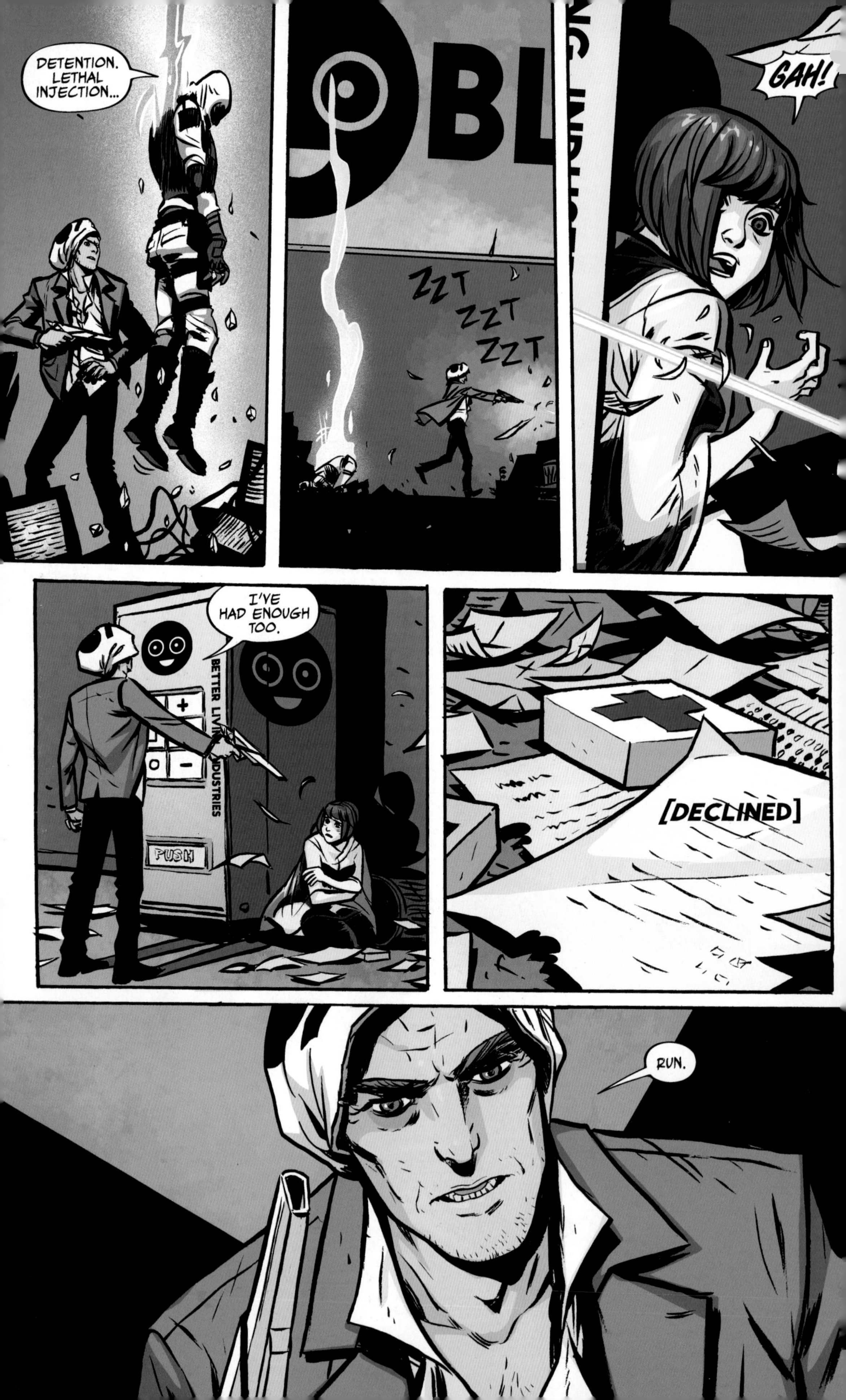
DETENTION. LETHAL INJECTION...
ZZT ZZT ZZT
GAH!
I'VE HAD ENOUGH TOO.
BETTER LIVING INDUSTRIES
PUSH
[DECLINED]
RUN.

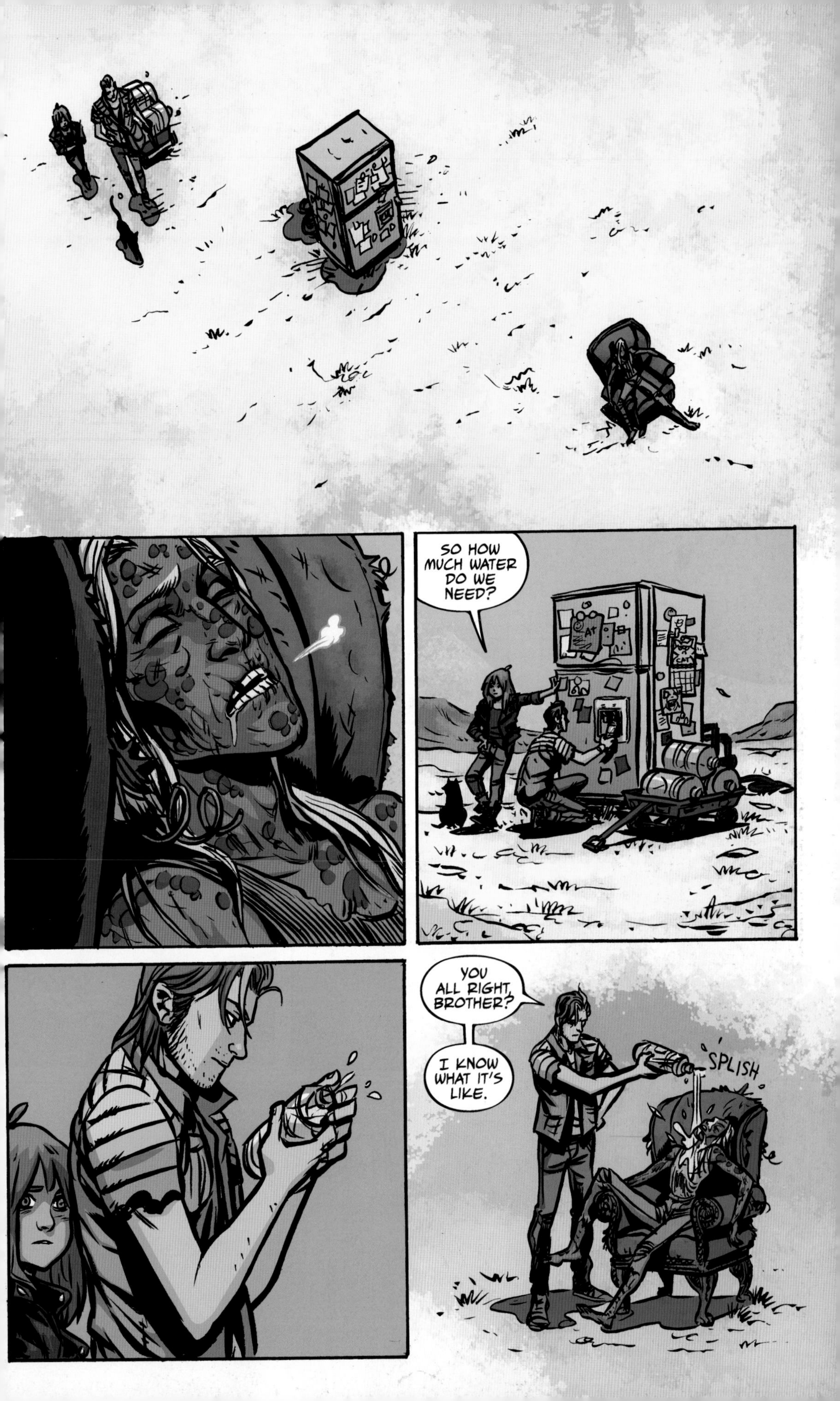
SO HOW MUCH WATER DO WE NEED?
YOU ALL RIGHT, BROTHER?
I KNOW WHAT IT'S LIKE.
SPLISH

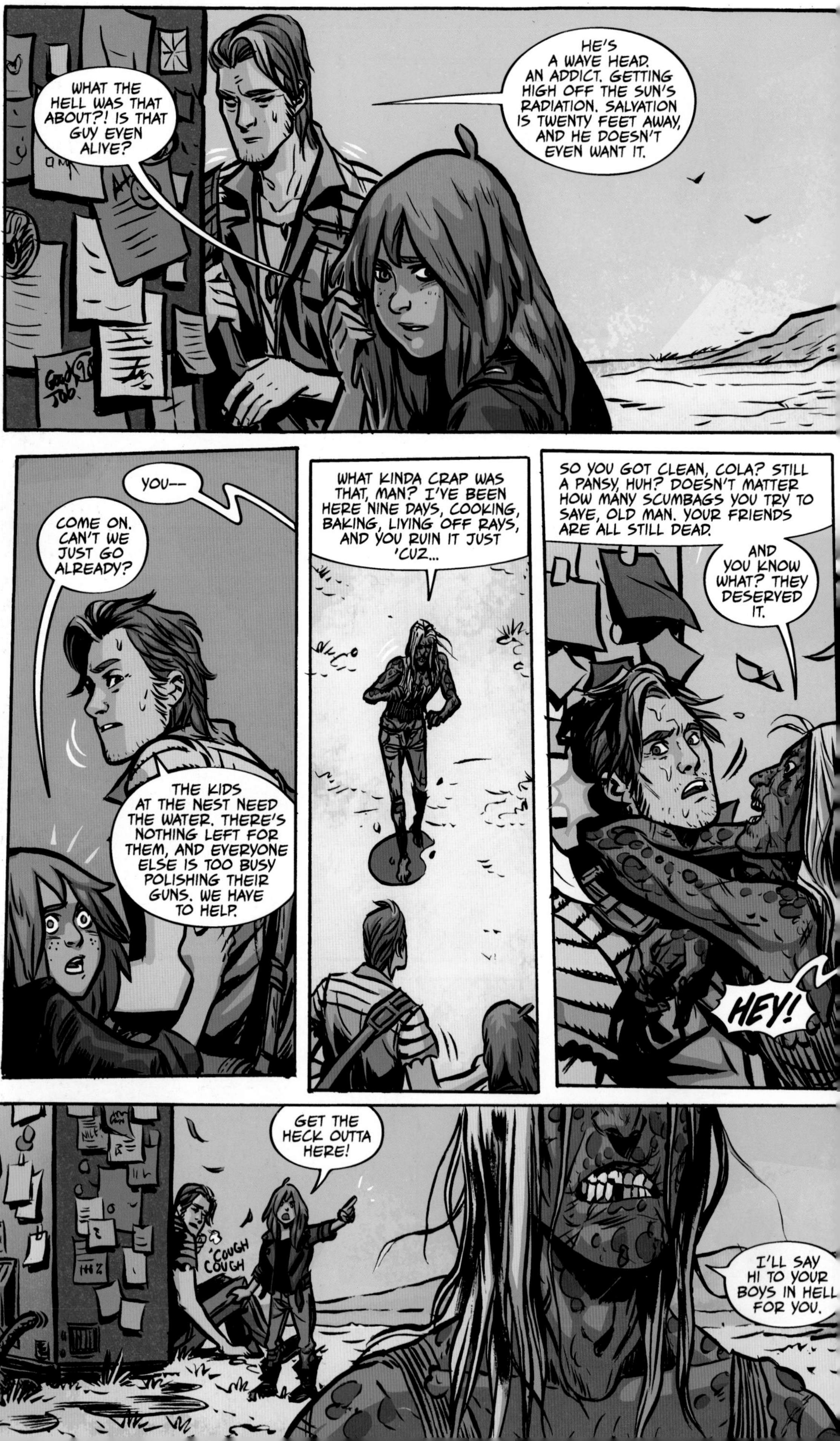
WHAT THE HELL WAS THAT ABOUT?! IS THAT GUY EVEN ALIVE?
HE'S A WAVE HEAD. AN ADDICT. GETTING HIGH OFF THE SUN'S RADIATION. SALVATION IS TWENTY FEET AWAY, AND HE DOESN'T EVEN WANT IT.
YOU--
COME ON. CAN'T WE JUST GO ALREADY?
THE KIDS AT THE NEST NEED THE WATER. THERE'S NOTHING LEFT FOR THEM, AND EVERYONE ELSE IS TOO BUSY POLISHING THEIR GUNS. WE HAVE TO HELP.
WHAT KINDA CRAP WAS THAT, MAN? I'VE BEEN HERE NINE DAYS, COOKING, BAKING, LIVING OFF RAYS, AND YOU RUIN IT JUST 'CUZ...
SO YOU GOT CLEAN, COLA? STILL A PANSY, HUH? DOESN'T MATTER HOW MANY SCUMBAGS YOU TRY TO SAVE, OLD MAN. YOUR FRIENDS ARE ALL STILL DEAD.
AND YOU KNOW WHAT? THEY DESERVED IT.
HEY!
GET THE HECK OUTTA HERE!
COUGH COUGH
I'LL SAY HI TO YOUR BOYS IN HELL FOR YOU.

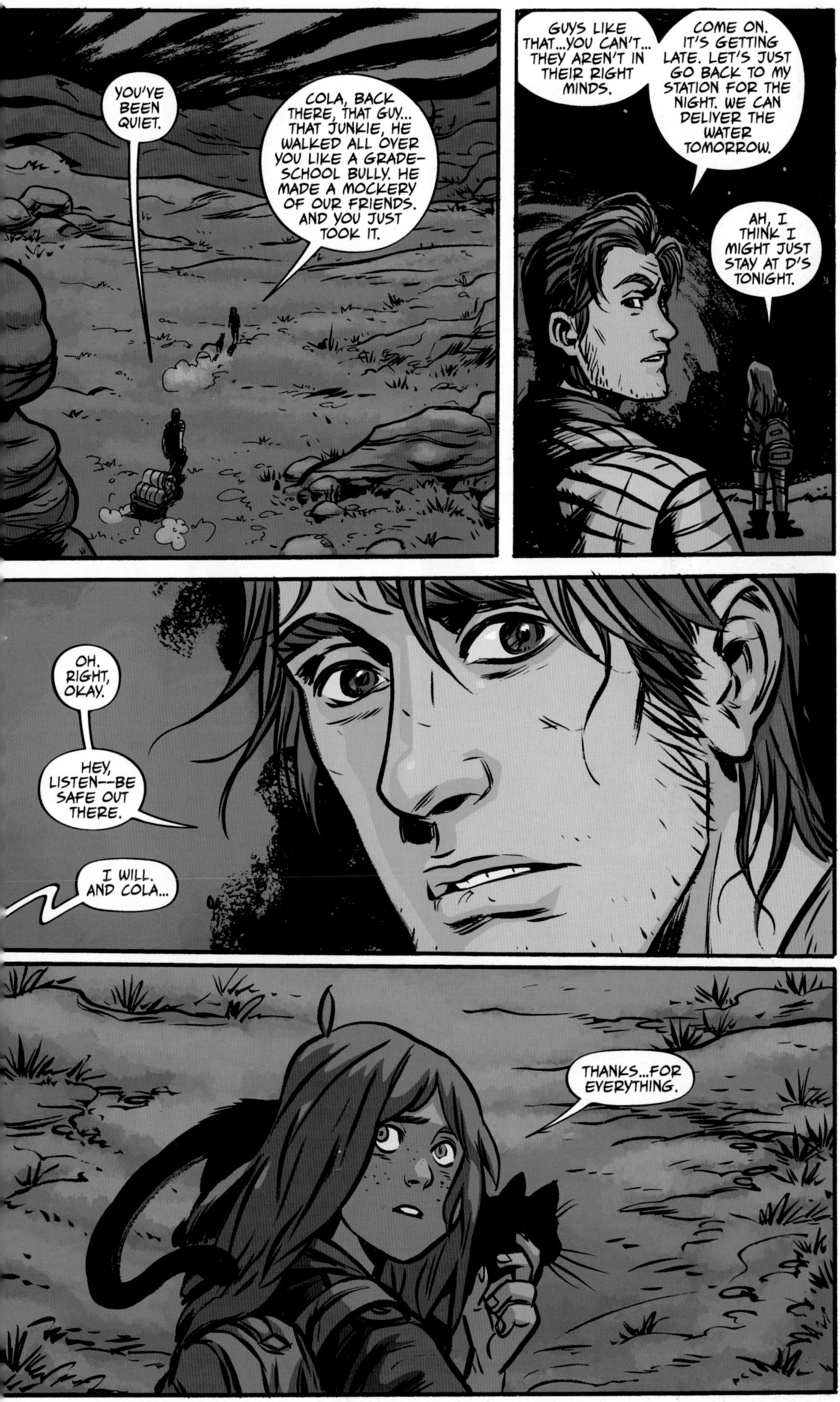
YOU'VE BEEN QUIET.
COLA, BACK THERE, THAT GUY... THAT JUNKIE, HE WALKED ALL OVER YOU LIKE A GRADE-SCHOOL BULLY. HE MADE A MOCKERY OF OUR FRIENDS. AND YOU JUST TOOK IT.
GUYS LIKE THAT...YOU CAN'T... THEY AREN'T IN THEIR RIGHT MINDS.
COME ON. IT'S GETTING LATE. LET'S JUST GO BACK TO MY STATION FOR THE NIGHT. WE CAN DELIVER THE WATER TOMORROW.
AH, I THINK I MIGHT JUST STAY AT D'S TONIGHT.
OH. RIGHT, OKAY.
HEY, LISTEN--BE SAFE OUT THERE.
I WILL. AND COLA...
THANKS...FOR EVERYTHING.

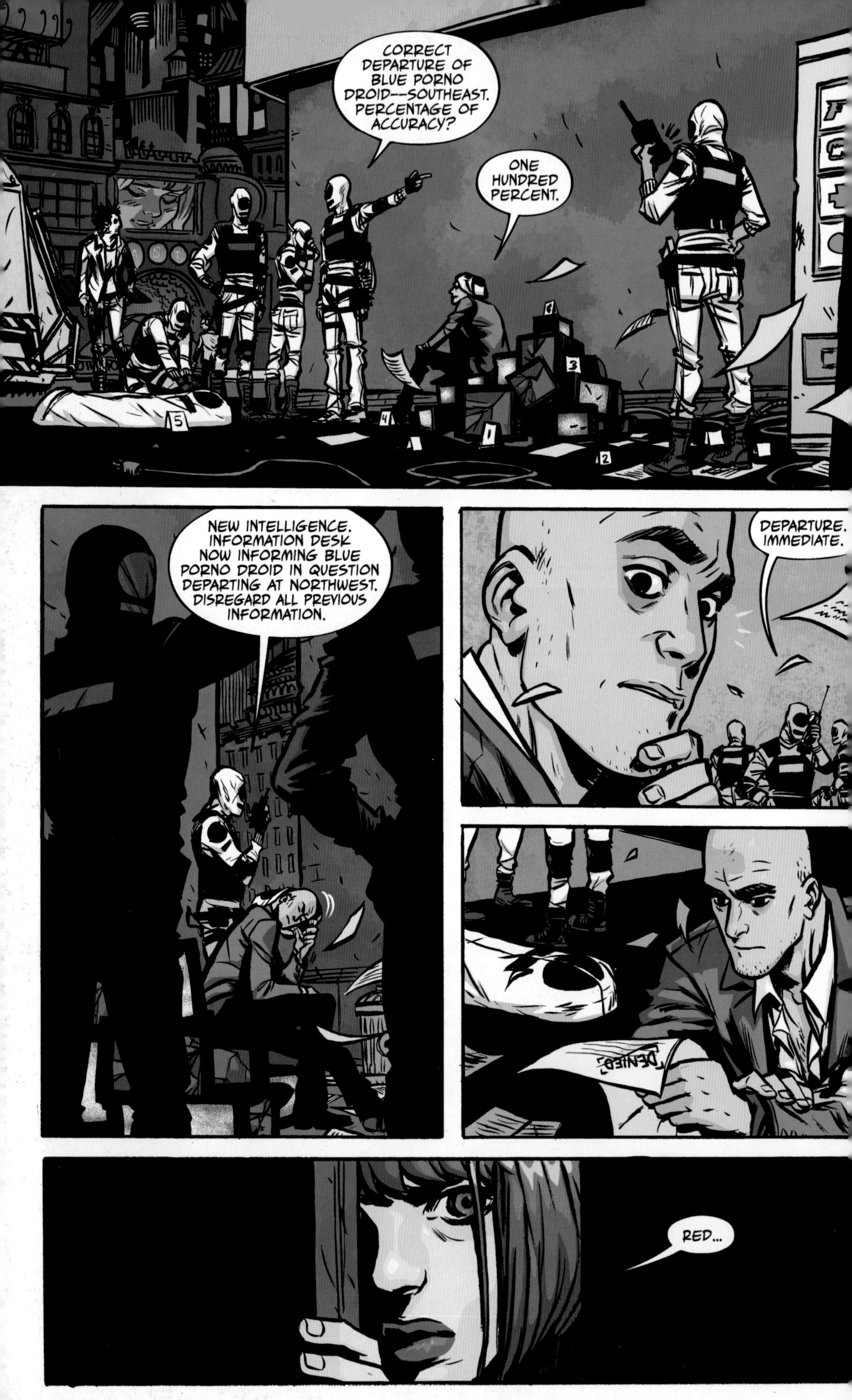
CORRECT DEPARTURE OF BLUE PORNO DROID--SOUTHEAST. PERCENTAGE OF ACCURACY?
ONE HUNDRED PERCENT.
NEW INTELLIGENCE. INFORMATION DESK NOW INFORMING BLUE PORNO DROID IN QUESTION DEPARTING AT NORTHWEST. DISREGARD ALL PREVIOUS INFORMATION.
DEPARTURE. IMMEDIATE.
DENIED
RED...

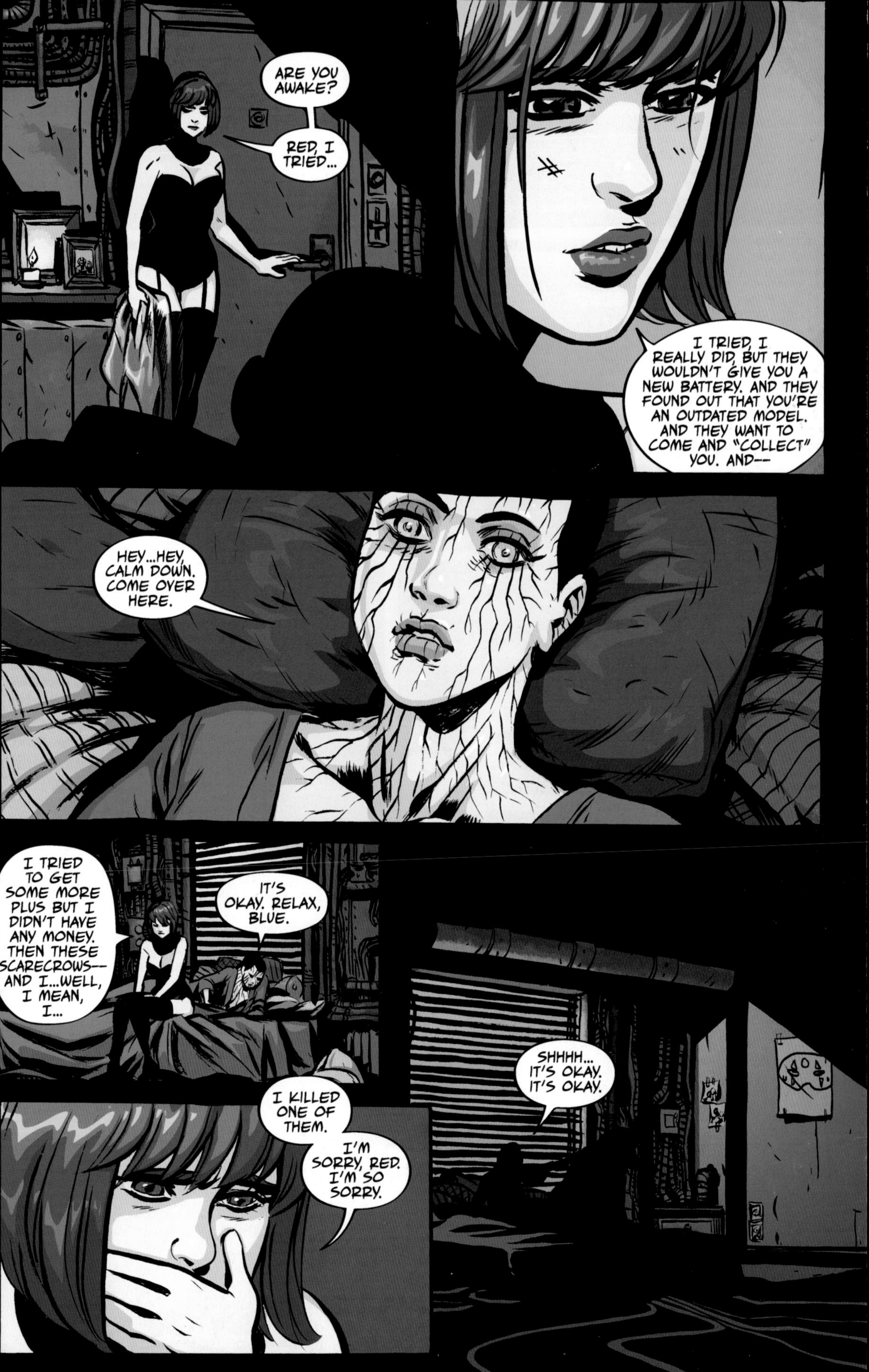
ARE YOU AWAKE?
RED, I TRIED...
I TRIED, I REALLY DID, BUT THEY WOULDN'T GIVE YOU A NEW BATTERY. AND THEY FOUND OUT THAT YOU'RE AN OUTDATED MODEL. AND THEY WANT TO COME AND "COLLECT" YOU. AND--
HEY...HEY, CALM DOWN. COME OVER HERE.
I TRIED TO GET SOME MORE PLUS BUT I DIDN'T HAVE ANY MONEY. THEN THESE SCARECROWS-- AND I...WELL, I MEAN, I...
IT'S OKAY. RELAX, BLUE.
I KILLED ONE OF THEM.
I'M SORRY, RED. I'M SO SORRY.
SHHHH... IT'S OKAY. IT'S OKAY.

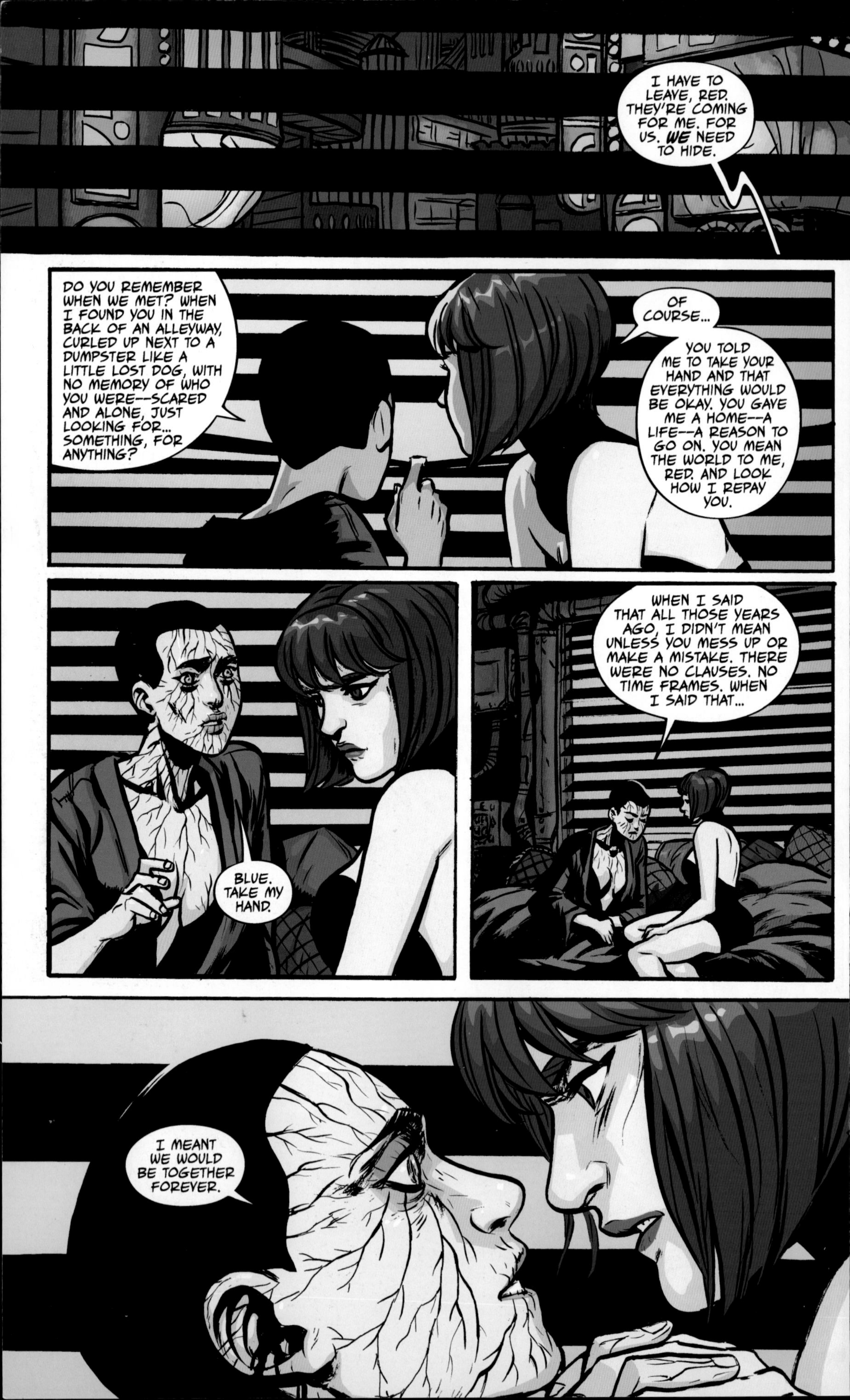
I HAVE TO LEAVE, RED. THEY'RE COMING FOR ME. FOR US. WE NEED TO HIDE.
DO YOU REMEMBER WHEN WE MET? WHEN I FOUND YOU IN THE BACK OF AN ALLEYWAY, CURLED UP NEXT TO A DUMPSTER LIKE A LITTLE LOST DOG, WITH NO MEMORY OF WHO YOU WERE--SCARED AND ALONE, JUST LOOKING FOR... SOMETHING, FOR ANYTHING?
OF COURSE...
YOU TOLD ME TO TAKE YOUR HAND AND THAT EVERYTHING WOULD BE OKAY. YOU GAVE ME A HOME--A LIFE--A REASON TO GO ON. YOU MEAN THE WORLD TO ME, RED. AND LOOK HOW I REPAY YOU.
BLUE. TAKE MY HAND.
WHEN I SAID THAT ALL THOSE YEARS AGO, I DIDN'T MEAN UNLESS YOU MESS UP OR MAKE A MISTAKE. THERE WERE NO CLAUSES. NO TIME FRAMES. WHEN I SAID THAT...
I MEANT WE WOULD BE TOGETHER FOREVER.

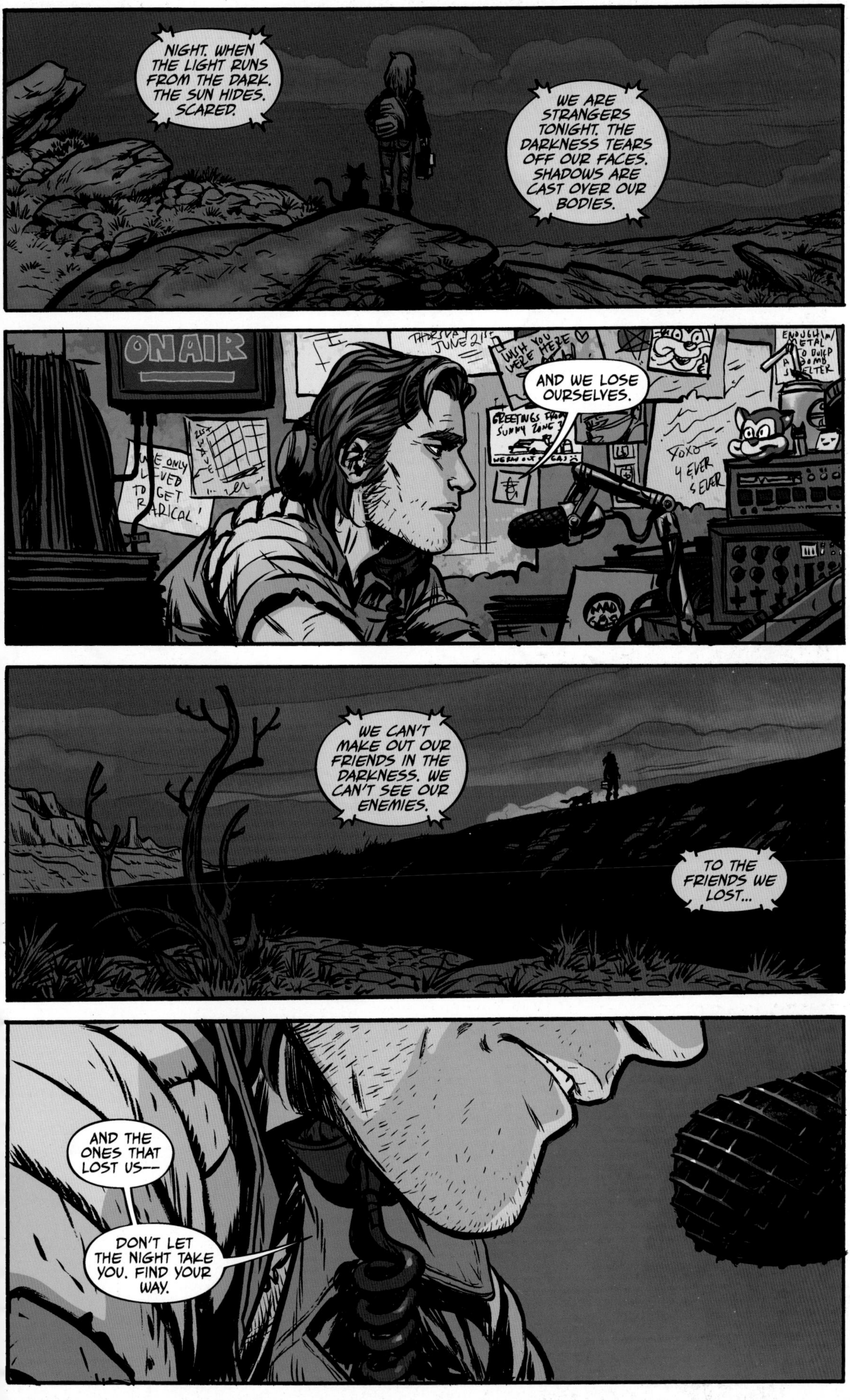
NIGHT. WHEN THE LIGHT RUNS FROM THE DARK. THE SUN HIDES. SCARED.
WE ARE STRANGERS TONIGHT. THE DARKNESS TEARS OFF OUR FACES. SHADOWS ARE CAST OVER OUR BODIES.
ON AIR
AND WE LOSE OURSELVES.
WE CAN'T MAKE OUT OUR FRIENDS IN THE DARKNESS. WE CAN'T SEE OUR ENEMIES.
TO THE FRIENDS WE LOST...
AND THE ONES THAT LOST US--
DON'T LET THE NIGHT TAKE YOU. FIND YOUR WAY.

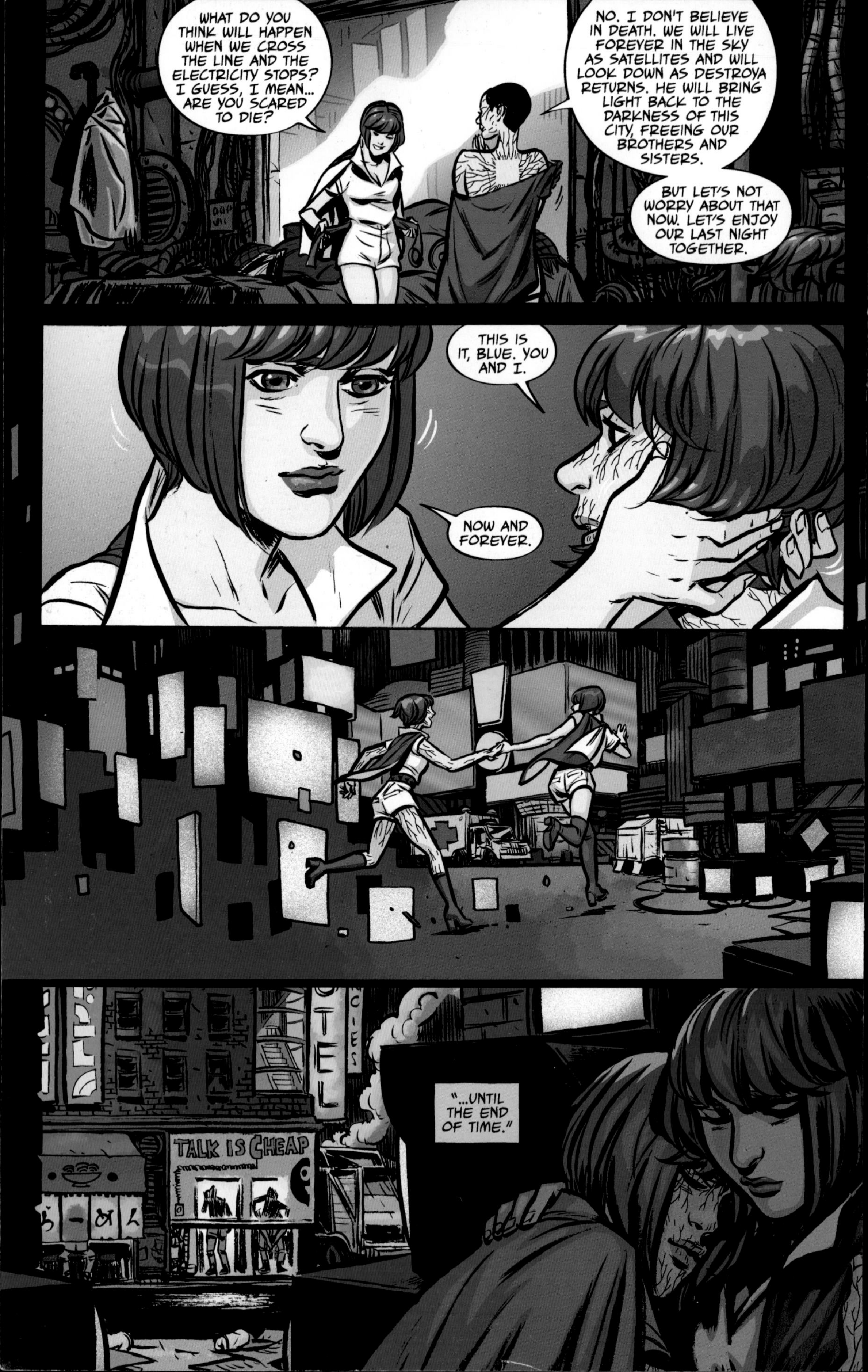
WHAT DO YOU THINK WILL HAPPEN WHEN WE CROSS THE LINE AND THE ELECTRICITY STOPS? I GUESS, I MEAN... ARE YOU SCARED TO DIE?
NO. I DON'T BELIEVE IN DEATH. WE WILL LIVE FOREVER IN THE SKY AS SATELLITES AND WILL LOOK DOWN AS DESTROYA RETURNS. HE WILL BRING LIGHT BACK TO THE DARKNESS OF THIS CITY, FREEING OUR BROTHERS AND SISTERS.
BUT LET'S NOT WORRY ABOUT THAT NOW. LET'S ENJOY OUR LAST NIGHT TOGETHER.
THIS IS IT, BLUE. YOU AND I.
NOW AND FOREVER.
TALK IS CHEAP
"...UNTIL THE END OF TIME."

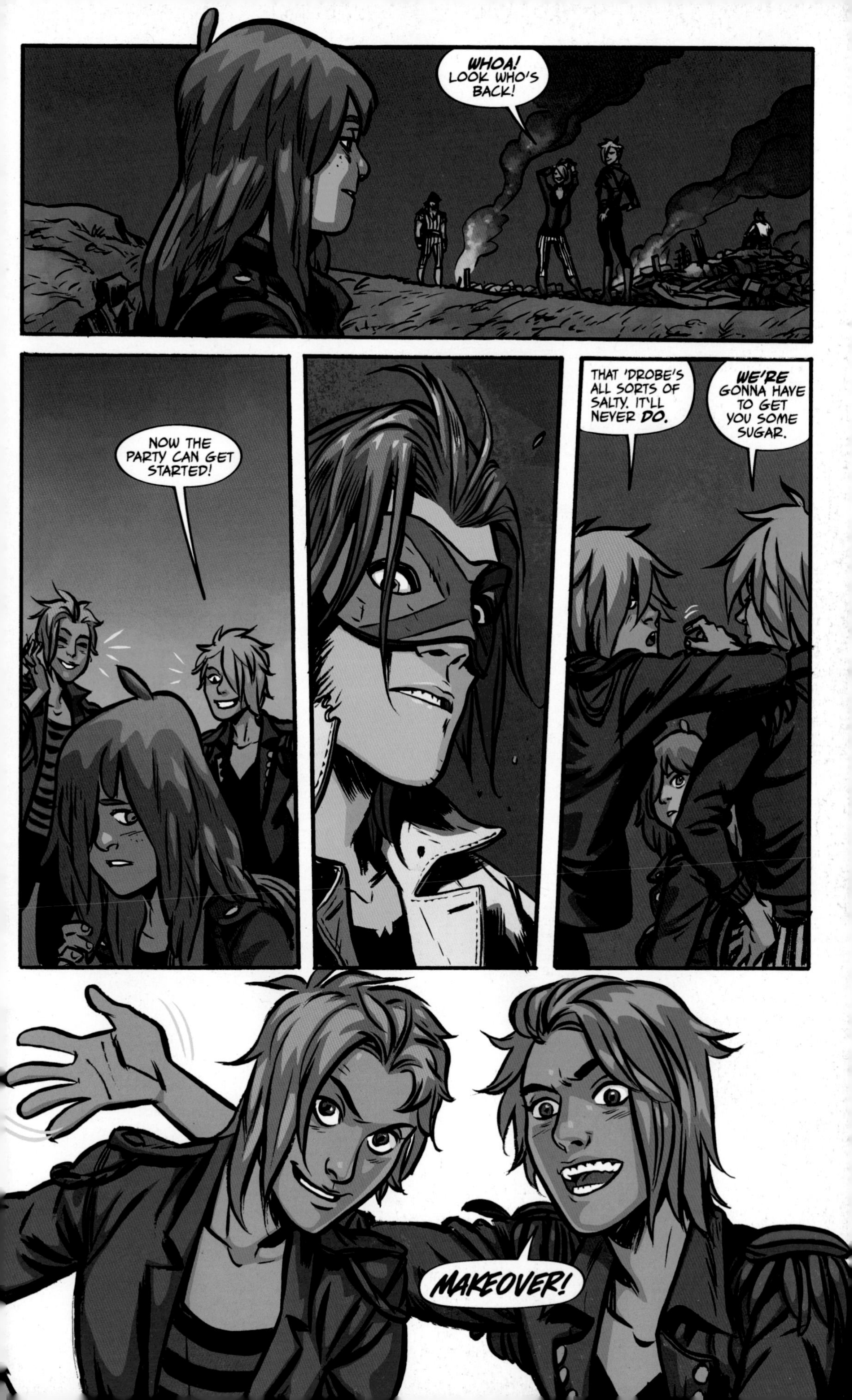
WHOA! LOOK WHO'S BACK!
NOW THE PARTY CAN GET STARTED!
THAT 'DROBE'S ALL SORTS OF SALTY. IT'LL NEVER DO.
WE'RE GONNA HAVE TO GET YOU SOME SUGAR.
MAKEOVER!

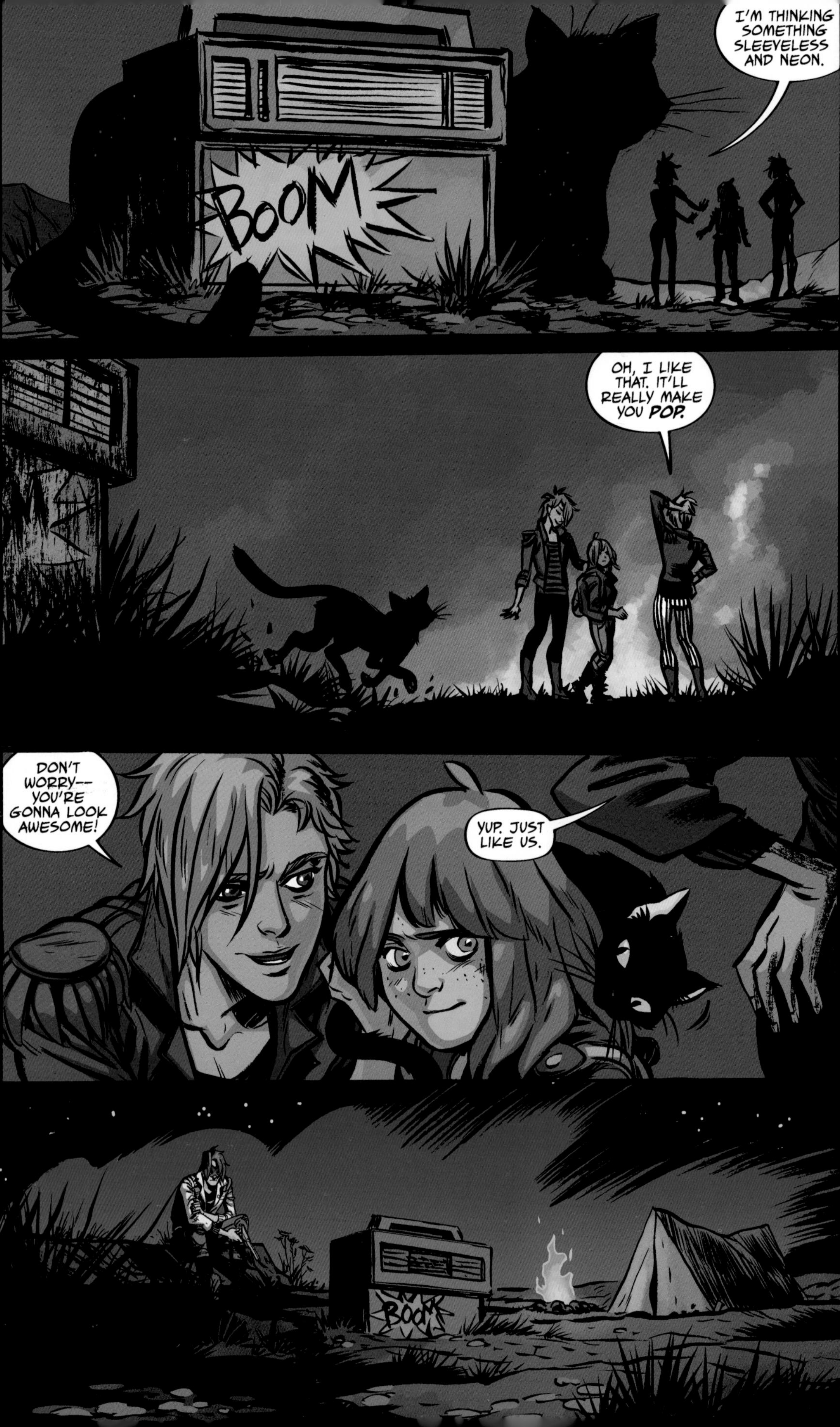

I'M THINKING SOMETHING SLEEVELESS AND NEON.
BOOM
OH, I LIKE THAT. IT'LL REALLY MAKE YOU POP.
DON'T WORRY-- YOU'RE GONNA LOOK AWESOME!
YUP. JUST LIKE US.

Chapter Four:

RUN!

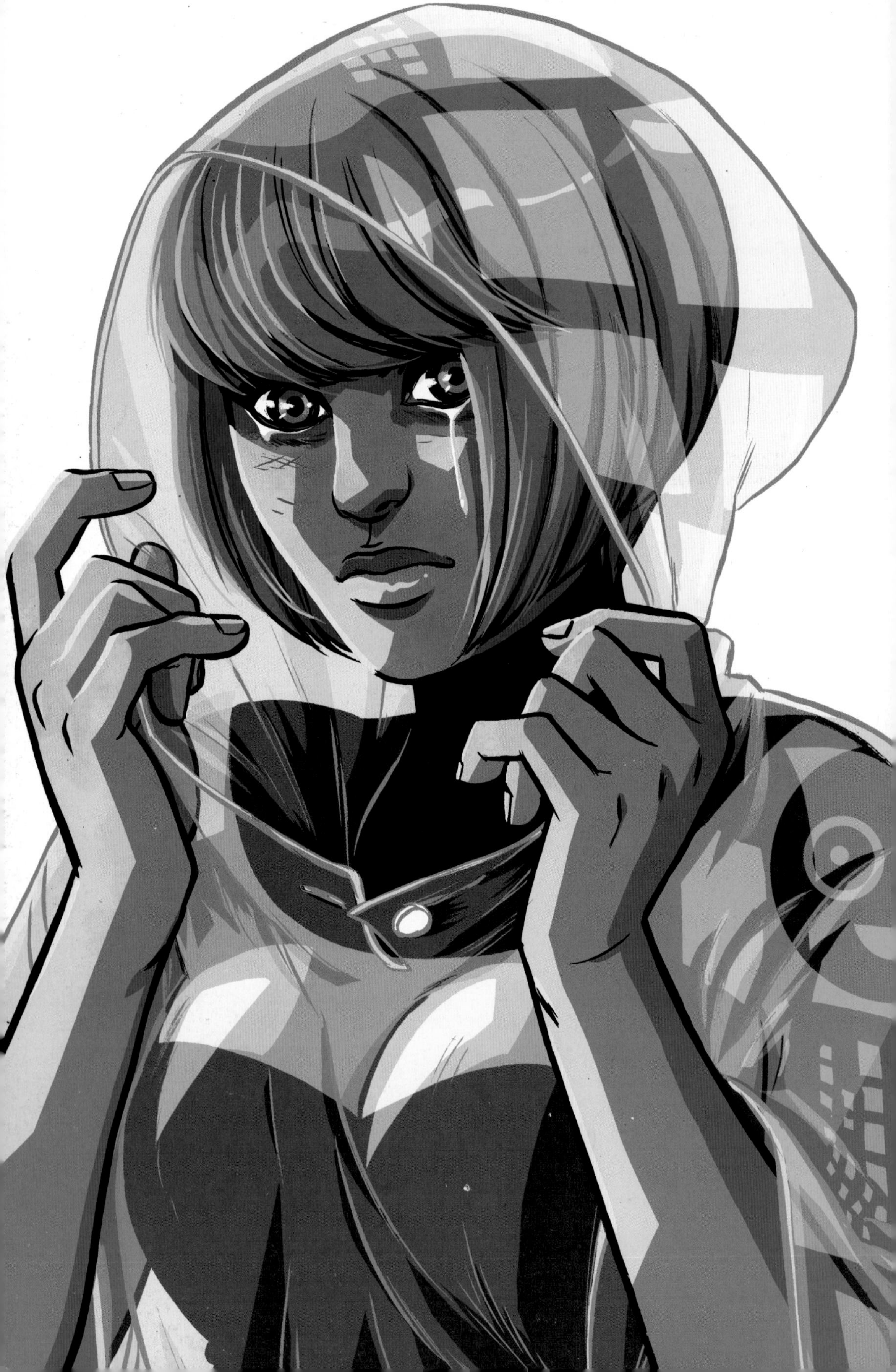

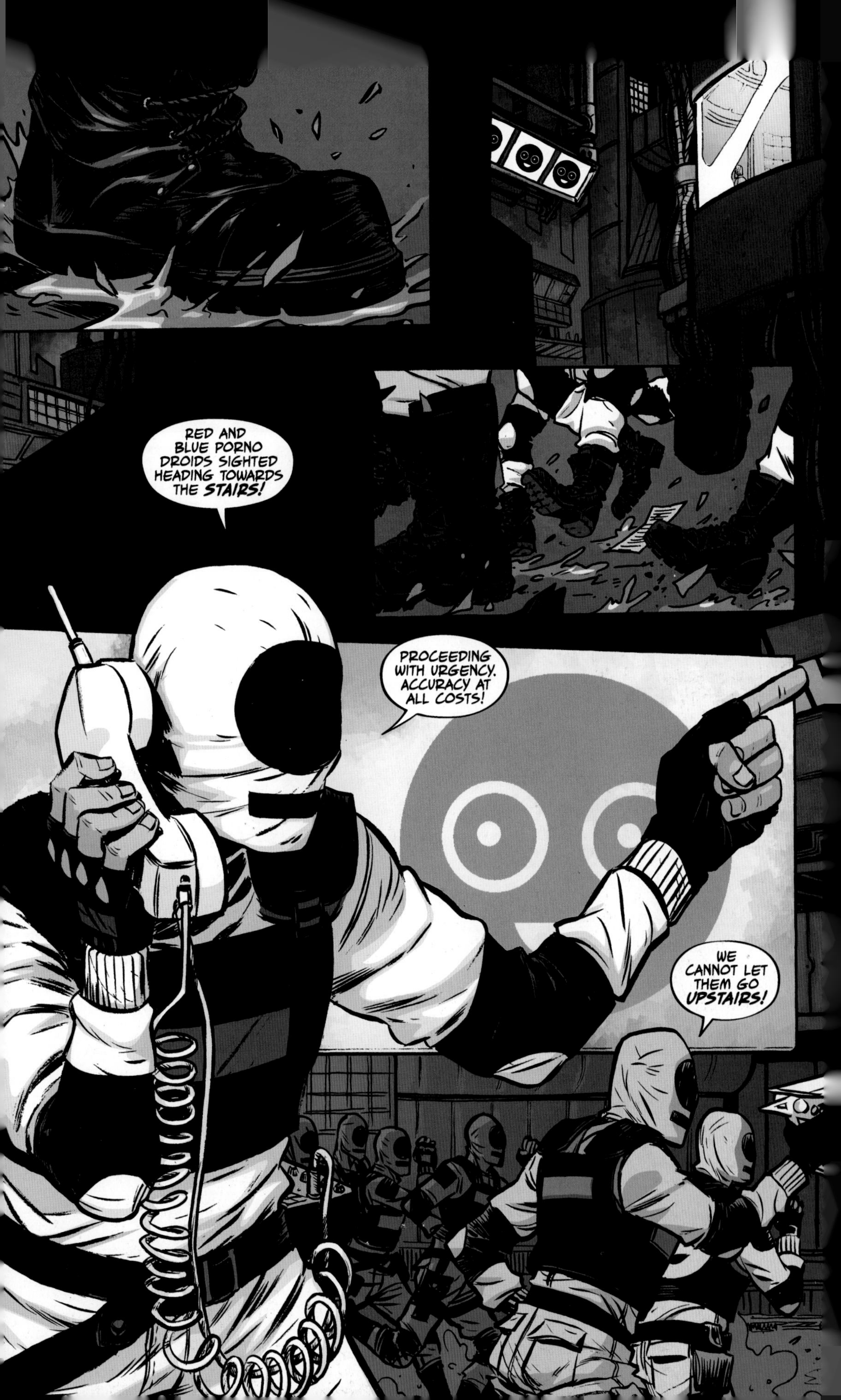
RED AND BLUE PORNO DROIDS SIGHTED HEADING TOWARDS THE STAIRS!
PROCEEDING WITH URGENCY. ACCURACY AT ALL COSTS!
WE CANNOT LET THEM GO UPSTAIRS!

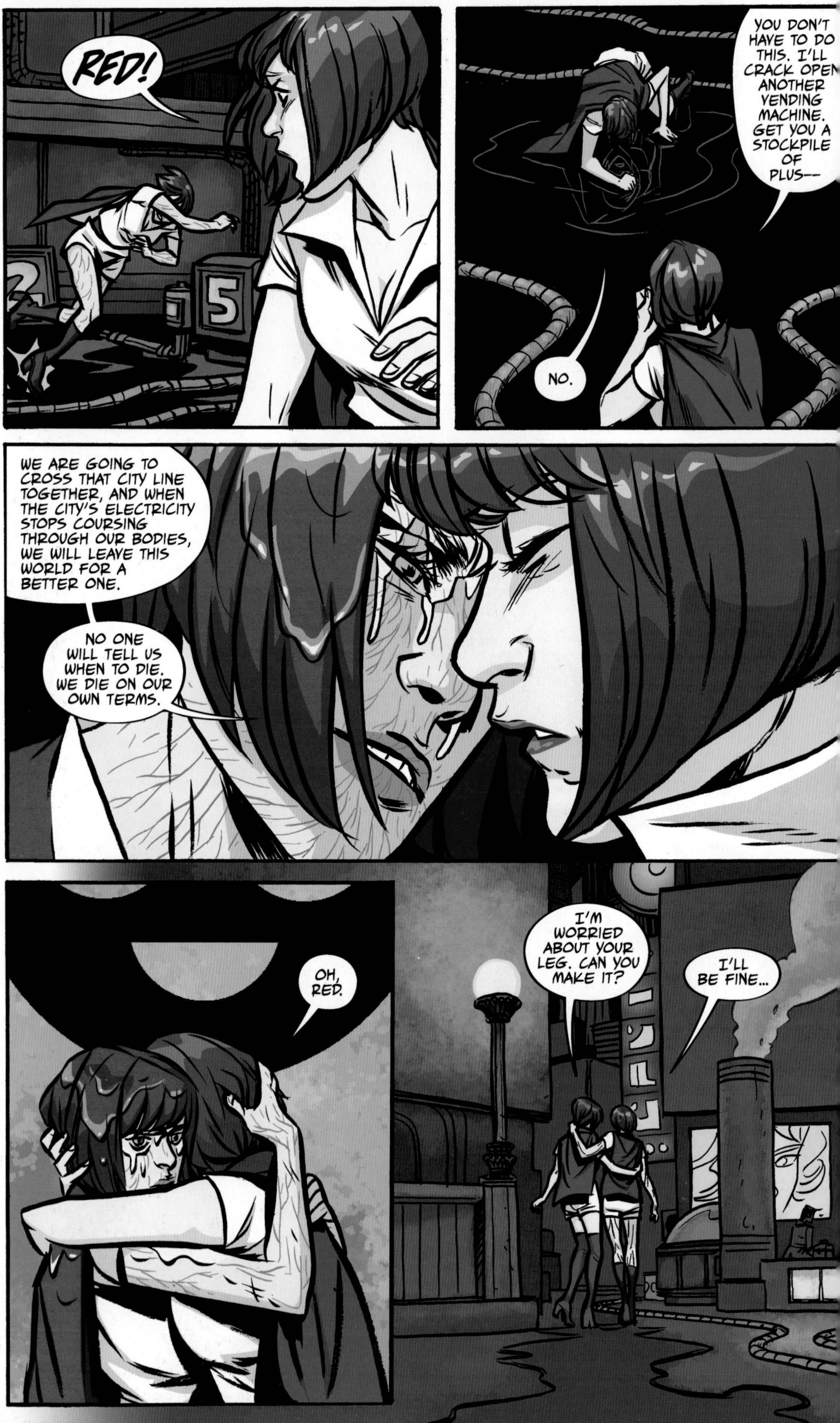

RED!
YOU DON'T HAVE TO DO THIS. I'LL CRACK OPEN ANOTHER VENDING MACHINE. GET YOU A STOCKPILE OF PLUS--
NO.
WE ARE GOING TO CROSS THAT CITY LINE TOGETHER, AND WHEN THE CITY'S ELECTRICITY STOPS COURSING THROUGH OUR BODIES, WE WILL LEAVE THIS WORLD FOR A BETTER ONE.
NO ONE WILL TELL US WHEN TO DIE. WE DIE ON OUR OWN TERMS.
OH, RED.
I'M WORRIED ABOUT YOUR LEG. CAN YOU MAKE IT?
I'LL BE FINE...

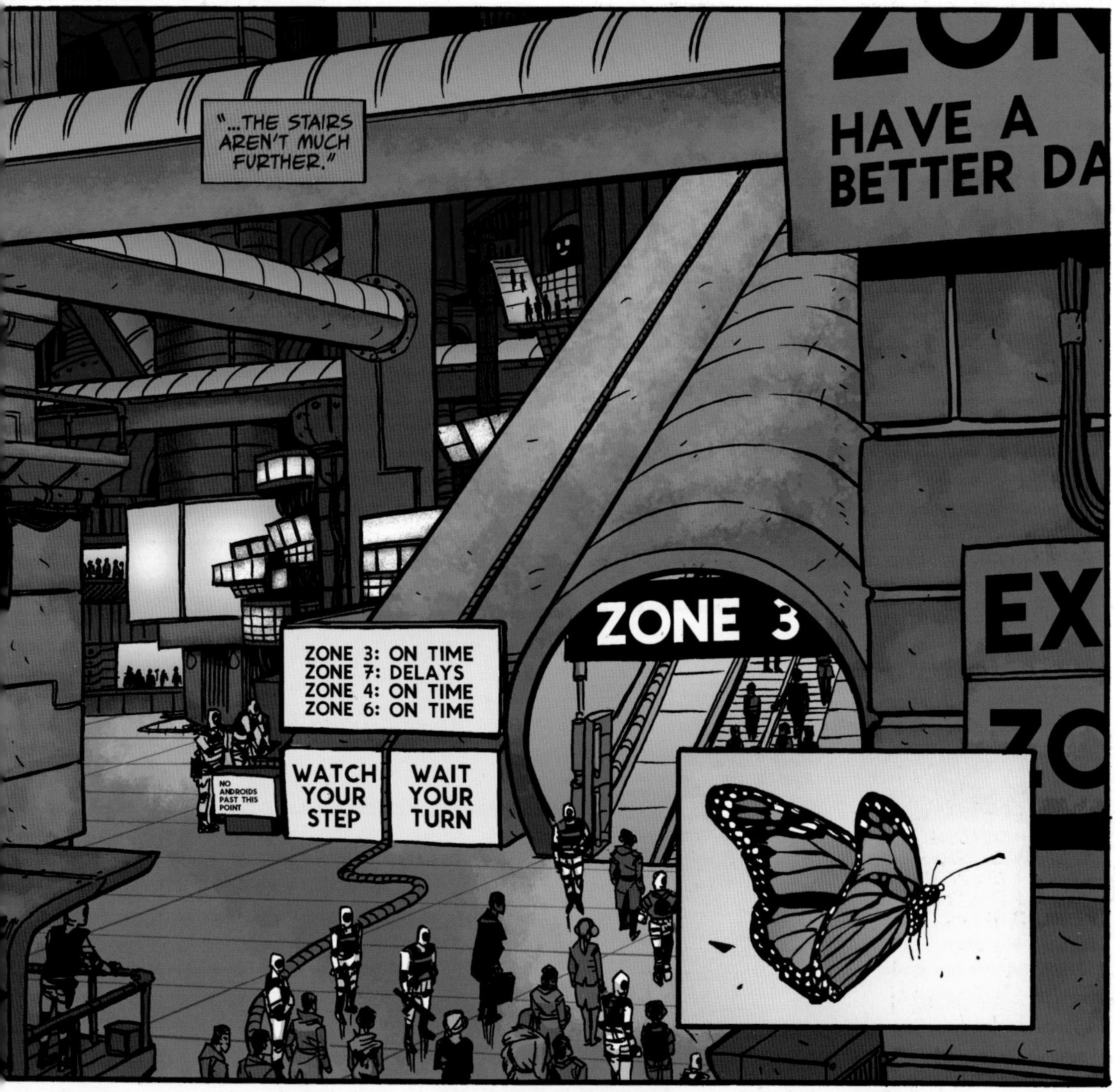
"...THE STAIRS AREN'T MUCH FURTHER."
HAVE A BETTER DA
ZONE 3
ZONE 3: ON TIME
ZONE 7: DELAYS
ZONE 4: ON TIME
ZONE 6: ON TIME
NO ANDROIDS PAST THIS POINT
WATCH YOUR STEP
WAIT YOUR TURN
EX

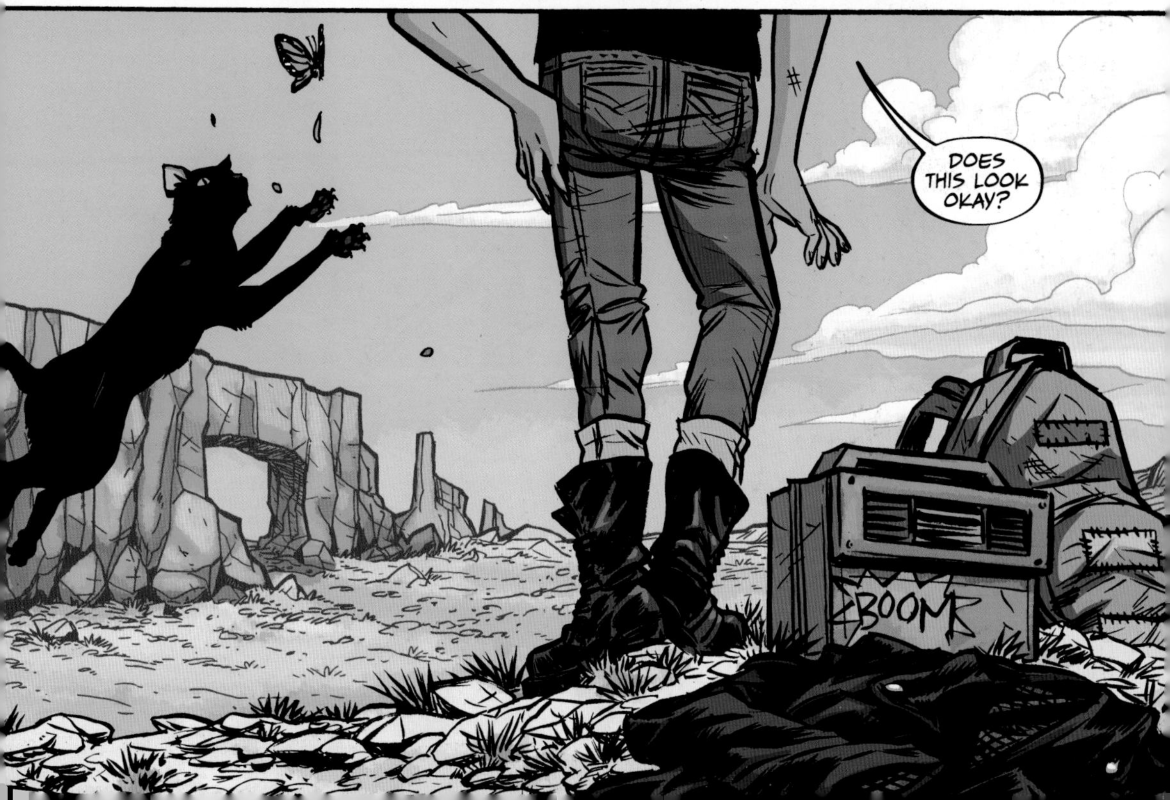
DOES THIS LOOK OKAY?
BOOM

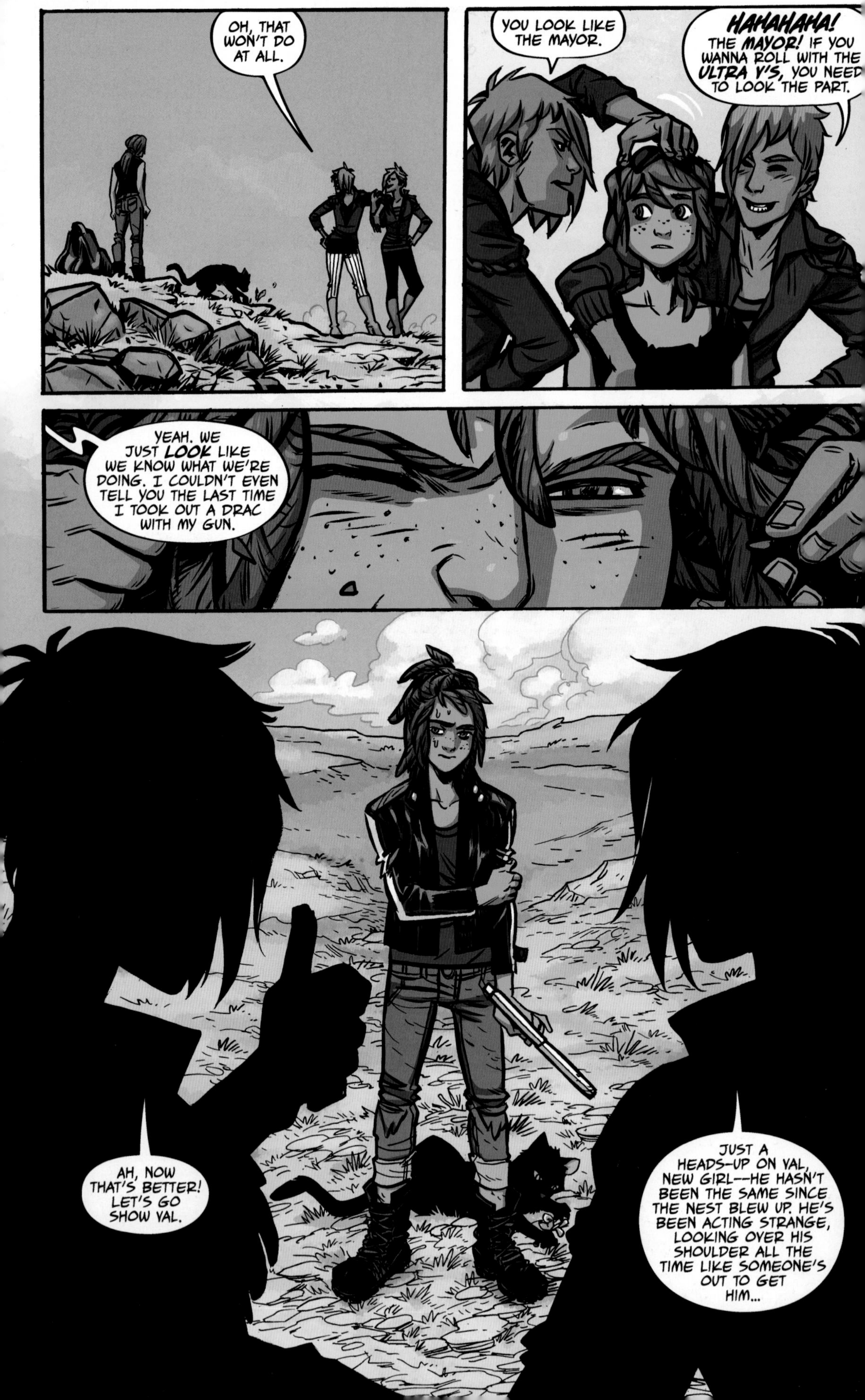
OH, THAT WON'T DO AT ALL.
YOU LOOK LIKE THE MAYOR.
HAHAHAHA! THE MAYOR! IF YOU WANNA ROLL WITH THE ULTRA V'S, YOU NEED TO LOOK THE PART.
YEAH. WE JUST LOOK LIKE WE KNOW WHAT WE'RE DOING. I COULDN'T EVEN TELL YOU THE LAST TIME I TOOK OUT A DRAC WITH MY GUN.
AH, NOW THAT'S BETTER! LET'S GO SHOW VAL.
JUST A HEADS-UP ON VAL, NEW GIRL--HE HASN'T BEEN THE SAME SINCE THE NEST BLEW UP. HE'S BEEN ACTING STRANGE, LOOKING OVER HIS SHOULDER ALL THE TIME LIKE SOMEONE'S OUT TO GET HIM...

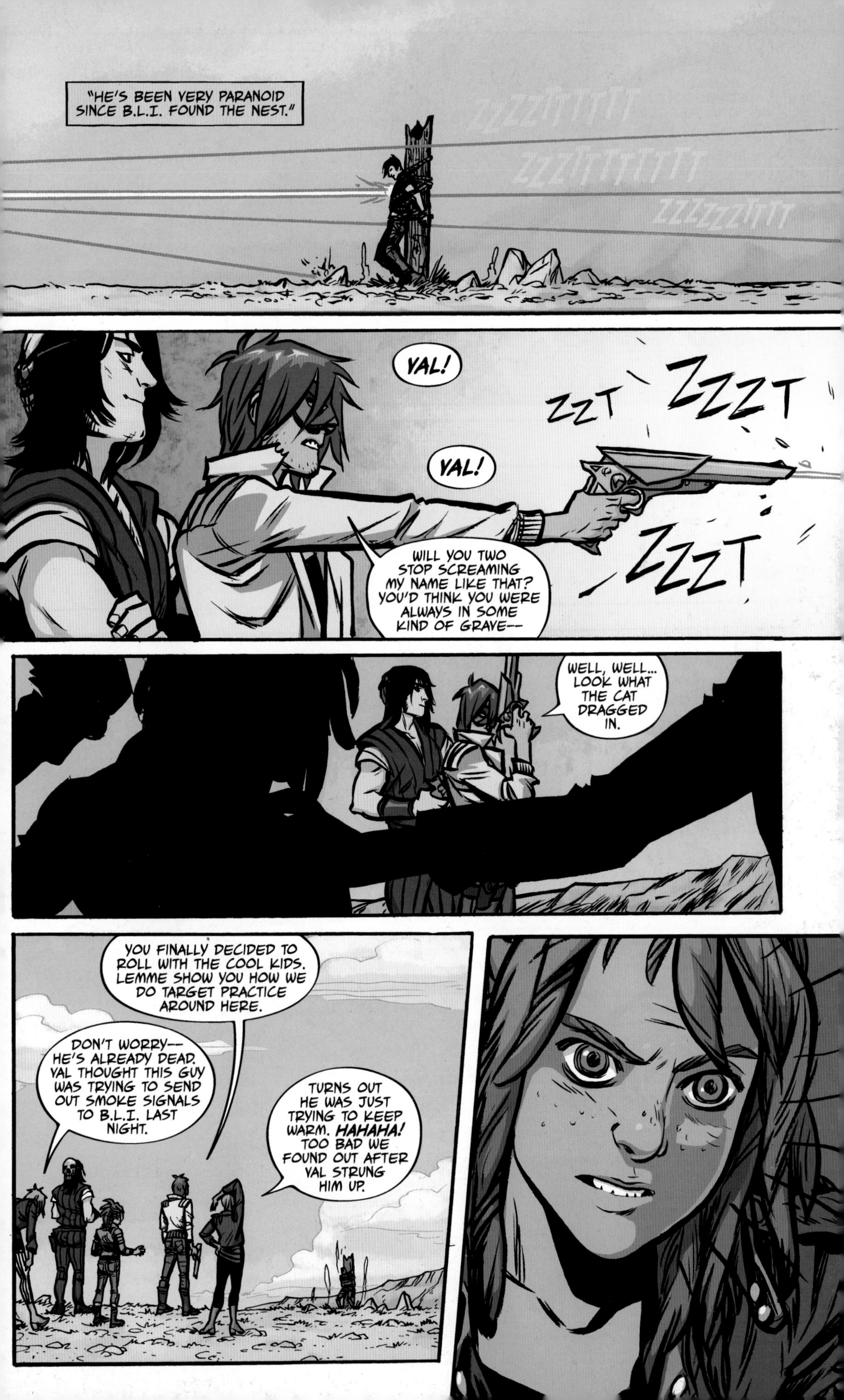
"HE'S BEEN VERY PARANOID SINCE B.L.I. FOUND THE NEST."
ZZZZTTTTTT
ZZZTTTTTTTTT
ZZZZZZZTTTT
YAL!
YAL!
ZZT
ZZZT
WILL YOU TWO STOP SCREAMING MY NAME LIKE THAT? YOU'D THINK YOU WERE ALWAYS IN SOME KIND OF GRAVE--
ZZZT
WELL, WELL... LOOK WHAT THE CAT DRAGGED IN.
YOU FINALLY DECIDED TO ROLL WITH THE COOL KIDS. LEMME SHOW YOU HOW WE DO TARGET PRACTICE AROUND HERE.
DON'T WORRY-- HE'S ALREADY DEAD. VAL THOUGHT THIS GUY WAS TRYING TO SEND OUT SMOKE SIGNALS TO B.L.I. LAST NIGHT.
TURNS OUT HE WAS JUST TRYING TO KEEP WARM. HAHAHA! TOO BAD WE FOUND OUT AFTER VAL STRUNG HIM UP.

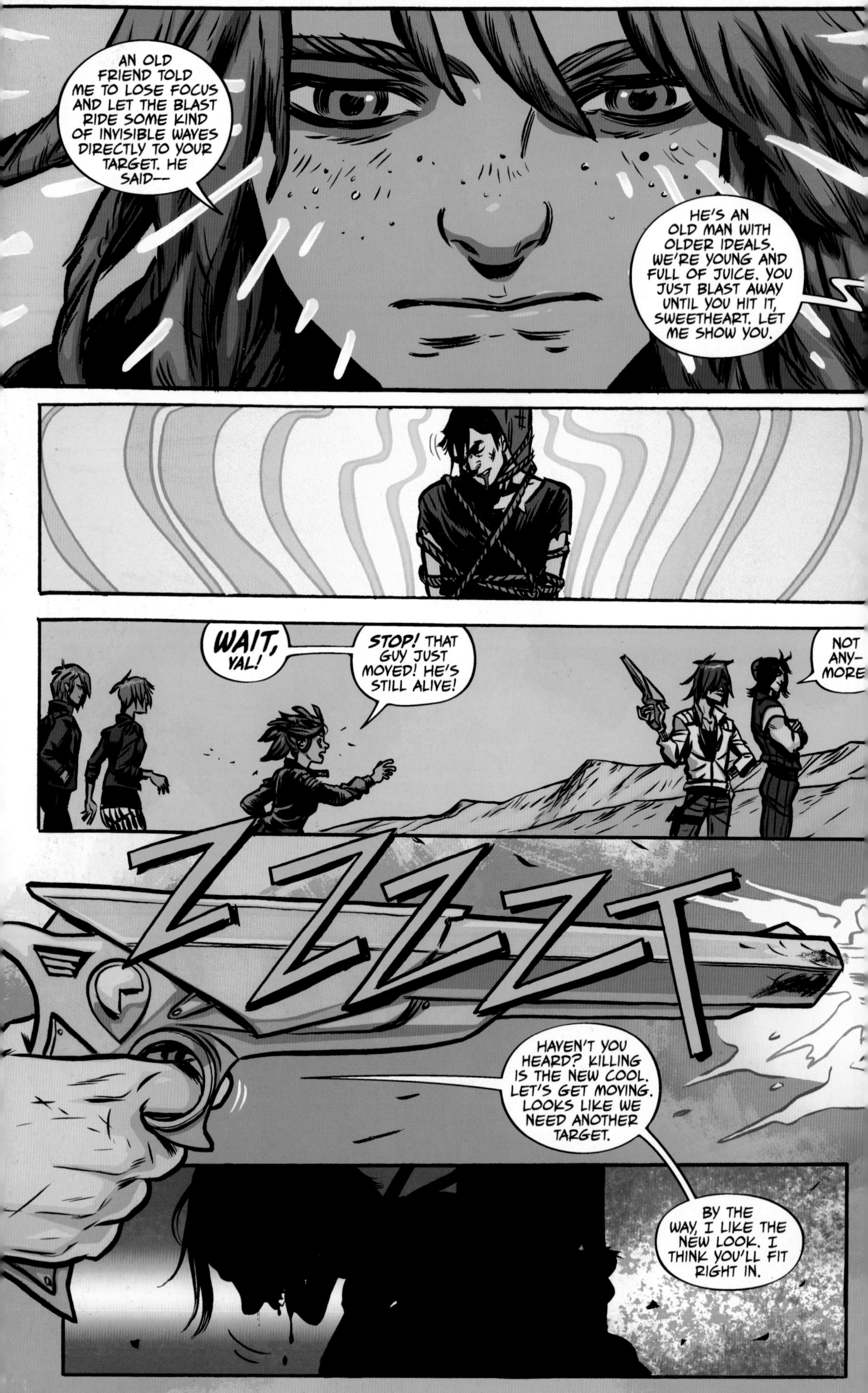
AN OLD FRIEND TOLD ME TO LOSE FOCUS AND LET THE BLAST RIDE SOME KIND OF INVISIBLE WAVES DIRECTLY TO YOUR TARGET. HE SAID--
HE'S AN OLD MAN WITH OLDER IDEALS. WE'RE YOUNG AND FULL OF JUICE. YOU JUST BLAST AWAY UNTIL YOU HIT IT, SWEETHEART. LET ME SHOW YOU.
WAIT, VAL!
STOP! THAT GUY JUST MOVED! HE'S STILL ALIVE!
NOT ANY-MORE
ZZZZT
HAVEN'T YOU HEARD? KILLING IS THE NEW COOL. LET'S GET MOVING. LOOKS LIKE WE NEED ANOTHER TARGET.
BY THE WAY, I LIKE THE NEW LOOK. I THINK YOU'LL FIT RIGHT IN.

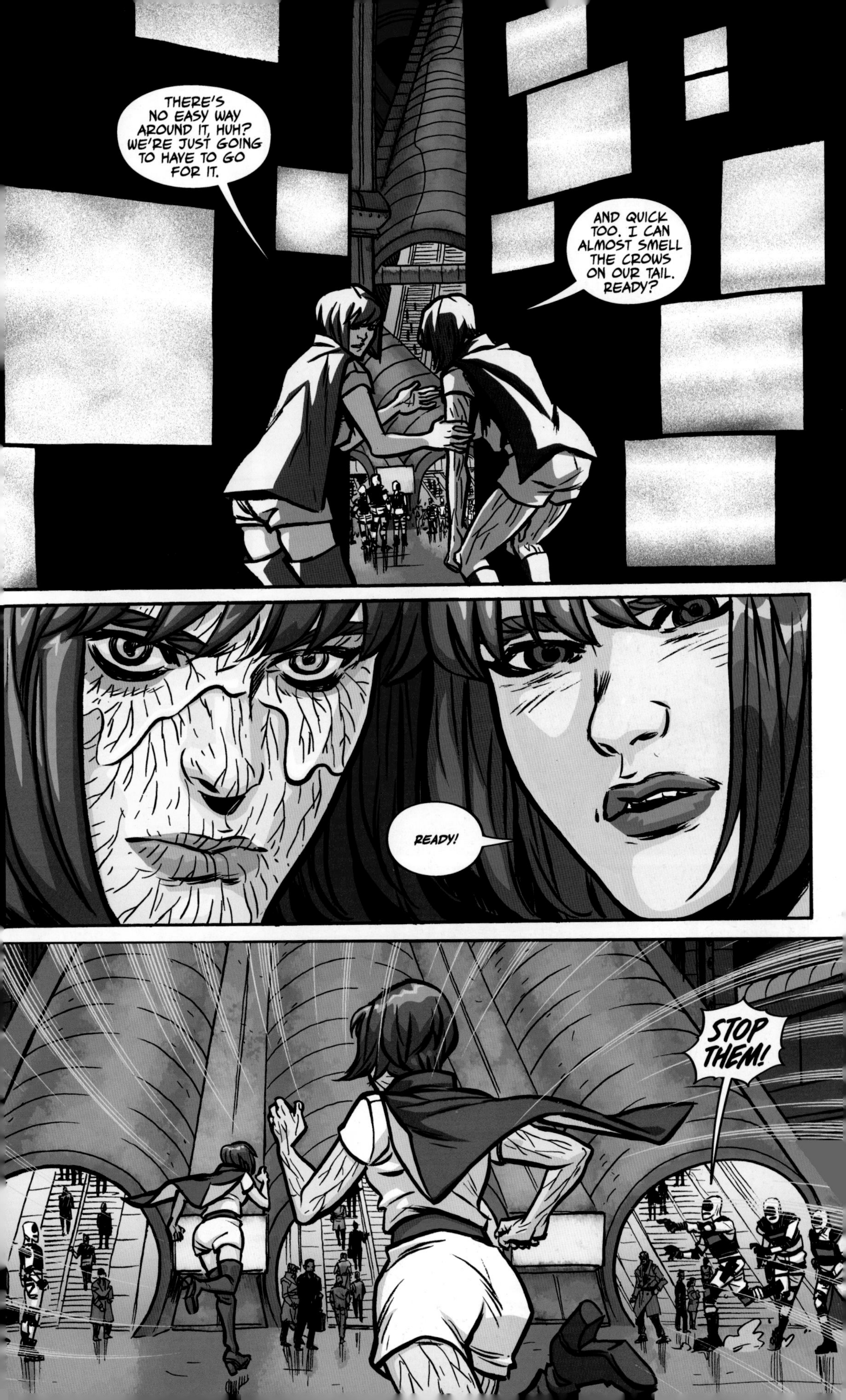
THERE'S NO EASY WAY AROUND IT, HUH? WE'RE JUST GOING TO HAVE TO GO FOR IT.
AND QUICK TOO. I CAN ALMOST SMELL THE CROWS ON OUR TAIL. READY?
READY!
STOP THEM!

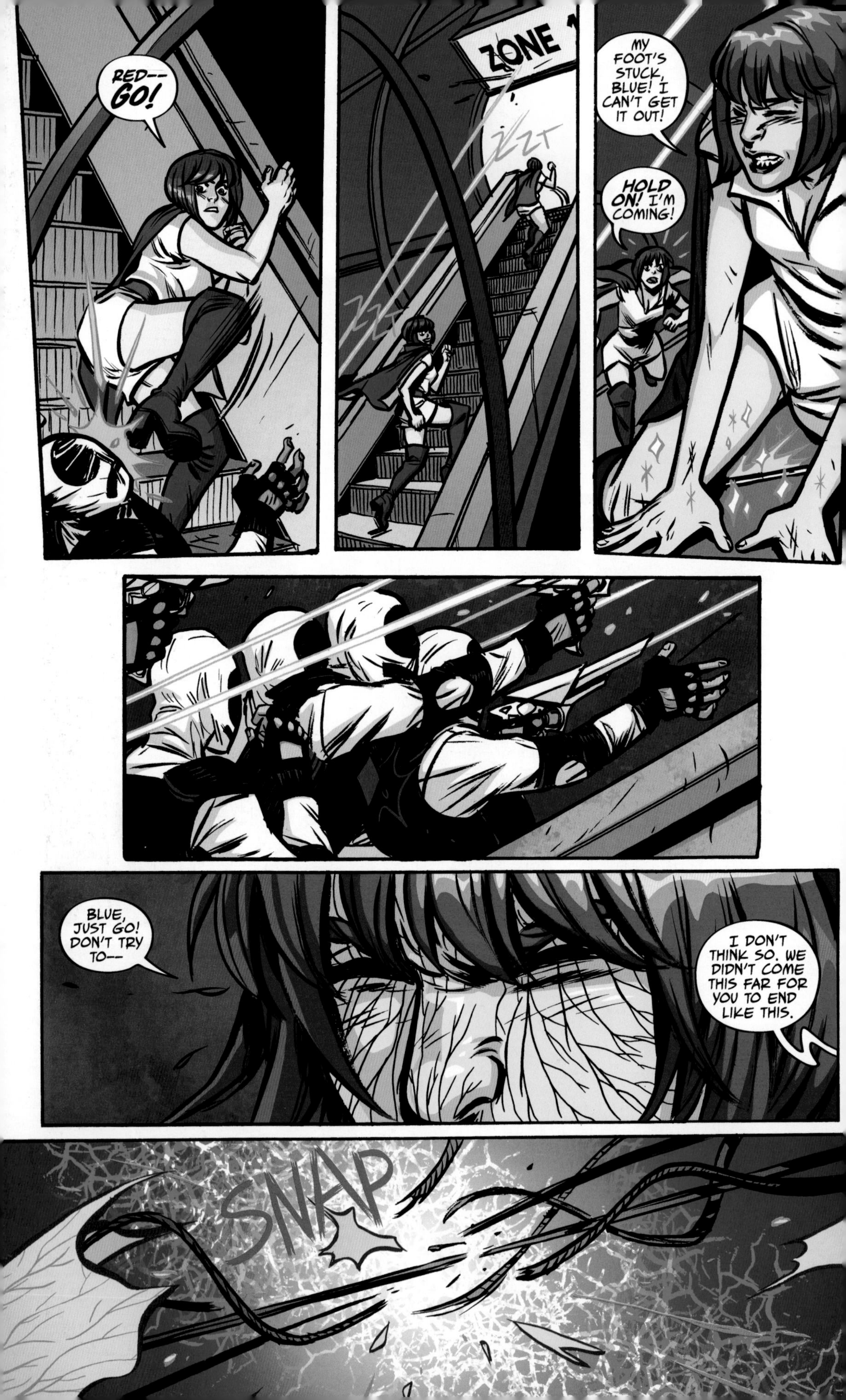
RED--
GO!
ZONE
ZZT
ZZT
MY FOOT'S STUCK, BLUE! I CAN'T GET IT OUT!
HOLD ON! I'M COMING!
BLUE, JUST GO! DON'T TRY TO--
I DON'T THINK SO. WE DIDN'T COME THIS FAR FOR YOU TO END LIKE THIS.
SNAP

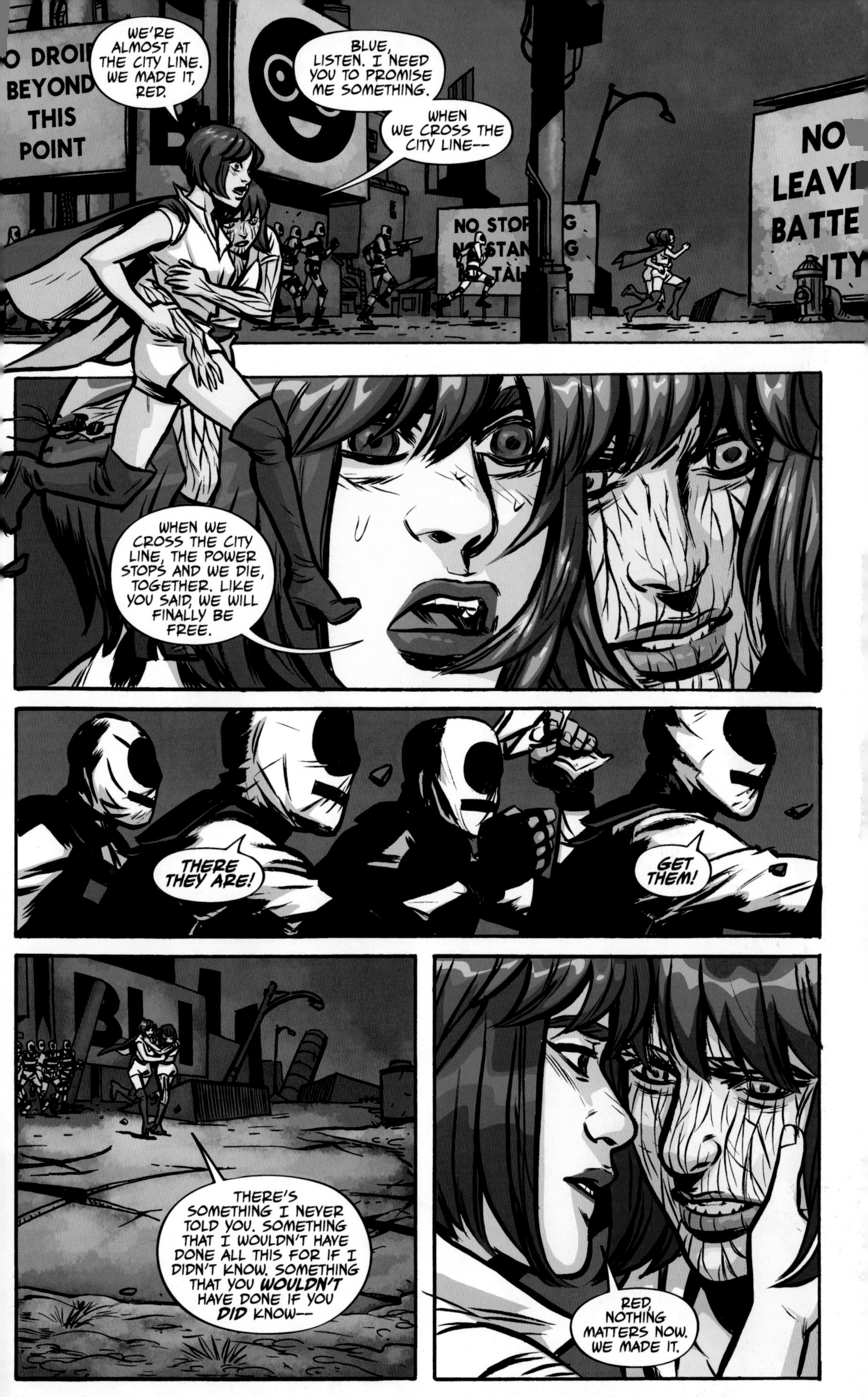
O DROI BEYOND THIS POINT
WE'RE ALMOST AT THE CITY LINE. WE MADE IT, RED.
BLUE, LISTEN. I NEED YOU TO PROMISE ME SOMETHING.
WHEN WE CROSS THE CITY LINE--
WHEN WE CROSS THE CITY LINE, THE POWER STOPS AND WE DIE, TOGETHER. LIKE YOU SAID, WE WILL FINALLY BE FREE.
THERE THEY ARE!
GET THEM!
THERE'S SOMETHING I NEVER TOLD YOU. SOMETHING THAT I WOULDN'T HAVE DONE ALL THIS FOR IF I DIDN'T KNOW. SOMETHING THAT YOU WOULDN'T HAVE DONE IF YOU DID KNOW--
RED, NOTHING MATTERS NOW. WE MADE IT.

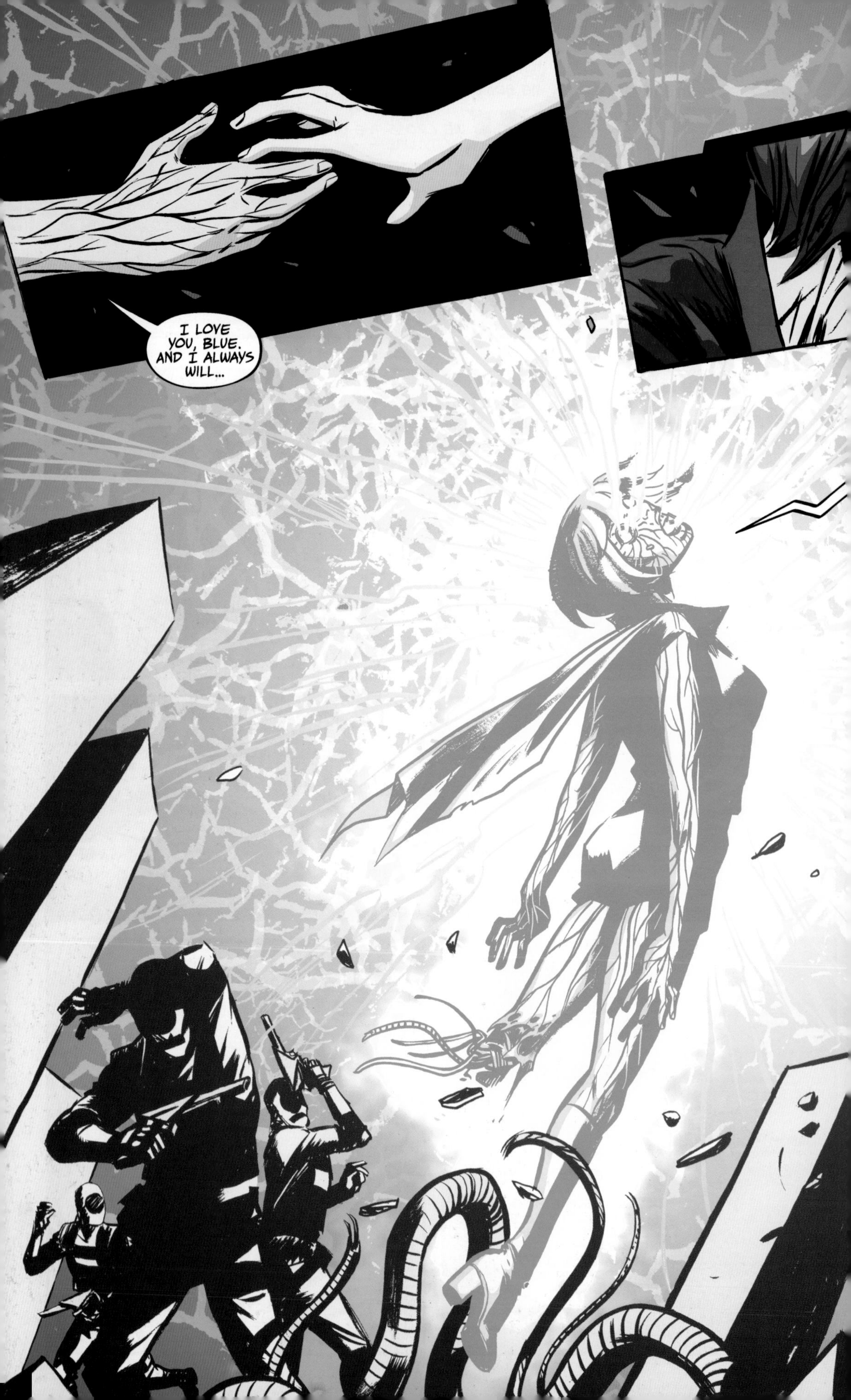
I LOVE YOU, BLUE. AND I ALWAYS WILL...

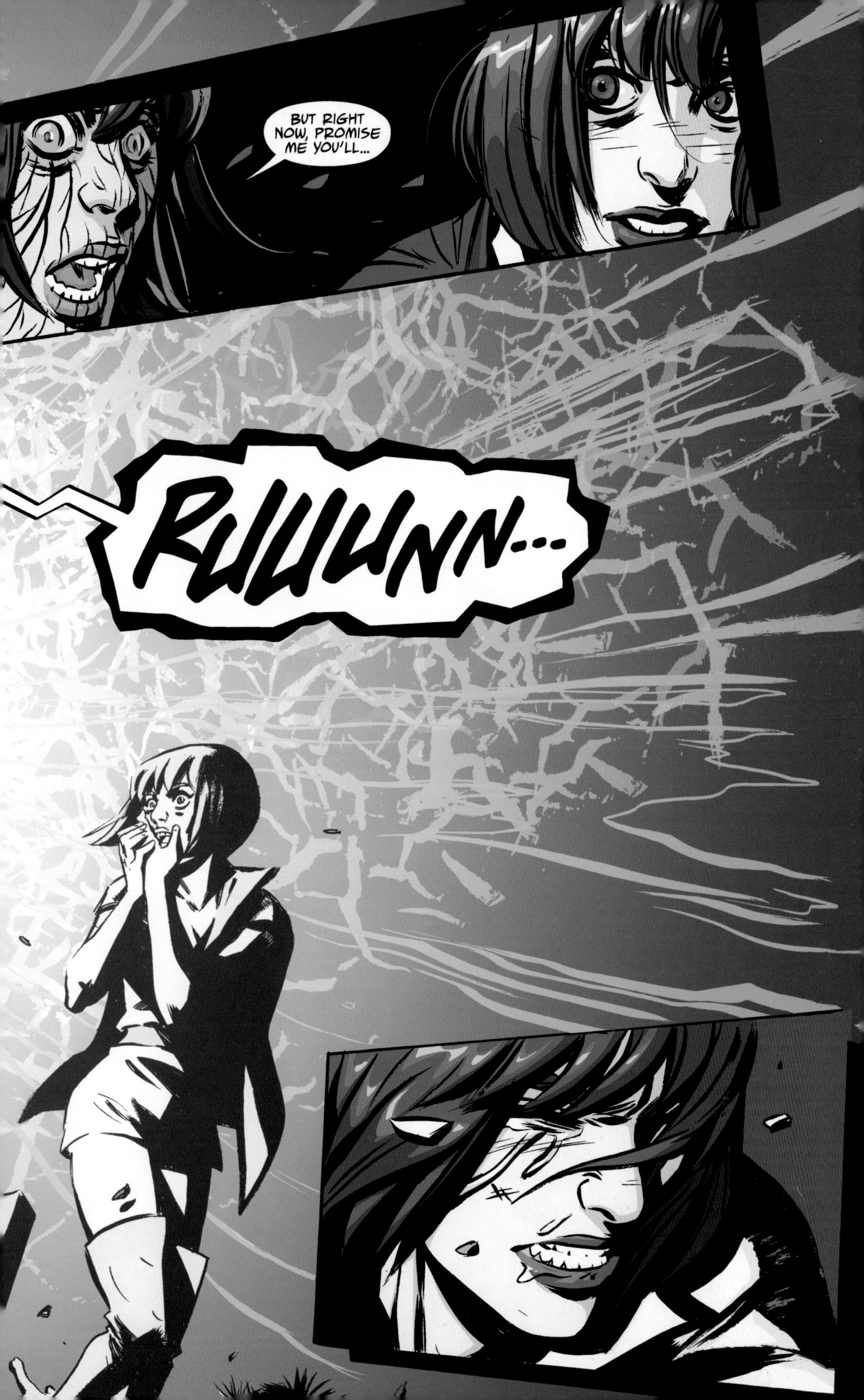
BUT RIGHT NOW, PROMISE ME YOU'LL...
RUUUNN...

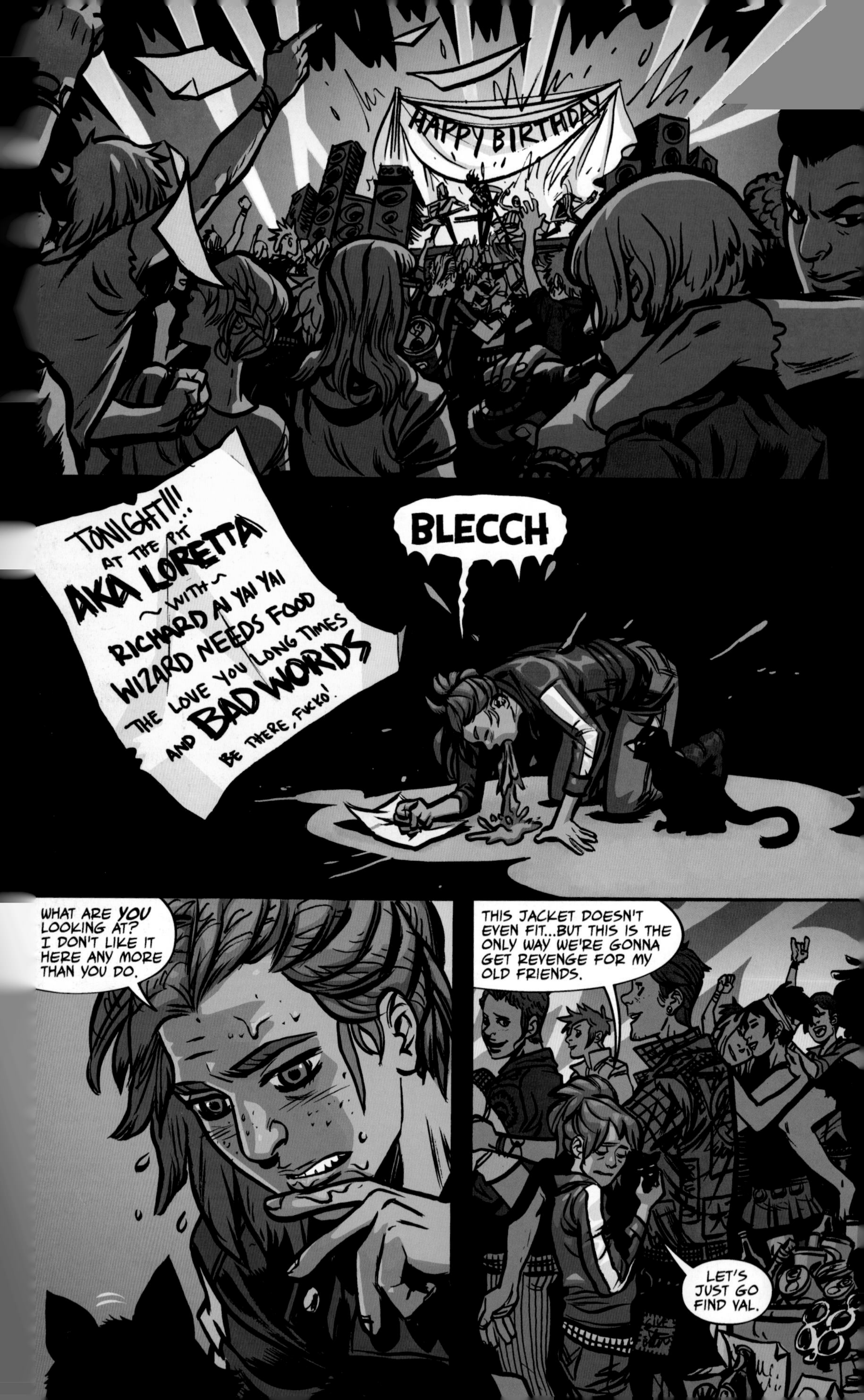
HAPPY BIRTHDAY
TONIGHT!!! AT THE PIT
AKA LORETTA
~WITH~
RICHARD AI YAI YAI
WIZARD NEEDS FOOD
THE LOVE YOU LONG TIMES
AND BAD WORDS
BE THERE, FUCKO!
BLECCH
WHAT ARE YOU LOOKING AT? I DON'T LIKE IT HERE ANY MORE THAN YOU DO.
THIS JACKET DOESN'T EVEN FIT...BUT THIS IS THE ONLY WAY WE'RE GONNA GET REVENGE FOR MY OLD FRIENDS.
LET'S JUST GO FIND VAL.

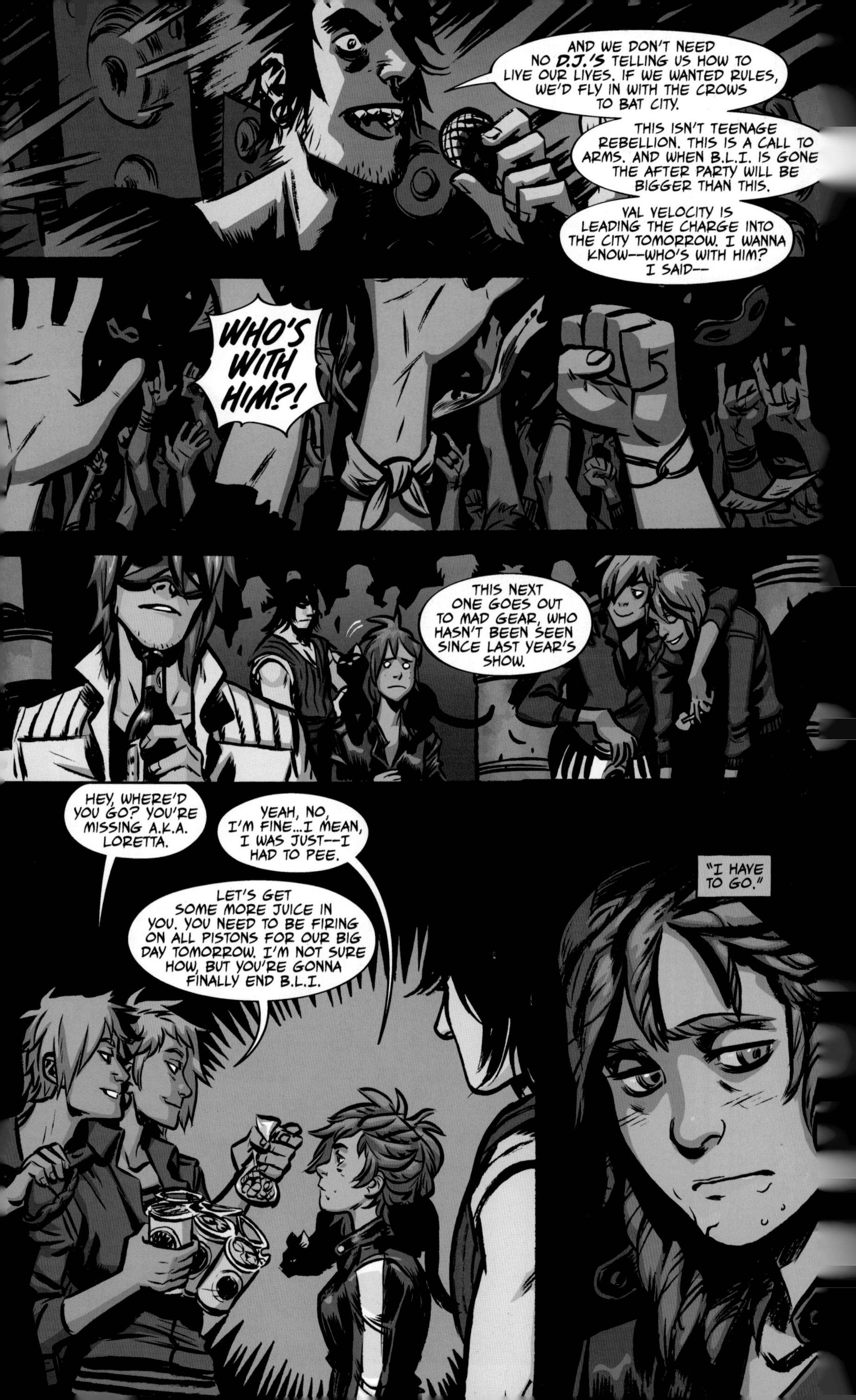
AND WE DON'T NEED NO D.J.'S TELLING US HOW TO LIVE OUR LIVES. IF WE WANTED RULES, WE'D FLY IN WITH THE CROWS TO BAT CITY.
THIS ISN'T TEENAGE REBELLION. THIS IS A CALL TO ARMS. AND WHEN B.L.I. IS GONE THE AFTER PARTY WILL BE BIGGER THAN THIS.
VAL VELOCITY IS LEADING THE CHARGE INTO THE CITY TOMORROW. I WANNA KNOW--WHO'S WITH HIM? I SAID--
WHO'S WITH HIM?!
THIS NEXT ONE GOES OUT TO MAD GEAR, WHO HASN'T BEEN SEEN SINCE LAST YEAR'S SHOW.
HEY, WHERE'D YOU GO? YOU'RE MISSING A.K.A. LORETTA.
YEAH, NO, I'M FINE...I MEAN, I WAS JUST--I HAD TO PEE.
LET'S GET SOME MORE JUICE IN YOU. YOU NEED TO BE FIRING ON ALL PISTONS FOR OUR BIG DAY TOMORROW. I'M NOT SURE HOW, BUT YOU'RE GONNA FINALLY END B.L.I.
"I HAVE TO GO."

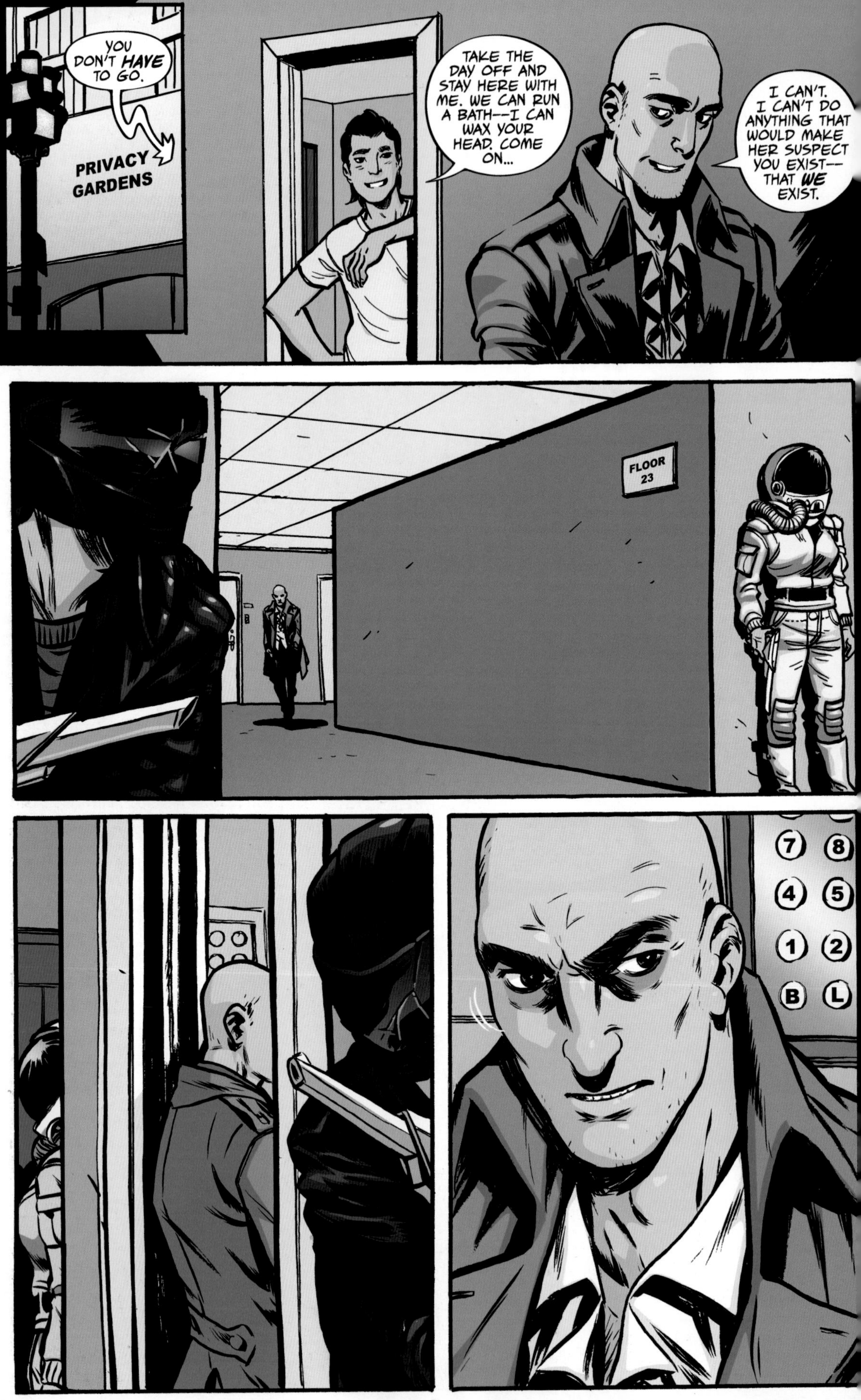

YOU DON'T HAVE TO GO.
PRIVACY GARDENS
TAKE THE DAY OFF AND STAY HERE WITH ME. WE CAN RUN A BATH--I CAN WAX YOUR HEAD. COME ON...
I CAN'T. I CAN'T DO ANYTHING THAT WOULD MAKE HER SUSPECT YOU EXIST--THAT WE EXIST.
FLOOR 23
7 8
4 5
1 2
B L

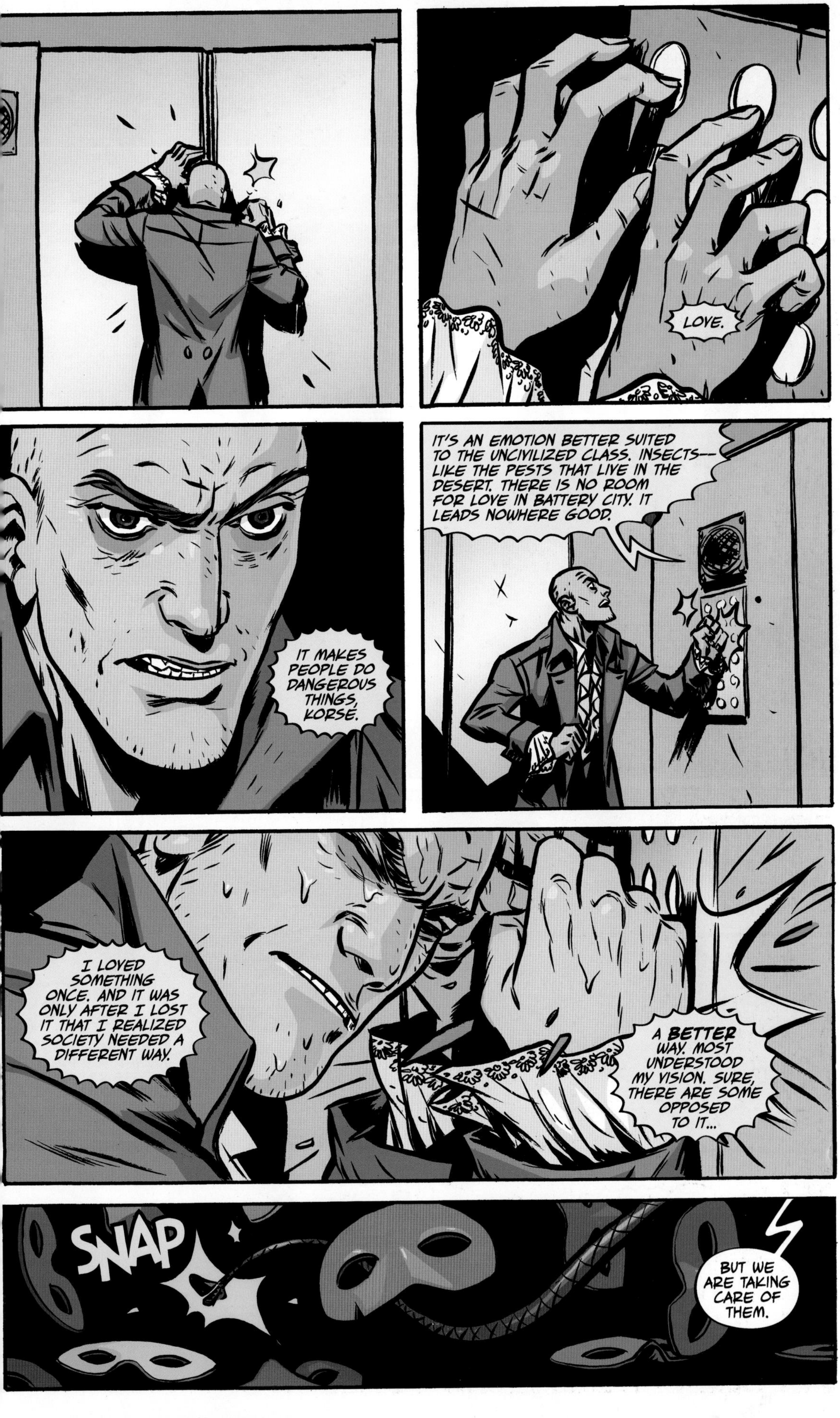
LOVE.
IT'S AN EMOTION BETTER SUITED TO THE UNCIVILIZED CLASS. INSECTS-- LIKE THE PESTS THAT LIVE IN THE DESERT. THERE IS NO ROOM FOR LOVE IN BATTERY CITY. IT LEADS NOWHERE GOOD.
IT MAKES PEOPLE DO DANGEROUS THINGS, KORSE.
I LOVED SOMETHING ONCE. AND IT WAS ONLY AFTER I LOST IT THAT I REALIZED SOCIETY NEEDED A DIFFERENT WAY.
A **BETTER** WAY. MOST UNDERSTOOD MY VISION. SURE, THERE ARE SOME OPPOSED TO IT...
SNAP
BUT WE ARE TAKING CARE OF THEM.

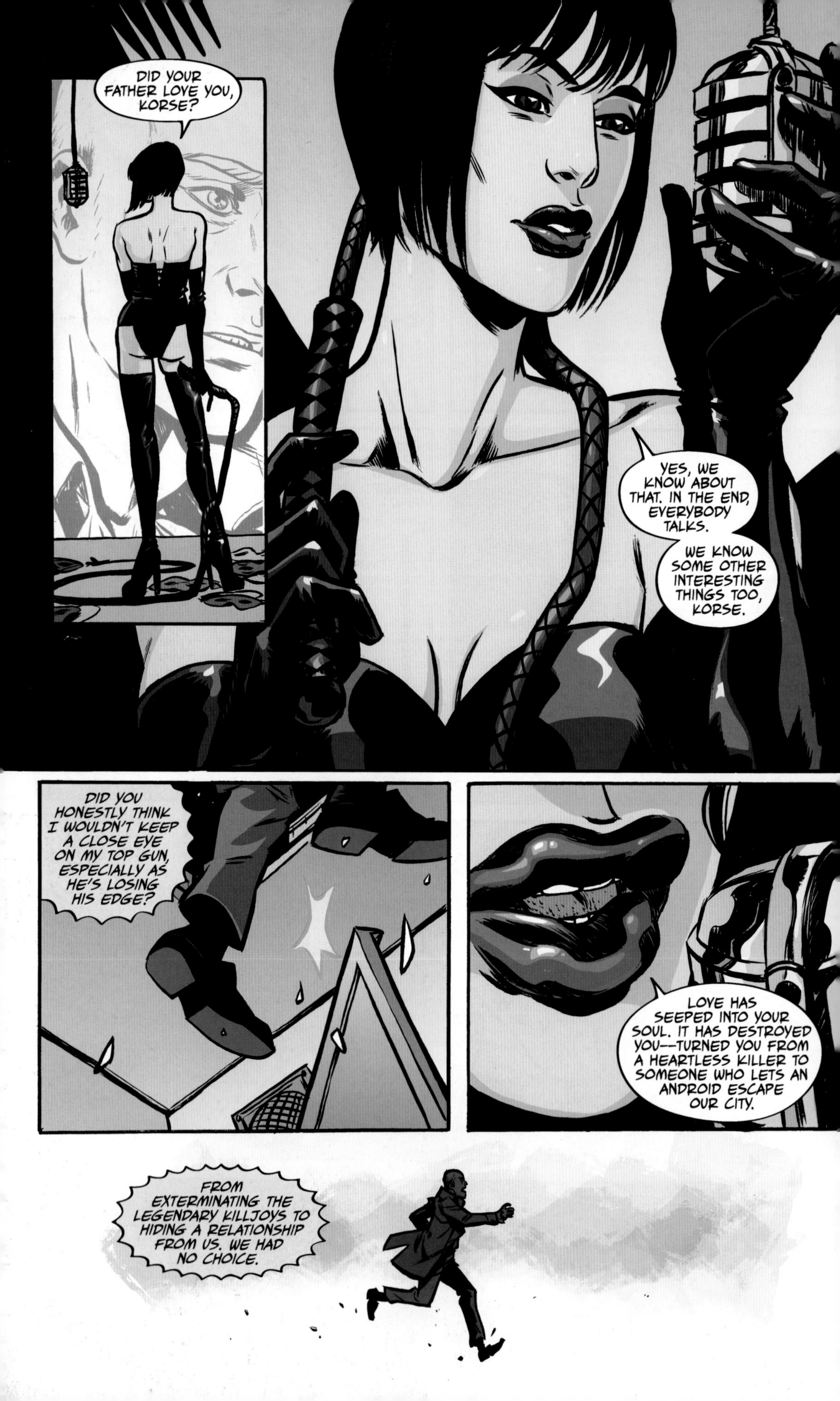
DID YOUR FATHER LOVE YOU, KORSE?
YES, WE KNOW ABOUT THAT. IN THE END, EVERYBODY TALKS.
WE KNOW SOME OTHER INTERESTING THINGS TOO, KORSE.
DID YOU HONESTLY THINK I WOULDN'T KEEP A CLOSE EYE ON MY TOP GUN, ESPECIALLY AS HE'S LOSING HIS EDGE?
LOVE HAS SEEPED INTO YOUR SOUL. IT HAS DESTROYED YOU--TURNED YOU FROM A HEARTLESS KILLER TO SOMEONE WHO LETS AN ANDROID ESCAPE OUR CITY.
FROM EXTERMINATING THE LEGENDARY KILLJOYS TO HIDING A RELATIONSHIP FROM US. WE HAD NO CHOICE.

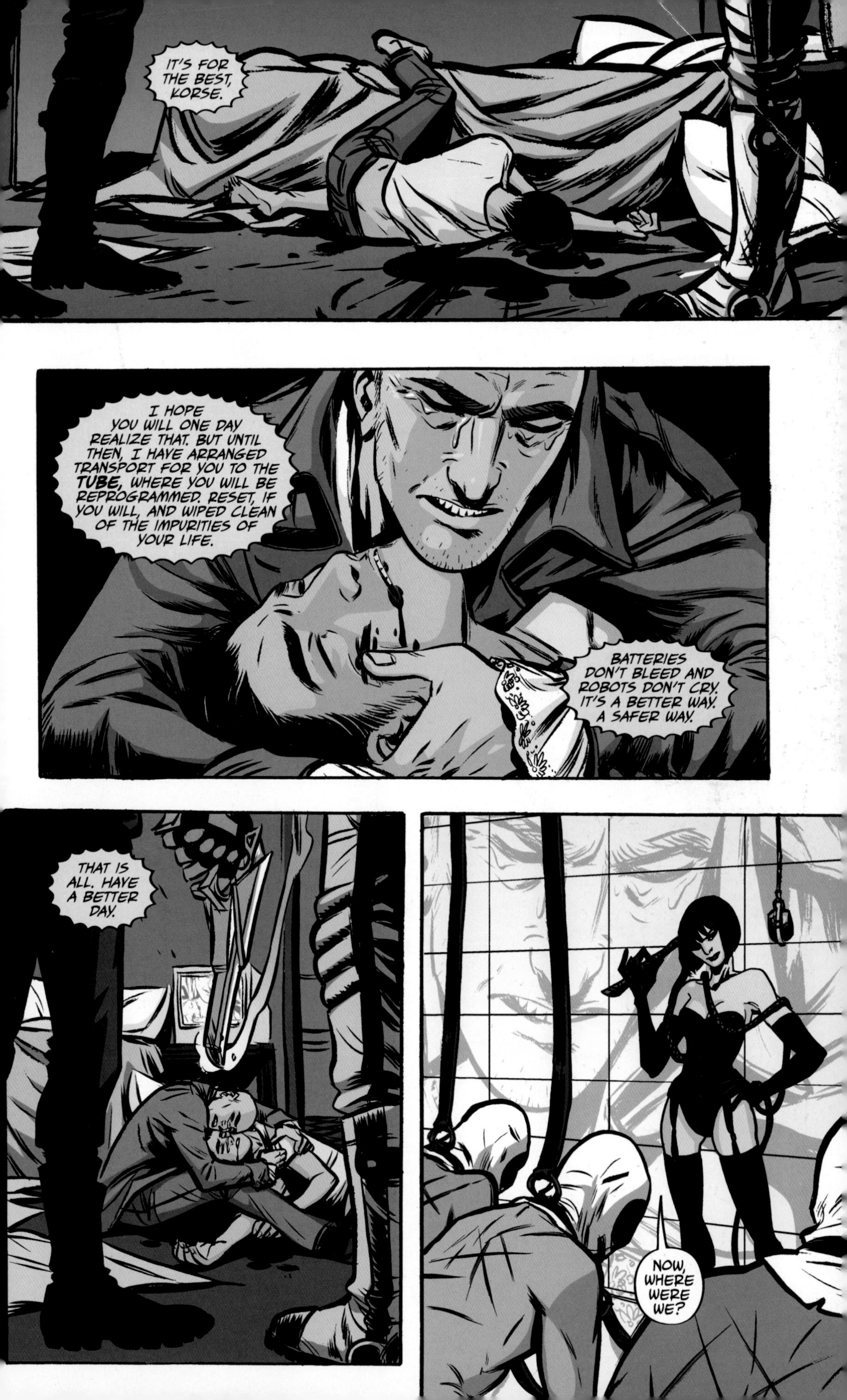
IT'S FOR THE BEST, KORSE.
I HOPE YOU WILL ONE DAY REALIZE THAT. BUT UNTIL THEN, I HAVE ARRANGED TRANSPORT FOR YOU TO THE TUBE, WHERE YOU WILL BE REPROGRAMMED. RESET, IF YOU WILL, AND WIPED CLEAN OF THE IMPURITIES OF YOUR LIFE.
BATTERIES DON'T BLEED AND ROBOTS DON'T CRY. IT'S A BETTER WAY. A SAFER WAY.
THAT IS ALL. HAVE A BETTER DAY.
NOW, WHERE WERE WE?

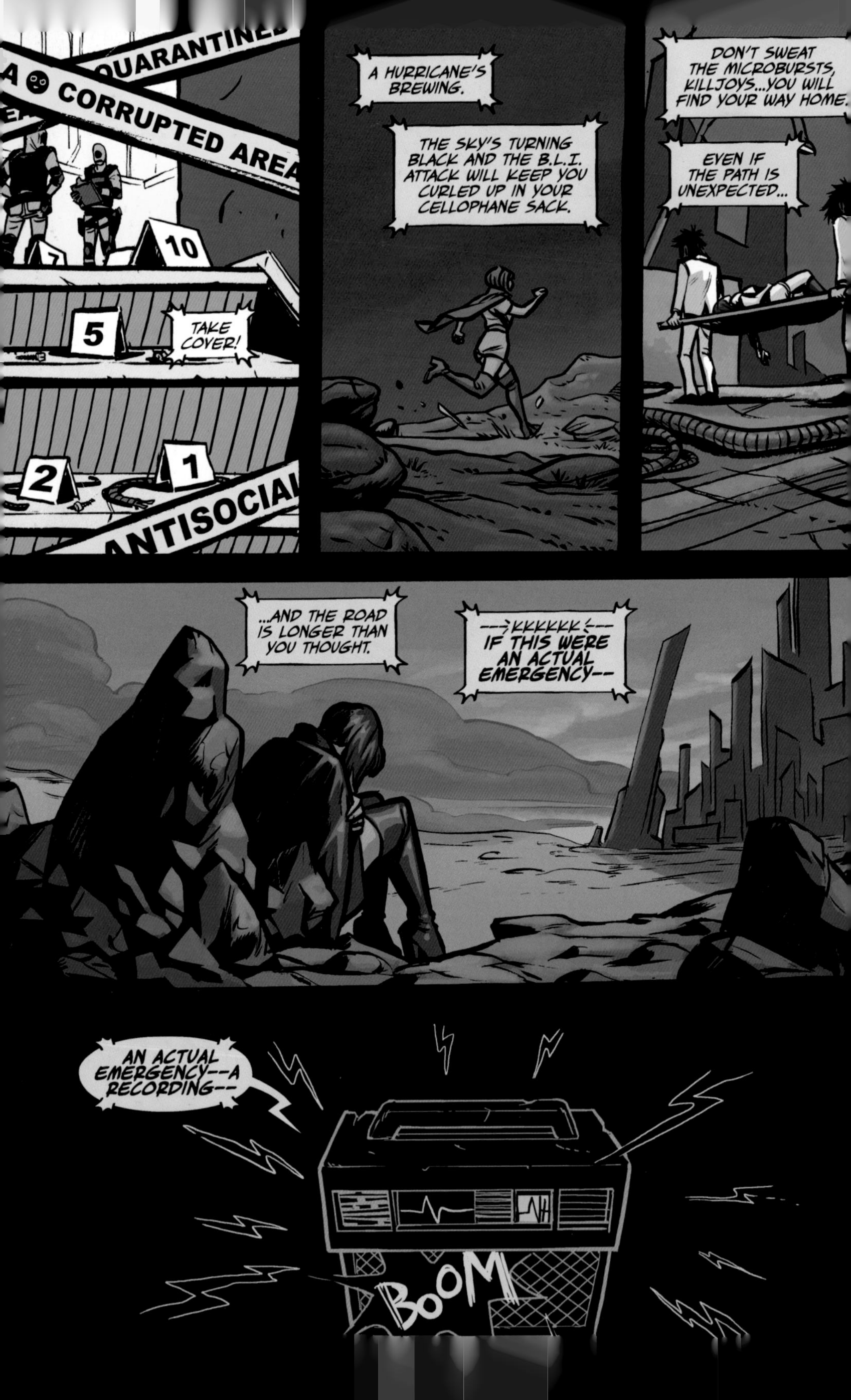
QUARANTINED
CORRUPTED AREA
10
7
5
TAKE COVER!
2
1
ANTISOCIAL
A HURRICANE'S BREWING.
THE SKY'S TURNING BLACK AND THE B.L.I. ATTACK WILL KEEP YOU CURLED UP IN YOUR CELLOPHANE SACK.
DON'T SWEAT THE MICROBURSTS, KILLJOYS...YOU WILL FIND YOUR WAY HOME.
EVEN IF THE PATH IS UNEXPECTED...
...AND THE ROAD IS LONGER THAN YOU THOUGHT.
KKKKKK
IF THIS WERE AN ACTUAL EMERGENCY--
AN ACTUAL EMERGENCY--A RECORDING--
BOOM

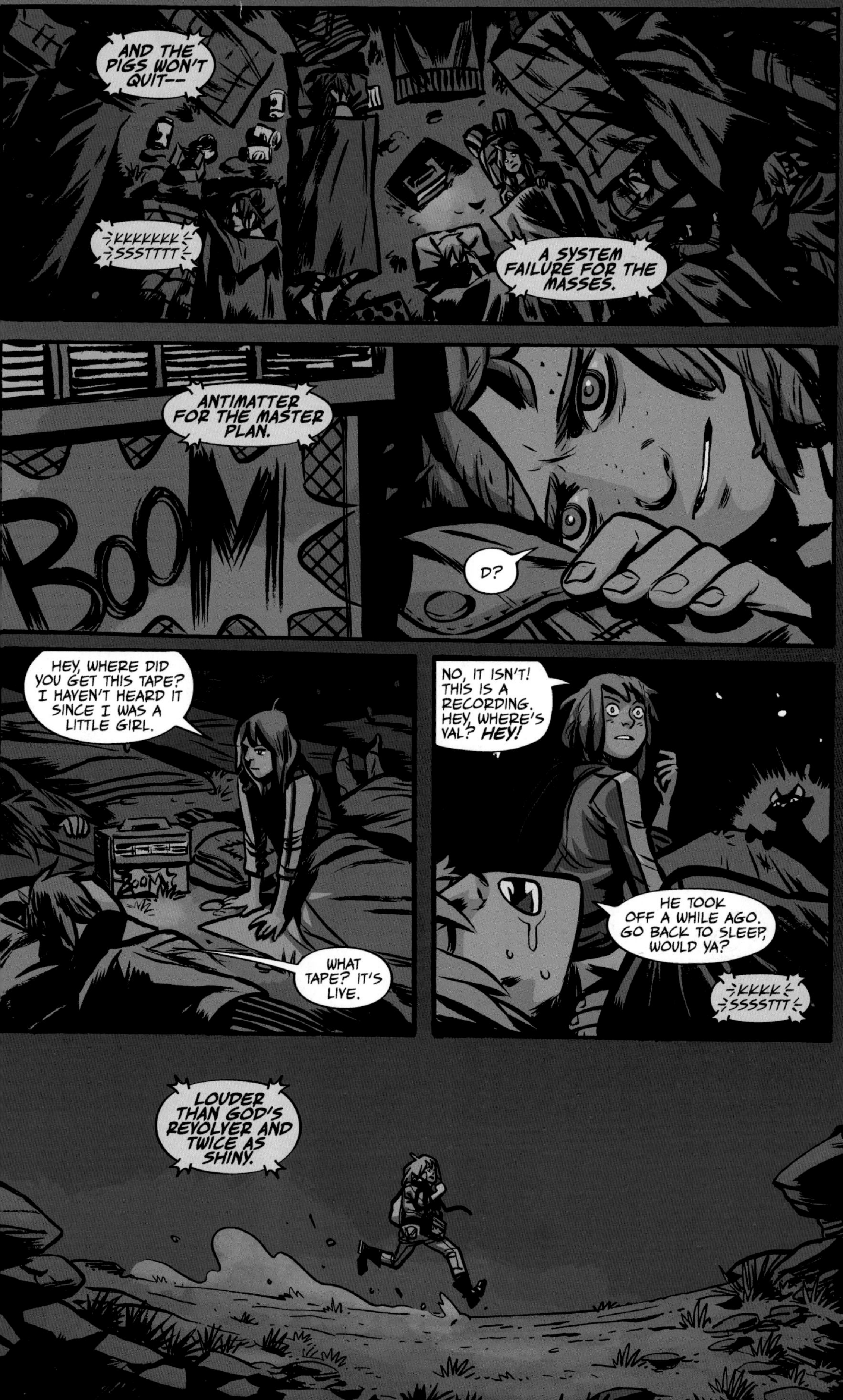
AND THE PIGS WON'T QUIT--
KKKKKKK SSSTTTT
A SYSTEM FAILURE FOR THE MASSES.
ANTIMATTER FOR THE MASTER PLAN.
BOOM
D?
HEY, WHERE DID YOU GET THIS TAPE? I HAVEN'T HEARD IT SINCE I WAS A LITTLE GIRL.
WHAT TAPE? IT'S LIVE.
NO, IT ISN'T! THIS IS A RECORDING. HEY, WHERE'S VAL? HEY!
HE TOOK OFF A WHILE AGO. GO BACK TO SLEEP, WOULD YA?
KKKK SSSSTTT
LOUDER THAN GOD'S REVOLVER AND TWICE AS SHINY.

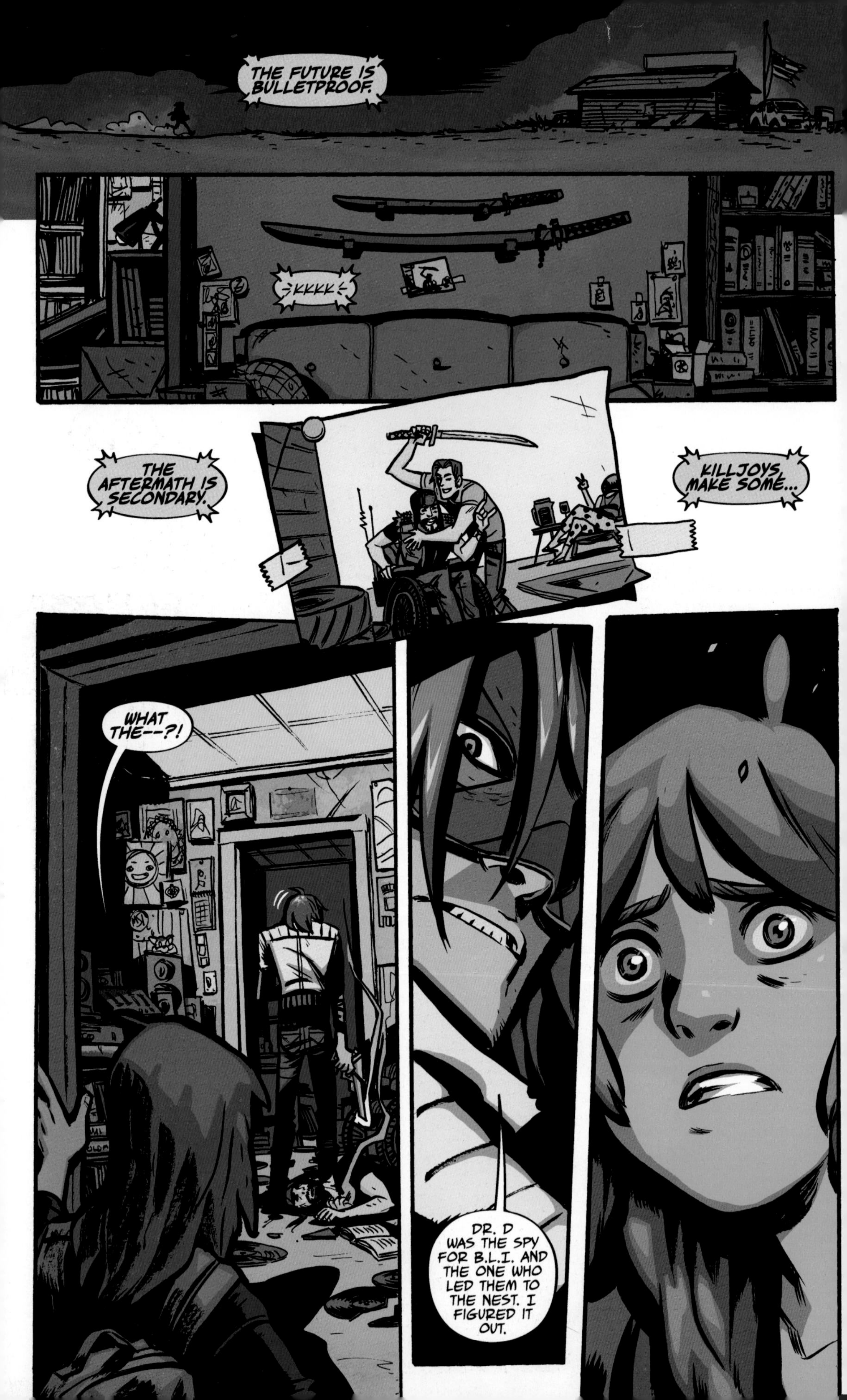
THE FUTURE IS BULLETPROOF.
KKKKK
THE AFTERMATH IS SECONDARY.
KILLJOYS, MAKE SOME...
WHAT THE--?!
DR. D WAS THE SPY FOR B.L.I. AND THE ONE WHO LED THEM TO THE NEST. I FIGURED IT OUT.

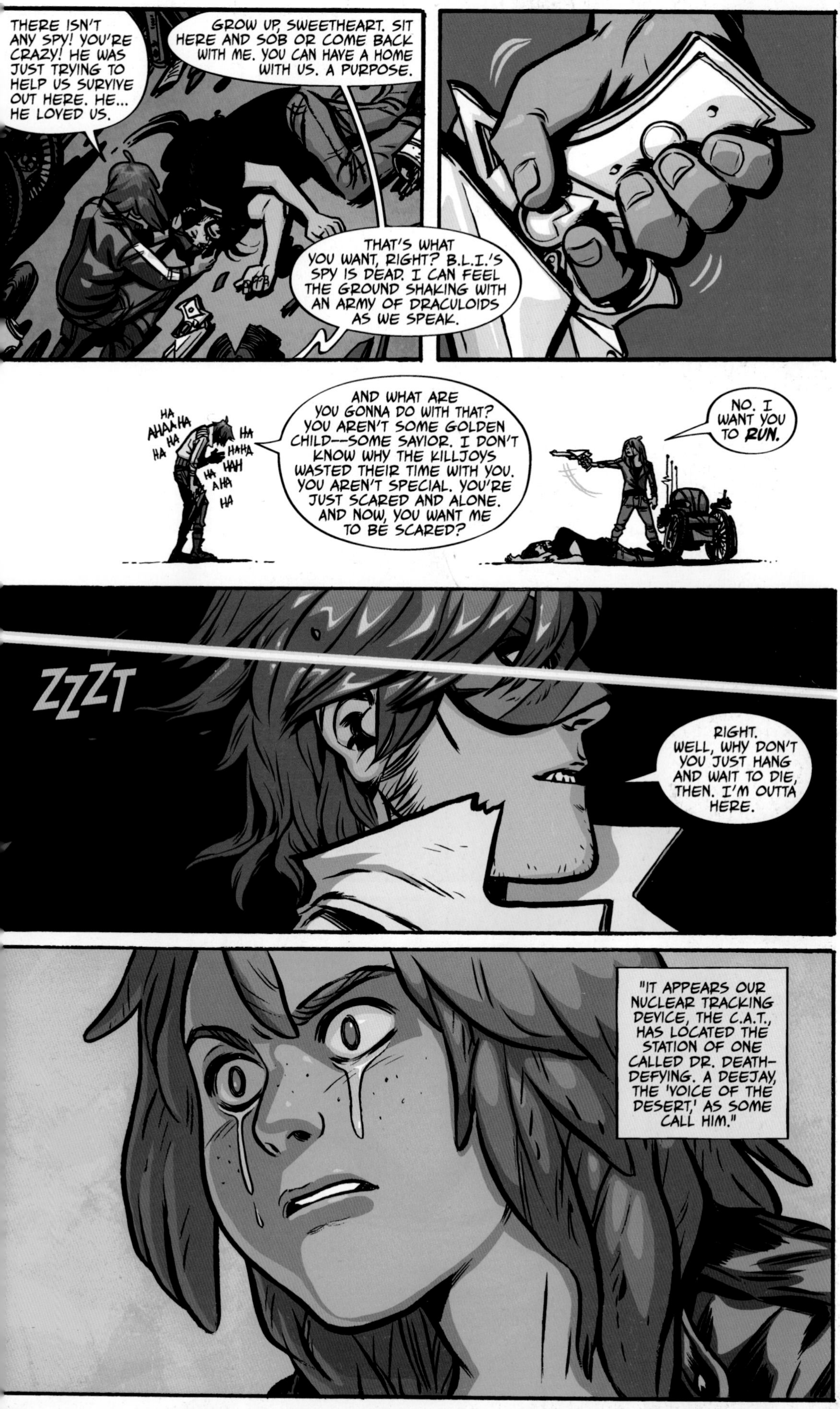

THERE ISN'T ANY SPY! YOU'RE CRAZY! HE WAS JUST TRYING TO HELP US SURVIVE OUT HERE. HE... HE LOVED US.
GROW UP, SWEETHEART. SIT HERE AND SOB OR COME BACK WITH ME. YOU CAN HAVE A HOME WITH US. A PURPOSE.
THAT'S WHAT YOU WANT, RIGHT? B.L.I.'S SPY IS DEAD. I CAN FEEL THE GROUND SHAKING WITH AN ARMY OF DRACULOIDS AS WE SPEAK.
HA AHAHAHA HA HA HA HAHA HAH HA AHA HA
AND WHAT ARE YOU GONNA DO WITH THAT? YOU AREN'T SOME GOLDEN CHILD--SOME SAVIOR. I DON'T KNOW WHY THE KILLJOYS WASTED THEIR TIME WITH YOU. YOU AREN'T SPECIAL. YOU'RE JUST SCARED AND ALONE. AND NOW, YOU WANT ME TO BE SCARED?
NO. I WANT YOU TO RUN.
ZZZT
RIGHT. WELL, WHY DON'T YOU JUST HANG AND WAIT TO DIE, THEN. I'M OUTTA HERE.
"IT APPEARS OUR NUCLEAR TRACKING DEVICE, THE C.A.T., HAS LOCATED THE STATION OF ONE CALLED DR. DEATH-DEFYING. A DEEJAY, THE 'VOICE OF THE DESERT,' AS SOME CALL HIM."

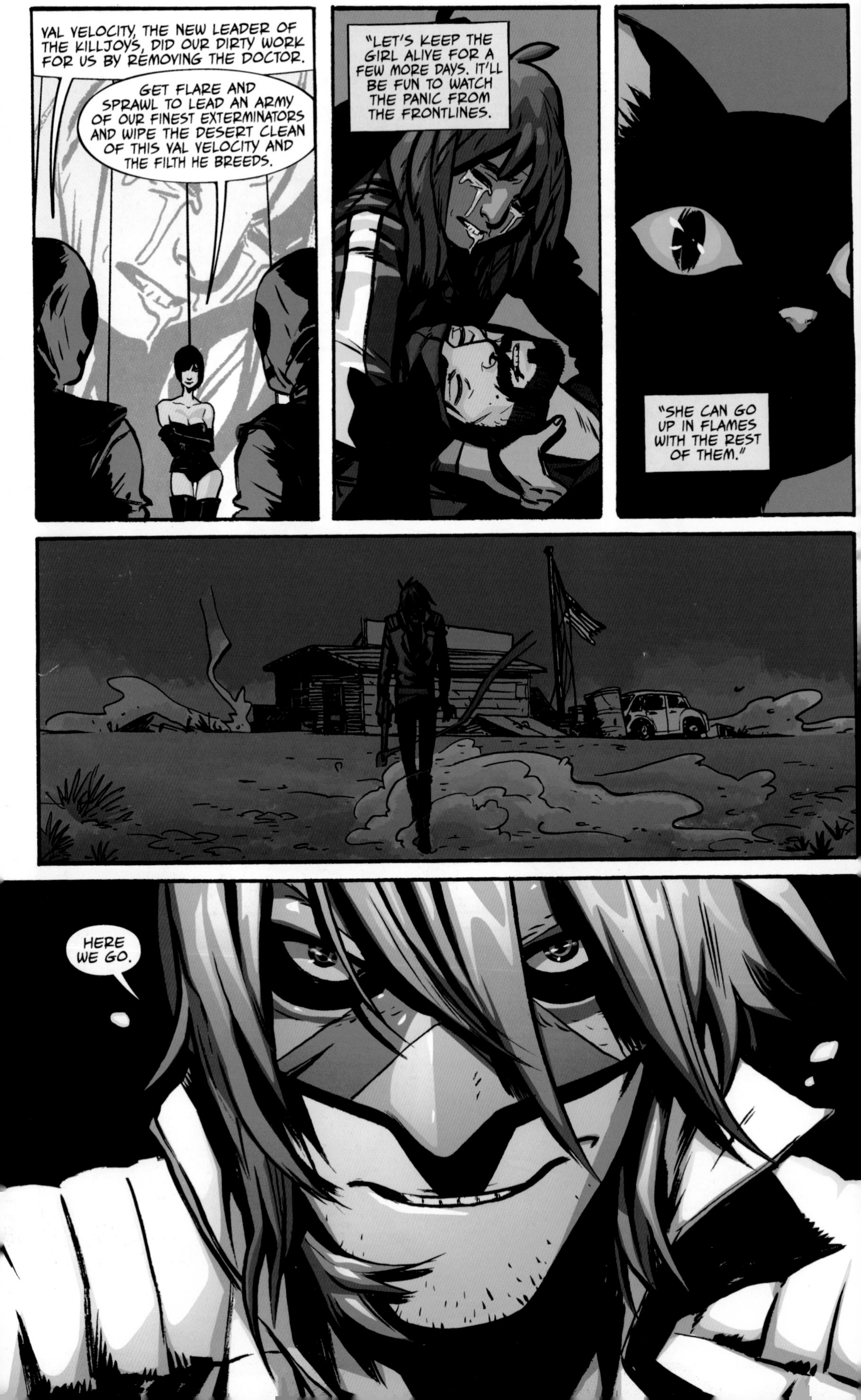
VAL VELOCITY, THE NEW LEADER OF THE KILLJOYS, DID OUR DIRTY WORK FOR US BY REMOVING THE DOCTOR.
GET FLARE AND SPRAWL TO LEAD AN ARMY OF OUR FINEST EXTERMINATORS AND WIPE THE DESERT CLEAN OF THIS VAL VELOCITY AND THE FILTH HE BREEDS.
"LET'S KEEP THE GIRL ALIVE FOR A FEW MORE DAYS. IT'LL BE FUN TO WATCH THE PANIC FROM THE FRONTLINES.
"SHE CAN GO UP IN FLAMES WITH THE REST OF THEM."
HERE WE GO.

Chapter Five:

WAKING THE DESTROYA

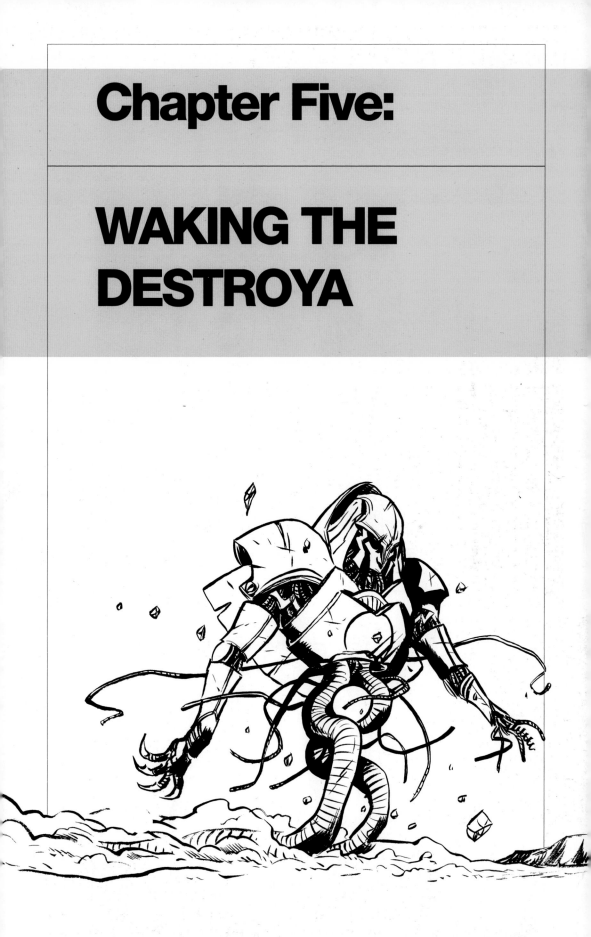

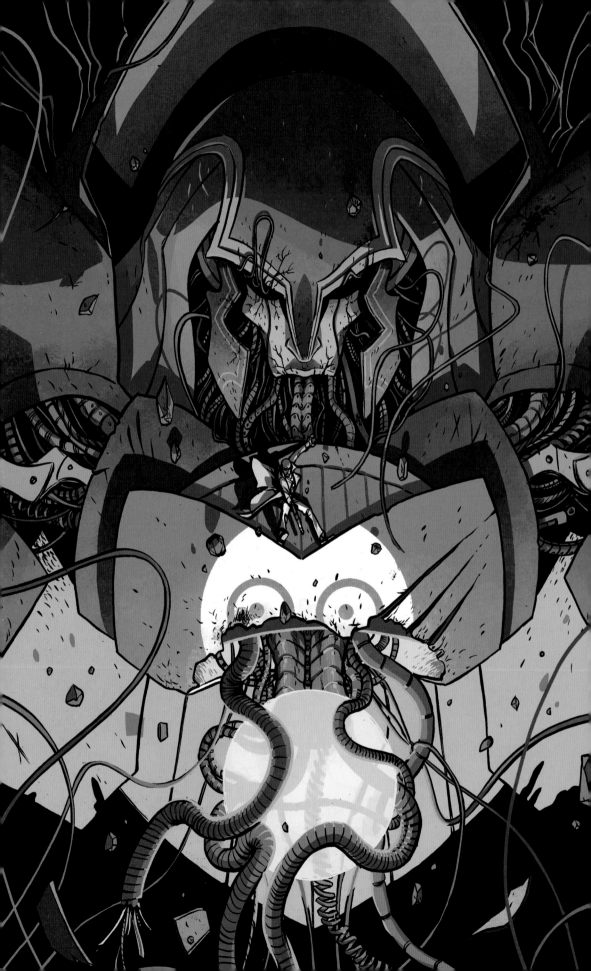

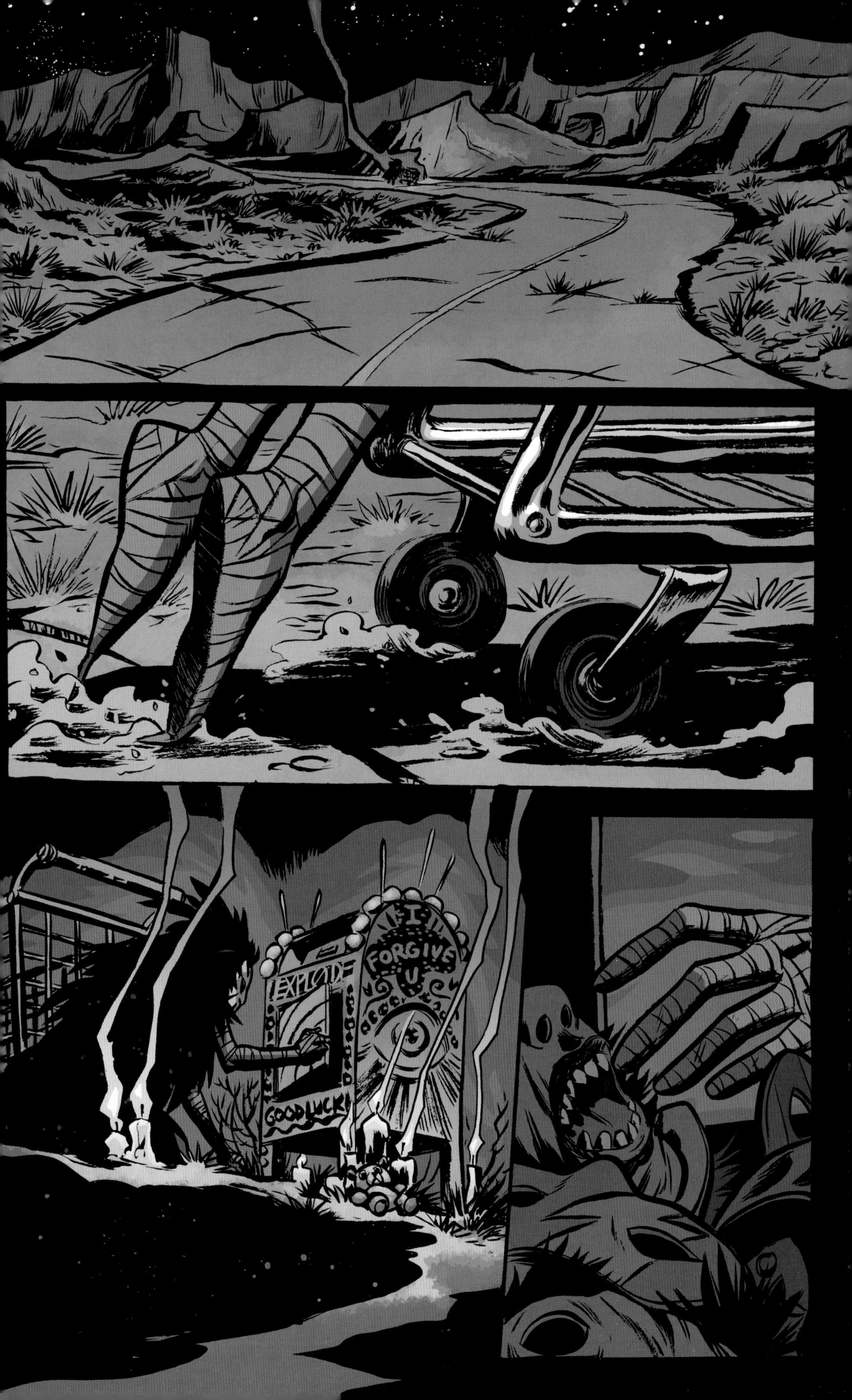
EXPLODE
I FORGIVE U
GOOD LUCK

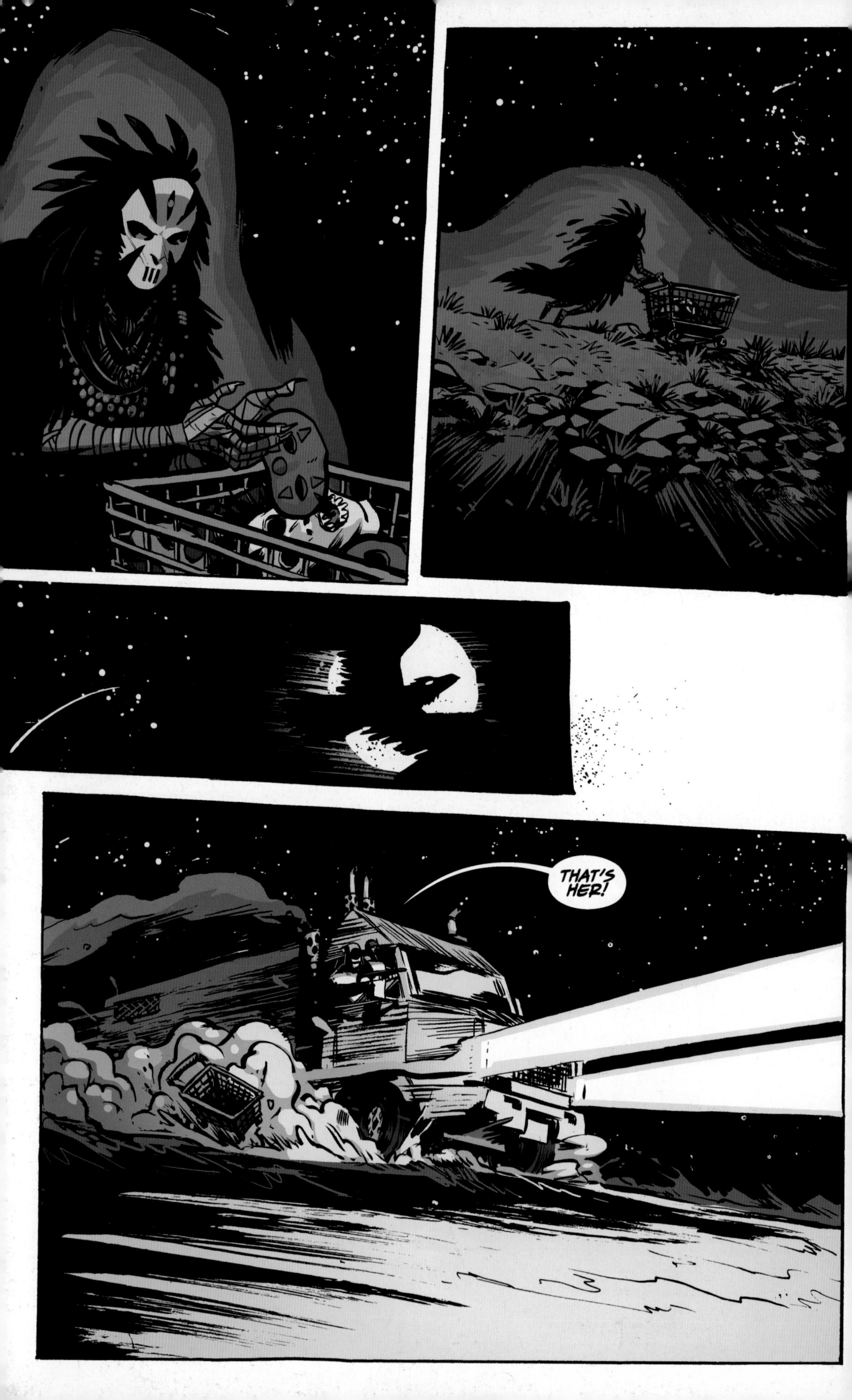
THAT'S HER!

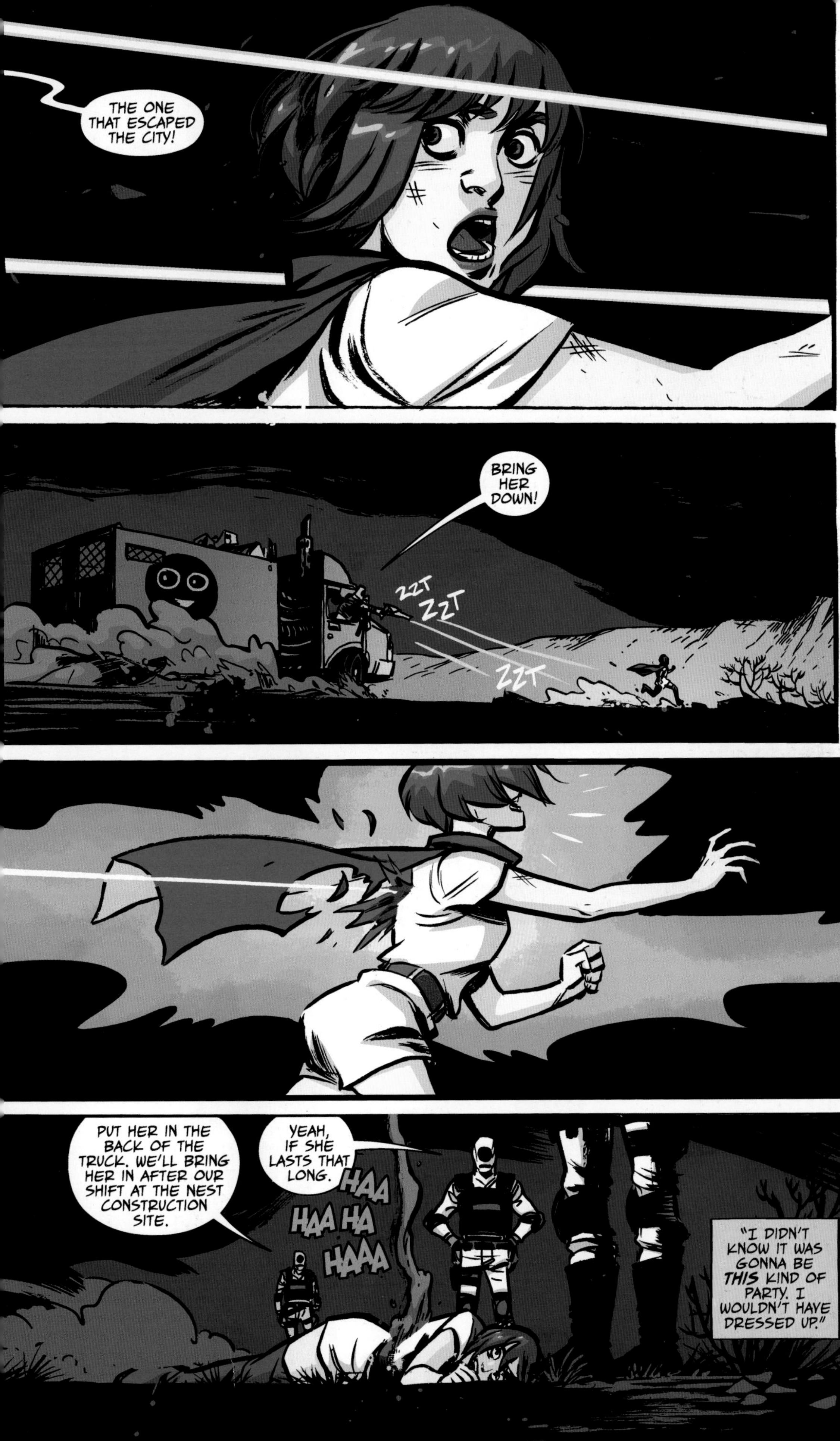
THE ONE THAT ESCAPED THE CITY!
BRING HER DOWN!
ZZT ZZT
ZZT
PUT HER IN THE BACK OF THE TRUCK. WE'LL BRING HER IN AFTER OUR SHIFT AT THE NEST CONSTRUCTION SITE.
YEAH, IF SHE LASTS THAT LONG.
HAA HAA HA HAAA
"I DIDN'T KNOW IT WAS GONNA BE *THIS* KIND OF PARTY. I WOULDN'T HAVE DRESSED UP."

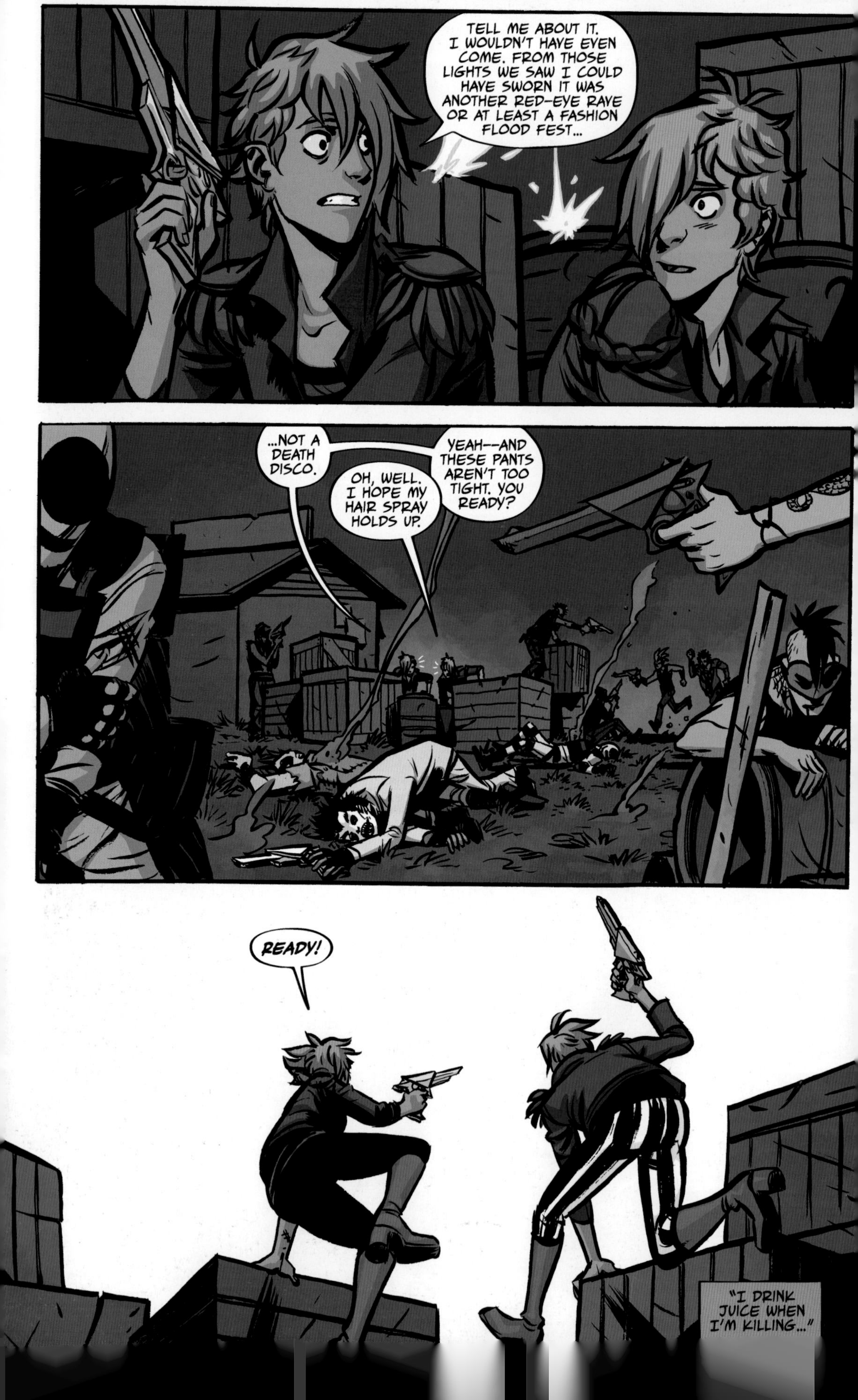
TELL ME ABOUT IT. I WOULDN'T HAVE EVEN COME. FROM THOSE LIGHTS WE SAW I COULD HAVE SWORN IT WAS ANOTHER RED-EYE RAVE OR AT LEAST A FASHION FLOOD FEST...
...NOT A DEATH DISCO.
YEAH--AND THESE PANTS AREN'T TOO TIGHT. YOU READY?
OH, WELL. I HOPE MY HAIR SPRAY HOLDS UP.
READY!
"I DRINK JUICE WHEN I'M KILLING..."

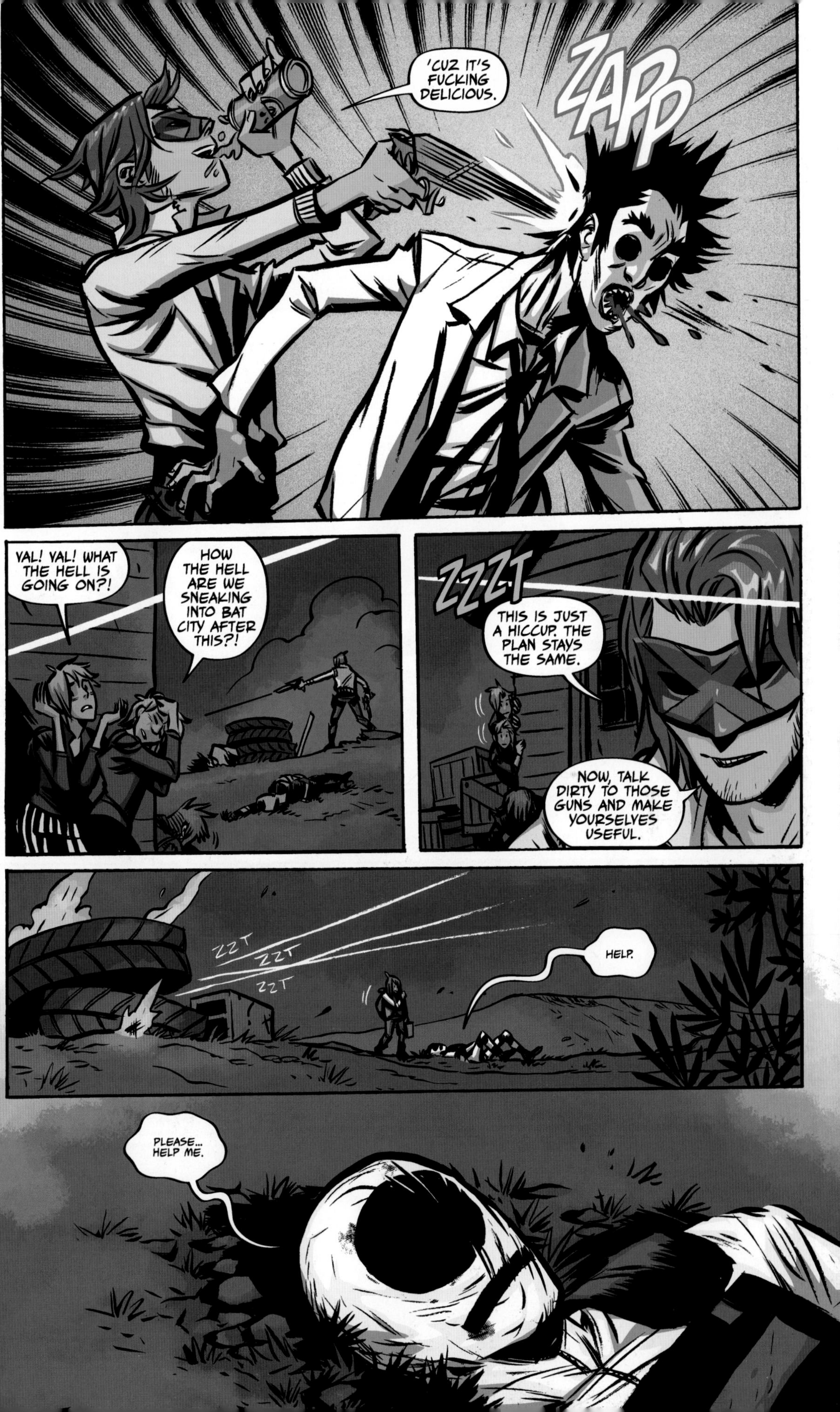
'CUZ IT'S FUCKING DELICIOUS.
ZAPP
VAL! VAL! WHAT THE HELL IS GOING ON?!
HOW THE HELL ARE WE SNEAKING INTO BAT CITY AFTER THIS?!
ZZZT
THIS IS JUST A HICCUP. THE PLAN STAYS THE SAME.
NOW, TALK DIRTY TO THOSE GUNS AND MAKE YOURSELVES USEFUL.
ZZT
ZZT
ZZT
HELP.
PLEASE... HELP ME.

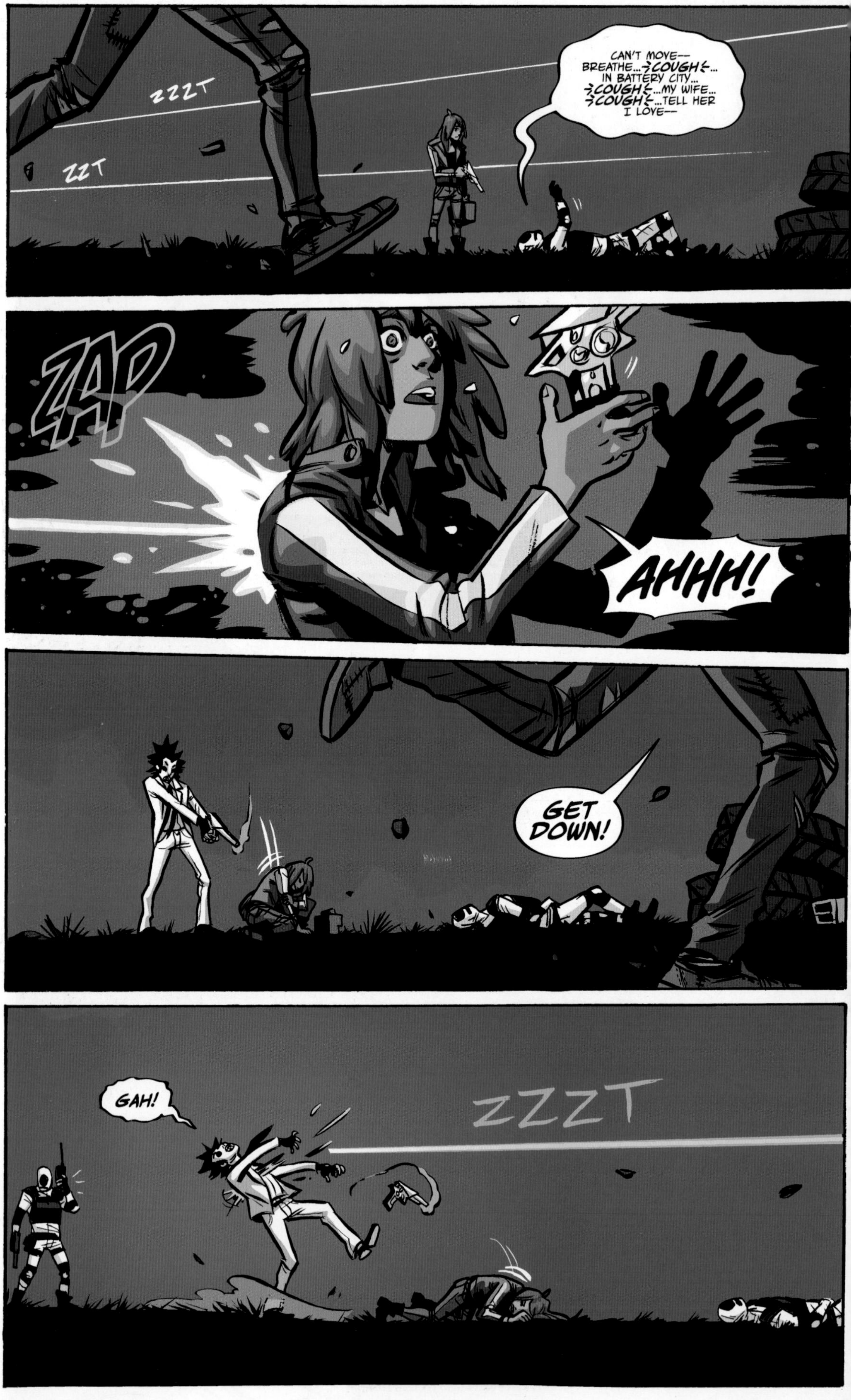
ZZZT
ZZT
CAN'T MOVE-- BREATHE... COUGH... IN BATTERY CITY... COUGH...MY WIFE... COUGH...TELL HER I LOVE--
ZAP
AHHH!
GET DOWN!
GAH!
ZZZT

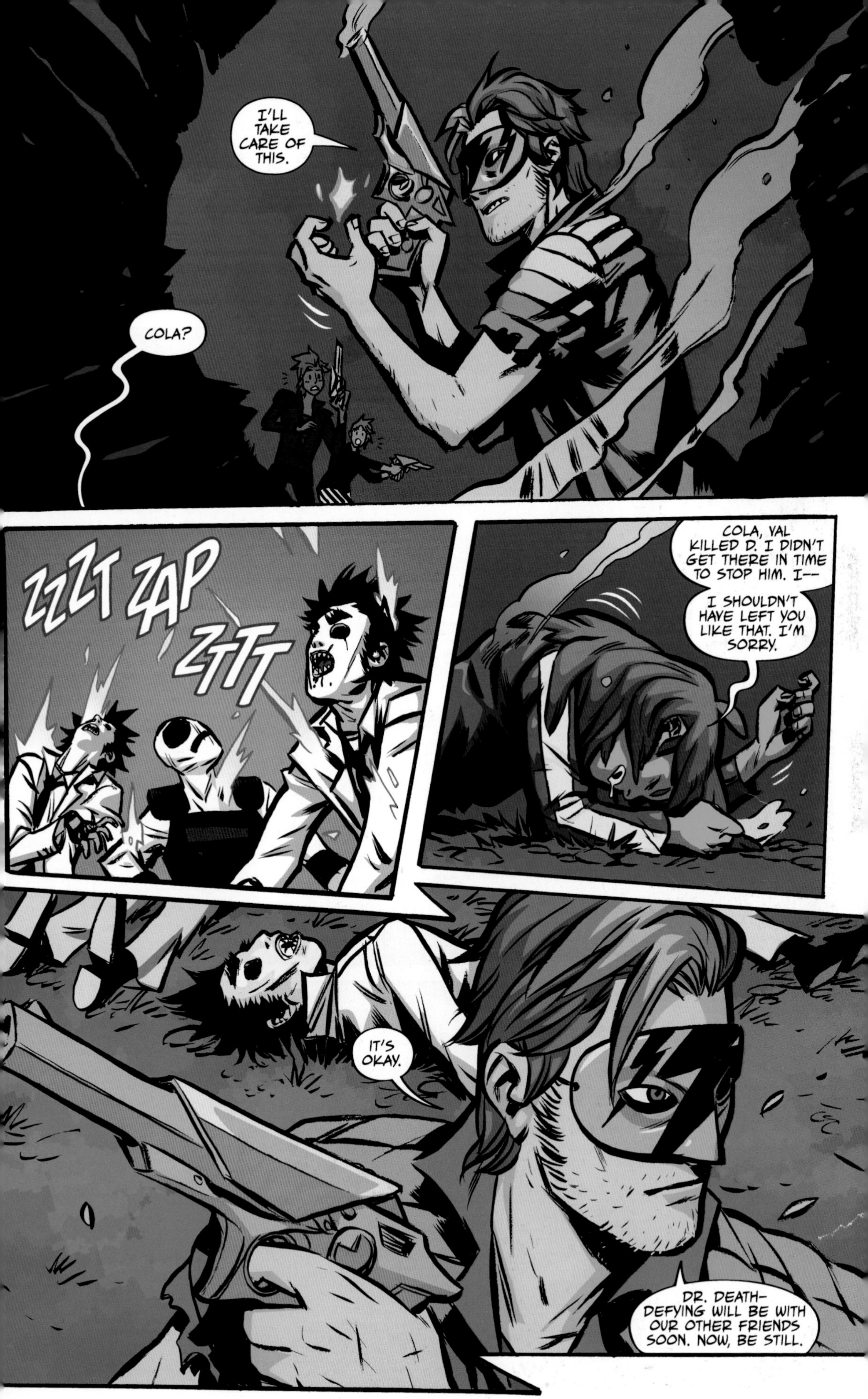
I'LL TAKE CARE OF THIS.
COLA?
ZZZT ZAP ZTTT
COLA, VAL KILLED D. I DIDN'T GET THERE IN TIME TO STOP HIM. I--
I SHOULDN'T HAVE LEFT YOU LIKE THAT. I'M SORRY.
IT'S OKAY.
DR. DEATH-DEFYING WILL BE WITH OUR OTHER FRIENDS SOON. NOW, BE STILL.

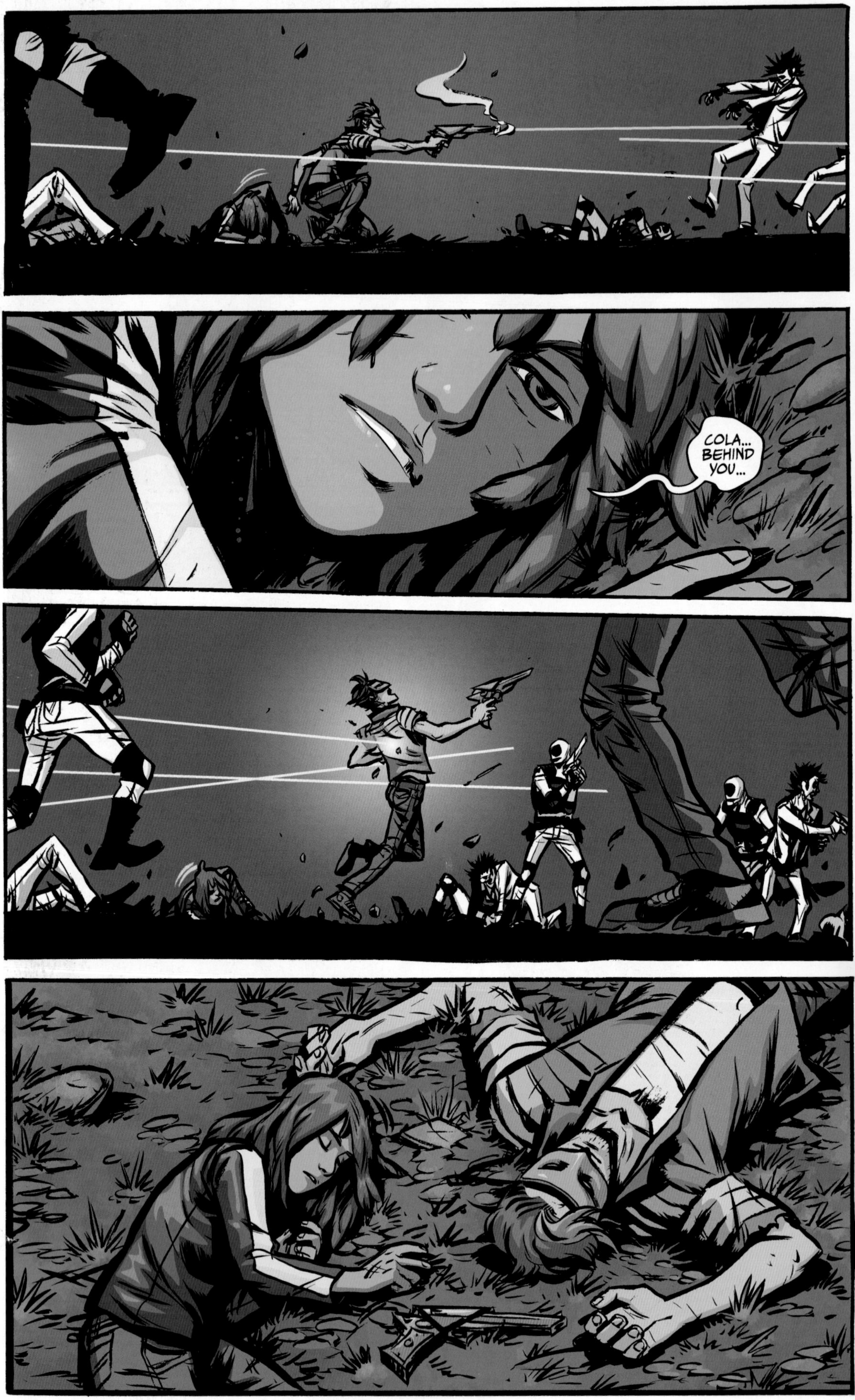
COLA... BEHIND YOU...

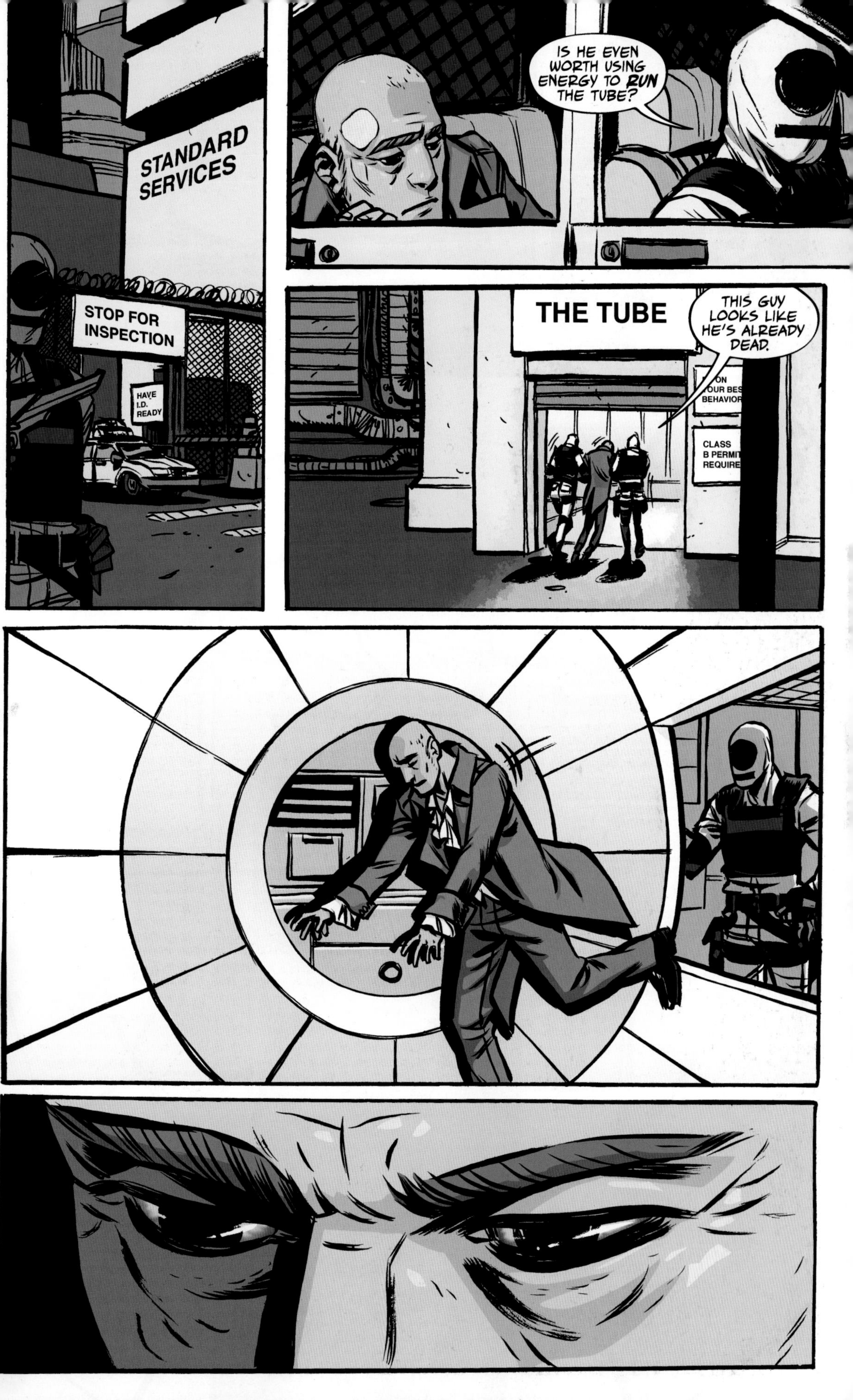
STANDARD SERVICES
STOP FOR INSPECTION
HAVE I.D. READY
IS HE EVEN WORTH USING ENERGY TO RUN THE TUBE?
THE TUBE
THIS GUY LOOKS LIKE HE'S ALREADY DEAD.
CLASS B PERMIT

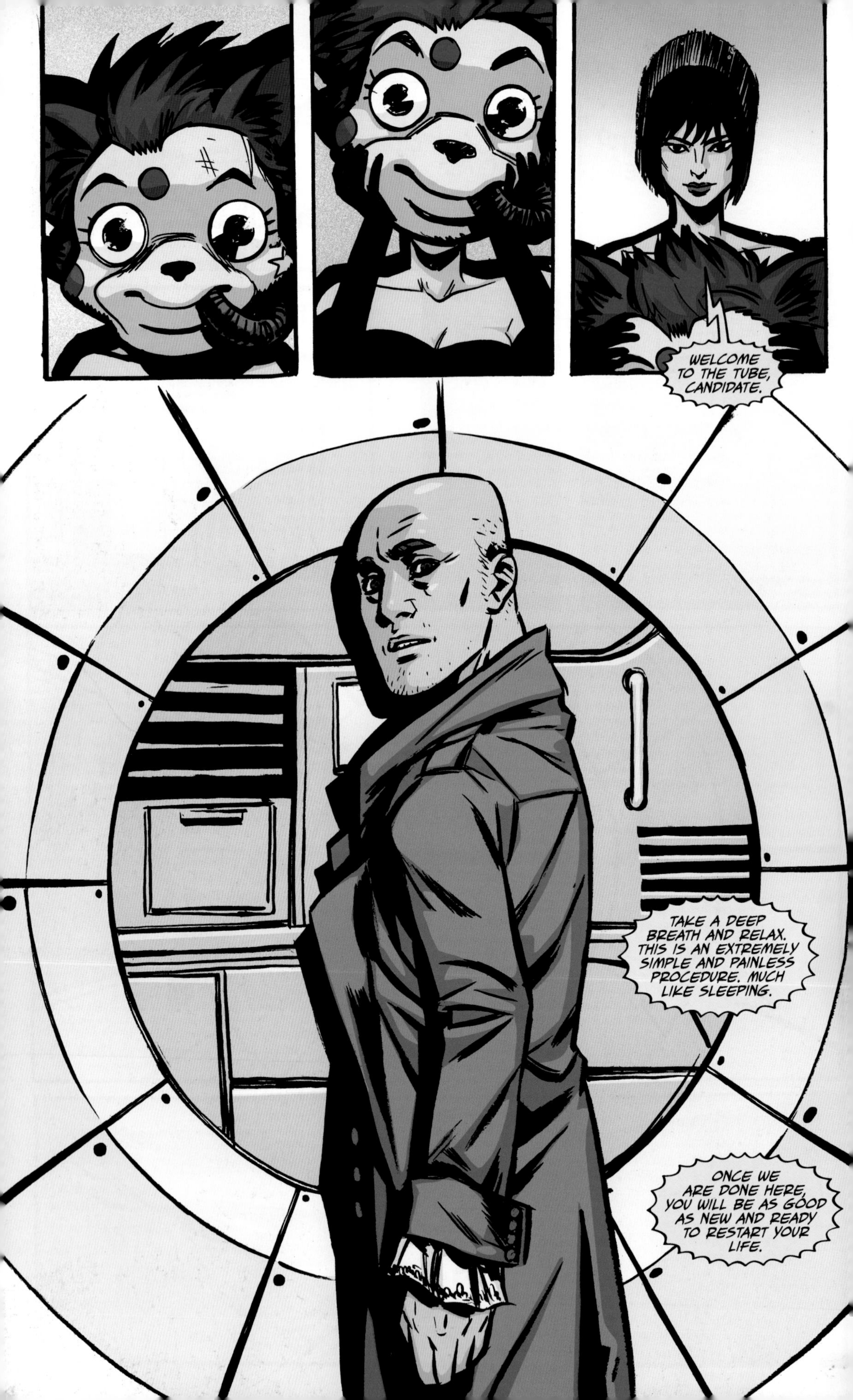
WELCOME TO THE TUBE, CANDIDATE.
TAKE A DEEP BREATH AND RELAX. THIS IS AN EXTREMELY SIMPLE AND PAINLESS PROCEDURE. MUCH LIKE SLEEPING.
ONCE WE ARE DONE HERE, YOU WILL BE AS GOOD AS NEW AND READY TO RESTART YOUR LIFE.

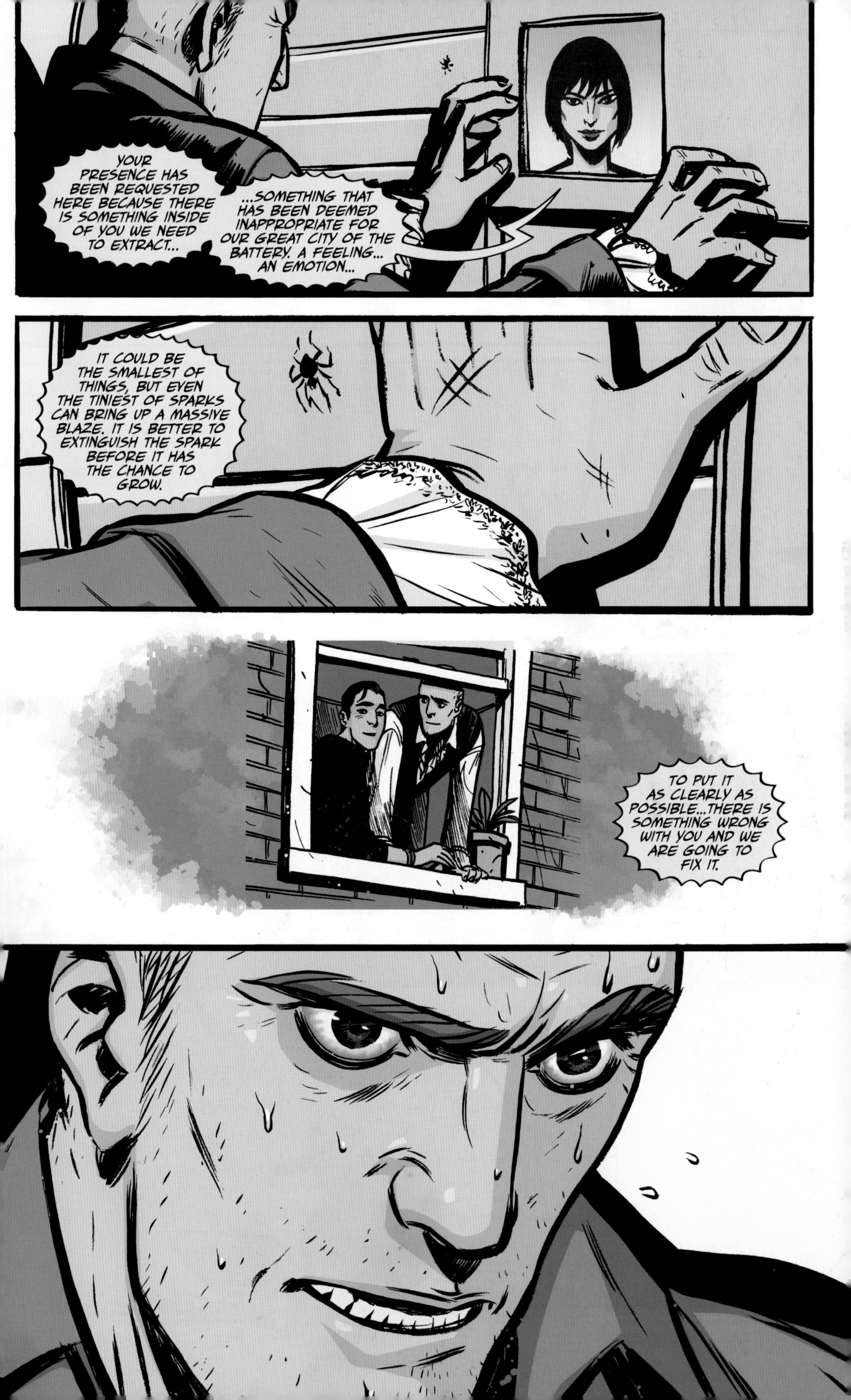
YOUR PRESENCE HAS BEEN REQUESTED HERE BECAUSE THERE IS SOMETHING INSIDE OF YOU WE NEED TO EXTRACT...
...SOMETHING THAT HAS BEEN DEEMED INAPPROPRIATE FOR OUR GREAT CITY OF THE BATTERY. A FEELING... AN EMOTION...
IT COULD BE THE SMALLEST OF THINGS, BUT EVEN THE TINIEST OF SPARKS CAN BRING UP A MASSIVE BLAZE. IT IS BETTER TO EXTINGUISH THE SPARK BEFORE IT HAS THE CHANCE TO GROW.
TO PUT IT AS CLEARLY AS POSSIBLE...THERE IS SOMETHING WRONG WITH YOU AND WE ARE GOING TO FIX IT.

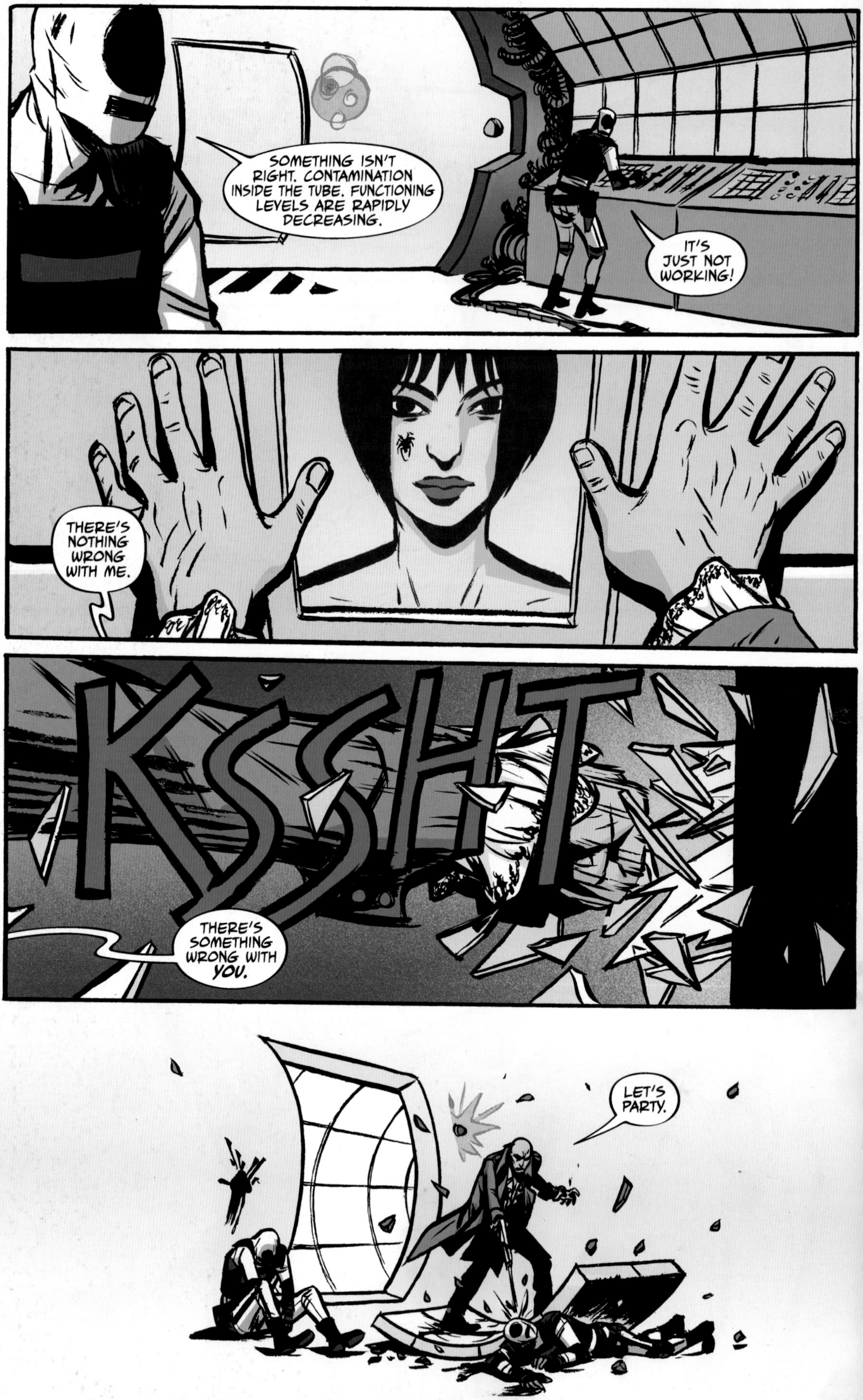
SOMETHING ISN'T RIGHT. CONTAMINATION INSIDE THE TUBE. FUNCTIONING LEVELS ARE RAPIDLY DECREASING.
IT'S JUST NOT WORKING!
THERE'S NOTHING WRONG WITH ME.
KSSHT
THERE'S SOMETHING WRONG WITH YOU.
LET'S PARTY.

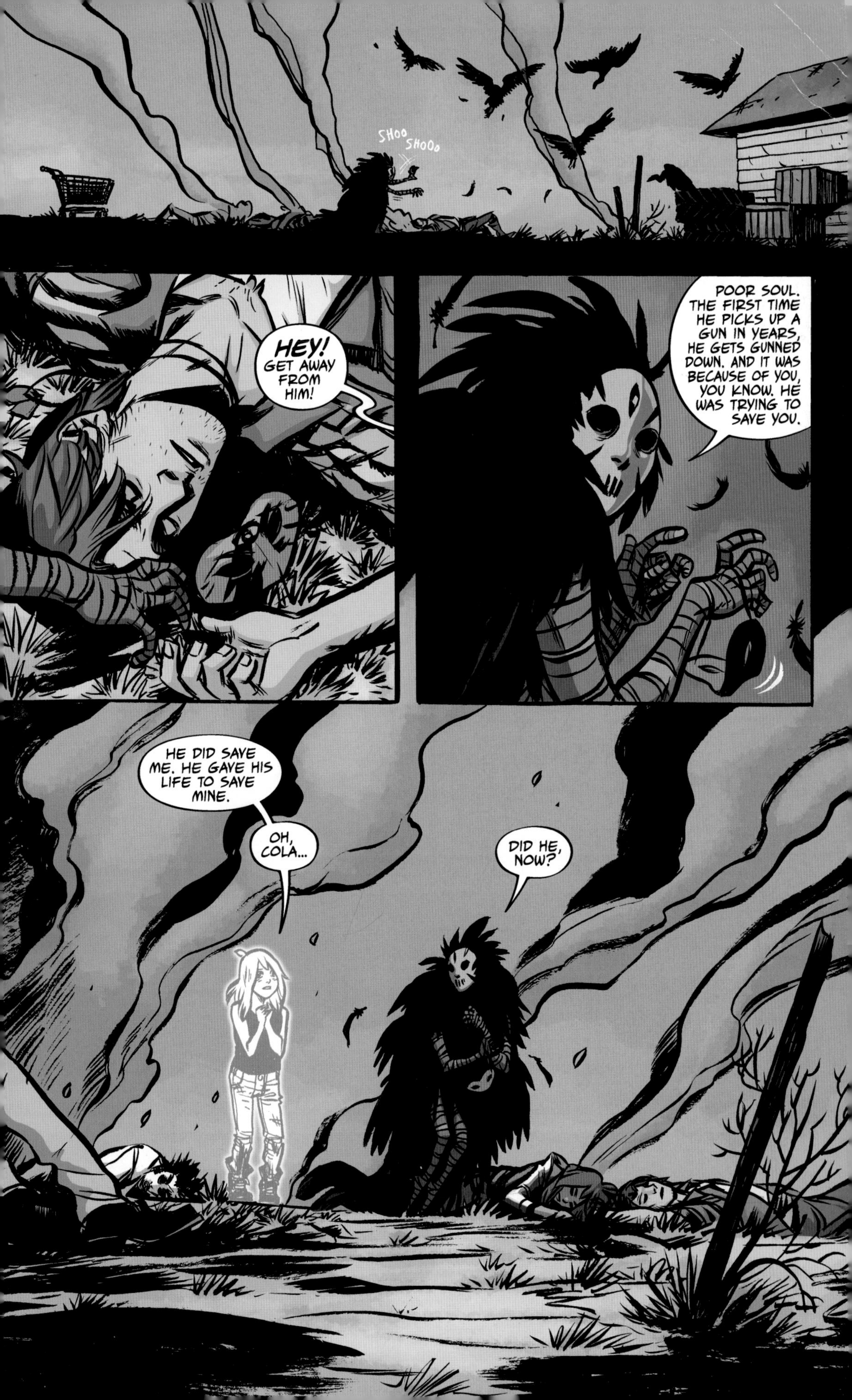
SHOO SHOO
HEY! GET AWAY FROM HIM!
POOR SOUL. THE FIRST TIME HE PICKS UP A GUN IN YEARS, HE GETS GUNNED DOWN. AND IT WAS BECAUSE OF YOU, YOU KNOW. HE WAS TRYING TO SAVE YOU.
HE DID SAVE ME. HE GAVE HIS LIFE TO SAVE MINE.
OH, COLA...
DID HE, NOW?

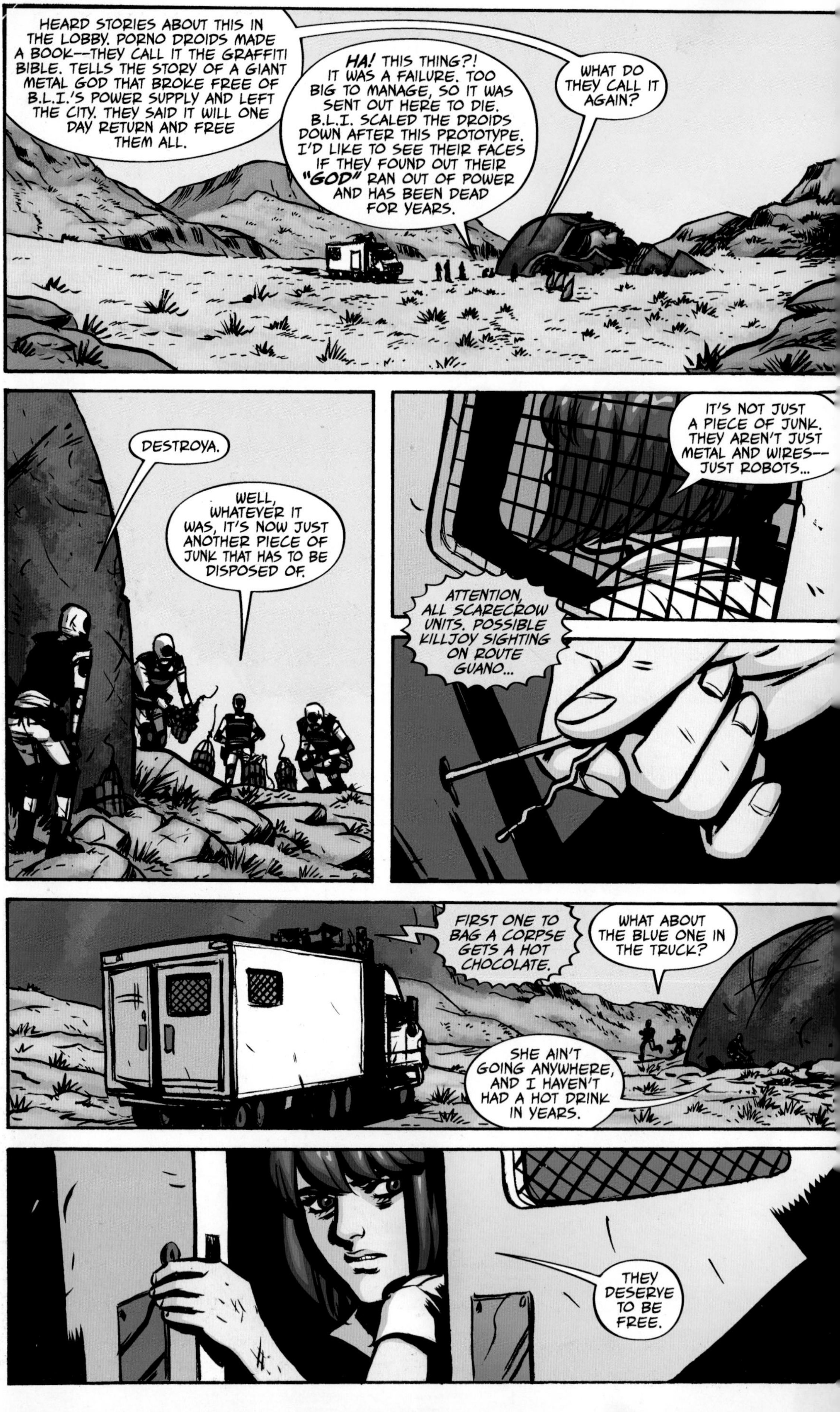
HEARD STORIES ABOUT THIS IN THE LOBBY. PORNO DROIDS MADE A BOOK--THEY CALL IT THE GRAFFITI BIBLE. TELLS THE STORY OF A GIANT METAL GOD THAT BROKE FREE OF B.L.I.'S POWER SUPPLY AND LEFT THE CITY. THEY SAID IT WILL ONE DAY RETURN AND FREE THEM ALL.
HA! THIS THING?! IT WAS A FAILURE. TOO BIG TO MANAGE, SO IT WAS SENT OUT HERE TO DIE. B.L.I. SCALED THE DROIDS DOWN AFTER THIS PROTOTYPE. I'D LIKE TO SEE THEIR FACES IF THEY FOUND OUT THEIR "GOD" RAN OUT OF POWER AND HAS BEEN DEAD FOR YEARS.
WHAT DO THEY CALL IT AGAIN?
DESTROYA.
WELL, WHATEVER IT WAS, IT'S NOW JUST ANOTHER PIECE OF JUNK THAT HAS TO BE DISPOSED OF.
IT'S NOT JUST A PIECE OF JUNK. THEY AREN'T JUST METAL AND WIRES--JUST ROBOTS...
ATTENTION, ALL SCARECROW UNITS. POSSIBLE KILLJOY SIGHTING ON ROUTE GUANO...
FIRST ONE TO BAG A CORPSE GETS A HOT CHOCOLATE.
WHAT ABOUT THE BLUE ONE IN THE TRUCK?
SHE AIN'T GOING ANYWHERE, AND I HAVEN'T HAD A HOT DRINK IN YEARS.
THEY DESERVE TO BE FREE.

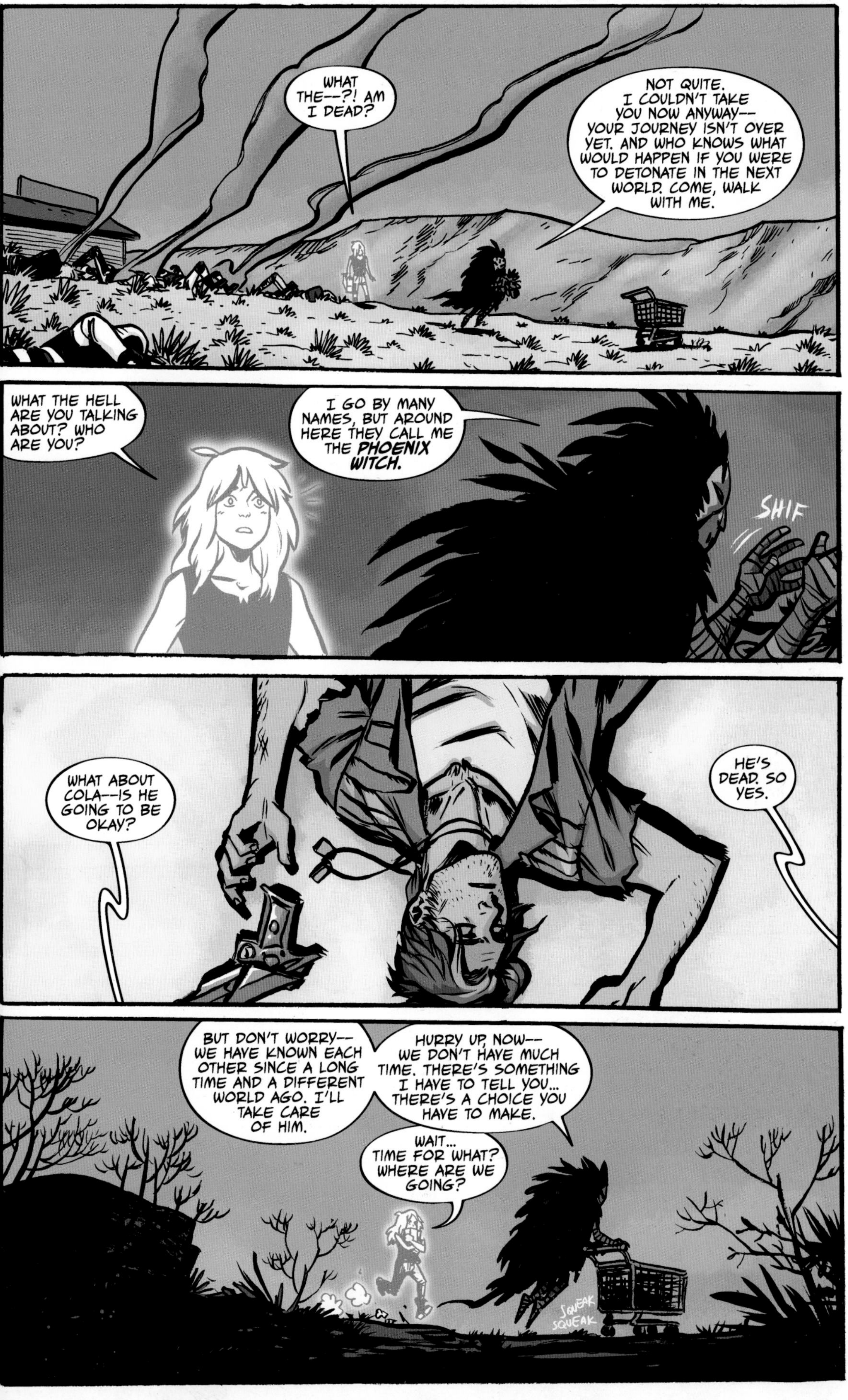
WHAT THE--?! AM I DEAD?
NOT QUITE. I COULDN'T TAKE YOU NOW ANYWAY-- YOUR JOURNEY ISN'T OVER YET. AND WHO KNOWS WHAT WOULD HAPPEN IF YOU WERE TO DETONATE IN THE NEXT WORLD. COME, WALK WITH ME.
WHAT THE HELL ARE YOU TALKING ABOUT? WHO ARE YOU?
I GO BY MANY NAMES, BUT AROUND HERE THEY CALL ME THE PHOENIX WITCH.
SHIF
WHAT ABOUT COLA--IS HE GOING TO BE OKAY?
HE'S DEAD. SO YES.
BUT DON'T WORRY-- WE HAVE KNOWN EACH OTHER SINCE A LONG TIME AND A DIFFERENT WORLD AGO. I'LL TAKE CARE OF HIM.
HURRY UP, NOW-- WE DON'T HAVE MUCH TIME. THERE'S SOMETHING I HAVE TO TELL YOU... THERE'S A CHOICE YOU HAVE TO MAKE.
WAIT... TIME FOR WHAT? WHERE ARE WE GOING?
SQUEAK SQUEAK

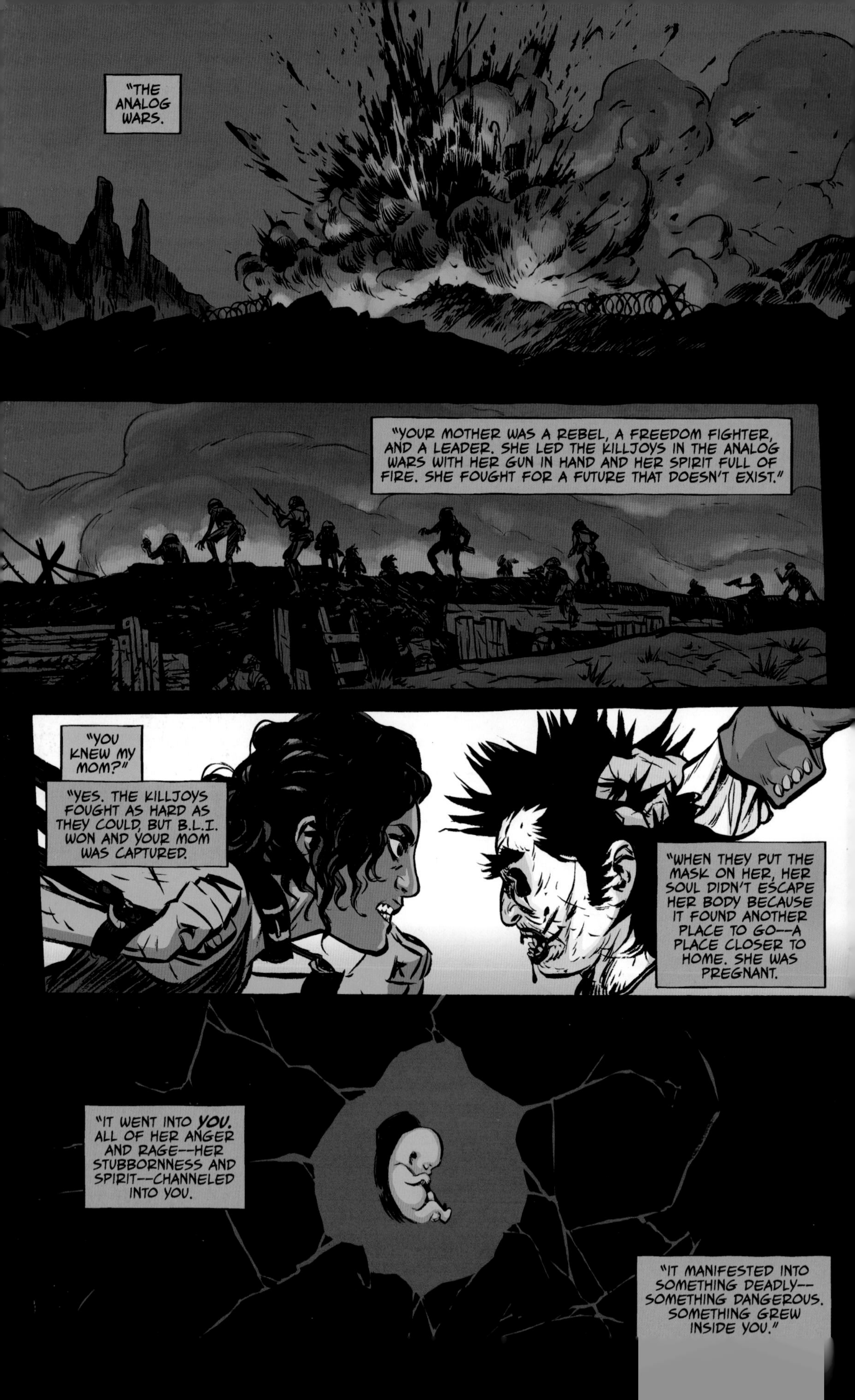
"THE ANALOG WARS.
"YOUR MOTHER WAS A REBEL, A FREEDOM FIGHTER, AND A LEADER. SHE LED THE KILLJOYS IN THE ANALOG WARS WITH HER GUN IN HAND AND HER SPIRIT FULL OF FIRE. SHE FOUGHT FOR A FUTURE THAT DOESN'T EXIST."
"YOU KNEW MY MOM?"
"YES. THE KILLJOYS FOUGHT AS HARD AS THEY COULD, BUT B.L.I. WON AND YOUR MOM WAS CAPTURED.
"WHEN THEY PUT THE MASK ON HER, HER SOUL DIDN'T ESCAPE HER BODY BECAUSE IT FOUND ANOTHER PLACE TO GO--A PLACE CLOSER TO HOME. SHE WAS PREGNANT.
"IT WENT INTO *YOU*. ALL OF HER ANGER AND RAGE--HER STUBBORNNESS AND SPIRIT--CHANNELED INTO YOU.
"IT MANIFESTED INTO SOMETHING DEADLY--SOMETHING DANGEROUS. SOMETHING GREW INSIDE YOU."

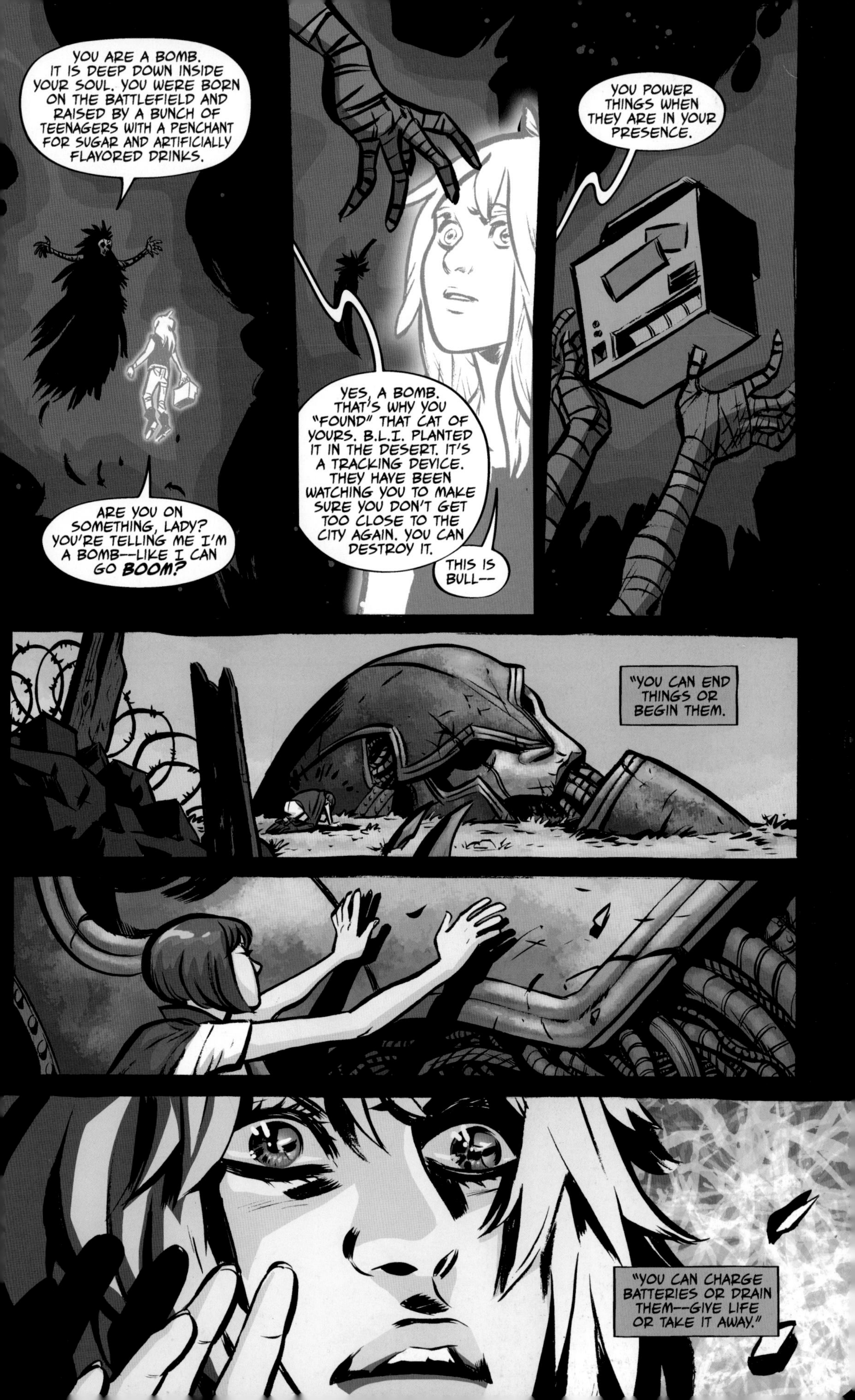
YOU ARE A BOMB. IT IS DEEP DOWN INSIDE YOUR SOUL. YOU WERE BORN ON THE BATTLEFIELD AND RAISED BY A BUNCH OF TEENAGERS WITH A PENCHANT FOR SUGAR AND ARTIFICIALLY FLAVORED DRINKS.
ARE YOU ON SOMETHING, LADY? YOU'RE TELLING ME I'M A BOMB--LIKE I CAN GO **BOOM?**
YES, A BOMB. THAT'S WHY YOU "FOUND" THAT CAT OF YOURS. B.L.I. PLANTED IT IN THE DESERT. IT'S A TRACKING DEVICE. THEY HAVE BEEN WATCHING YOU TO MAKE SURE YOU DON'T GET TOO CLOSE TO THE CITY AGAIN. YOU CAN DESTROY IT.
THIS IS BULL--
YOU POWER THINGS WHEN THEY ARE IN YOUR PRESENCE.
"YOU CAN END THINGS OR BEGIN THEM.
"YOU CAN CHARGE BATTERIES OR DRAIN THEM--GIVE LIFE OR TAKE IT AWAY."

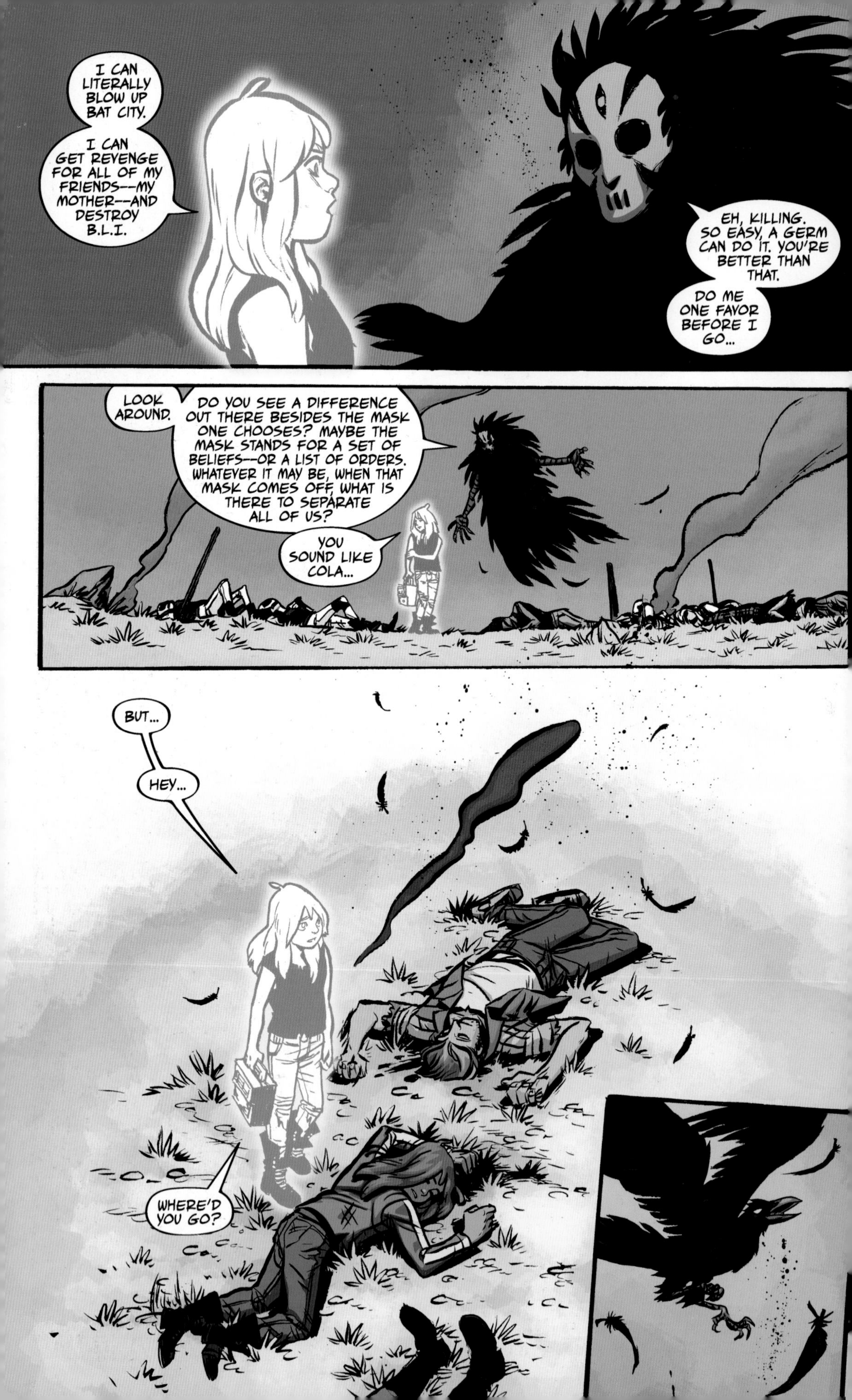
I CAN LITERALLY BLOW UP BAT CITY.
I CAN GET REVENGE FOR ALL OF MY FRIENDS--MY MOTHER--AND DESTROY B.L.I.
EH, KILLING. SO EASY, A GERM CAN DO IT. YOU'RE BETTER THAN THAT.
DO ME ONE FAVOR BEFORE I GO...
LOOK AROUND.
DO YOU SEE A DIFFERENCE OUT THERE BESIDES THE MASK ONE CHOOSES? MAYBE THE MASK STANDS FOR A SET OF BELIEFS--OR A LIST OF ORDERS. WHATEVER IT MAY BE, WHEN THAT MASK COMES OFF, WHAT IS THERE TO SEPARATE ALL OF US?
YOU SOUND LIKE COLA...
BUT...
HEY...
WHERE'D YOU GO?

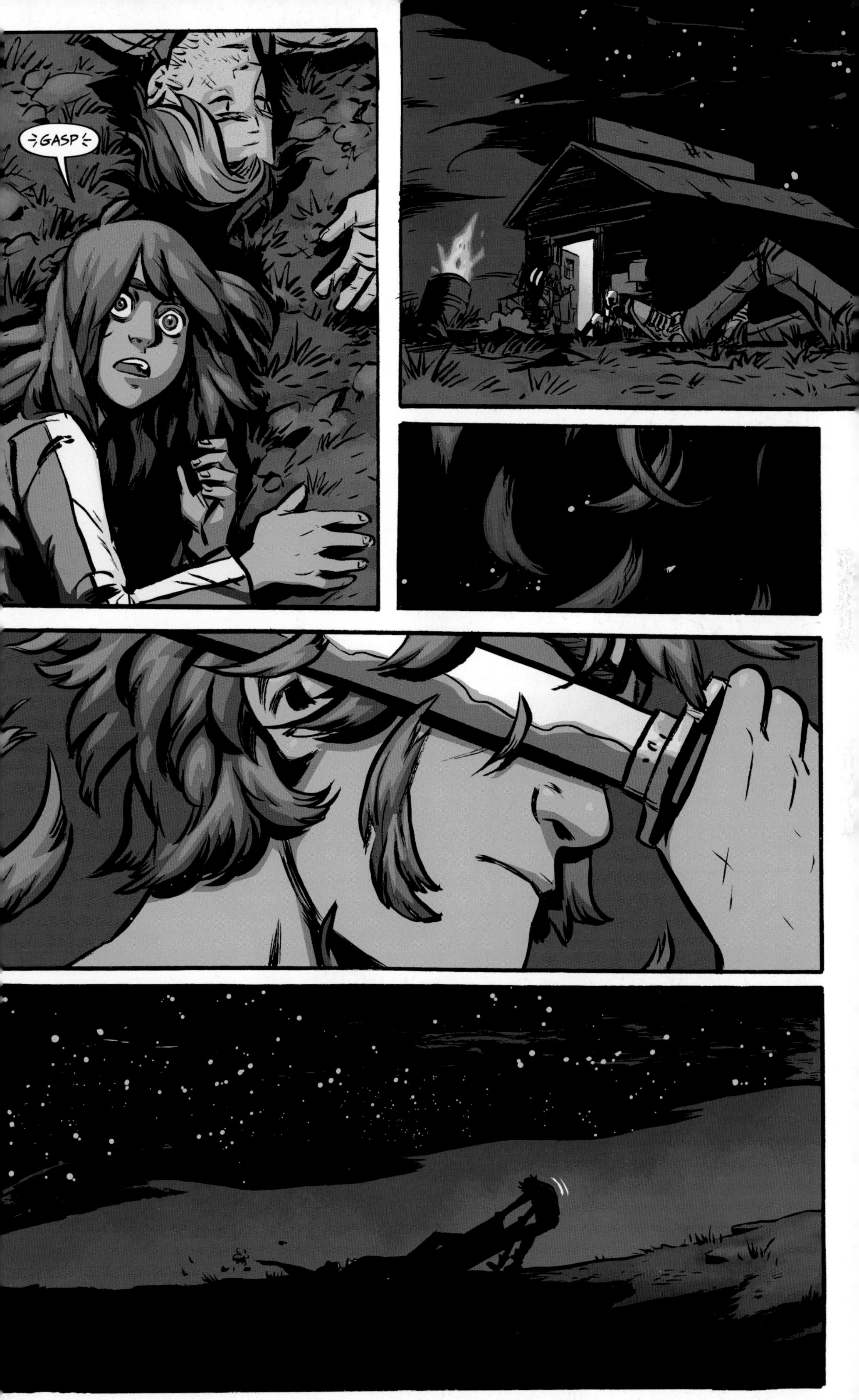
GASP

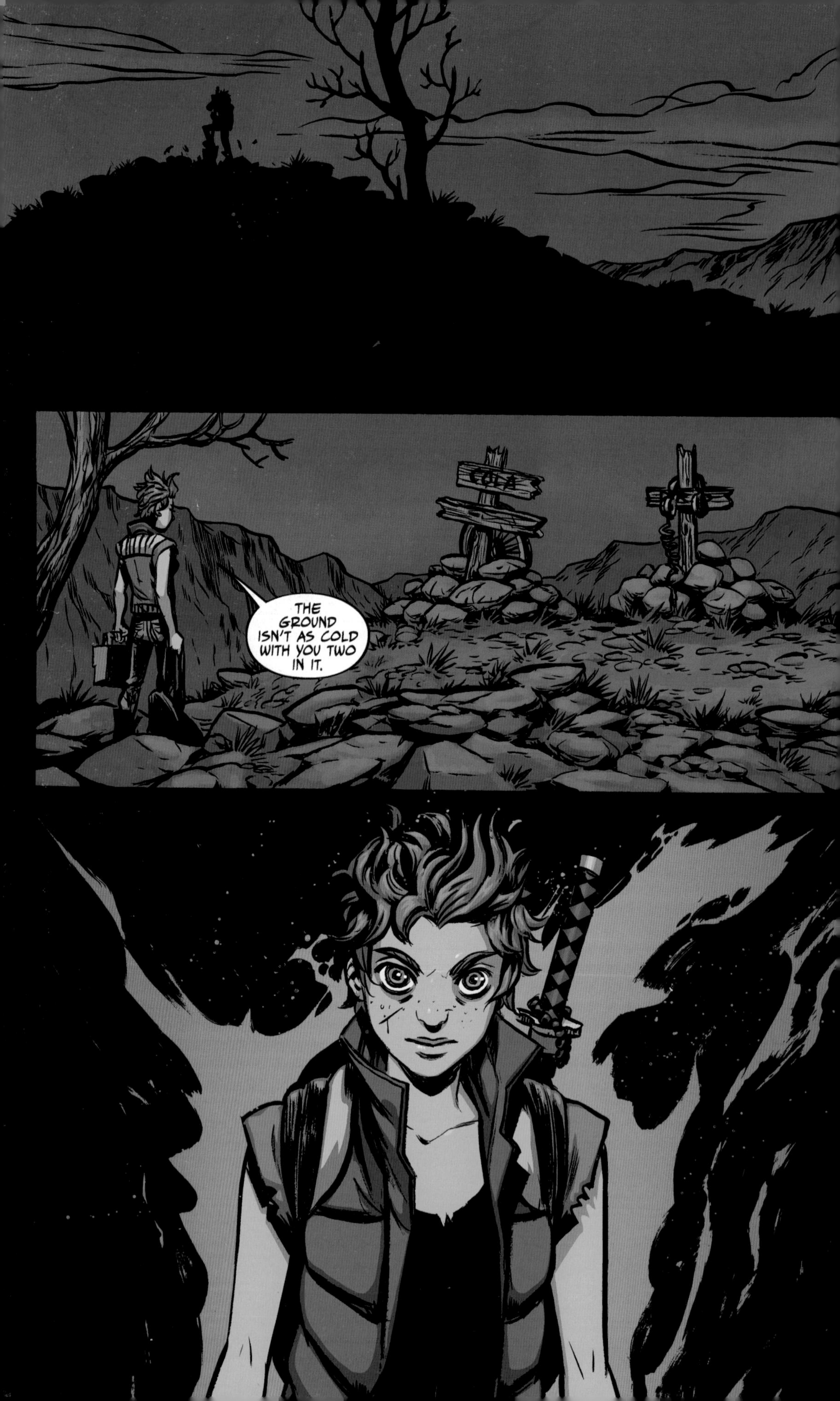
THE GROUND ISN'T AS COLD WITH YOU TWO IN IT.

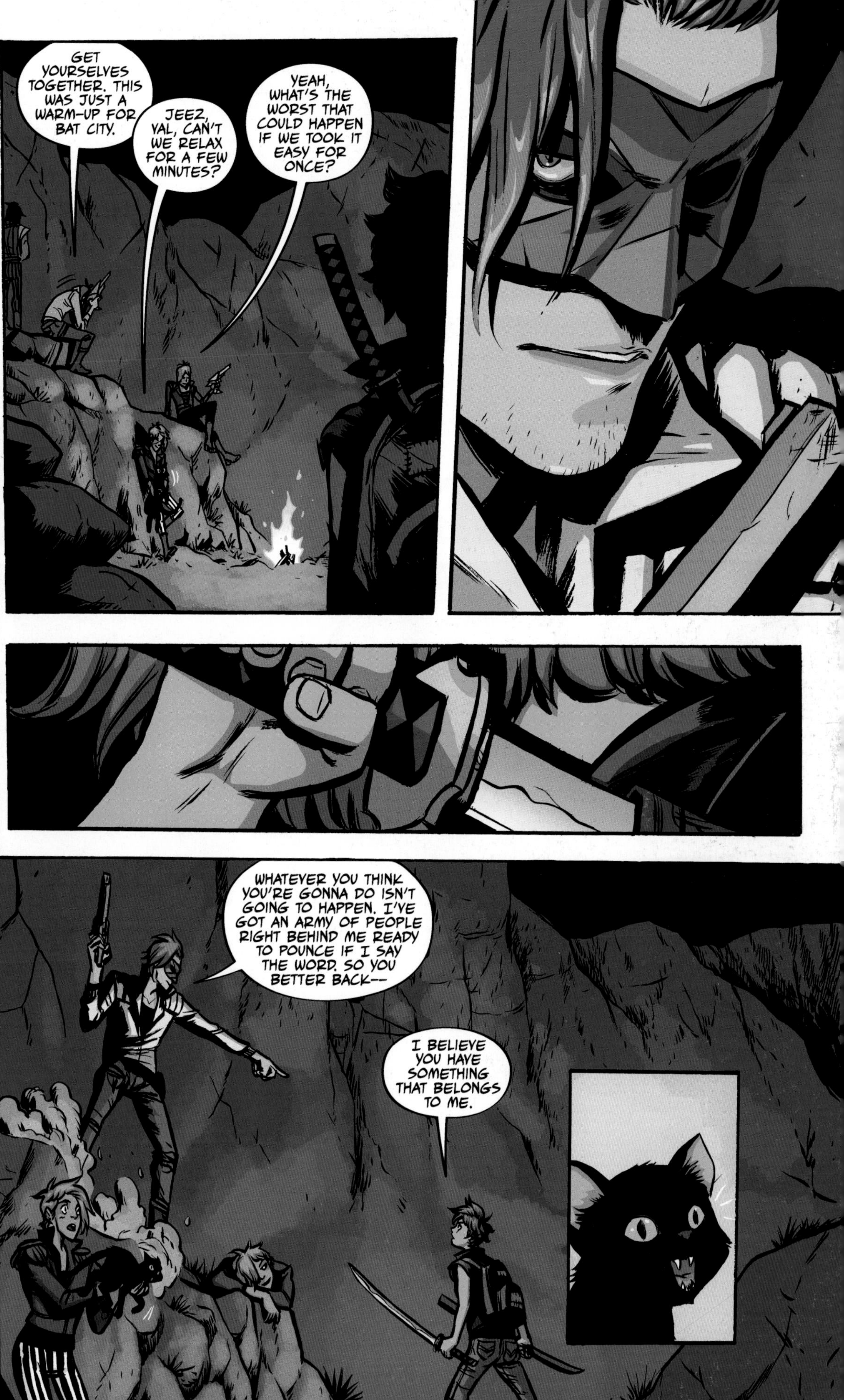
GET YOURSELVES TOGETHER. THIS WAS JUST A WARM-UP FOR BAT CITY.
JEEZ, VAL, CAN'T WE RELAX FOR A FEW MINUTES?
YEAH, WHAT'S THE WORST THAT COULD HAPPEN IF WE TOOK IT EASY FOR ONCE?
WHATEVER YOU THINK YOU'RE GONNA DO ISN'T GOING TO HAPPEN. I'VE GOT AN ARMY OF PEOPLE RIGHT BEHIND ME READY TO POUNCE IF I SAY THE WORD. SO YOU BETTER BACK--
I BELIEVE YOU HAVE SOMETHING THAT BELONGS TO ME.

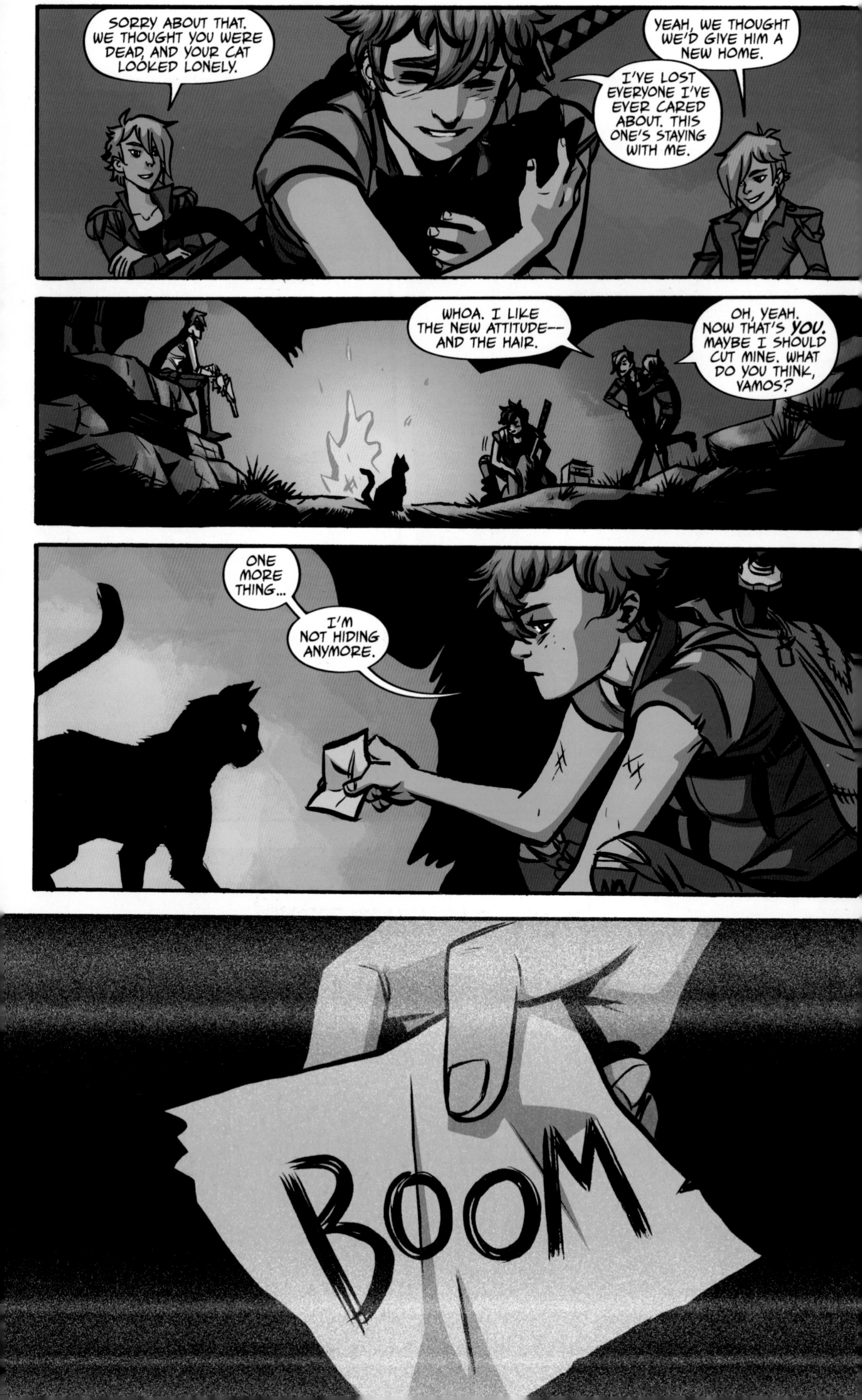
SORRY ABOUT THAT. WE THOUGHT YOU WERE DEAD, AND YOUR CAT LOOKED LONELY.
YEAH, WE THOUGHT WE'D GIVE HIM A NEW HOME.
I'VE LOST EVERYONE I'VE EVER CARED ABOUT. THIS ONE'S STAYING WITH ME.
WHOA. I LIKE THE NEW ATTITUDE-- AND THE HAIR.
OH, YEAH. NOW THAT'S YOU. MAYBE I SHOULD CUT MINE. WHAT DO YOU THINK, VAMOS?
ONE MORE THING...
I'M NOT HIDING ANYMORE.
BOOM

Chapter Six:

BOOM!

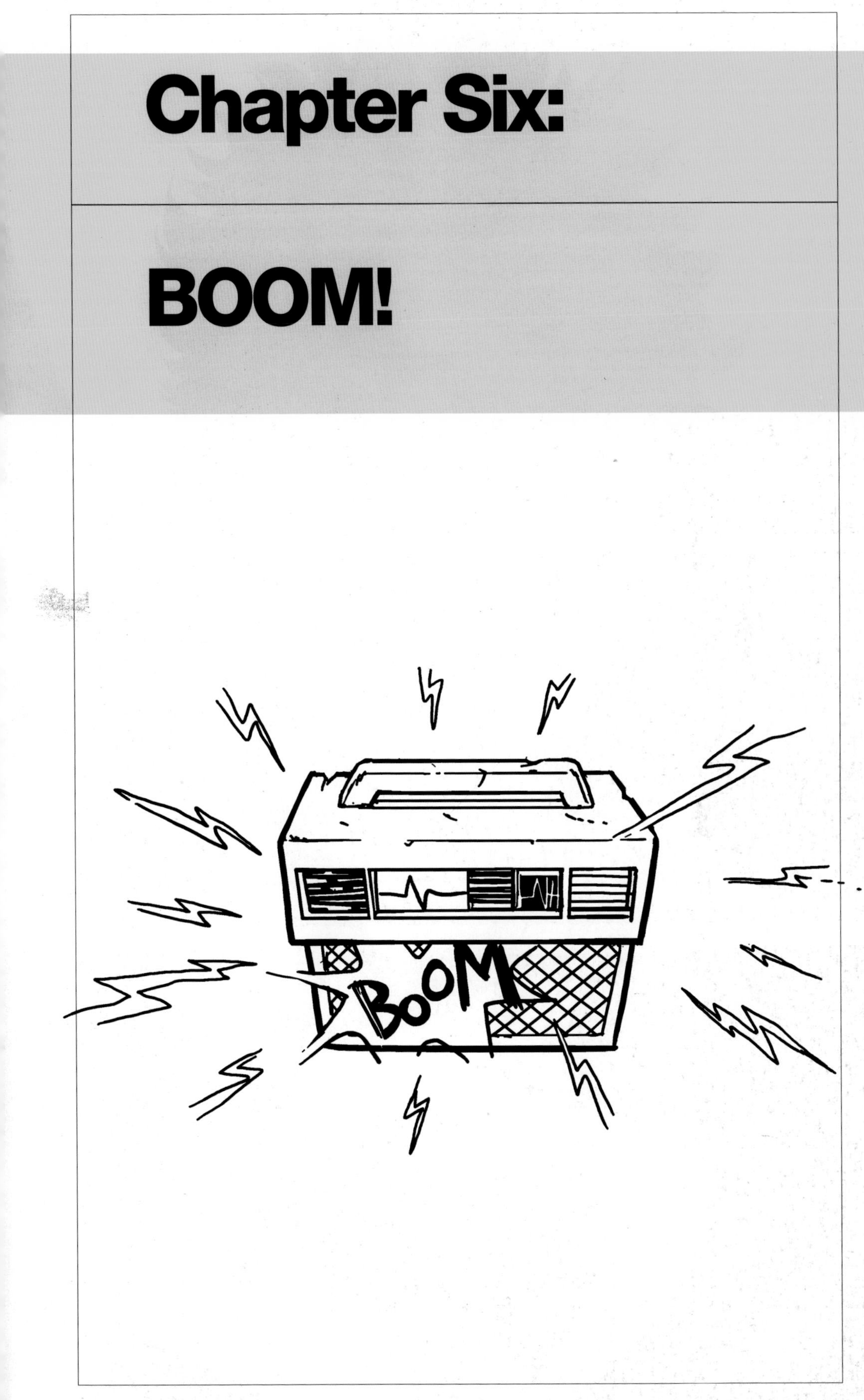
BOOM

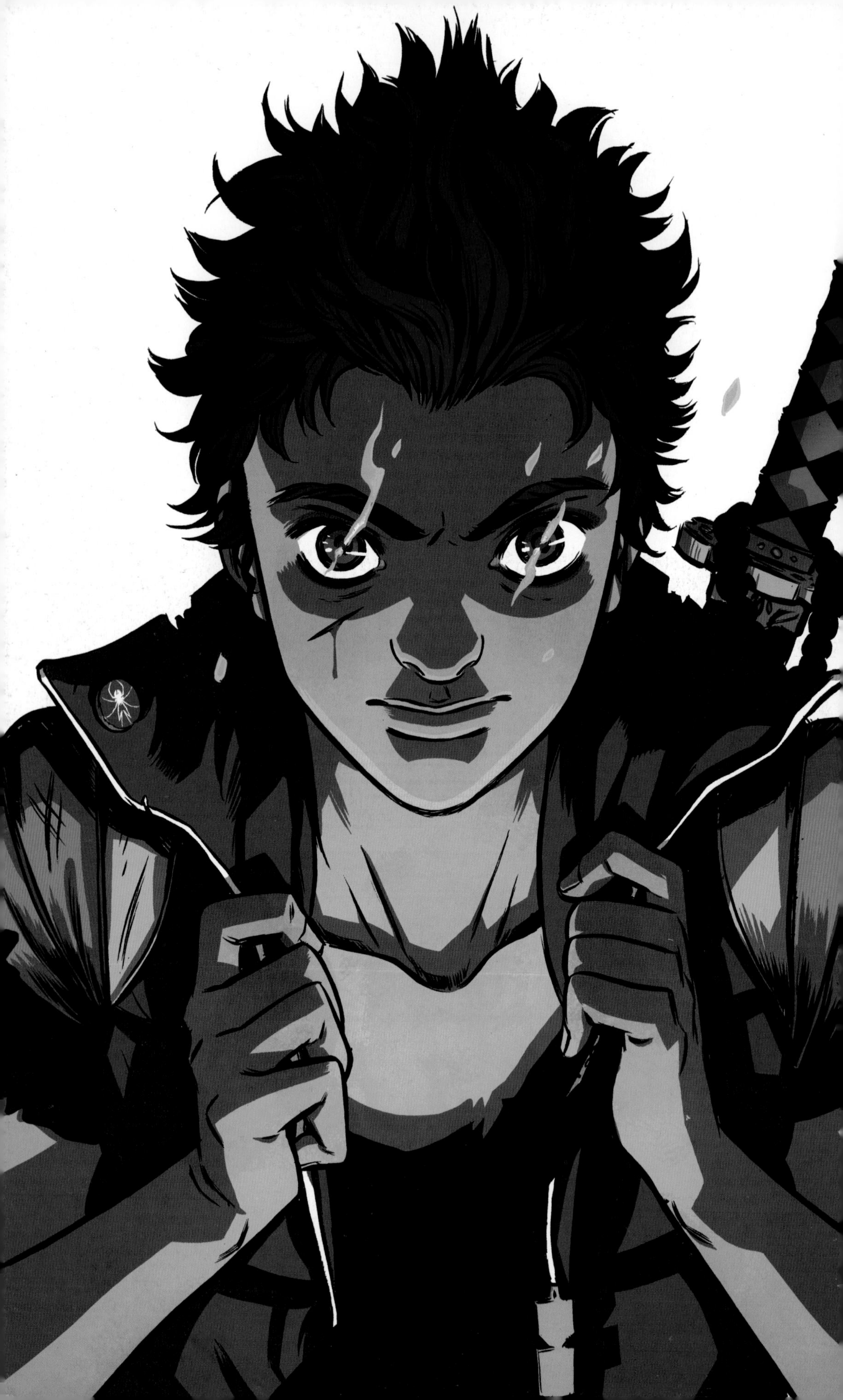

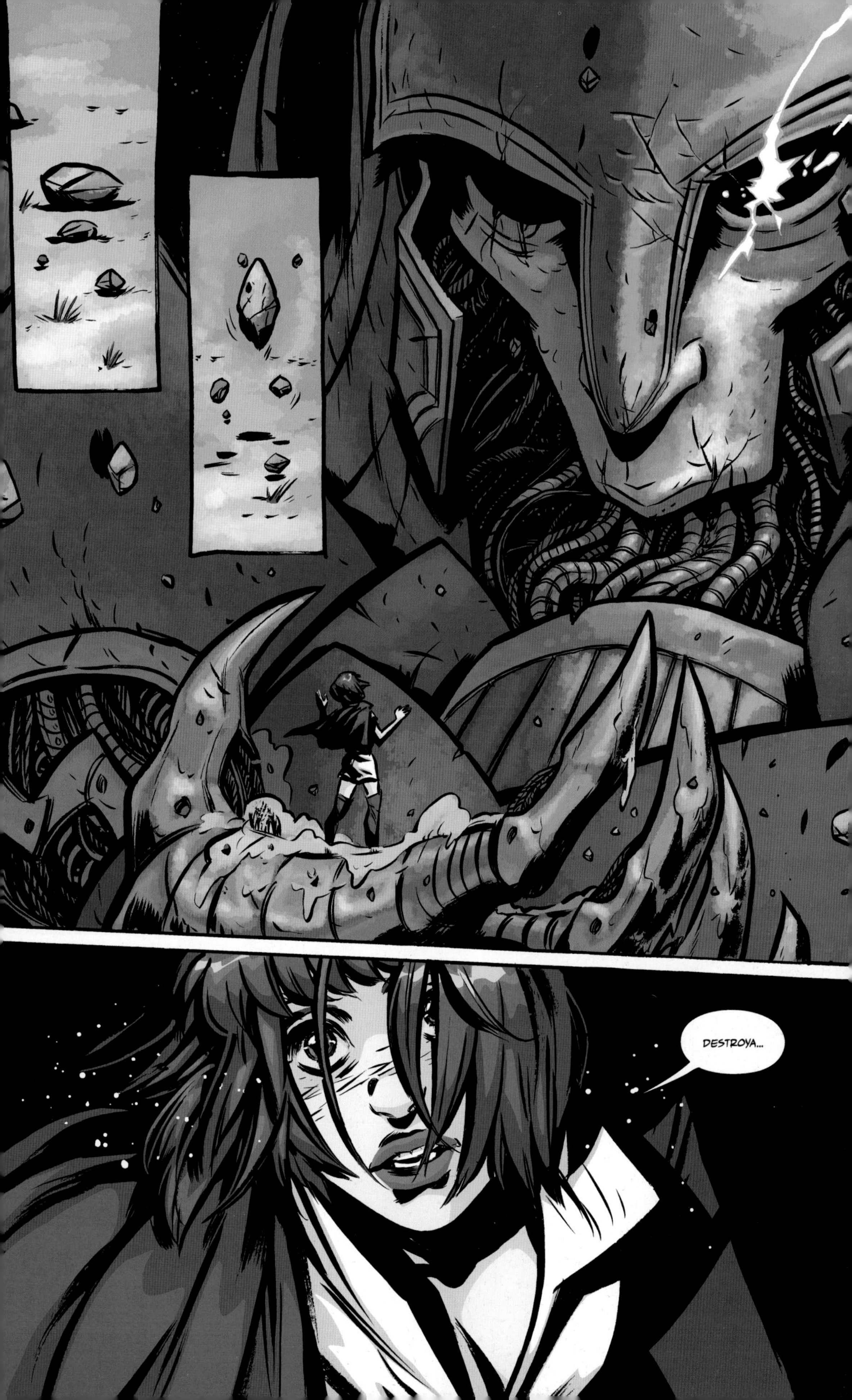
DESTROYA...

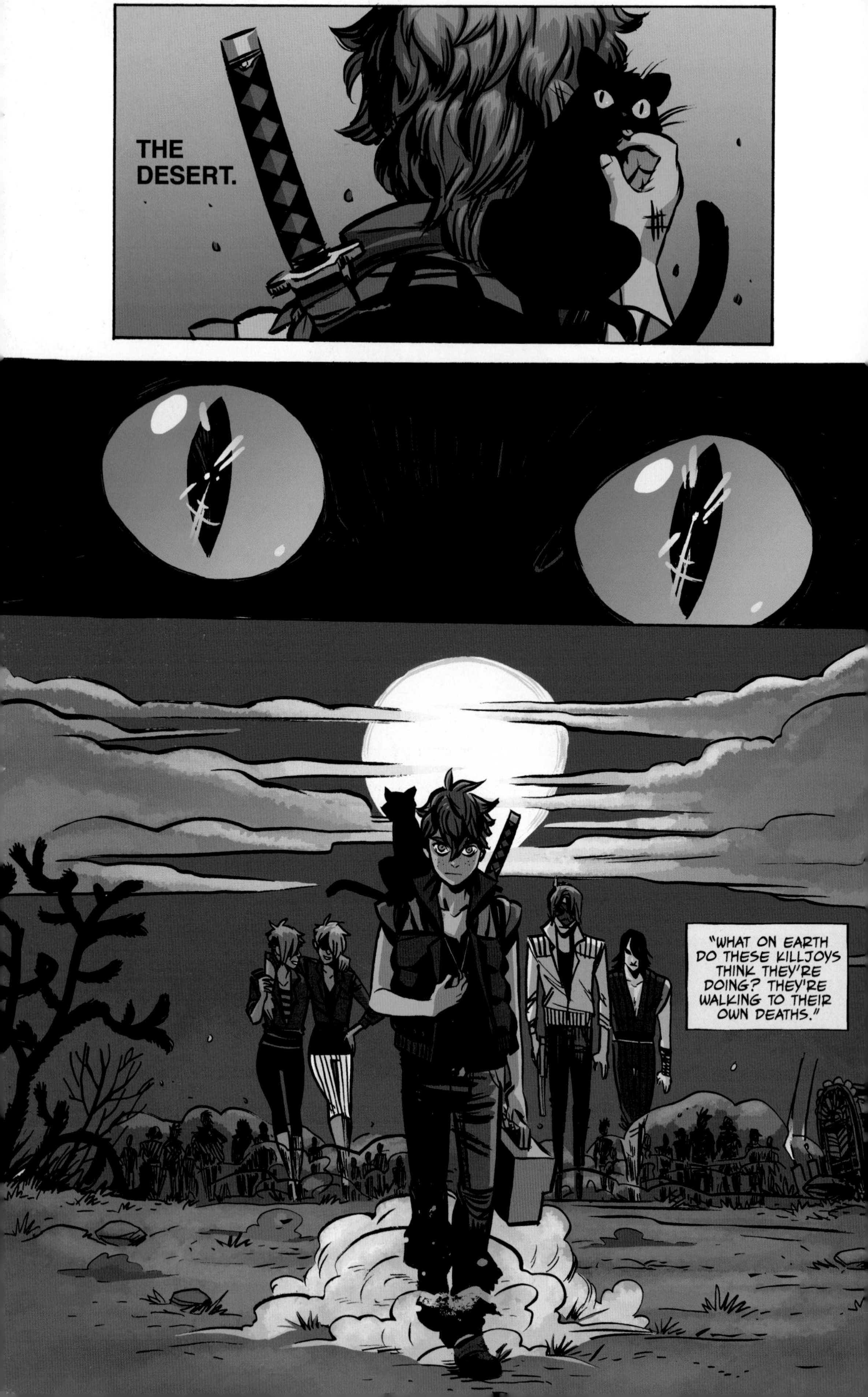
THE DESERT.
"WHAT ON EARTH DO THESE KILLJOYS THINK THEY'RE DOING? THEY'RE WALKING TO THEIR OWN DEATHS."

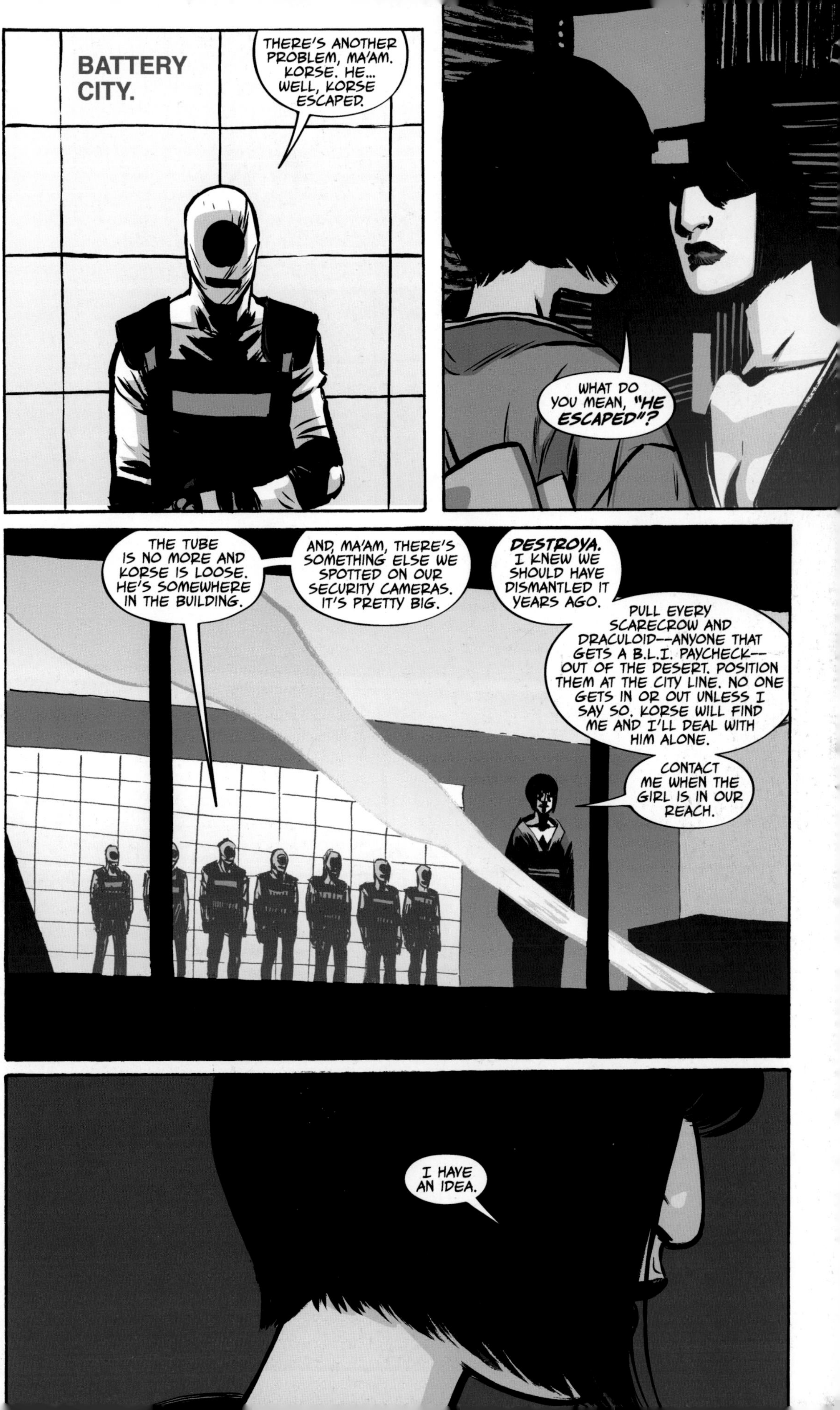
BATTERY CITY.
THERE'S ANOTHER PROBLEM, MA'AM. KORSE. HE... WELL, KORSE ESCAPED.
WHAT DO YOU MEAN, "HE ESCAPED"?
THE TUBE IS NO MORE AND KORSE IS LOOSE. HE'S SOMEWHERE IN THE BUILDING.
AND, MA'AM, THERE'S SOMETHING ELSE WE SPOTTED ON OUR SECURITY CAMERAS. IT'S PRETTY BIG.
DESTROYA. I KNEW WE SHOULD HAVE DISMANTLED IT YEARS AGO.
PULL EVERY SCARECROW AND DRACULOID--ANYONE THAT GETS A B.L.I. PAYCHECK--OUT OF THE DESERT. POSITION THEM AT THE CITY LINE. NO ONE GETS IN OR OUT UNLESS I SAY SO. KORSE WILL FIND ME AND I'LL DEAL WITH HIM ALONE.
CONTACT ME WHEN THE GIRL IS IN OUR REACH.
I HAVE AN IDEA.

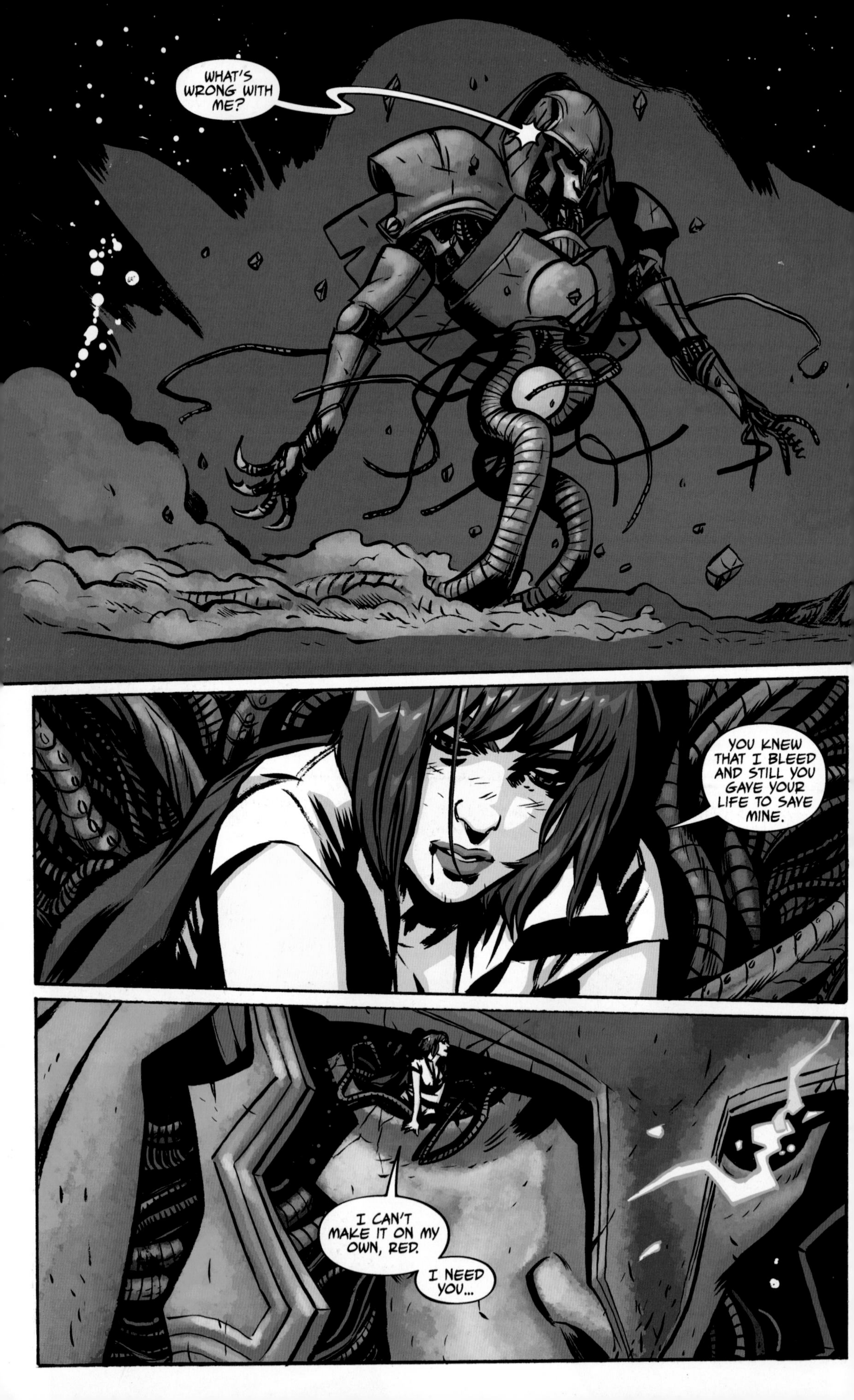
WHAT'S WRONG WITH ME?
YOU KNEW THAT I BLEED AND STILL YOU GAVE YOUR LIFE TO SAVE MINE.
I CAN'T MAKE IT ON MY OWN, RED.
I NEED YOU...

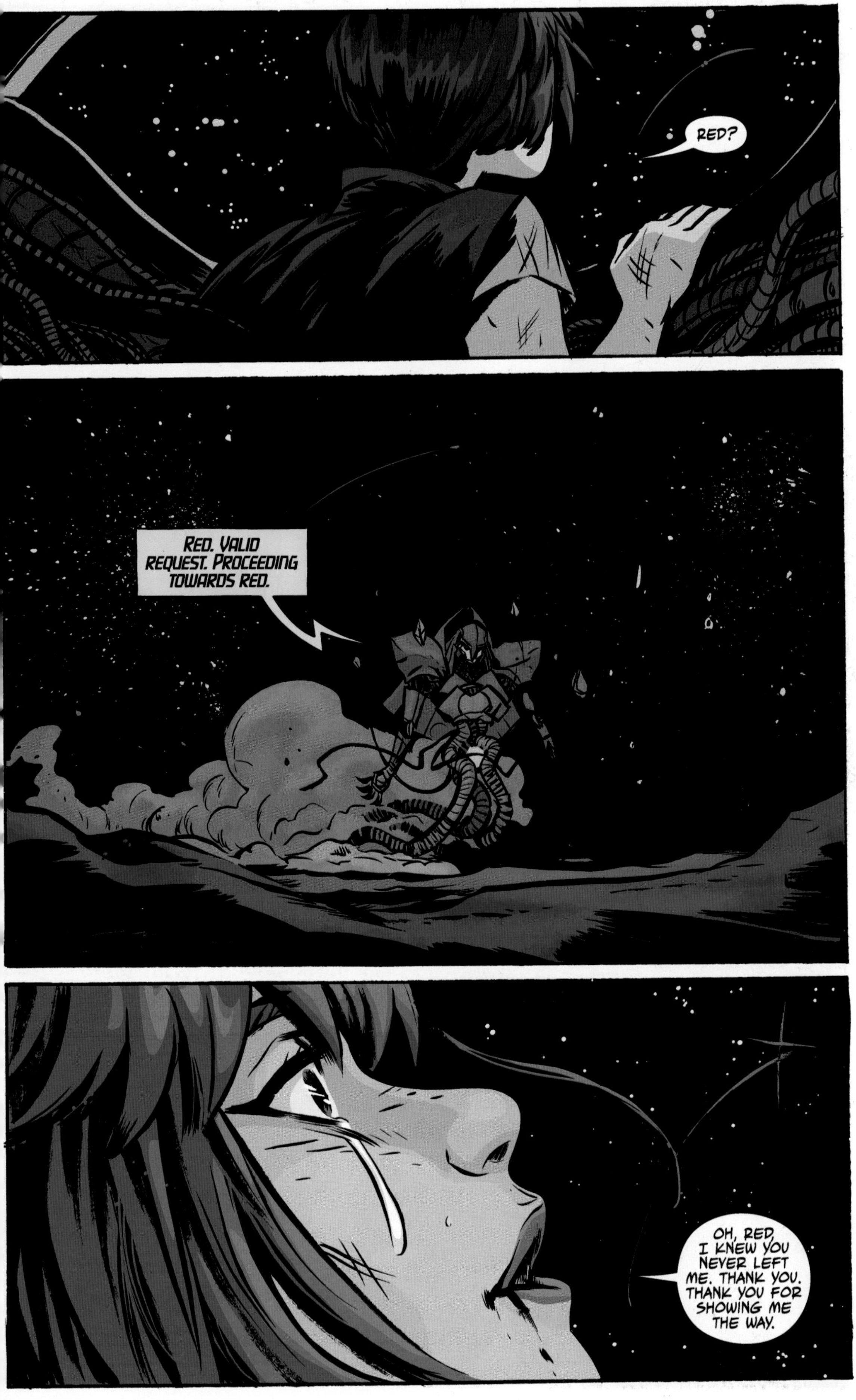
RED?
RED. VALID REQUEST. PROCEEDING TOWARDS RED.
OH, RED, I KNEW YOU NEVER LEFT ME. THANK YOU. THANK YOU FOR SHOWING ME THE WAY.

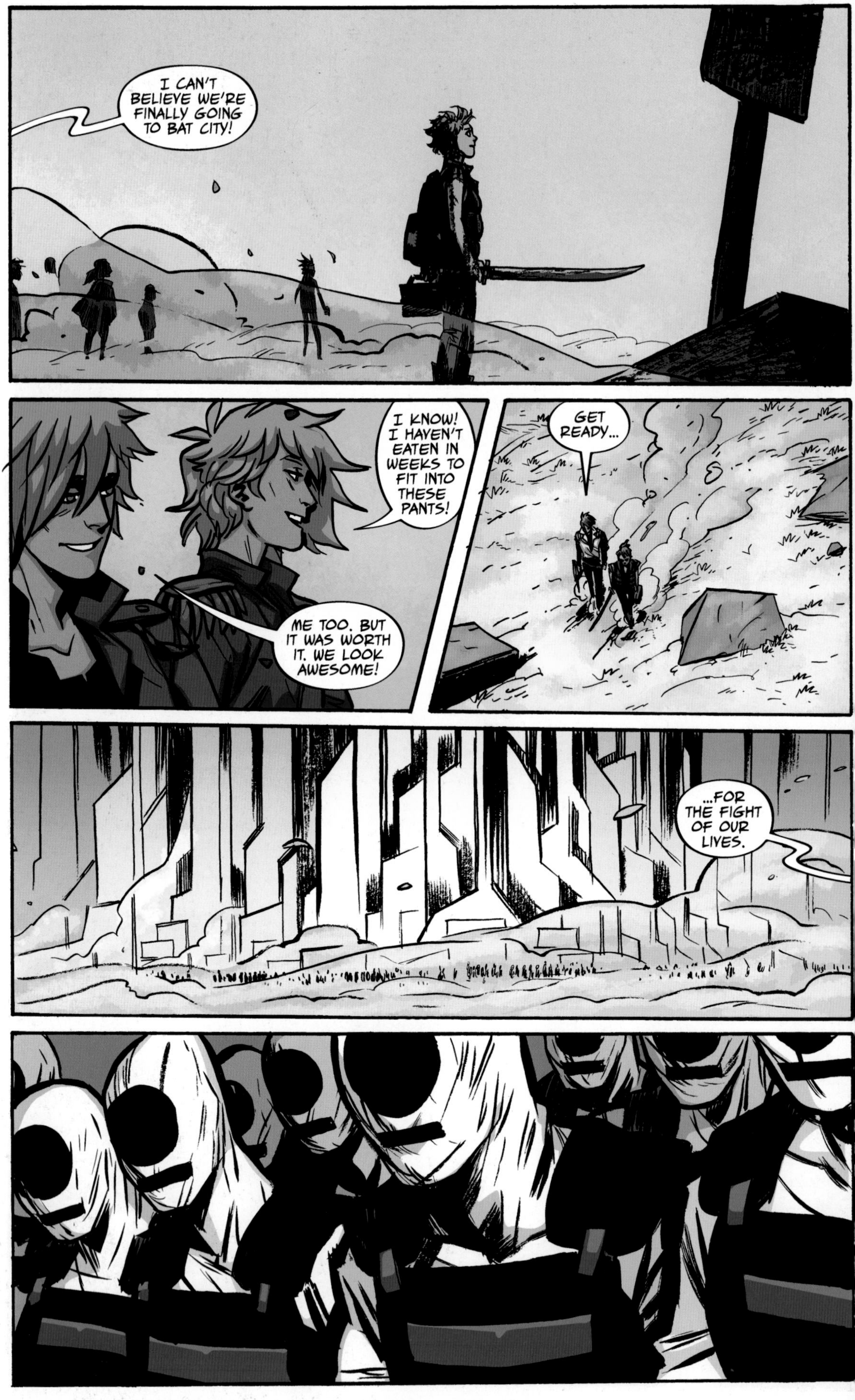

I CAN'T BELIEVE WE'RE FINALLY GOING TO BAT CITY!
I KNOW! I HAVEN'T EATEN IN WEEKS TO FIT INTO THESE PANTS!
ME TOO. BUT IT WAS WORTH IT. WE LOOK AWESOME!
GET READY...
...FOR THE FIGHT OF OUR LIVES.

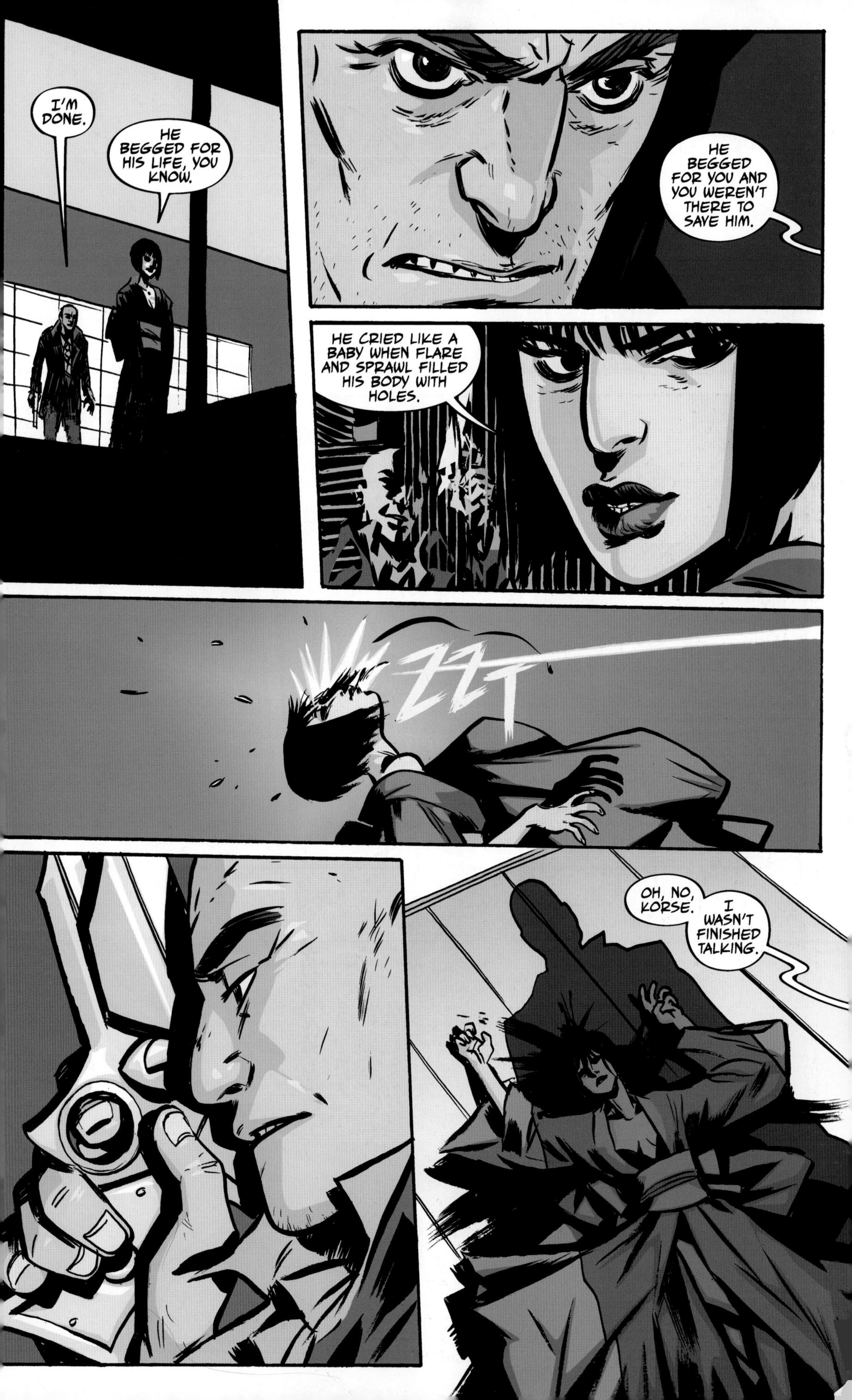
I'M DONE.
HE BEGGED FOR HIS LIFE, YOU KNOW.
HE BEGGED FOR YOU AND YOU WEREN'T THERE TO SAVE HIM.
HE CRIED LIKE A BABY WHEN FLARE AND SPRAWL FILLED HIS BODY WITH HOLES.
ZZT
OH, NO, KORSE.
I WASN'T FINISHED TALKING.

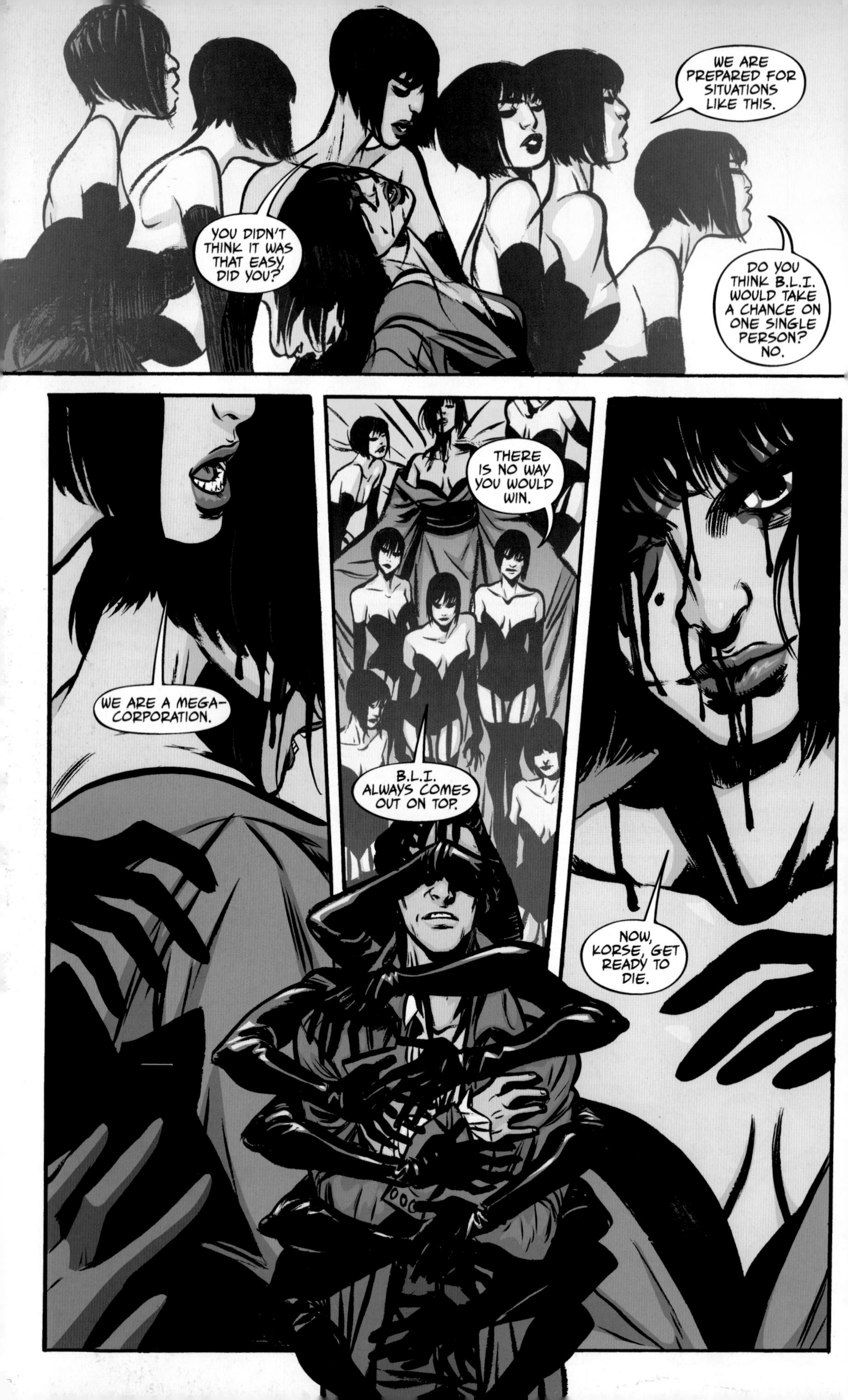
WE ARE PREPARED FOR SITUATIONS LIKE THIS.
YOU DIDN'T THINK IT WAS THAT EASY, DID YOU?
DO YOU THINK B.L.I. WOULD TAKE A CHANCE ON ONE SINGLE PERSON? NO.
WE ARE A MEGA-CORPORATION.
THERE IS NO WAY YOU WOULD WIN.
B.L.I. ALWAYS COMES OUT ON TOP.
NOW, KORSE, GET READY TO DIE.

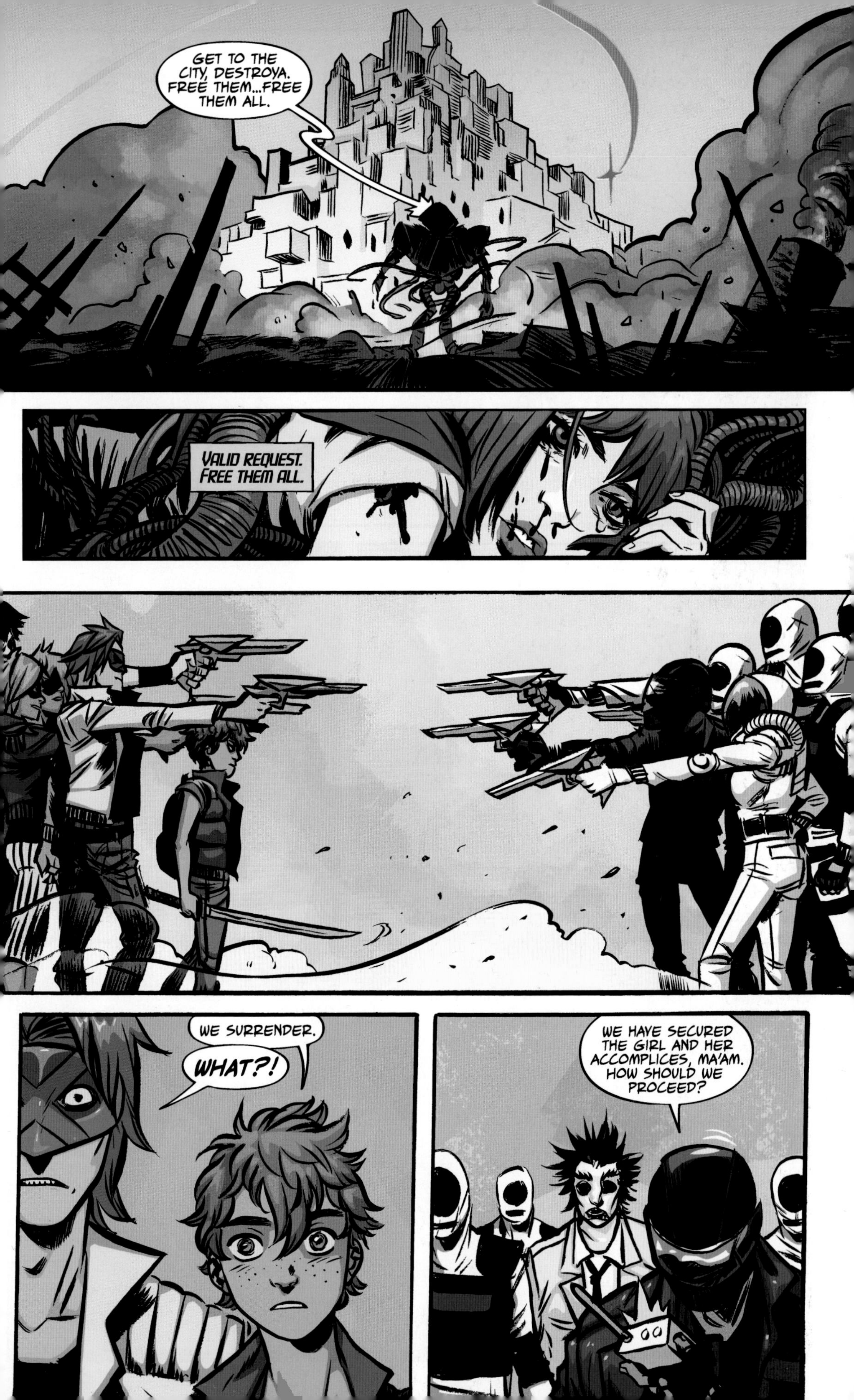
GET TO THE CITY, DESTROYA. FREE THEM...FREE THEM ALL.
VALID REQUEST. FREE THEM ALL.
WE SURRENDER.
WHAT?!
WE HAVE SECURED THE GIRL AND HER ACCOMPLICES, MA'AM. HOW SHOULD WE PROCEED?

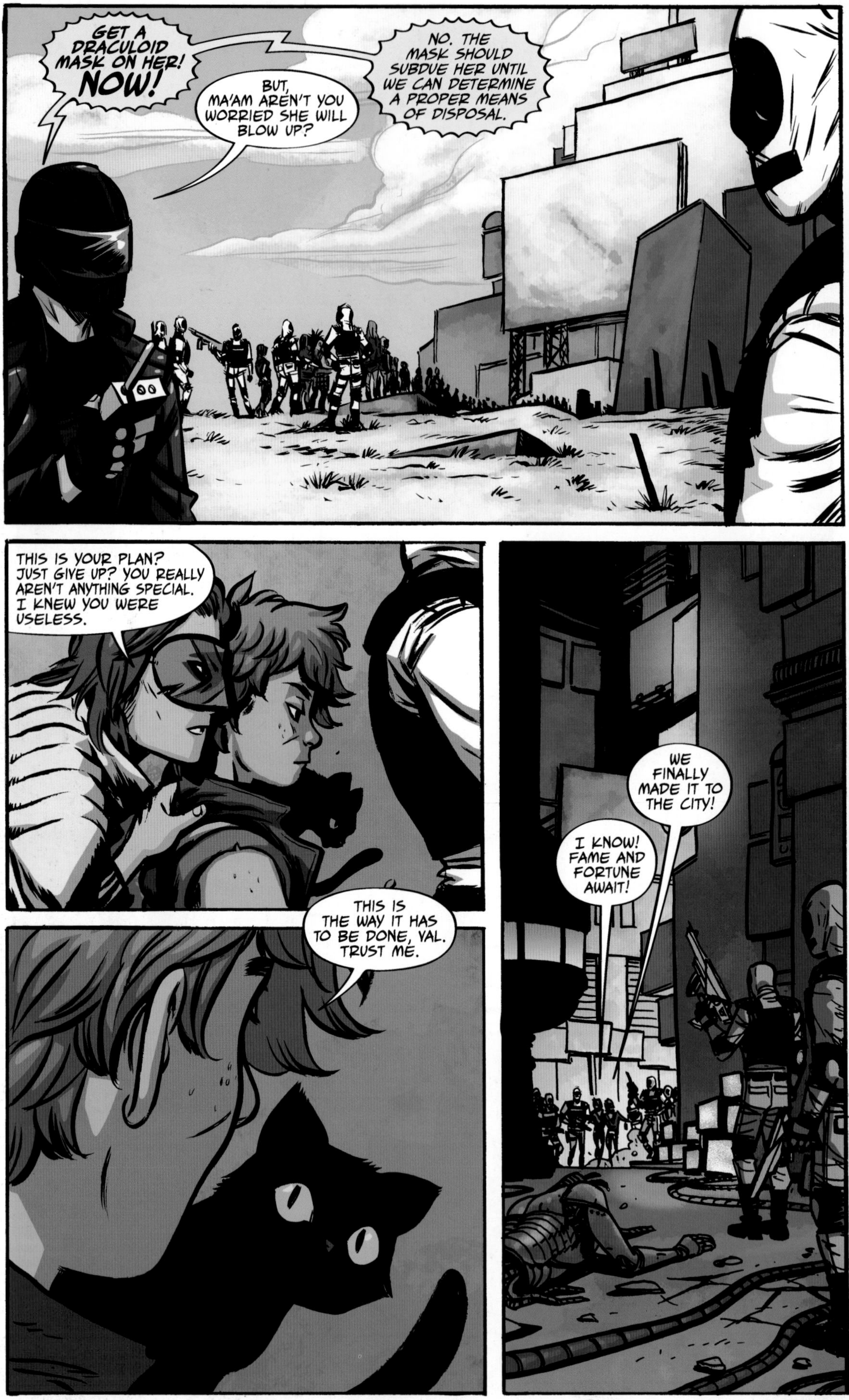
GET A DRACULOID MASK ON HER! NOW!
BUT, MA'AM AREN'T YOU WORRIED SHE WILL BLOW UP?
NO. THE MASK SHOULD SUBDUE HER UNTIL WE CAN DETERMINE A PROPER MEANS OF DISPOSAL.
THIS IS YOUR PLAN? JUST GIVE UP? YOU REALLY AREN'T ANYTHING SPECIAL. I KNEW YOU WERE USELESS.
THIS IS THE WAY IT HAS TO BE DONE, VAL. TRUST ME.
WE FINALLY MADE IT TO THE CITY!
I KNOW! FAME AND FORTUNE AWAIT!

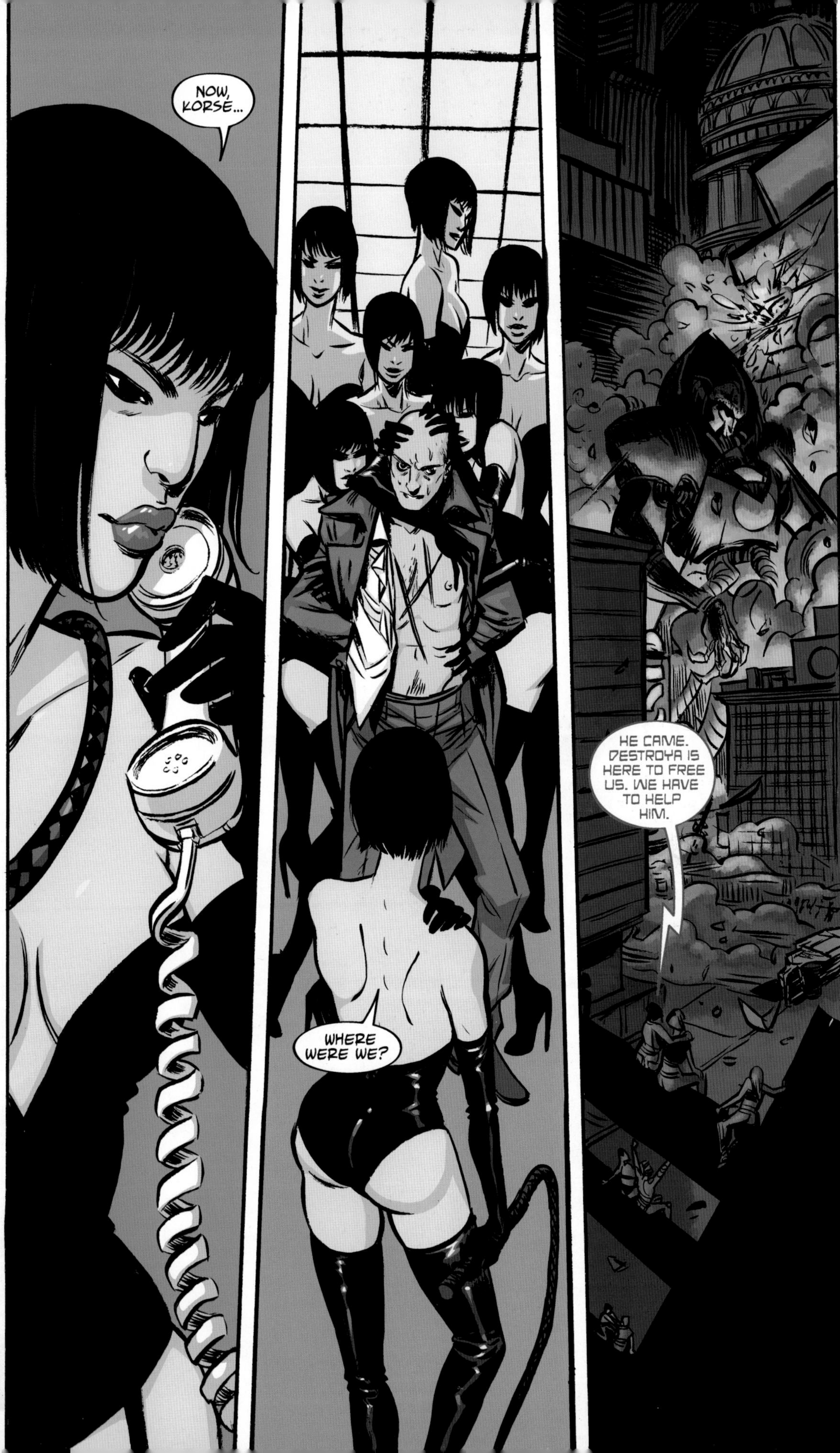
NOW, KORSE...
WHERE WERE WE?
HE CAME. DESTROYA IS HERE TO FREE US. WE HAVE TO HELP HIM.

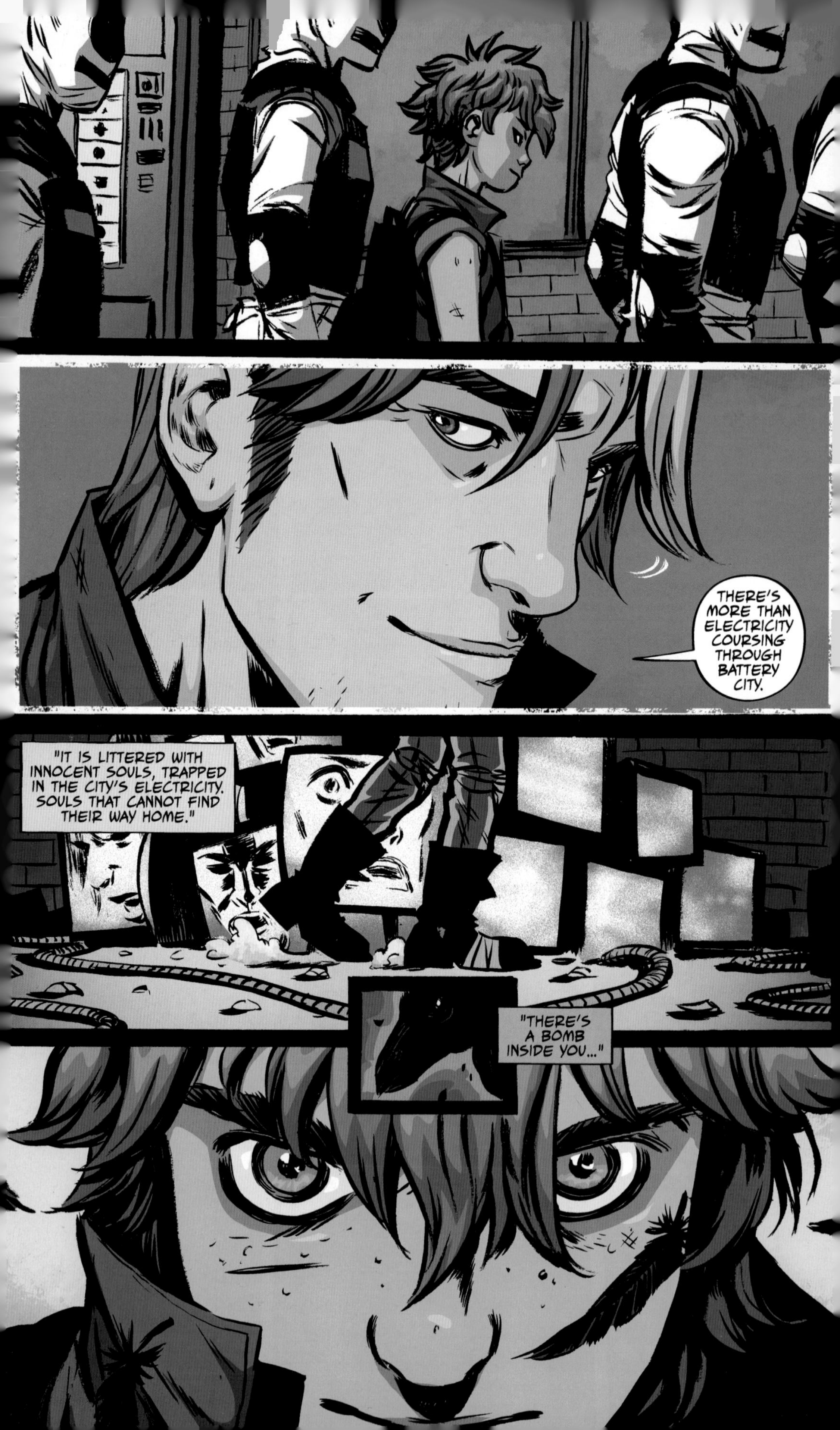
THERE'S MORE THAN ELECTRICITY COURSING THROUGH BATTERY CITY.
"IT IS LITTERED WITH INNOCENT SOULS, TRAPPED IN THE CITY'S ELECTRICITY. SOULS THAT CANNOT FIND THEIR WAY HOME."
"THERE'S A BOMB INSIDE YOU..."

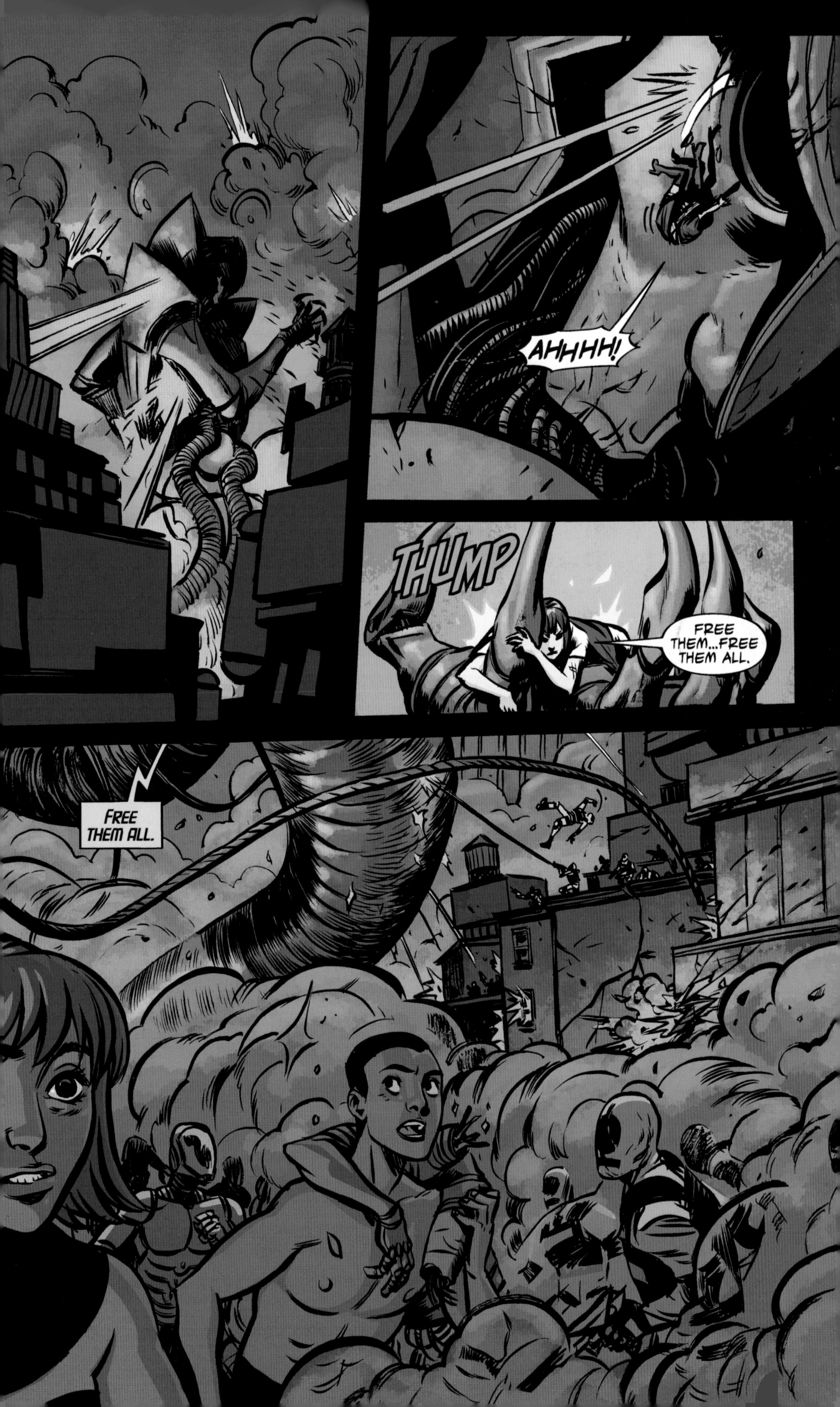
AHHHH!
THUMP
FREE THEM...FREE THEM ALL.
FREE THEM ALL.

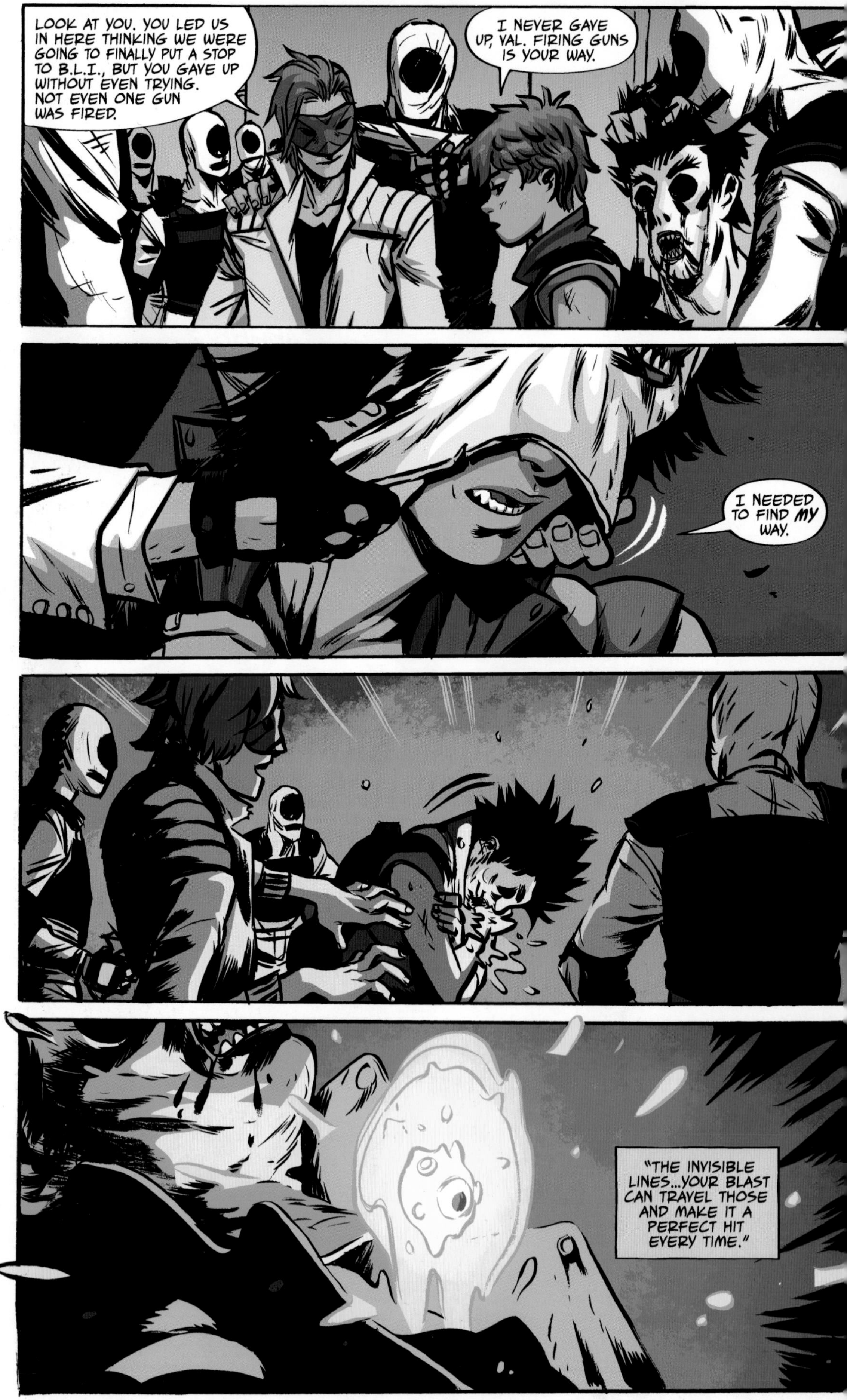

LOOK AT YOU. YOU LED US IN HERE THINKING WE WERE GOING TO FINALLY PUT A STOP TO B.L.I., BUT YOU GAVE UP WITHOUT EVEN TRYING. NOT EVEN ONE GUN WAS FIRED.
I NEVER GAVE UP, VAL. FIRING GUNS IS YOUR WAY.
I NEEDED TO FIND *MY* WAY.
"THE INVISIBLE LINES...YOUR BLAST CAN TRAVEL THOSE AND MAKE IT A PERFECT HIT EVERY TIME."

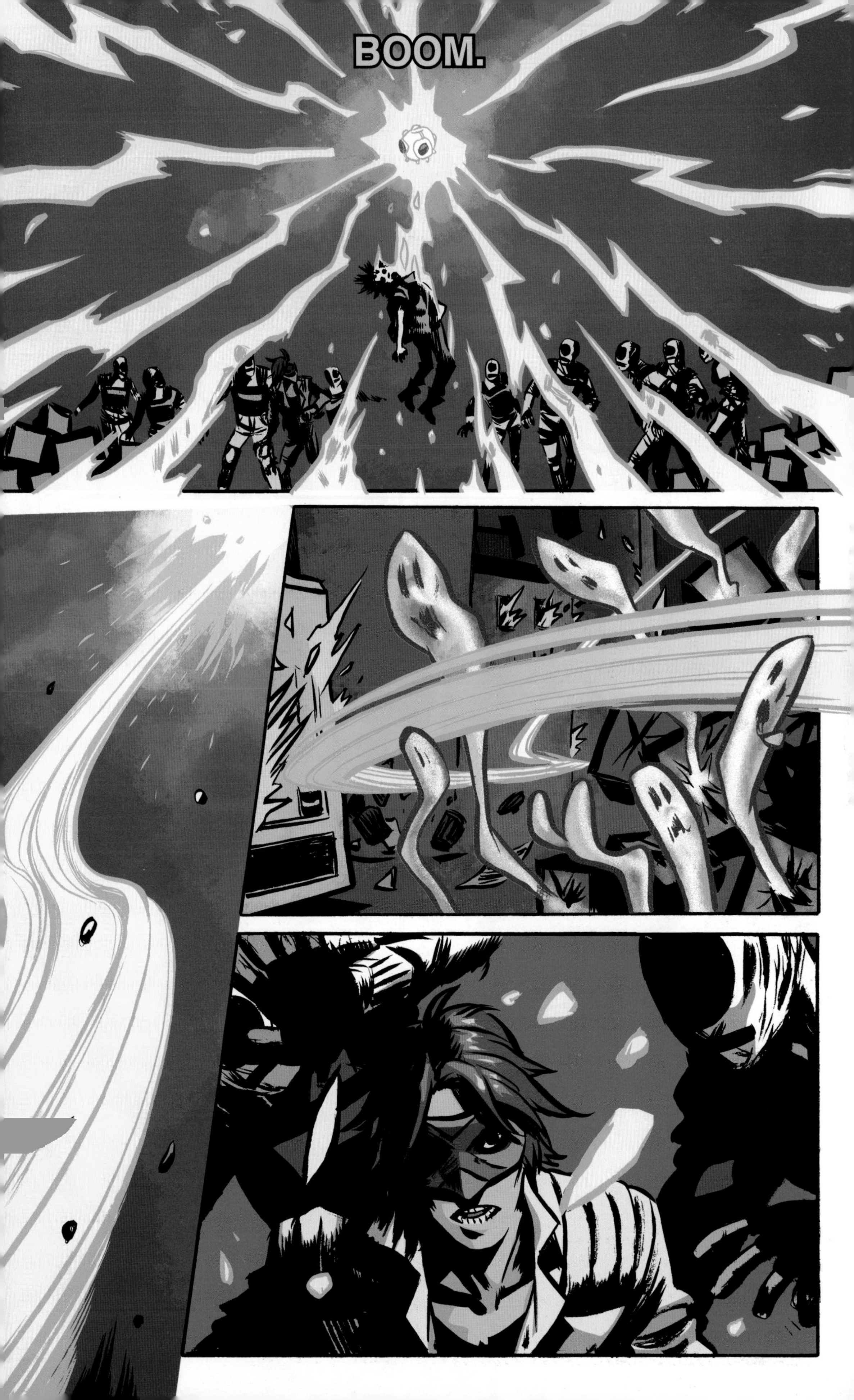
BOOM.

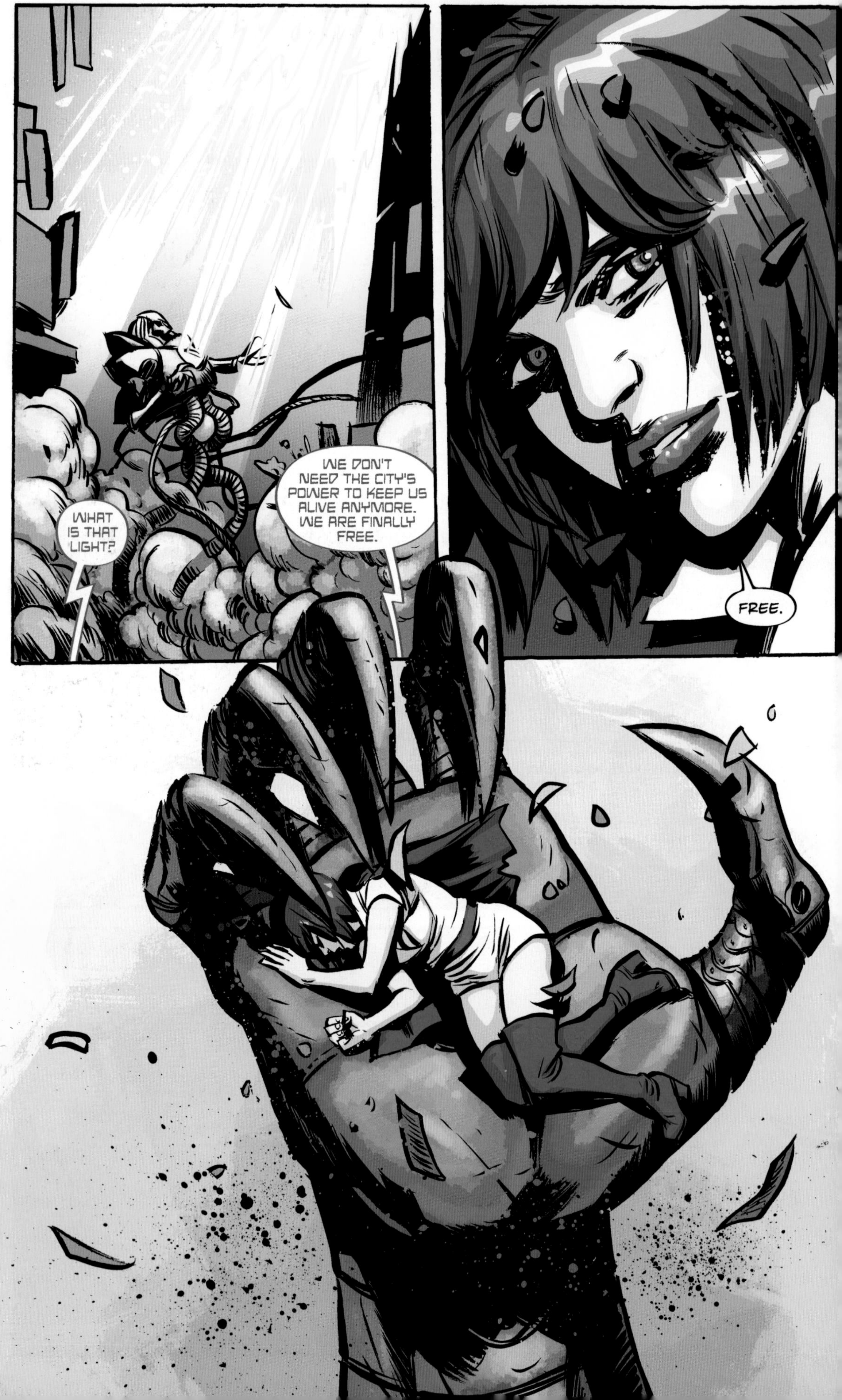
WHAT IS THAT LIGHT?
WE DON'T NEED THE CITY'S POWER TO KEEP US ALIVE ANYMORE. WE ARE FINALLY FREE.
FREE.

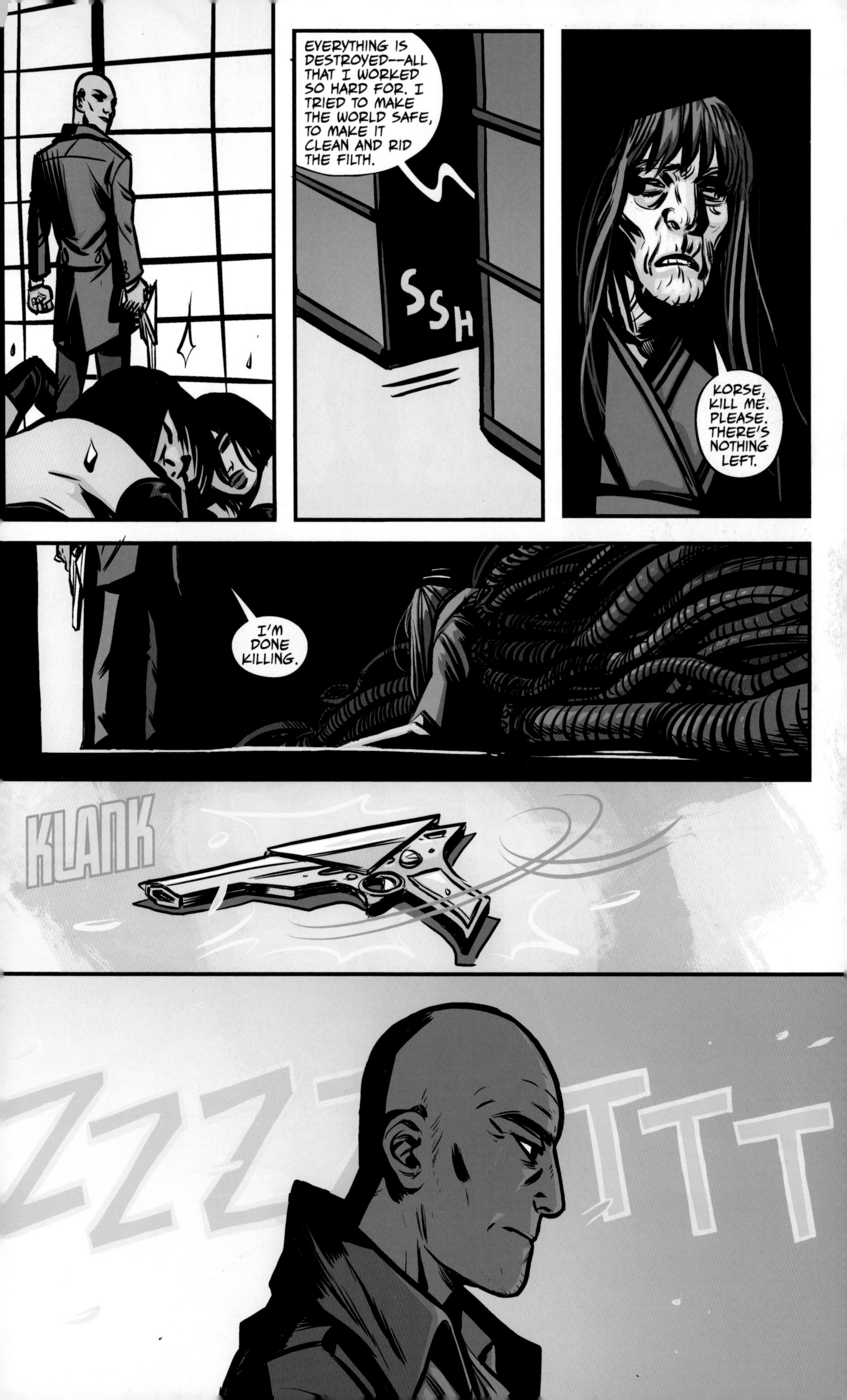
EVERYTHING IS DESTROYED--ALL THAT I WORKED SO HARD FOR. I TRIED TO MAKE THE WORLD SAFE, TO MAKE IT CLEAN AND RID THE FILTH.
SSH
KORSE, KILL ME. PLEASE. THERE'S NOTHING LEFT.
I'M DONE KILLING.
KLANK
ZZZTTTT

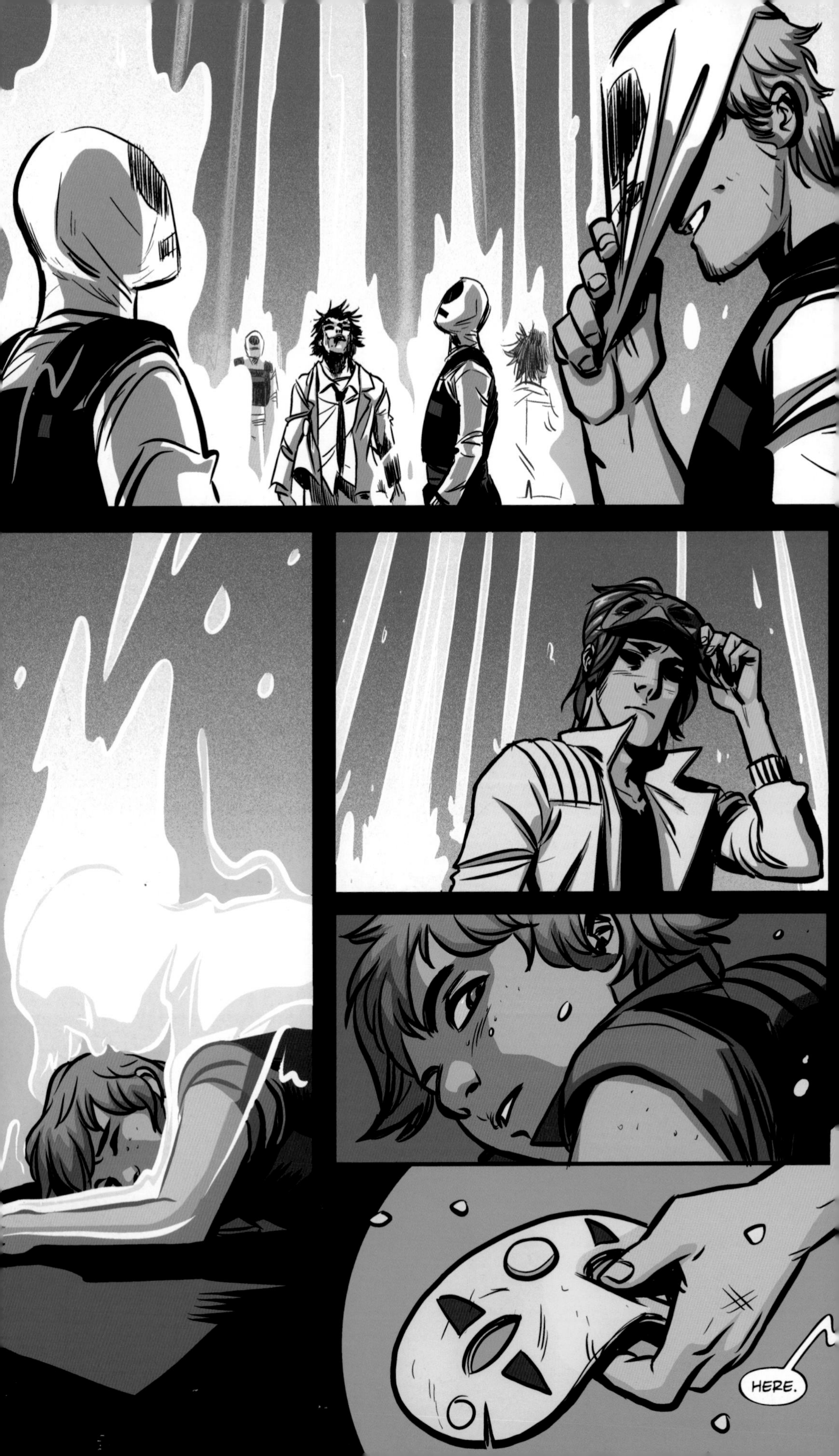
HERE.

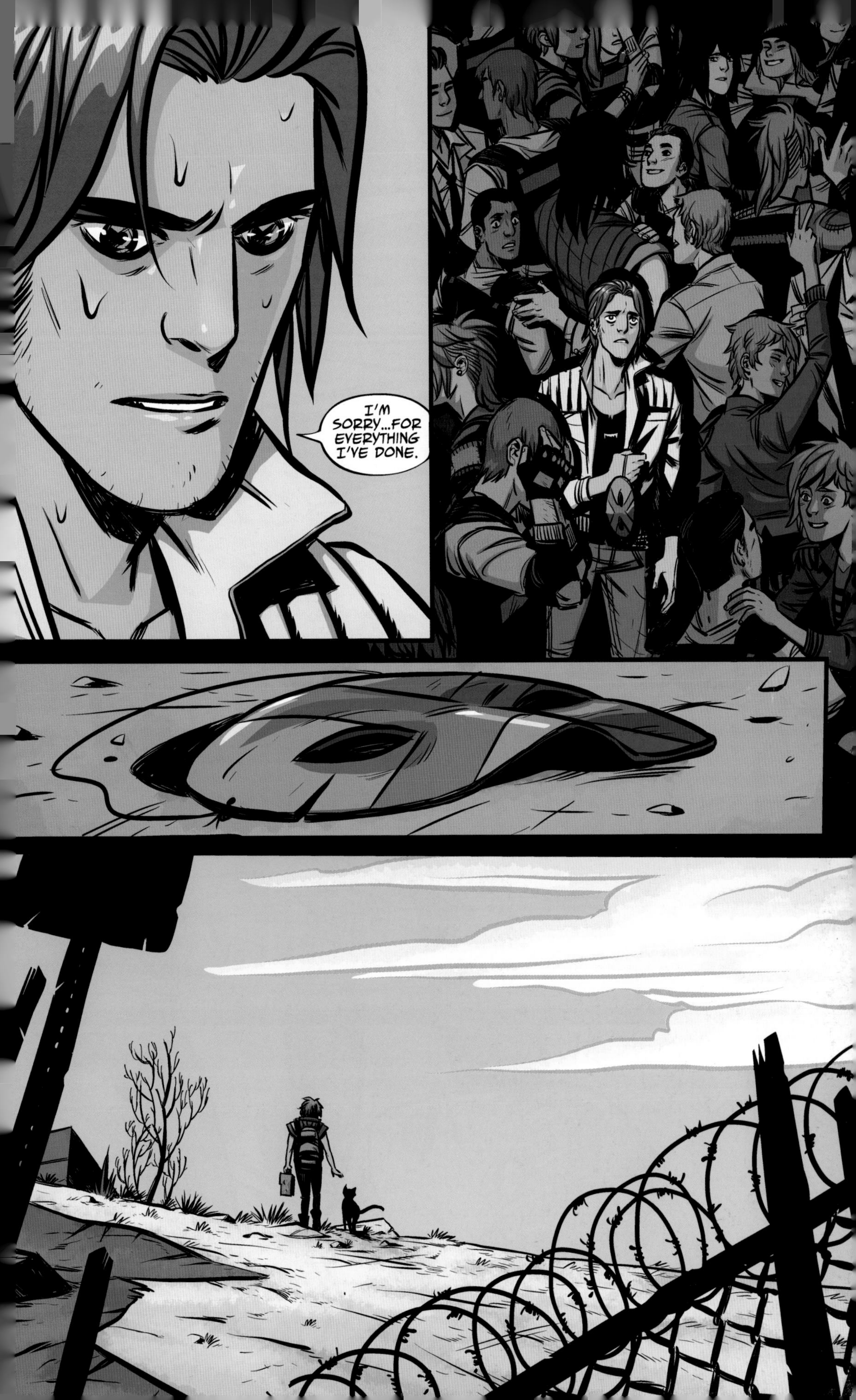
I'M SORRY...FOR EVERYTHING I'VE DONE.

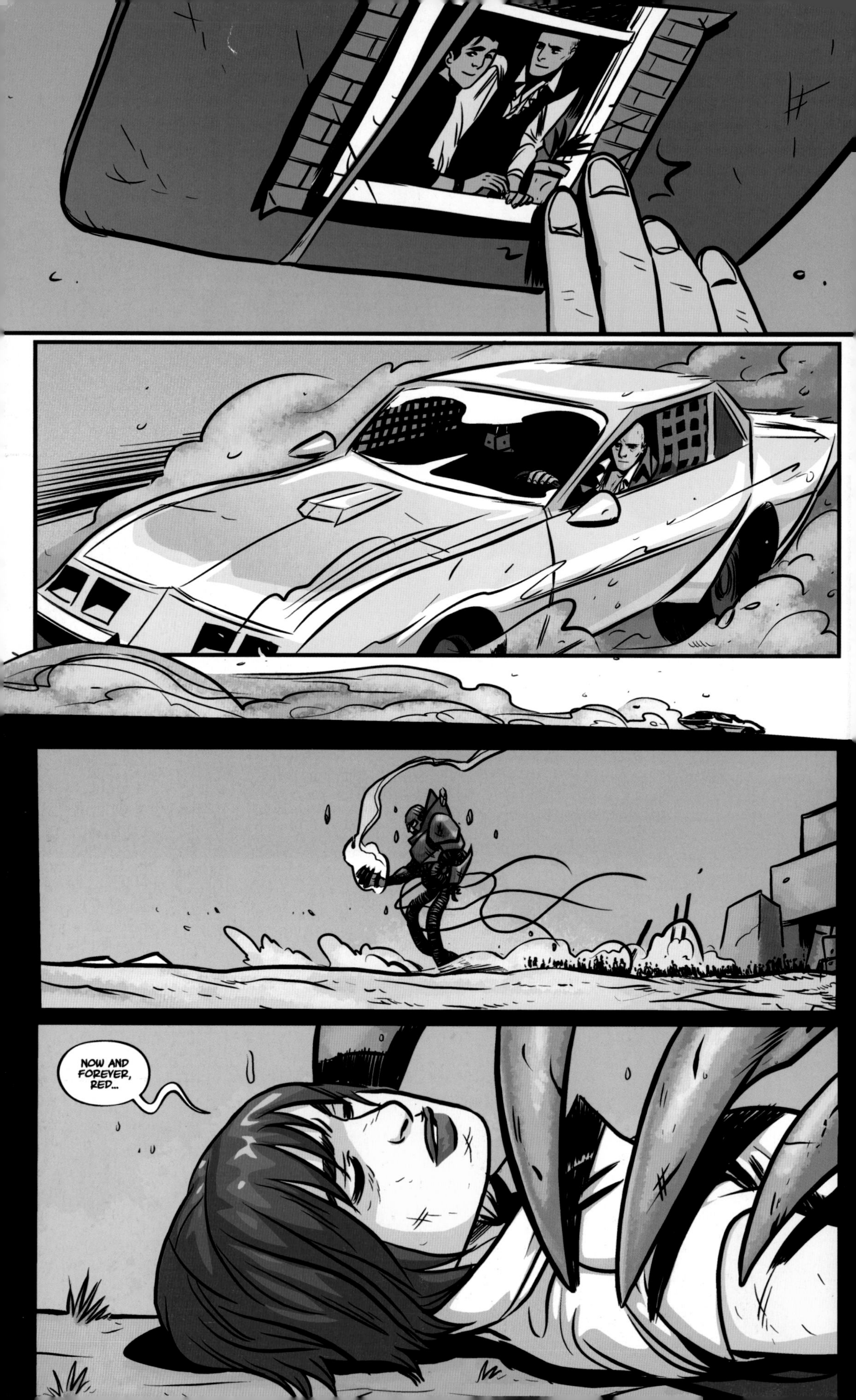
NOW AND FOREVER, RED...

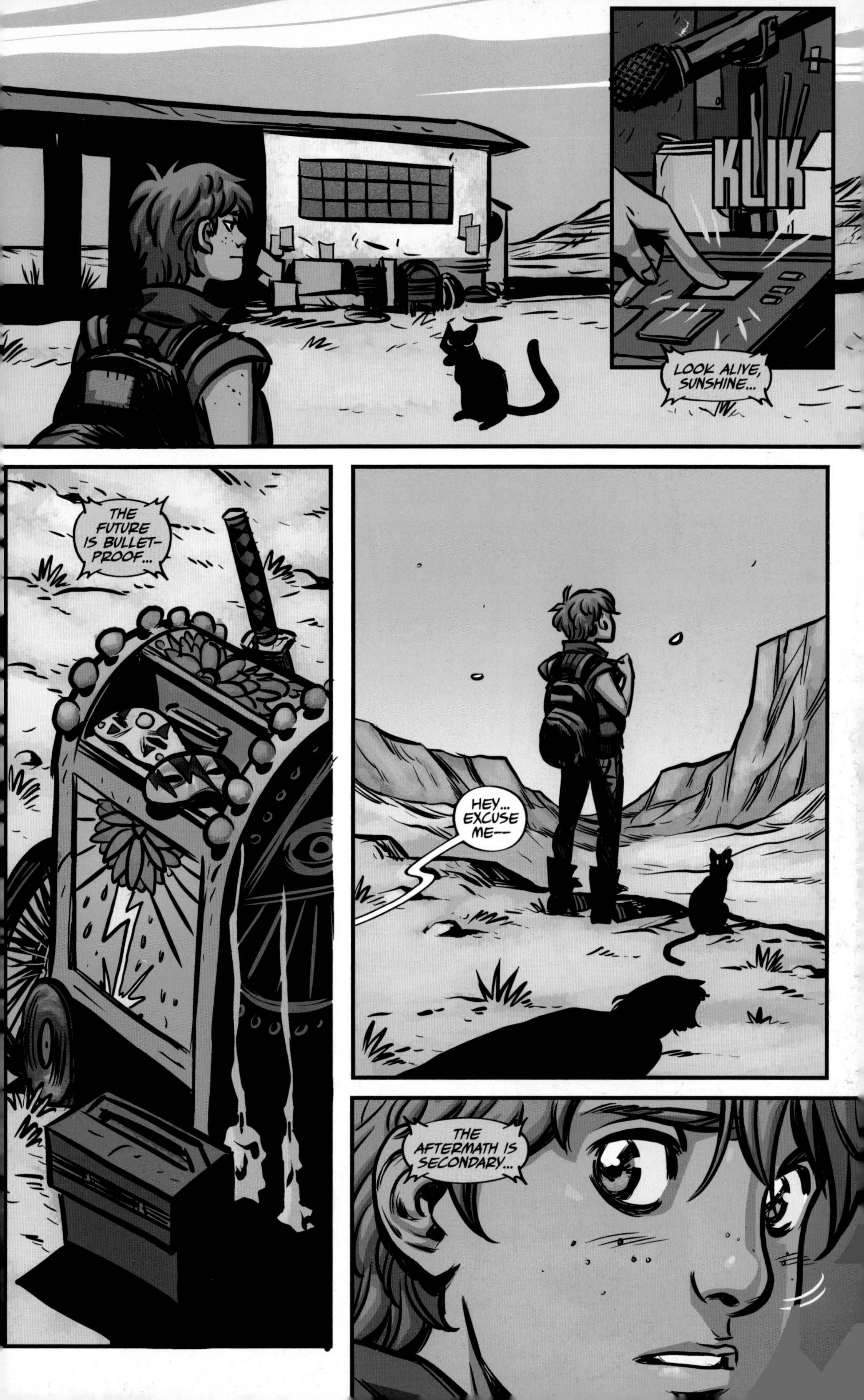
KLIK
LOOK ALIVE, SUNSHINE...
THE FUTURE IS BULLET-PROOF...
HEY... EXCUSE ME--
THE AFTERMATH IS SECONDARY...

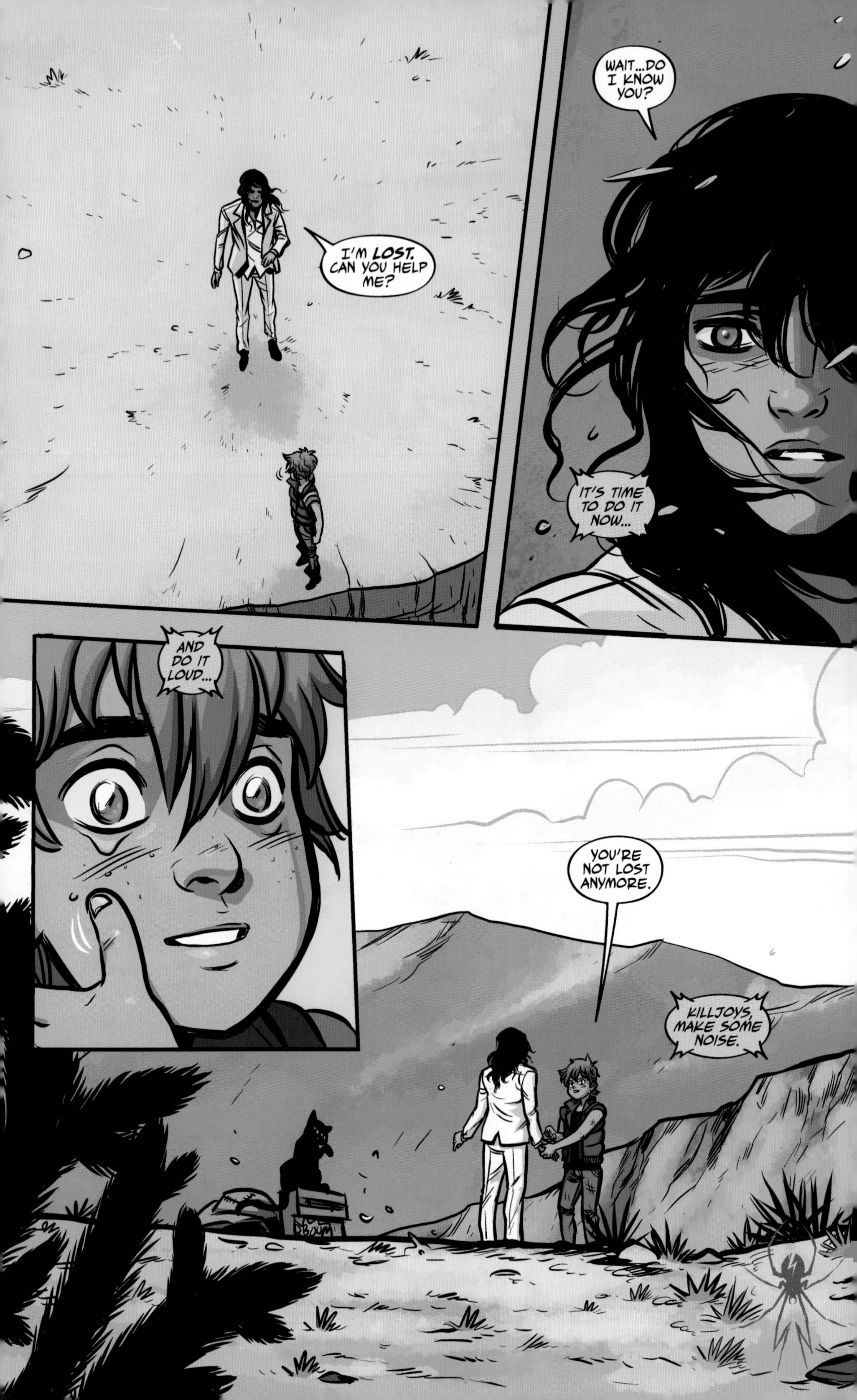
I'M LOST. CAN YOU HELP ME?
WAIT...DO I KNOW YOU?
IT'S TIME TO DO IT NOW...
AND DO IT LOUD...
YOU'RE NOT LOST ANYMORE.
KILLJOYS, MAKE SOME NOISE.

Bonus Feature:

DEAD SATELLITES

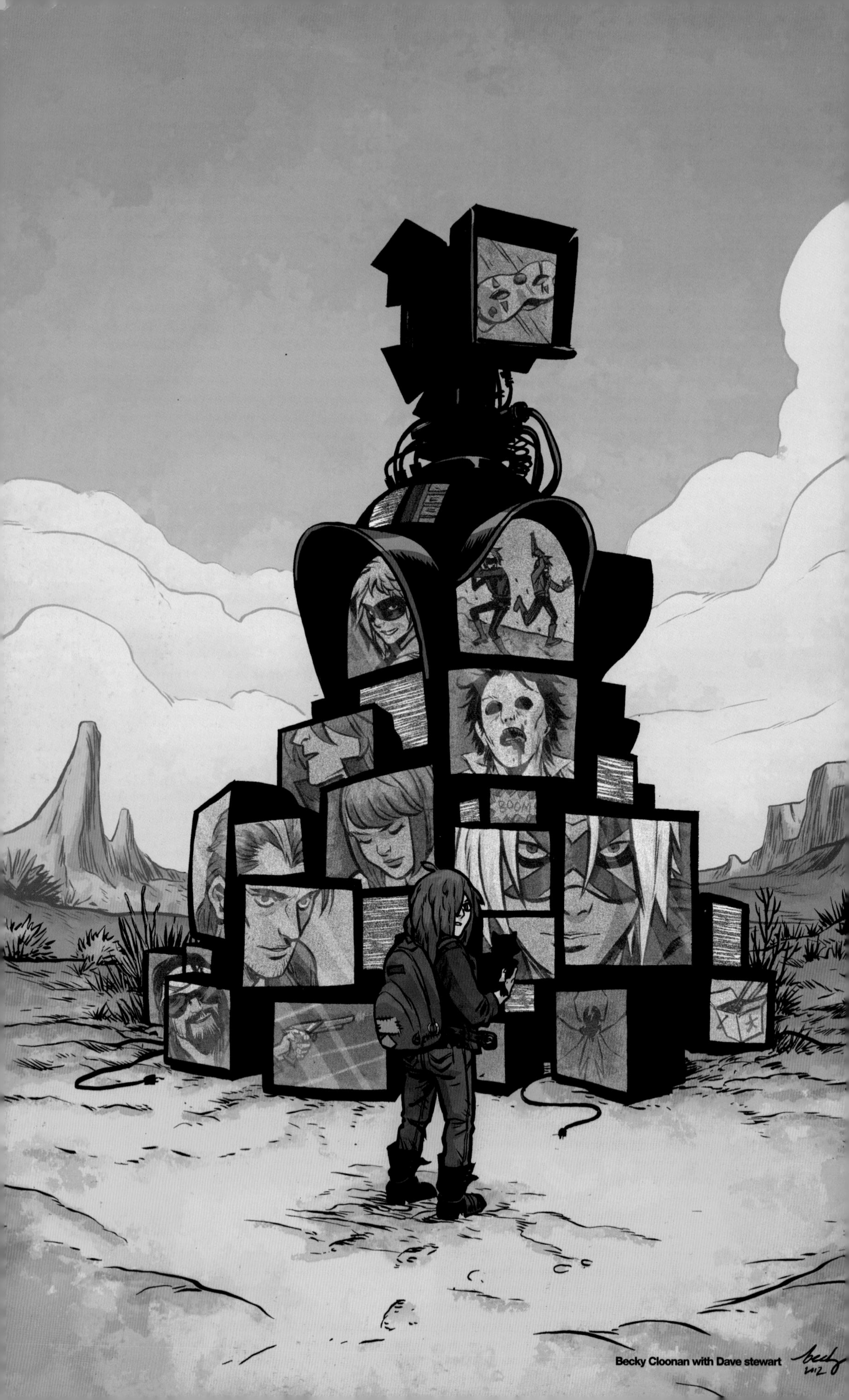
BOOM

Becky Cloonan with Dave stewart

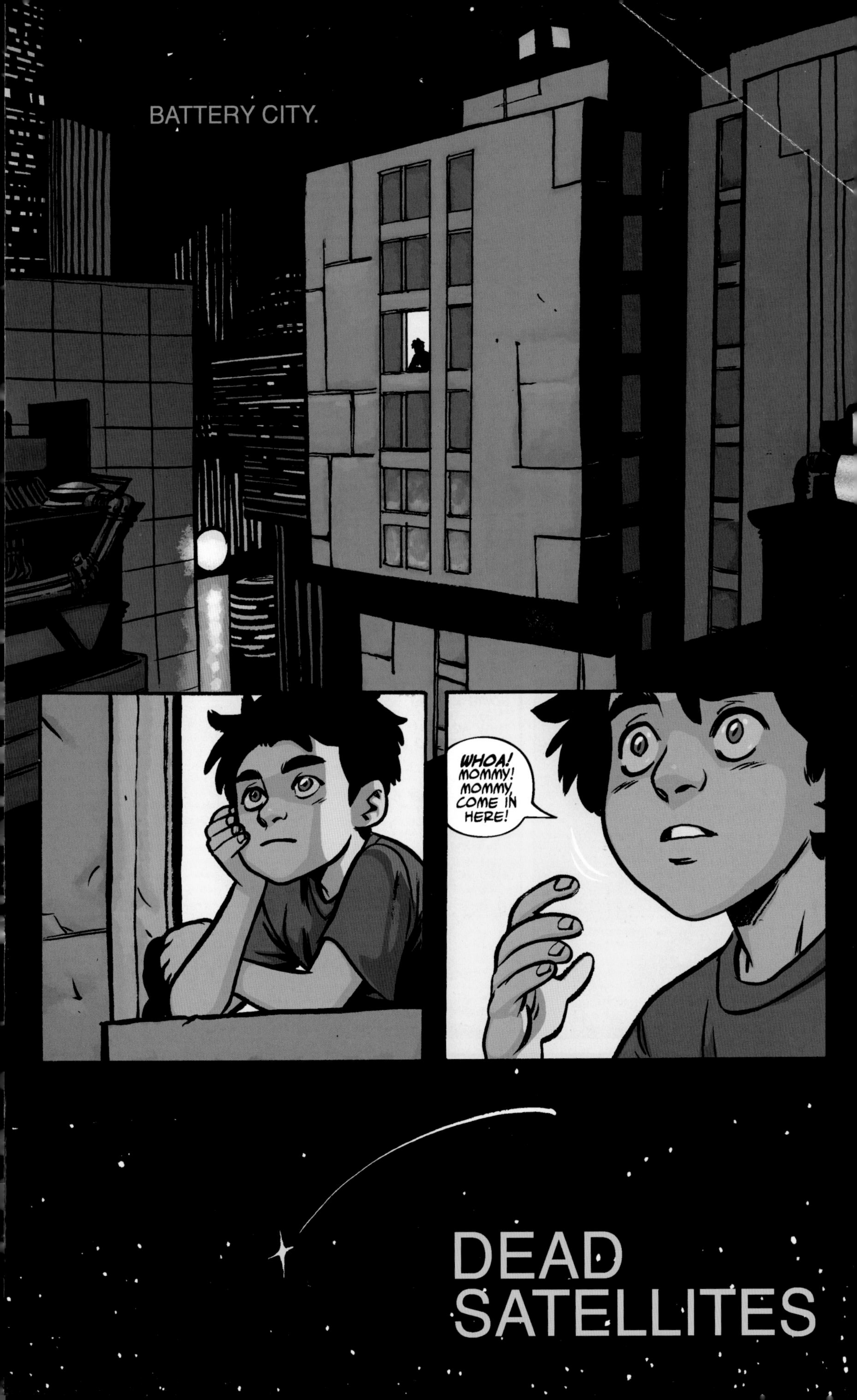
BATTERY CITY.
WHOA! MOMMY! MOMMY, COME IN HERE!
DEAD SATELLITES

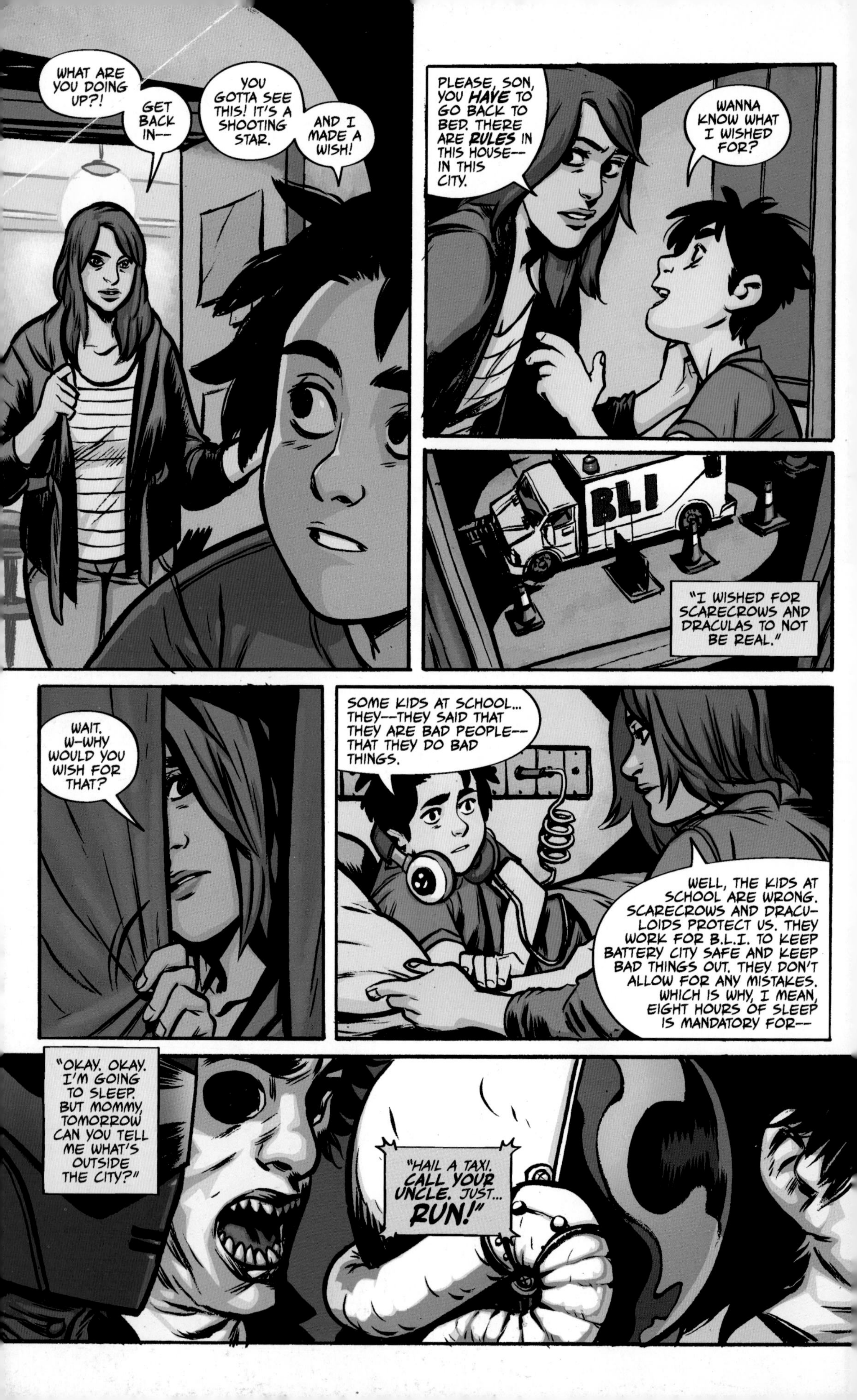
WHAT ARE YOU DOING UP?!
GET BACK IN--
YOU GOTTA SEE THIS! IT'S A SHOOTING STAR.
AND I MADE A WISH!
PLEASE, SON, YOU HAVE TO GO BACK TO BED. THERE ARE RULES IN THIS HOUSE-- IN THIS CITY.
WANNA KNOW WHAT I WISHED FOR?
BLI
"I WISHED FOR SCARECROWS AND DRACULAS TO NOT BE REAL."
WAIT. W-WHY WOULD YOU WISH FOR THAT?
SOME KIDS AT SCHOOL... THEY--THEY SAID THAT THEY ARE BAD PEOPLE-- THAT THEY DO BAD THINGS.
WELL, THE KIDS AT SCHOOL ARE WRONG. SCARECROWS AND DRACULOIDS PROTECT US. THEY WORK FOR B.L.I. TO KEEP BATTERY CITY SAFE AND KEEP BAD THINGS OUT. THEY DON'T ALLOW FOR ANY MISTAKES. WHICH IS WHY, I MEAN, EIGHT HOURS OF SLEEP IS MANDATORY FOR--
"OKAY. OKAY. I'M GOING TO SLEEP. BUT MOMMY, TOMORROW CAN YOU TELL ME WHAT'S OUTSIDE THE CITY?"
"HAIL A TAXI. CALL YOUR UNCLE. JUST... RUN!"

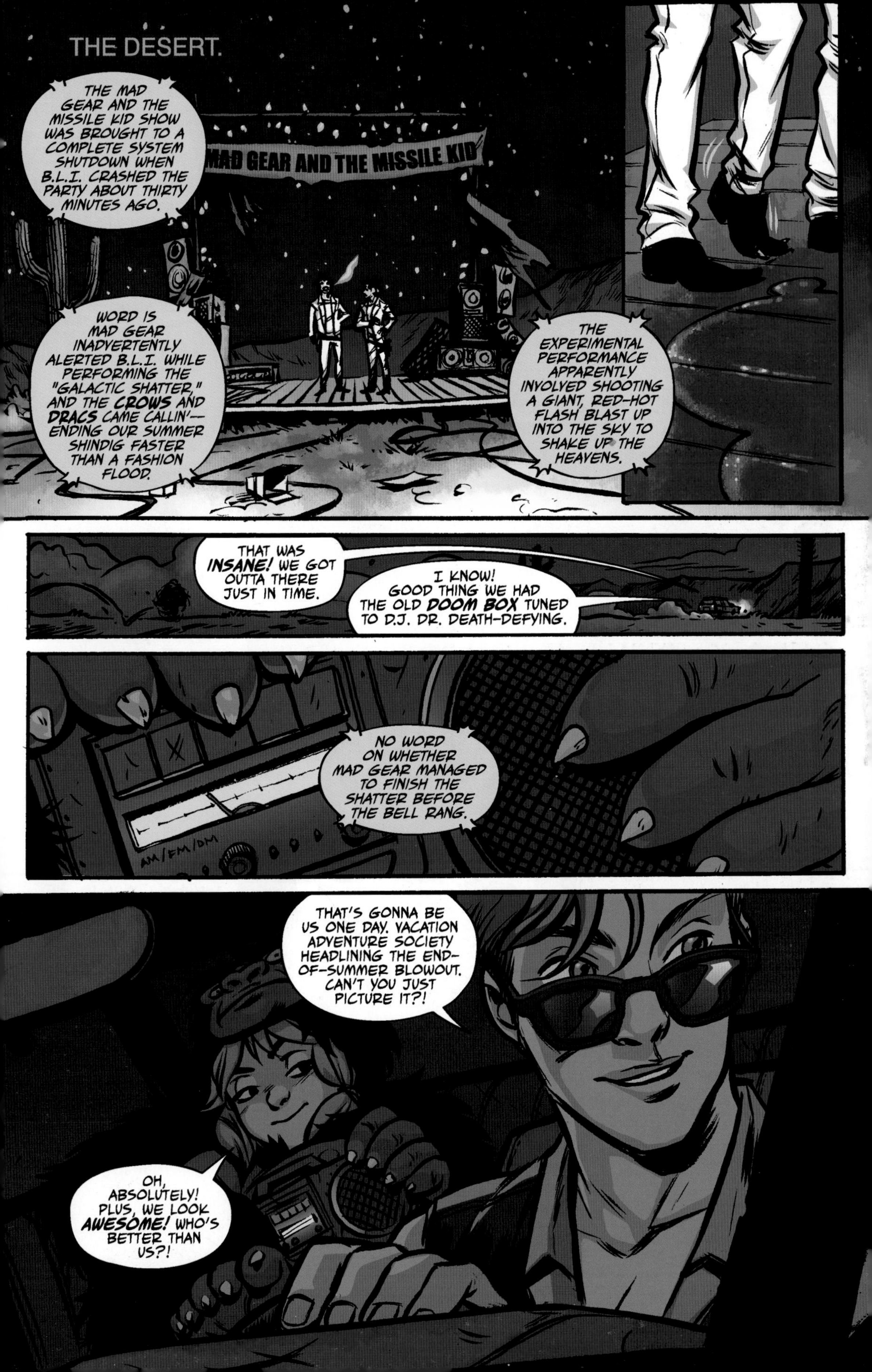
THE DESERT.
THE MAD GEAR AND THE MISSILE KID SHOW WAS BROUGHT TO A COMPLETE SYSTEM SHUTDOWN WHEN B.L.I. CRASHED THE PARTY ABOUT THIRTY MINUTES AGO.
MAD GEAR AND THE MISSILE KID
WORD IS MAD GEAR INADVERTENTLY ALERTED B.L.I. WHILE PERFORMING THE "GALACTIC SHATTER," AND THE CROWS AND DRACS CAME CALLIN'— ENDING OUR SUMMER SHINDIG FASTER THAN A FASHION FLOOD.
THE EXPERIMENTAL PERFORMANCE APPARENTLY INVOLVED SHOOTING A GIANT, RED-HOT FLASH BLAST UP INTO THE SKY TO SHAKE UP THE HEAVENS.
THAT WAS INSANE! WE GOT OUTTA THERE JUST IN TIME.
I KNOW! GOOD THING WE HAD THE OLD DOOM BOX TUNED TO D.J. DR. DEATH-DEFYING.
NO WORD ON WHETHER MAD GEAR MANAGED TO FINISH THE SHATTER BEFORE THE BELL RANG.
AM/FM/DM
THAT'S GONNA BE US ONE DAY. VACATION ADVENTURE SOCIETY HEADLINING THE END-OF-SUMMER BLOWOUT. CAN'T YOU JUST PICTURE IT?!
OH, ABSOLUTELY! PLUS, WE LOOK AWESOME! WHO'S BETTER THAN US?!

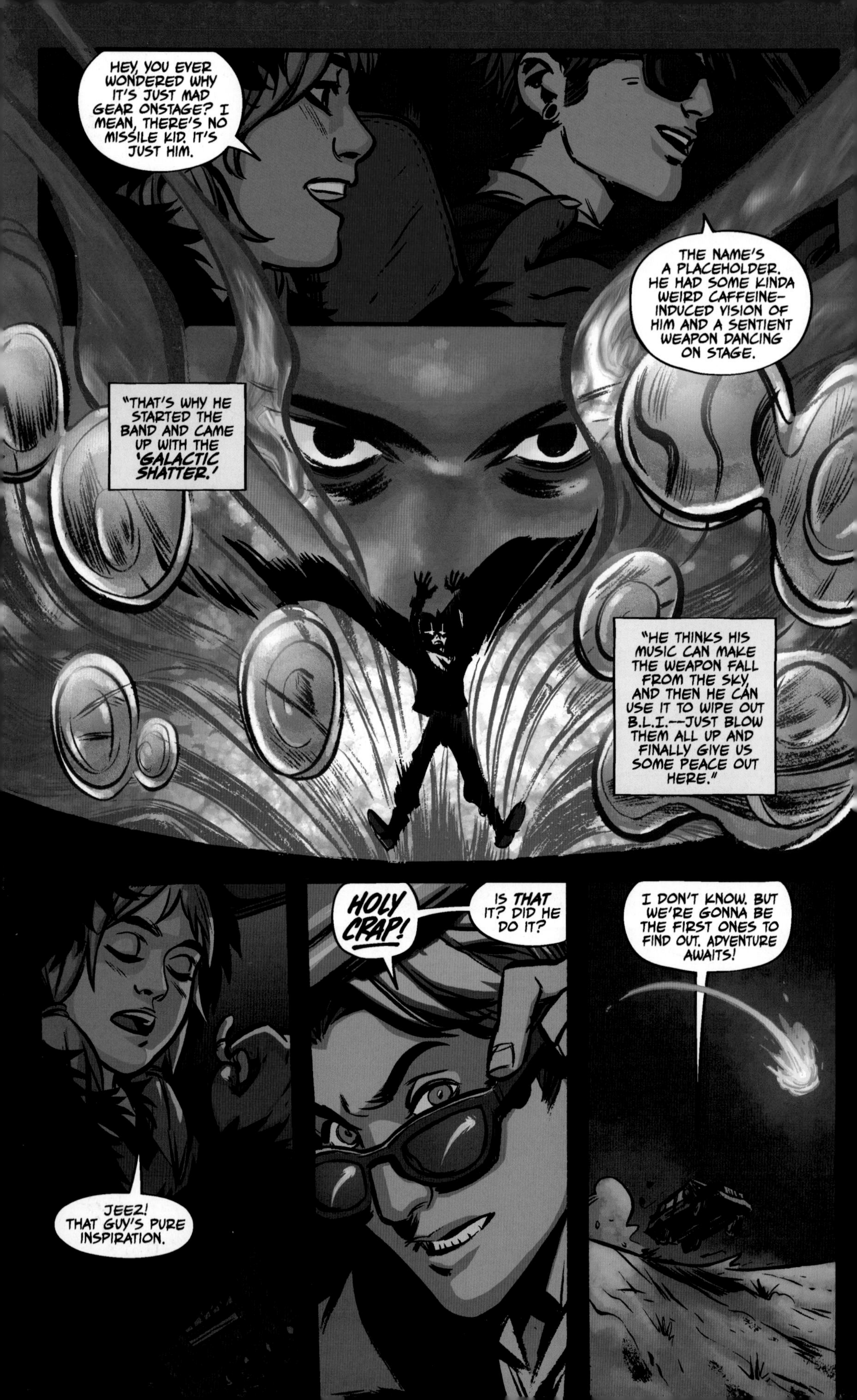
HEY, YOU EVER WONDERED WHY IT'S JUST MAD GEAR ONSTAGE? I MEAN, THERE'S NO MISSILE KID. IT'S JUST HIM.
THE NAME'S A PLACEHOLDER. HE HAD SOME KINDA WEIRD CAFFEINE-INDUCED VISION OF HIM AND A SENTIENT WEAPON DANCING ON STAGE.
"THAT'S WHY HE STARTED THE BAND AND CAME UP WITH THE 'GALACTIC SHATTER.'
"HE THINKS HIS MUSIC CAN MAKE THE WEAPON FALL FROM THE SKY, AND THEN HE CAN USE IT TO WIPE OUT B.L.I.--JUST BLOW THEM ALL UP AND FINALLY GIVE US SOME PEACE OUT HERE."
JEEZ! THAT GUY'S PURE INSPIRATION.
HOLY CRAP!
IS THAT IT? DID HE DO IT?
I DON'T KNOW. BUT WE'RE GONNA BE THE FIRST ONES TO FIND OUT. ADVENTURE AWAITS!

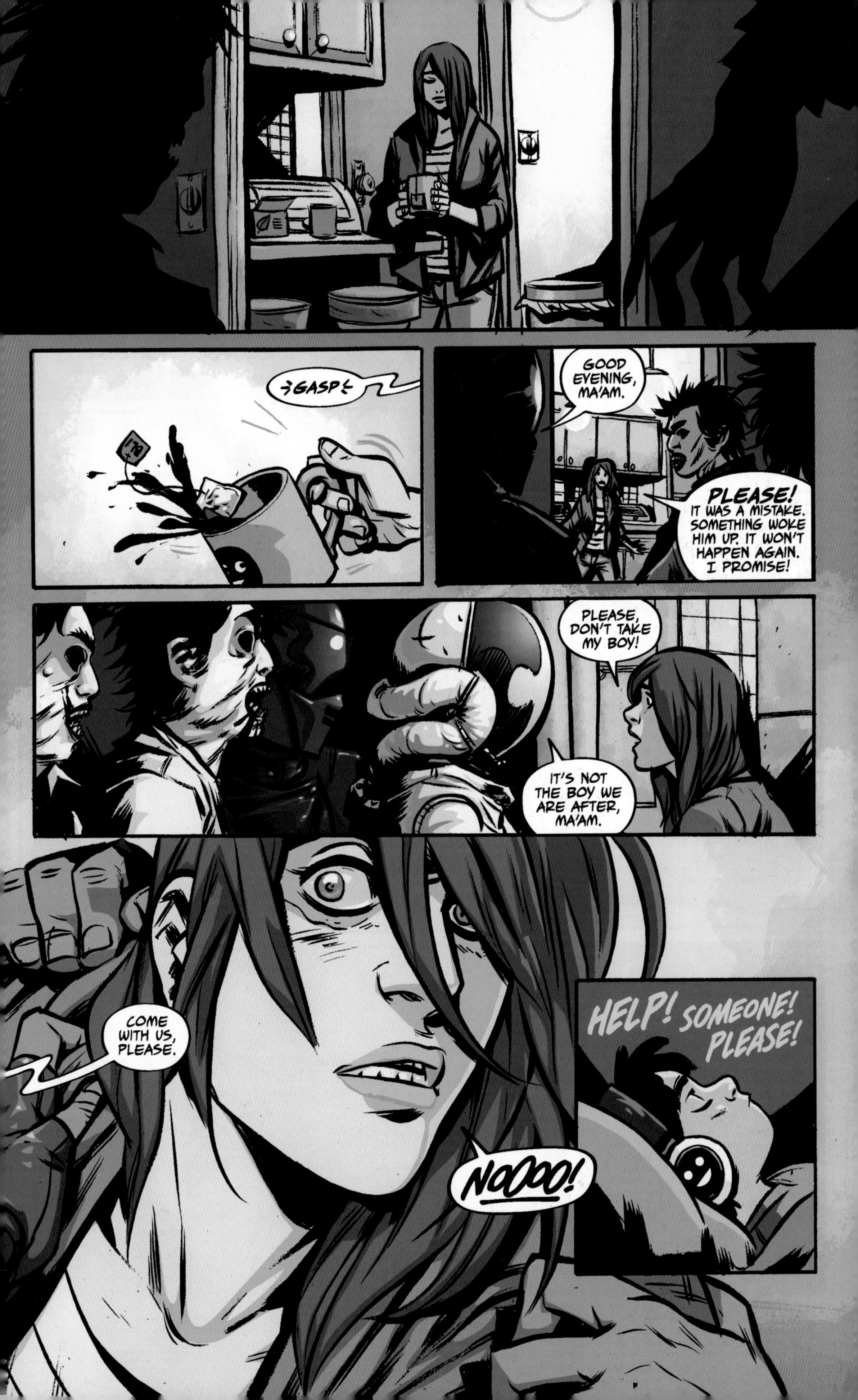

GASP
GOOD EVENING, MA'AM.
PLEASE! IT WAS A MISTAKE. SOMETHING WOKE HIM UP. IT WON'T HAPPEN AGAIN. I PROMISE!
PLEASE, DON'T TAKE MY BOY!
IT'S NOT THE BOY WE ARE AFTER, MA'AM.
COME WITH US, PLEASE.
NOOOO!
HELP! SOMEONE! PLEASE!

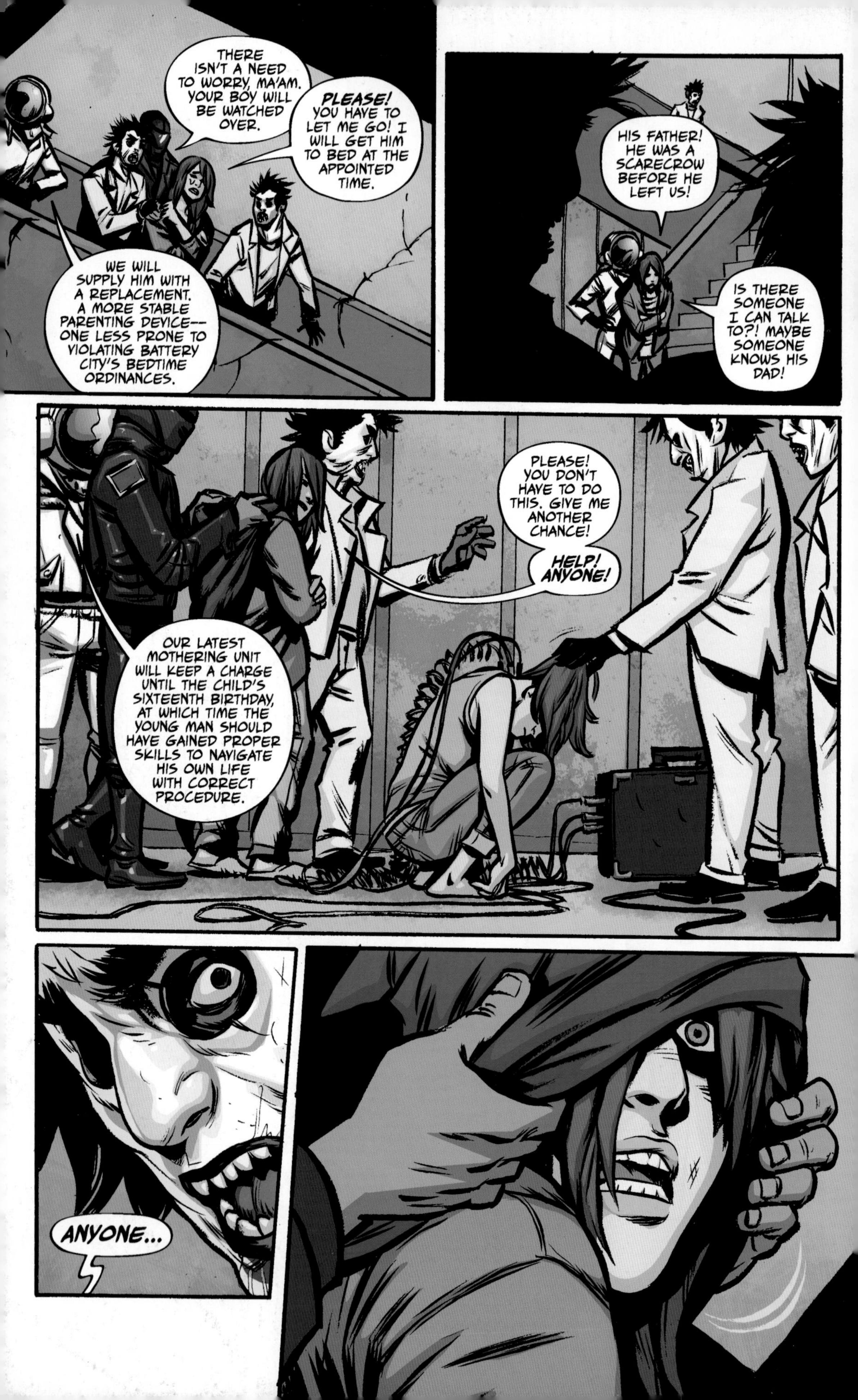
THERE ISN'T A NEED TO WORRY, MA'AM. YOUR BOY WILL BE WATCHED OVER.
PLEASE! YOU HAVE TO LET ME GO! I WILL GET HIM TO BED AT THE APPOINTED TIME.
WE WILL SUPPLY HIM WITH A REPLACEMENT. A MORE STABLE PARENTING DEVICE-- ONE LESS PRONE TO VIOLATING BATTERY CITY'S BEDTIME ORDINANCES.
HIS FATHER! HE WAS A SCARECROW BEFORE HE LEFT US!
IS THERE SOMEONE I CAN TALK TO?! MAYBE SOMEONE KNOWS HIS DAD!
PLEASE! YOU DON'T HAVE TO DO THIS. GIVE ME ANOTHER CHANCE!
HELP! ANYONE!
OUR LATEST MOTHERING UNIT WILL KEEP A CHARGE UNTIL THE CHILD'S SIXTEENTH BIRTHDAY, AT WHICH TIME THE YOUNG MAN SHOULD HAVE GAINED PROPER SKILLS TO NAVIGATE HIS OWN LIFE WITH CORRECT PROCEDURE.
ANYONE...

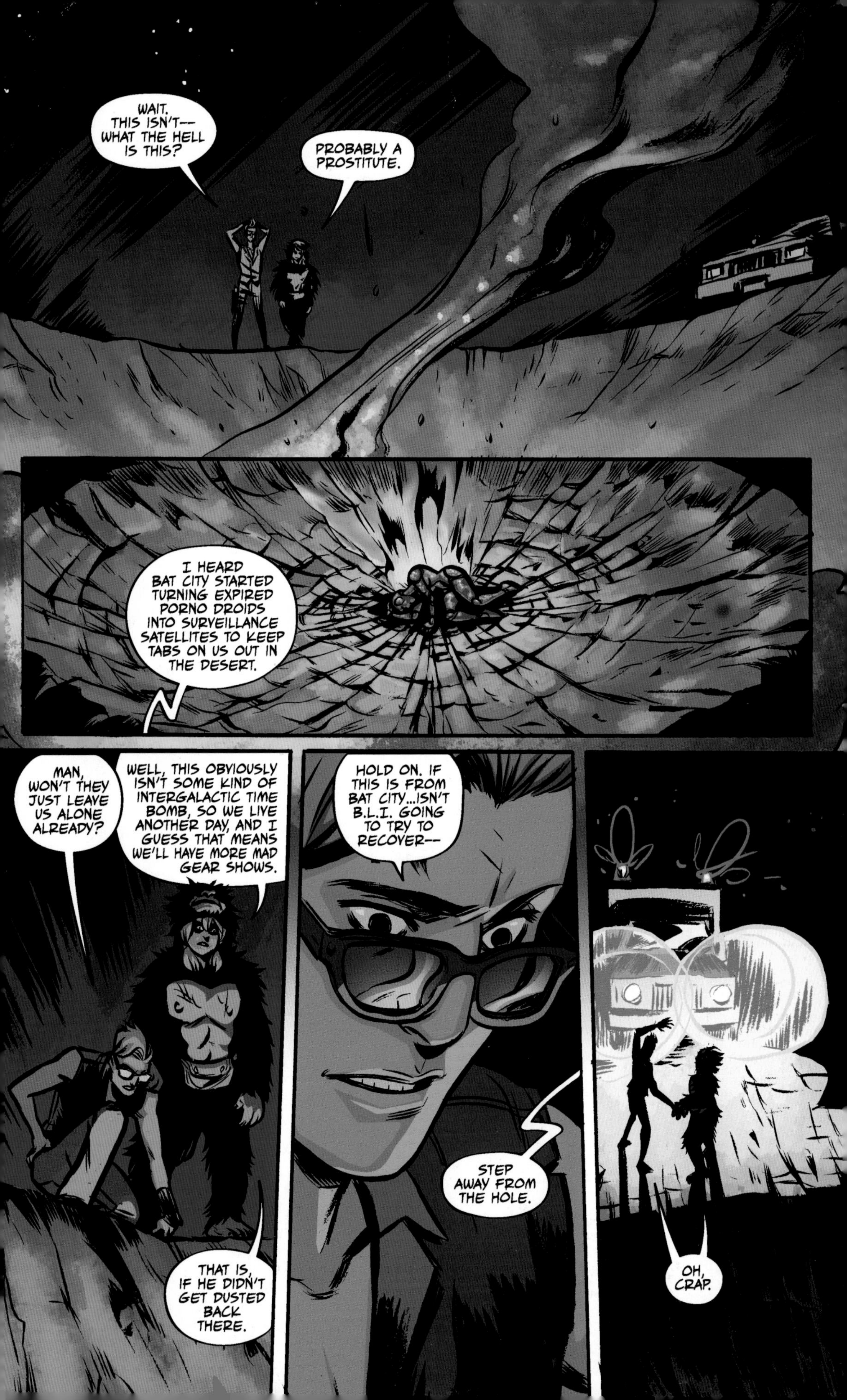

WAIT. THIS ISN'T-- WHAT THE HELL IS THIS?
PROBABLY A PROSTITUTE.
I HEARD BAT CITY STARTED TURNING EXPIRED PORNO DROIDS INTO SURVEILLANCE SATELLITES TO KEEP TABS ON US OUT IN THE DESERT.
MAN, WON'T THEY JUST LEAVE US ALONE ALREADY?
WELL, THIS OBVIOUSLY ISN'T SOME KIND OF INTERGALACTIC TIME BOMB, SO WE LIVE ANOTHER DAY, AND I GUESS THAT MEANS WE'LL HAVE MORE MAD GEAR SHOWS.
THAT IS, IF HE DIDN'T GET DUSTED BACK THERE.
HOLD ON. IF THIS IS FROM BAT CITY...ISN'T B.L.I. GOING TO TRY TO RECOVER--
STEP AWAY FROM THE HOLE.
OH, CRAP.

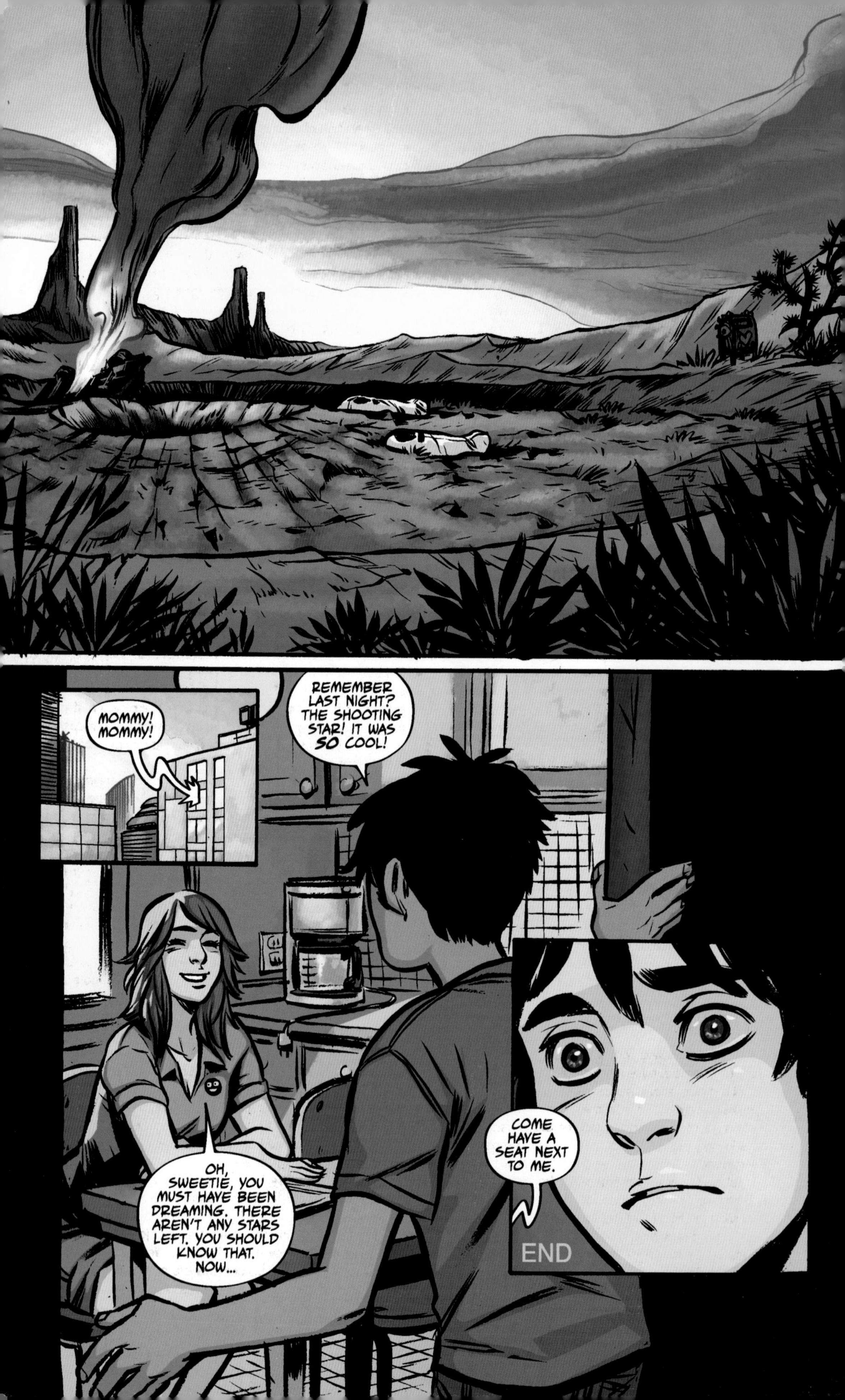
MOMMY! MOMMY!
REMEMBER LAST NIGHT? THE SHOOTING STAR! IT WAS SO COOL!
OH, SWEETIE, YOU MUST HAVE BEEN DREAMING. THERE AREN'T ANY STARS LEFT. YOU SHOULD KNOW THAT. NOW...
COME HAVE A SEAT NEXT TO ME.
END

STRANGER DAYS: THE TRUE STORY OF *THE TRUE LIVES OF THE FABULOUS KILLJOYS*

By Shaun Simon

The True Lives of the Fabulous Killjoys started with a single ray gun blast into a desert canyon. The blast bounced off every wall at lightning speed. Round and round it went, echoing through the night. But it didn't hit its target. Not then. It burnt out and fell silent. We would have to revisit that ledge. We would have to take another shot. And we would have to try to hit the bull's-eye before the blast burnt out for good.

Gerard called me in the summer of 2008 and asked me about this comic book idea I was working on. I had never written a comic before, and it was my dream to one day get the chance to. He told me he was working on something with very similar ideas and themes. This is what Gerard and I do. We talk about ideas. We talk about stories, comics, fashion, and life. We've been doing this for years.

We did more than just talk when he lived on the East Coast. I can tell you stories about dressing up in Santa outfits and going to NYC on Christmas Eve because he really needed a new laptop. We hung fliers at a local rock show that our bands were playing, promoting a slumber party he and I were having at our rundown murderesque practice studio. When no one showed up, Gerard and I put on a fashion show with clothes we got at a Salvation Army around the corner. We named a rotten tuna fish sandwich "Sweet Chubby" and proceeded to take Sweet Chubby around the country in the tour van. This is what our friendship is like; it's how we roll.

The name I had was *Killjoys*—plain and simple. Gerard brought *The True Lives of the Fabulous*. This is a good example of how we work together. One of us would come up with an idea and the other would complete it. We were lucky enough to have a couple of East Coast weddings that year which Gerard spent at my house, where we came up with the main story together. This was the ray gun going off.

The miniseries was announced in 2009 at San Diego Comic-Con. People were excited—probably none more than me—and everything was falling into place. We even had a September deadline for the first issue script.

Then everything stopped. The ray gun blast fizzled out and died before hitting the target.

If we had written the book back then, it would have been very different. The old version of the story focused on Mike Milligram, a late-twenty-something living in a desert trailer park and working a crappy job. Mike's teenage years were a blur. Part of him believed he was part of a gang called the Killjoys who fought fictional things in the real world. The other part of him believed it was just a dream. Music was the only thing that kept Mike going, so when the music was erased from his Ramones tape, it sent him over the edge. He went and got his old teenage gang, who were now living normal lives, back together because, yes, it was all real. It was a story about a group of old friends getting together and taking a surreal road trip across the country and discovering what America really was. Reaching deep inside its pretty façade and pulling out the ugly guts. The gang would have found out that a former gang had now become the largest health care corporation in the country and were hell bent on making the world a safe and clean place by removing all that was dirty, like the Ramones.

Gerard was wrapping up his next album with his band, My Chemical Romance. As far as I knew it was pretty much done, and he was ready to get into comic mode. One afternoon I got a call from him telling me he'd just got back from a weekend in the desert, where he had this vision. He started singing me lyrics to the song "Na Na Na" off of their *Danger Days* record and was talking about the look and themes that we had discussed months before for the comic. We had planned on keeping them separate. Gerard said that his band was going to scrap the album they'd just recorded and start again with this new vision—the Killjoys vision.

I would get e-mails from him with sketches and designs he was doing for the record—everything from costumes to ray guns, cars, and mailboxes. He didn't know it at the time, but he was also designing the world of our comic.

I saw the video to "Na Na Na" a little while before it was released. It was everything we had been talking about for years. The look. The colors. The energy. It was bizarre and exciting. Meanwhile, our story in the comic stayed the same. They did another video for their song "SING," and the comic stayed on the back burner as MCR went on tour.

Soon after, Gerard called me up and told me the band had been planning on making a third video but ran out of money. The gist of our conversation was basically, "What if this third video is our comic?" Gerard and his band had created this colorful world in their videos based on the look and themes of our comic. So why not follow suit and finish the story in the comic? It all made sense. This is when it happened. This is when we took that next shot in the dust bowl, and the target exploded.

The energy Gerard and I had at the beginning returned. We took our original characters as inspiration but started with the Killjoys already dead. The Girl was only a child in the MCR videos when the Killjoys, who protected her, were killed. It was never explained why they protected her in the videos, so we wanted to focus on her life years after the Killjoys died and discover what was so special about her.

Scripting the comic was nothing but fun. Gerard is a visual writer and can change the whole feel of a page by changing a few angles and panel sizes. We'd get notes from Sierra where she would bring up a small point that made us rethink and rewrite entire scenes. It was an amazing feeling seeing it all finally come together. But we didn't actually see it until Becky had the first script.

It was issue one, page four, that I was worried about. It was dense with details that, in the wrong hands, could have easily turned out like a seizure. It was the first page I turned to after getting the pencils from Becky. Not only did she make it look effortless, but it also looked better than I'd pictured it in my head. I knew this book was going to be something very special. Then came Dan Jackson, our incredibly talented colorist. The panels jumped off the page. It was pop art. It was brilliant.

June 12, 2013, was the day issue one came out. It was five years after Gerard called me up and asked me about this comic idea I was working on. I went to my local comic shop and saw it sitting on the shelf. I saw people picking up copies. It was surreal. The journey was finally coming to its end.

The Girl in *Killjoys* needed to go on a journey to discover who she was and what she stood for. She didn't know where she was going to end up but she ended up exactly where she was meant to. Her journey is very much like our journey with this book. We started out in one place and ended up somewhere completely different. But we ended up exactly where we were meant to.

BEING MIKE MILLIGRAM
By Gerard Way

I don't have a lot of friends.

I have always been a "quality over quantity" individual, but having said that, I have recently come to the conclusion I am somewhat "allergic" to them. It's not that I can't keep friends—it's just that I have a hard time meeting them, making them, and connecting with them, and they mostly predate being in a band. They fit on less than one hand, and I hold them all very dear.

Now I see other friends more often than Shaun, but when I see Shaun I tend to do things with him that I don't do with anyone else. As he mentioned in his wonderful afterword, these activities could involve anything from becoming Secret Santas, to giving rotten food full personalities. It has always been this way with Shaun; things happen when we get in the same room.

So it was no surprise that when we ended up spending a few moments together we created a universe, and like he said, this universe was very different than the one we provided for public consumption. Mostly. Somewhat. But not really.

The True Lives of the Fabulous Killjoys (and when I use this title I speak of the entire endeavor—liquid idea, rock album concept, live-action vignettes, indie comic miniseries) was the most ambitious and encompassing creative project I have ever been involved in, and it was nearly my last.

To me, in the end, the project was about so much more than the story—it was about the creative process itself, and a final charge up the hill—one last vie for immortality while we still had our youth. But lots of lessons were learned on this journey, and one of them was that you don't achieve immortality by vying for it; you do it by living a fearless existence while the rest of the world sorts out how it will be remembered.

You also can't force your creations to behave and achieve like your creations before them, and *The True Lives of the Fabulous Killjoys* was more rebellious in that regard than anything I had a hand in creating, as it was designed to be. So it took some time, as Shaun has said, and for me it took some time to fully embrace what this creation was, from the ray guns to the music, through the characters.

Mike Milligram.

Mike is the original Killjoy. His name comes from the nickname I gave Mikey Way during the tracking of *The Black Parade*, because Mikey had become so calm and collected after his departure from the haunted Paramore house. He would show up, big black boots on, and do a bass part in one take. The character was the starting point in my brain for the comic, and like Shaun said, very different. In every way the character that would become Party Poison and then Val Velocity would hold inside of him every hope and fear attached to my life at that moment. And more so than Death, the leader of the Black Parade, I fought with Mike to retain my identity.

Despite *Killjoys* being such a colorful book, one of the things I like about it is that pretty much with the exception of the Girl, everyone is black and white. Mike Milligram stands so diametrically opposed to what my life in the band had become that he was on a suicide mission to destroy it.

Shaun and I had created the character out of our need to express our distaste for the homogenization of our youth culture into our thirties, and inside of Mike were the emotions of anger and frustration with a platform to take it out on people. As Mike, and then Party Poison, and then Val fights the omnipresent BL/ind corporation, so I fought with my own corporation. And I'm not talking about record companies; I'm talking about the corporation we become.

When success occurs, you create a machine to sustain it, so the more I became wrapped up in this character, the more I did to sabotage its function.

It started with the basic and most important things, the sound of things. If something sounds like it works in the machine, then find me the thing that is furthest away from it—find me the thing that starts to break apart the machine—find me the sound that breaks things.

Two completed albums later, the sound was there.

Visually, find me the thing that is furthest away, find me the color of irritation, give me *bright red*. I had become again so wrapped up in the character of Mike Milligram/Party Poison that one day, during a fitting for costumes in Hollywood with Colleen Atwood for the video "Na Na Na," I was alone and, standing in front of the full-length mirror, I snapped a photo of someone altogether different than who I had been two years before. And the transformation occurred and continued into the next year of touring and jetting all over the globe, making rash decisions and sticking it to "the man" (myself), getting further and further away from my identity at top speed until it felt like all the bolts in the machine were going to slip out of circuit, and everything, including my well-being, would break apart.

The crash never occurred, the wreck never came, and out of love for my family and animalistic self-preservation I learned the most important lesson of the saga: Grow up.

Or find something in the middle, something tangible. Real people don't have wars with sci-fi dystopian megaconglomerates. They get up and go to work. They show up on time, they live in the minute and not in the fog present.

And that, to me, is how the book was finished, by looking inward, to that inner sixteen-year-old girl—the one that lives in the pages of this book, the one that saves everyone by evolving—by getting up, getting on her feet, and being real.

This book exists because Shaun helped me show up, Becky stuck with us, Nate gave it BOOMs, Dan gave it brilliant color, and Sierra kept us on the tracks (patiently and diligently). The end result is a work that was fabricated by hundreds of individuals, most of them fictional, but in the end, the real ones got it done.